Whitechapel

A Period Thriller Surrounding the Infamous 'Jack the Ripper' Murders

Bryan Lightbody

Bloomington, IN　　Milton Keynes, UK
authorHOUSE®

AuthorHouse™
1663 Liberty Drive, Suite 200
Bloomington, IN 47403
www.authorhouse.com
Phone: 1-800-839-8640

AuthorHouse™ *UK Ltd.*
500 Avebury Boulevard
Central Milton Keynes, MK9 2BE
www.authorhouse.co.uk
Phone: 08001974150

© *2007 Bryan Lightbody. All rights reserved.*

No part of this book may be reproduced, stored in a retrieval system, or transmitted by any means without the written permission of the author.

First published by AuthorHouse 3/1/2007

ISBN: 978-1-4259-6181-7 (sc)

Printed in the United States of America
Bloomington, Indiana

This book is printed on acid-free paper.

Author's Note

Whitechapel is a historical novel. It is a work of fiction based on true events. For that reason it includes mostly factual characters that interplay with a small number of fictional creations. To that end I must stress that although the descriptions of crime scenes, the geography of the East End of London and the resultant injuries to the victims are generally accurate, and the roles of the various factual characters are correct, their actions and conversations are in the main speculative and hypothetical. These actions and interactions are an invention of the author for the purposes of creating the novel and if they bear relationship to previously unreported events that is pure co-incidence. *Whitechapel* is written to allow the reader to enter the world of Victorian London, learn of the events of the autumn of 1888 and to link together some of the enigmas of the case to perhaps provide a tangible answer to the enduring mystery of 'Jack the Ripper.' Its overall purpose is to entertain.

ACKNOWLEDGEMENTS

I would like to thank the following people. It would be ideal to explain their part in the completion of this book but unfortunately that is impractical, needless to say they have all provided invaluable input.

Christine Lightbody, Stuart & Cathy Lightbody, Mark and Sandy Lightbody, Daniel & Susanna Shadrake, Paul Tracey (your constant interest helped get the job done), Sasha Lee at Authorhouse, Steve Scruton and BBC Essex, all those who have endured walks around Whitechapel and Spitalfields (you know who you are, Mark Goodenough being the first). Cathy at Hannay's in Braintree, Kurt, Gary, Paul, Justin, Tony, Scott and Dave from One Team at Maltby Street, and all of those that I have worked with at some point who have quizzed me and cajoled me to get it done.

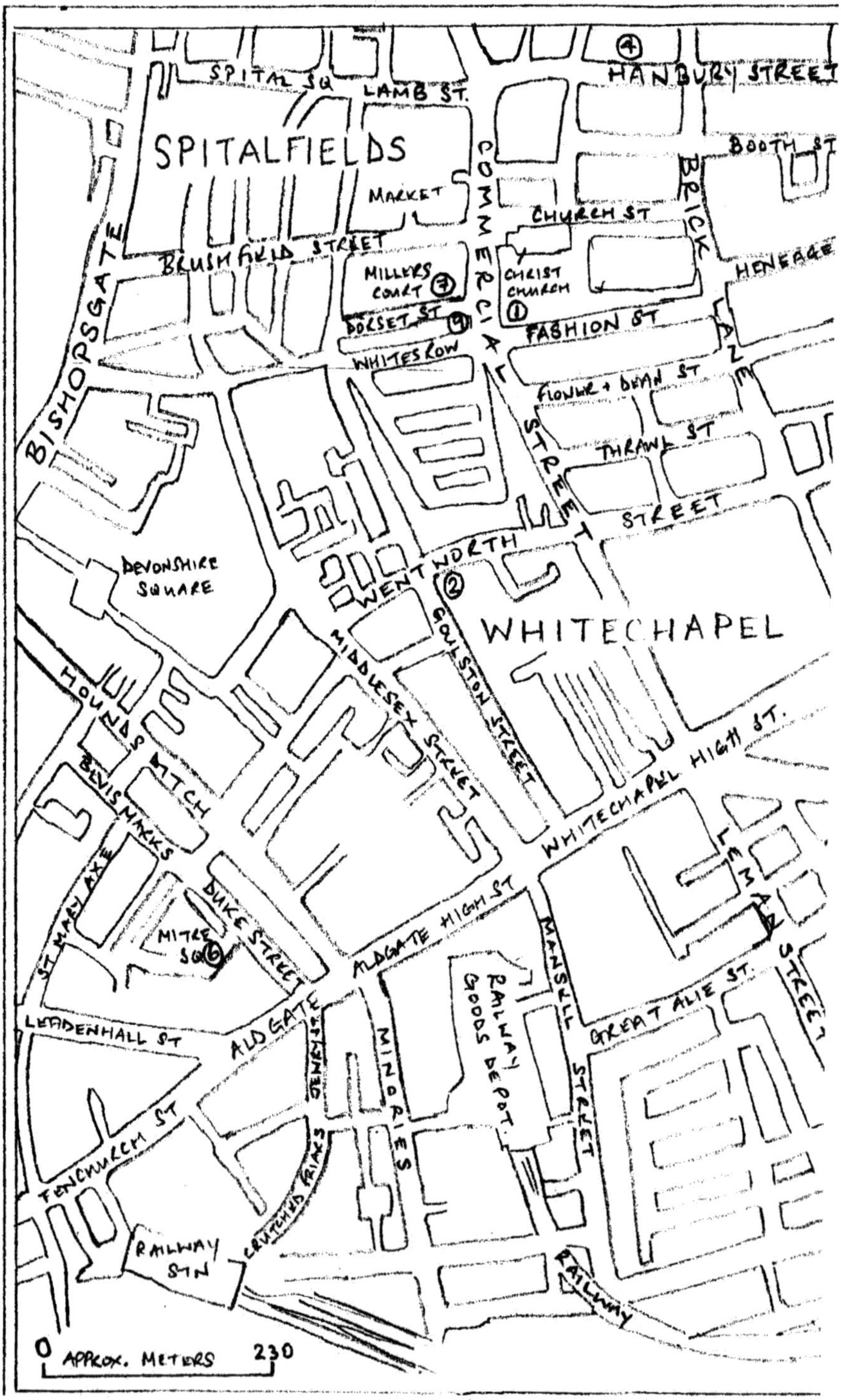
SPITAL SQ
LAMB ST.
HANBURY STREET
SPITALFIELDS
MARKET
COMMERCIAL STREET
BOOTH ST
BRICK LANE
CHURCH ST
BRUSHFIELD STREET
MILLERS COURT 7
CHRIST CHURCH 1
HENEAGE
DORSET ST
FASHION ST
WHITES ROW
FLOWER + DEAN ST
THRAWL ST
BISHOPSGATE
WENTWORTH STREET
DEVONSHIRE SQUARE
WHITECHAPEL
GOULSTON STREET
MIDDLESEX STREET
HOUNDSDITCH
BEVIS MARKS
WHITECHAPEL HIGH ST.
LEMAN STREET
ST MARY AXE
DUKE STREET
MITRE SQ 6
ALDGATE HIGH ST
MANSELL STREET
RAILWAY GOODS DEPOT.
GREAT ALIE ST.
LEADENHALL ST
ALDGATE
JEWRY ST
MINORIES
FENCHURCH ST
CRUTCHED FRIARS
RAILWAY STN
RAILWAY
0 APPROX. METERS 230

ix

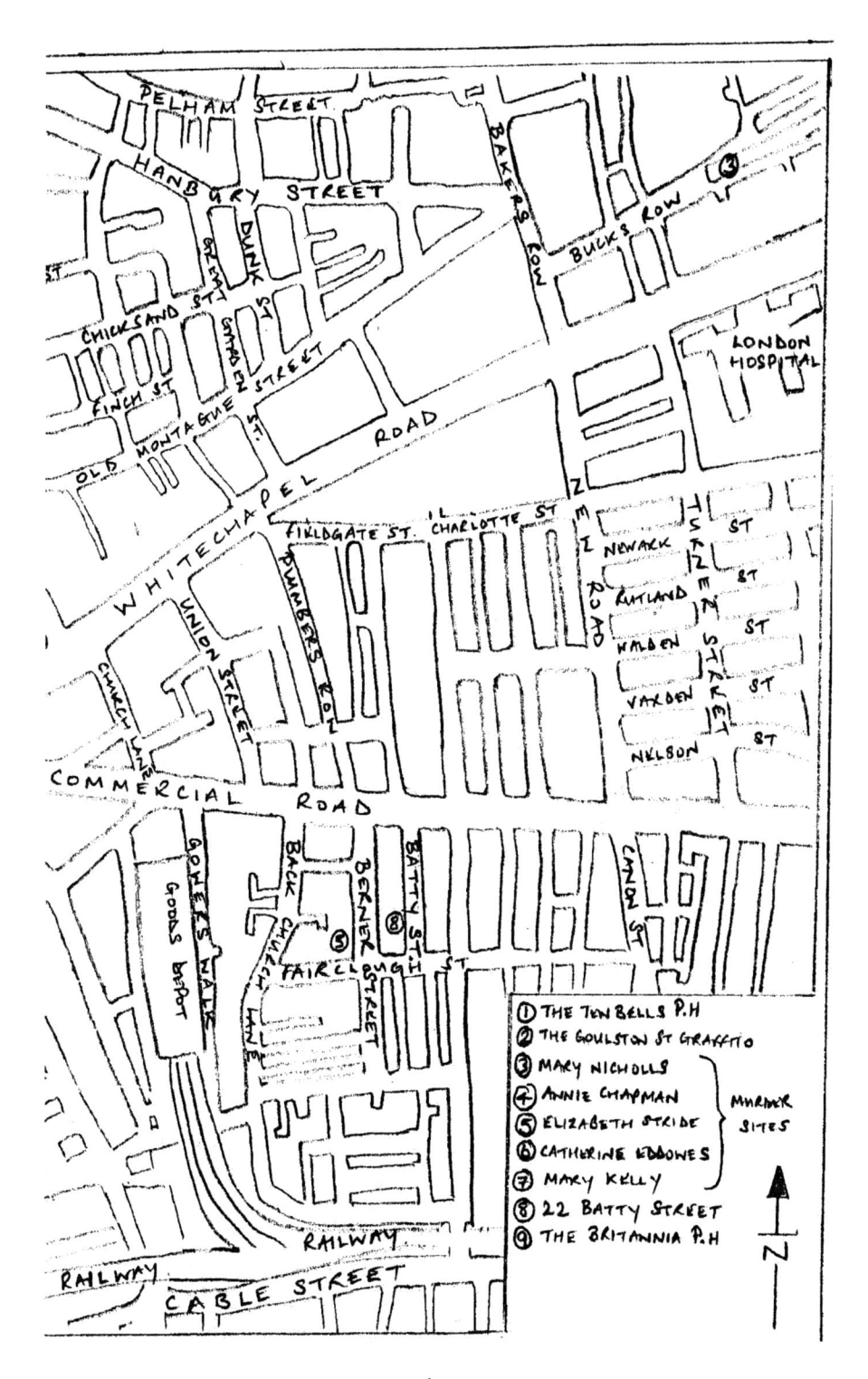

CHAPTER ONE

Bank holiday Monday 6th August 1888, 2.a.m. Martha Tabrum a forty-one year old haggard Whitechapel prostitute, or 'unfortunate' to coin a commonly used phrase, staggered out of the White Swan public house in Whitechapel High Street. She was in the company of another prostitute Mary Ann 'Pearly Poll' Connolly, fifty years old, broad with a drink reddened face, reeking of alcohol and body odour, mildly disguised by a cheap perfume. They were in the company of two men in military uniforms; the party of four split two ways, with Pearly Poll walking off into Angel Alley for a quick knee trembler of a screw which would give her doss money for the night. Her would-be lover was tall, lean, well groomed in his uniform with a neatly trimmed moustache obviously out for a cheap gutter thrill.

He pushed her against the wall and as he did so she lifted her bustling skirt and then proceeded to unbutton the fly on his trousers. He spat saliva onto his palm as a makeshift lubricant and entered her with little thought of comfort for her, but the pain this caused her was very much dulled by the alcohol. They rocked rhythmically against the wall breathing stale alcohol drenched breath over each other. Within a matter of a couple of minutes the whole wretched act was over, him withdrawing and wiping himself on the edge of her skirt as he did so, her then slumping to the cold cobbles dropping down the wall as she fought to gain control of her spinning drunken mind. She had the money from her client already; he had paid her in the White Swan and eventually dragged herself to her feet to head off to her lodgings at Crossingham's Doss House. Her military client then waited on the main road near the junction with Wentworth Street for his friend.

Martha had taken her client off to George Yard, again just off of Whitechapel High Street, to indulge him in her carnal wares little knowing it would be the last time she offered them. He was an older man with a much fancier uniform than his friend and a big handlebar moustache. She walked away from him as they entered the yard and tried to be seductive in beckoning him with her finger up to the wall which she now had her back to. She began hitching up the layers of her bustle skirt whilst he approached her undoing his trouser fly. He spoke to her in a strange accent before they began.

"Say, angel, will you kiss me there before we start?" He was pointing to below his waist. She had thought that he had paid her generously for a street 'shag' when they were still in the pub, so with this in mind and knowing having plied her trade over many years that with him moistened it would not hurt as much, so she obliged for several minutes. He then stood up and she directed him with her hand and felt his penetration. As a result of her initial work and the use of her finger in his anal passage to put pressure on his prostate gland to bring about a swift climax, hence the name 'prostitutes', intercourse lasted a matter of about a minute.

He withdrew and put himself away and avoided the common practice she had found with many clients of wiping themselves on her skirt. Again she found this quite considerate. Not as heavily drunk as Pearly Poll, she straightened her skirt out and looked up to see her client still stood in front of her staring directly at her. He had his right hand now behind his back.

"What's the matter wiv you then?" she said in a typical cockney accent. He said nothing, just continuing to stare.

"Say somefink, you bloody freak."

"Do you know Mary Kelly?"

"Who" she replied quizzically.

"Ginger, Mary Kelly, Fair Emma?"

"I dunno what you're bleedin' on about. Thought I was good enough.........."

Her words tailed off. He lunged at her with a large pocket knife and in so doing clasped his left hand over her mouth to destroy any hope she had of alerting anyone to her plight.

He plunged the knife repeatedly into her torso in a totally random fashion striking her chest, her stomach and her sides with blood now seeping heavily through her clothes and beginning to soil his. He just kept stabbing with an unabated ferocity for a couple of minutes. For some time she had still tried to scream and it had been hard for him to control this reflex in her. She fell to the floor silent and limp, his right hand now aching from its fervent work. He looked around frantically following the violent struggle between them but fortunately there was still no one in sight. He had a second knife which he pulled from a scabbard on his belt that was in fact a military bayonet; he thought it would help remove things from her better. His right arm was really in pain now from the attack as the adrenaline that had coursed around his body was wearing off so he would have to go to work with his left hand to finish the job.

He sat down on the floor next to the warm lifeless body just looking at his handiwork contemplating his next move. It seemed like an eternity he was in thought as he considered what he had done; it was the first time he had killed someone. He sat by the body lost in his thoughts for nearly an hour and his friend waiting in Wentworth Street had long since gone. Just as he was about to get to his feet and begin his grisly work, he saw a cab pull up in the main road at the far end of the yard. Furious at his delay he delivered a massive final blow with his left arm brandishing the bayonet. He plunged it into her sternum and made off in the opposite direction simply melting into the night.

* * *

Robert Ford woke from his deep slumber to a mild August morning, a Tuesday, the 28th in fact, rubbing the sleep from his eyes and rolling back the covers from the soft bed in his lodgings. His feet made contact with the rough and bare wooden floorboards and were naked except for a few blisters from his new work boots. He looked across at the tin mechanical alarm clock that had brought consciousness to his tired body and weary mind and saw the time. Twenty minutes to six in the morning. Could that be right? Twenty minutes before he had to be at work? He had forgotten to set the alarm correctly; placing his blistered feet in his tough new boots they would have to carry him swiftly to Commercial Street Police Station from his lodgings in Bakers Row.

Robert Ford, a Metropolitan Police Constable with four years service. One of the new lads still at 'The Street,' the name by which Commercial Street Police Station was known by those who worked there and an officer troubled by the murder earlier in the month of prostitute Martha Tabram. He had known her in passing as he did most of the women who frequent the streets for work as indeed he did himself as a beat constable. An inoffensive woman, why had she been so brutally murdered?

Robert, being only twenty-five years old and fit by the standards of the day as a result of not drinking heavily or smoking and trying to eat regularly around shifts, pulled on his uniform, his unforgiving boots and took hold of his beat duty helmet and made for the door of his room. Tripping over Boson the brindle coloured English Bull Terrier belonging to Mrs Williams, his landlady, and receiving a growl and an attempted nip too close for comfort to his left ankle, he entered the street and ran north along Bakers Row towards Bethnal Green Road.

There were still many cabs around with their tired and forlorn looking horses, a few drunks and the market traders were now out in force along Bethnal Green Road. Many of them knew young Robert as a local police constable or 'copper' and shouted typical East End encouragement to him along his route.

"Afternoon, Bobby boy, late shift today?" or "What do coppers say about being up early and not getting caught out?"

The air carried the curious 19th century East End stench, a mixture of fresh and rotten vegetables, flowers and meat all of which blended with the smell of the less than sanitary local streets.

His heart now pumping hard after over a half a mile of running he was at the junction with Wheler Street, just a left turn and a two hundred yard dash to the front door of the 'nick'. Born and bred around the streets which he now patrolled, he knew them like the back of his hands from the days when he was a noted teenage pugilist. As a profession he knew that it would either kill him or leave him a punch drunk destitute and so he had 'thrown in the towel' early to make a proper lawful life for himself. The blisters were rubbing red raw inside of his boots and beads of perspiration were now rolling down his face on this warm August morning. Just as he got to the junction with Commercial Street he fell, heavily, winding himself and grazing his hands. His helmet rolled dangerously close to the wheels of a 'hansom' or cab and he could hear female laughter to his right. Looking over he saw two of the local girls now giggling at his predicament. It was Mary 'Polly' Nichols and the unusually attractive Mary Kelly. Nichols was a typical haggard looking forty-three year old prostitute whilst Kelly, relatively new to the area by comparison, was an attractive auburn haired Irish girl of about twenty-five who Robert knew well in passing and always seemed to greet him with a lovely smile and wink. In her beautifully rounded Limerick accent she spoke to Robert.

"Mind your step, constable, are you in a rush or falling for me?" Robert looked up at her red faced and smiled. If only she knew. Despite the fact she was a prostitute Robert admired her from afar. She was the same age as him and had been to France with an artist and seemed so much more sophisticated than her profession belied. She charmed, fascinated and bewitched him. He had spent many evenings chatting with Mary outside of The Britannia or The Ten Bells pubs in Spitalfields about life and ambitions, and was on the verge of plucking up the courage to ask her for a drink together one evening, away from either of their professional capacities. Too early in the day for him to think of a witty reply he grabbed his helmet and lunged for the doors of the nick.

With a few minutes at least to spare before parade he went into the constables toilets to check his appearance. He brushed the dirt by hand from his helmet, did up his tunic and straightened his whistle chain. Checking his pockets he had his note book, truncheon, china graph pencil and of course his whistle. Finally looking in the mirror, damn it! He hadn't shaved. Sergeant Kerby the duty sergeant taking parade would go mad. He would have to pull the peak of his helmet down low and keep his head down.

The shout came up "Get on parade!" and a sea of constables washed through the corridors bumping and jostling each other, exchanging both good humoured and miserable banter as they burst into the parade room and stood to in front of the afore mentioned Sergeant Kerby and Inspector Spratling. Before reading through the standing orders, the collator's notices and the Police Gazette, the men were inspected by Spratling, not Kerby. Robert almost physically breathed a sigh of relief as he knew that Spratling was generally very cursory with his examination of the assembled officers' appearances.

As the inspector passed along the rank of twelve men, Robert could see Kerby glance across at him, but not at his shave shadow but at his legs. Looking down Robert then noticed he had a torn knee on his left trouser leg, obviously from his earlier fall. Spratling then confronted him looking him up and down.

"New style summer trousers, son? Allow a bit of a breeze in do they?" sneered Spratling.

"No, sir. Had a fall outside. Sorry."

"Get them sorted before you represent the Queen out on the street."

"Yes, sir."

Kerby then addressed the constables with the relevant information for the day. This took the form of highlighting areas of recent crime increase for attention, local wanted thieves to look for and apprehend any changes in practices in policing matters and new high profile criminal personalities seen on the 'ground'.

"So, a murder this month of one of the ladies of the night. One Martha Tabrum, thirty-nine years old of George Street, Spitalfields. No apparent reasoning, she was found slain in George Yard in the early hours of the 7th August having last been seen with a Grenadier Guardsman. She was found with numerous stab wounds, possibly from a bayonet. I want you all to pay attention to any squaddies in the area.

"Next item, Willy Brannigan has been seen on the ground and he is well known as a burglar. Special attention to areas with high value property, and yes, I know they are few and far between here, as he is wanted in connection with a string of West End crimes."

Kerby rambled on in Robert's mind with some more Police Gazette bulletins whilst he drifted off thinking about the murder of Martha Tabrum. He hoped that the detective branch cracked the case soon to keep the local people placated. The East End was an area of massive social deprivation with most of the people there believing that the powers that be cared nothing for it as a region of London, and felt it was perceived as a human dumping ground. He then paid attention to Kerby once more as he continued.

"The Polish-Jew confidence trickster and thief Michael Ostrog is back in town along with Aaron Kosminski another of the same persuasion. Both of 'em are known for violence on occasions and bizarre public behaviour, so look out. Ostrog is also wanted to failing to answer to bail, so if you see him, swift him. He's easy to spot, he normally wear's a cleric's type suit and be careful he often carries a knife, thinks he's a surgeon apparently used to practice with the Russian army 'til he allegedly killed some Russian in a duel. Now Kosminski, on the other hand, is as bloody mad as you like hairdresser who's not adverse to eating food out of the gutter, is by all accounts a self abuser, or to you lot a 'wanker' which has apparently fuelled a hatred of women." There was a unanimous bought of laughter following Kerby's translation of 'self abuser' amongst the constables.

"All right, settle down," said Spratling, "Carry on please, Sergeant."

"A Dr M J Druitt has been seen by the river down at Wapping Steps recently staring blankly at the water. He's been moved on a couple of times by some of the lads and seems very reasonable but distant, lets see if any further types of behaviour develop. Outside of that he's seen knocking about with a military type on our ground here. In relation to the Tabrum murder, no description of a suspect but just to emphasise that her last client she was seen with was maybe a guardsman. Is there a uniform connection?" With typical police sarcasm and cynicism Kerby added, "Narrows it down to about 7000 suspects," bringing another laugh and a smile to the sombre early morning proceedings. "Time for a cup of tea, lads, before you go out then," were Kerby's parting words.

The men all started filing out of the parade room and as they did so Kerby grabbed Robert's arm. "And by the way, boy, get a bleedin' shave as well as sorting out your trousers or it'll be a reprimand in your pocket book."

"Yes, sarg, sorry," replied Robert. He then shuffled off with the rest of them to have a welcome cup of tea and find a needle and cotton. He looked for Liz the cleaning lady at the nick who although unreliable and likely to lose her job as a result of too much drunkenness, had a heart of gold. Robert thought that she would probably be able to help sort out his trousers. Nick-named 'Long Liz,' Elizabeth Stride was known to be a part time local prostitute too.

Robert found Liz in the basement just swilling out a dirty bucket by a sink and coughing loudly. Although plain to look at now at forty-five, she had faired better than most of the others of her age and probably up to ten years previously had been an attractive woman with good facial bone structure and even now a slim physique.

"Liz, you got any black cotton and a needle, love?" asked Robert in his innocent way. The motherly Liz looked him up and down seeing the tear in his trousers and smiled.

"Do you want me to stitch it for you too, little wounded soldier?" What did she mean? He looked at his leg again and could see how red raw it was from a nasty graze taking off a large piece of skin.

"Liz, you are an angel."

"Well get 'em off then, boy, can't do'em in place, not unless you want wear then permanently,"

Robert looked at her gulped and decided the embarrassment would be worth it.

He took his trousers off much to her delight, with Liz laughing and shouting 'and the rest!' as he handed them over to her.

Robert decided to engage her in a bit of conversation, "Liz, did you know Martha?"

"No, darling," she replied "but I understand she was someone on the game, all a bit worrying really a killer being out there. Still could be hit by one of them bleedin' horse drawn bus's tomorrow."

"Yes, I suppose you're right." Robert wondered if he would be so philosophical later in life. "Liz, why do you do what you do away from here?"

The tall fair haired woman paused for a moment and then spoke with a hint of shame avoiding any eye contact.

"Money. That's all. I've got to live and there is little else I can do." Robert pondered the answer and realised that he was one of the more fortunate locals to have found a career for himself. Five minutes later an his trousers were done, he pulled them on quickly, went up to Liz and kissed her on the cheek and whispered "Thanks," into her ear and ran off to the mess room to get a cup of tea with the lads on his 'relief' or shift.

The banter between him and his mates began as soon as he entered the room, with suggestions readily being made about his whereabouts for the last five minutes and how good he must be with a needle and cotton.

"Oi, Bobby boy, I hope you were careful with that needle and didn't feel a prick?" Came the smug comment from Derek 'Del boy' Lake, actually a close friend of Robert's from the Police Training School of Peel House. Del boy was twenty-five and a resident originally of South London, unlike Robert born in the East. A larger than life character always with something to say, they had enjoyed many good days walking the streets of Whitechapel together.

"Well then, boyo, that old tart stitch you up good and proper did she?"

"She is not just an old tart, and besides, is that the best you can come up with then, Taffy?" Robert replied scornfully to the last comment from Taffy Williams an older constable on the relief, some forty years old with lots of service in Central London and now in the East End. He resembled a typical Victorian Bobby, portly with a ruddy complexion, a big bushy moustache and mutton chop sideburns. "Listen, pal, I don't have to be funny, just nasty. I've got more days leave than you've got in this job."

Robert's real feelings were to tell Taffy exactly what he was, a nasty, rude, uncaring has-been. Unfortunately, thought Robert, he would probably retaliate with more spiteful abuse. He sat down with Del to enjoy the hot steaming tea pushed in front of him on the table.

"Well then, son," began Del, "we're both posted number two beat together, fancy strolling and enjoying a bit of lively good-natured company?" Robert looked pensive for a minute, scratched his head and then replied with mocking authority and experience.

"Yeah, okay. Come with me, son and watch and learn!" They laughed heartily at his comment, finished slurping their tea, donned their helmets and headed for the front door of the nick.

It was now 6.35.a.m. Commercial Street was bustling with activity, cabs travelling up and down taking the bankers and city gents into town, trams full of the regular work force being pulled along by strong brawny horses and the market traders and newspaper vendors shouting as everyone passed by. Few, if any, of the ladies of the night were now to be seen on the streets, having made their money they had found lodgings and a bed to sleep off the night's excesses of vile and rough sex subdued by alcohol.

Robert and Del turned right from the nick and headed south-east towards The Ten Bells public house and Spitalfields Flower Market. The aroma of the air was quite bizarre as before, but this time also with a stronger smell of fresh flowers as they neared Spitalfields, horse deposits from all the various forms of transport and the smell of human refuse decaying from some of the local slums all running east from Commercial Street.

However, it is a time of great social upheaval due to the appalling condition of the East End slums, the lawlessness of the area at times and the rise in Irish or 'Fenian' terrorism in London. Despite this it is still a time when those passing constables patrolling in the street acknowledge their presence and wish them a good day. One such person accustomed to greeting 'The Law' was Ralph a grubby street urchin of a paper boy.

Ralph had stumbled from his makeshift bedding in his mother's rooms at around 5.a.m. He knew he had to be at the offices of 'The Star' by 5.30 each day to collect his one hundred copies of the paper to sell on the streets of his home area of Spitalfields. Not having the luxury of a proper bed Ralph slept on the hard wooden floor with the companionship of two rough brown woollen blankets his late father had dragged home from the army and the additional warmth of 'Bruiser,' a Welsh border collie now very old and grey being some twelve years old as was young Ralph, but in dog years he was the equivalent of a grandparent not a sibling as the skinny East End boy regarded him.

Bruiser stirred slightly as Ralph pulled himself from under his covers; dirty and fully clothed except for his ill fitting and worn out boots and a tatty old serge winter coat, two sizes too big for him. Being the old dog that he now was Bruiser licked the boy's face before he stood and then nestled himself into the warm blankets now being left unattended. Ralph rubbed the sleep from his eyes with characteristic mucky hands and pulled on his boots around feet already covered by two pairs of patch work tatty socks. His coat dragged along the floor as he entered the ramshackle pantry and grabbed a piece of dry bread from the table and slurped some water from a cold iron kettle. He knew he would only need his coat until he started work and got accustomed to the sometimes fresh August early morning air.

He then exited the half broken door of one of the rundown flats that made up Millers Court along with some single room bed sits. None of these habitations were maintained by their landlords whose sole interest was in rent and not welfare or comfort. Ralph hated this life but he knew nothing different other than East End squalor with the only light from time to time being the smiling face of Mary the auburn haired Irish girl who lived next door and to Ralph had the voice of angel when she sang. To hear her made up for all of the drunken tantrums he would have to tolerate from his alcoholic mother who had caused him from her life style to be born syphilitic after a brief affair with a young infantryman. He knew little of his father who had died when Ralph was only four, but he had seemed like a kind man who had always tried to give the boy something when he came home on leave. Sometimes it would be a wooden toy or other times old clothes or something like his valued blankets. When she arrived home drunk late at night he would huddle in the corner with Bruiser his only real friend and companion. Bruiser, Mary Kelly and Constable Ford were the only people who showed him any interest in life. Ralph admired Constable Ford as he was a local boy made good by gaining a basic education and joining the Police Force. In so doing he seemed never to forget his roots and was always approachable with any of the local people. He found Ralph a great source of information and everyday bought a paper from the lad who he referred to as a 'local businessman' to boost the lad's self esteem.

Ralph ran to the offices of The Star and collected his hundred copies from Mr Haddaway the sales manager. In Ralph's eyes Haddaway was typical of some of the selfish business owning people around the East End, just wanting something out of everyone.

"Now don't you forget lad, one hundred papers go and you gets your wages. And I expect to see the proper monetary return before you do."

"Yes, Mr Haddaway," Ralph really had to bite his tongue to be civil to such a man he described to others as a 'blood sucker'. Still, things could be worse he thought; he could be stuck cleaning chimneys.

By 6.35.a.m he was at his regular pitch in Commercial Street at the junction with Lamb Street right next to Spitalfields Flower Market.

"Getchaya Star read all about it, London gripped by a wave of Irish terrorism, Fenians vow revenge..." Ralph bellowed at the top of his voice and he would always get waves of traders from the market and then city gents coming by and buying his papers, but then he could get periods of quiet before the next wave of buyers. As he turned in the direction of the police station he saw Robert and Del on patrol coming towards him. To the young boy they looked so fine and important in their 'Bobbies' uniform with their helmets and high necked tunics, lined top to bottom with shiny metal buttons and a whistle chain across the chest.

Ralph's attention was taken from his gaze at the two 'Bobbies' for a moment as he saw movement in the alley across the way, Red Lion Court. He saw a very furtive figure who he could have sworn was dressed as a priest dart away down the alley at the sight of the police with very sunken eyes and a beard. He was quite familiar with the locals and this was someone he could be almost certain that he had never seen before.

Robert and Del were almost upon him now and Ralph's face broadened into a big smile to greet them followed by a hearty 'Good morning, constables.'

"Mornin' to you young Ralph, how's business?" Replied Robert enquiringly.

"Brisk, I will say, Constable Ford, very brisk just the way we business people likes it," said Ralph in the most adult way he could.

"Well, lad," said Del "how long 'til you knock off for the day?"

"I never knocks off completely as I've got the evenin's to do too, but I'm down to my last twenty this morning before I'm through."

"Nineteen now," said Robert offering Ralph tuppence for a copy of The Star.

Ralph quickly reciprocated by passing Robert his copy. As he did so he thought about the strange figure he'd seen. A good source of information for the police on occasions, he thought perhaps it should wait, and he'd see if he saw the bearded man again.

"Thank you, Constable Ford have a good day, sir"

"And to you, Ralph. You can call me Robert"

"Can't get too familiar with the customers now can I?" Del and Robert chuckled with Ralph at that last comment and then walked on. Robert tucked the paper into the inside pocket of his police tunic and turned to Del and said "What a nice lad, hope he makes it away from all this shit one day."

Michael Ostrog watched very carefully as the two constables walked off along Commercial Street towards Aldgate. He would have to be cautious as he knew they would be looking for him for jumping bail. He considered he may have to leave London, but he had only just arrived and his work had hardly begun. There had only been the one murder, and death on the streets of London's East End was not an uncommon occurrence so the streets would not be any busier with the accursed police so maybe he would be all right for a while. He shuffled along Red Lion Court looking for somewhere to get some semblance of food. He had been up all night and now he was tired and hungry, a mere petty thief at times, he eventually found himself in Brick Lane after a few minutes and spied a bakers shop.

He watched in a very calculating manner through the shop window at the activity inside. It was early with hardly anyone around and inside was just the baker and what he considered was a 'ripe' young girl. He looked up and down the street and could see no one in his immediate vicinity. In the gutter he spotted a lump of broken wood, most probably a broken chair leg, what it came from was not important, the fact it was a weapon was. Ostrog bent down and took a hold of the piece of stained and chipped shaped timber and looked it up and down smiling. Looking along the road again he saw no one for a hundred yards or so in either direction and turned and dashed into the shop. The young girl looked up startled, the baker, her father had his back turned and knew nothing as Ostrog clubbed him viciously over the head just once and with immense force knocking him unconscious and drawing blood. Almost before the girl could scream Ostrog dropped the club and lunged at her covering her mouth, all she could now do was shiver and sob, paralysed by fear.

His left hand covering her mouth and his body pinning her to the back wall of the shop he began a deep resonant laugh revealing foul and decrepit teeth and drooled. She was so young, so innocent, what an opportunity. He thrust his right hand up under her skirt and apron and felt for the inside of her undergarments. He ripped them away from her body violently and she clenched her eyes tightly shut and began sobbing harder. His stubby rough fingers fumbled within her garments and he felt himself begin to shake with excitement, he hissed at her and spoke in a low and sickening tone.

"You are so fresh and ripe, my lovely, mmm?" Her eyes opened and widened with terror. He continued in a loathsome accent "Now I only want bread, I shall return another time for dessert," he pushed the now hysterical girl to the floor and grabbed four loaves of bread shoving them under his coat. Almost hyperventilating, the girl watched as he left the shop back into Brick Lane and disappeared. Her gaze then fell to her father, motionless and his head lying in a pool of blood.

Chapter Two

Millers Court, 7.30.a.m and the auburn haired Mary Kelly was returning to her slum of what would now be called a bed sit. At twenty-five and being attractive even she could not fathom why she was working the streets of East London as a common whore. She rationalised and realised that for the past four years it was all she had known. Born in Limerick in Ireland, she had come to the mainland in Wales as a child when her father had come to work in an ironworks in Caernarvonshire. Her closest sibling, Henry, had gone off and joined the Scots Guards a matter she had always considered strange with their family heritage, while she had met a lovely young lad called Gareth Davies. Gareth was a miner, and when she was sixteen she married him. Three years later she fell pregnant, and then cruelly, as fate would often have it, Gareth was killed within a matter of months in a pit explosion. The subsequent distress had caused her to lose the child and once recovered from the physical drain of the two catastrophes she fled to Cardiff where she first fell into prostitution. Some say the oldest profession, once into the cycle of it seemed you could never escape.

After a long illness, caused by the real emotional trauma of her life to date catching up with her and her body trying to fight off infection and disease from the physical and sexual abuse she had found herself receiving, she eloped to Liverpool and eventually to London in hope of a fresh start. She found one initially in domestic service in London's well to do West End where she had got on with her work well and had made a good impression on the family for whom she worked.

Unfortunately, this was doomed to come to an end when she took up with a man called Bill Morganstone, a thief and a drunk. She fell into ways of drunkenness quickly and became slacking in her work for her employers in Knightsbridge. They asked her to leave as a result and she was forced to move full time to London's East End where she now found herself struggling to make ends meet. With Morganstone's drunken and often violent ways she very quickly left him and fell back into prostitution to live. With her looks she was fortunate to be able to be more selective with 'clients' and command a better price.

However, time with Morganstone had left its mark with Mary; she never fully was able to kick the alcohol habit. Living with a succession of men on and off she finally took up with a local man called Joe Barnett. Although they appeared to get on as a friendly couple, Mary, who was also known as 'Black Mary' due to her frequent choices of clothing, 'Fair Emma', due to her complexion or sometimes just as 'Ginger', they also had frequent disagreements and separations. Mary was lucky that the years of abuse had so far not taken their toll on her looks.

She had parted company with Mary Nichols in Commercial Street not long after seeing Robert Ford and now turned up at 13 Miller's Court surprisingly sober and was greeted by Barnett just as he was going off to work, a local grave digger.

"Mary, love, why can't you give it up? We could move away and make a new start if you did," pleaded Barnett. He knew only too well of the profession that Mary plied on the filthy streets of Whitechapel. Although uncomfortable, it was not unusual for wives or partners to sell themselves in this way.

"I like it here and we've got to eat. Can you think of what else I could do? I'll hardly get a reference from that old banshee Mrs Buki now, will I?" Mrs Buki had been her former employer in Knightsbridge.

"Then get yourself a sewing job or something else local **and honest.**"

"Oh, get to work with you, Joe Barnett; I am too tired to bicker about it now. If you keep on about it I'll go back to Paris."

Mary had eloped to Paris for a short time between her time of living in Liverpool, albeit briefly, and then coming to London. She only stayed a fortnight having travelled out there with a 'gentleman' that she met whilst working in Liverpool, who after a short time in the French capital started to scare her and make her feel uncomfortable. He had claimed to be an artist having travelled many parts of the world including British colonial Africa and he insisted on sketching her frequently which she enjoyed, but one day as a result of her own suggestion she posed naked. The whole incident was bizarre and she discovered he was paying obsessive attention to the parts of her body that made her a woman. This, he claimed, was because that not only was he an artist but also a medical practitioner specialising in gynaecological issues. He persisted in wearing a very flashy uniform wherever they went and would scurry off to hospitals by himself and come back with specimen jars all wrapped up and never let her see what was in them. The jars were kept in a kind of leather carpet bag that he referred to as his 'art materials' bag, an item of luggage he was very possessive about and asked her to refrain from touching it 'and messing my art things and instruments.'

He was an American and sported a long bushy moustache and boasted of his medical achievements in various parts of the United States saying he had perfected many miracle cures for common yet persistent ailments. He frequently complained of missing his hunting hounds while they were in Paris and whenever in the street with dogs around he would pay them more attention than anything else. It didn't take too much time before she grew very tired with his company let alone being disturbed by his medical obsessions.

One day when he was out and she was on her own in the hotel accommodation they shared in the Monmartre district of Paris, known for its association as the artist's centre of the city, she opened the art materials bag. Below the pencils, pastels and brushes with paint she found a false bottom. Curiosity now aroused, she removed it and on seeing the contents felt a chill run down her spine. Already disturbed by his behaviour she now found what seemed to her untrained eye to be surgeon's knives, some forceps and one of his mysterious specimen jars wrapped in brown paper. Ripping the packaging away from around the jar she exposed what was floating inside it in a light brown coloured medical fluid. Not having any anatomical knowledge Mary initially saw the contents merely as folds of flesh, disturbing enough to her before the shock realisation of what these folds of flesh were. Although a simple girl she knew enough to recognise these folds on one side with its orifice as being the same as she possessed to ply her trade. Mary almost paralysed with fear and beginning to panic, considered in her mind his possibly horrific intentions for her. She hurriedly and chaotically gathered and packed her meagre belongings, shoving them with no methodology into her one battered leather case.

She realised during this process that she needed money to return to England and with her pulse now beginning to quicken s a result of her discovery, she rifled through her companions belongings finding £50 in Dr Tumblety's brief case. Whilst searching for his travel papers, Mary came across a dark blue leather jewellery box just the right size to house a necklace and broach or perhaps a dress watch. Dr Tumblety had never expressed any interest in such finery only ever making use of a fob watch on a silver chain, which puzzled Mary as to what he might keep in the box. It was locked with a small brass padlock really more for show than as a deterrent as it appeared too weak to stop it being opened. Mary grabbed her own bag and pulled out a nail file with a hooked cuticle end jammed this hook into the lock's key hole and with a brisk turn of the nail file the latch popped opened and fell away onto to the richly carpeted French hotel's floor.

Her heart started to pound as one hand continued to grasp the base of the box and the other dropping the file now took hold of the lid to pull it open. Initially very stiff, the spring loaded lid began to ease back to reveal its hidden secret inside. Her eyes widened and her lower jaw fell open as she spied for the first time the contents of the box, fearing he maybe likely to return at any minute her amazed admiration was short. Inside sat on a bed of crushed black velvet were the largest single diamond and two huge pieces of emerald stone she had ever seen in her life. These precious gems were surrounded by a ring of what appeared to be smaller diamonds round them in a circle. The large diamond itself was about one and a half inches round and cut in a perfect circular fashion. Knowing that diamonds were very valuable and they could resolve all her troubles, especially the largest, she pulled the centre stone from the box and took a handful of the small diamonds and tossed the now significantly emptier jewellery box back into Tumblety's bag.

Looking out of the hotel room's window to see what the weather was doing she saw that it was dry and bright accentuating the beauty of the classical Paris skyline; but sending a shiver through her body, Mary also noticed that Tumblety was returning along the road she overlooked in a carriage. She grabbed her case from the bed that she had now unceremoniously packed and fled the room. Finding the back staircase she made her way down the stairs but too quickly losing her footing and falling as she neared the bottom from becoming entangled in the voluminous skirt of her typically Victorian dress. With grazed knees and palms, bruises all along her right side from the fall, she sobbed to herself as she grabbed her now even more battered case and ran out from the back of the building through an alley way and into one of the busy Parisian streets melting into the crowd.

Days later having fled the bohemian Monmartre district of Paris her imagination took a jaundiced view of the French capital and she swore never to return. She found herself passage on a ship from Calais boarding a mixed passenger and cargo vessel bound for Dover. Within a week Mary was settled in London and taking up an engagement in service in the fashionable and affluent Knightsbridge in West London with a lady called Mrs Buki, ironically a French matriarch

Unfortunately for Mary this promising position ended in disaster with her being accused of theft whilst in service for the family in Knightsbridge. She always felt aggrieved by this accusation as she had not taken anything from them and it seemed that they may have discovered her past link to prostitution and making up the accusation of stealing dismissed her.

Barnett carried on talking to Mary as she was lost in another world recalling those events in her mind. For a few minutes as she pondered her life to date, and what to do with the diamonds she had taken from Tumblety and now had hidden in a case below the floor boards of Millers Court. She had pawned one of them for money to buy some best clothes, but what about the rest? Would he be coming to look for her? Could she cut her obsessive links to the street life she was now so accustomed to? But most of all, if she could make a new start where could she go to exchange the largest diamond for it's financial value to start afresh without creating any unwarranted interest? Joe Barnett was just a passing phase, in truth she desperately needed someone in her life to love and spend the rest of her life with.

"Joe, I need to sleep. Will you away to work, darling, and we'll discuss it later."

"Yeah, well just and stay sober so that it is a discussion and not the usual drunken argument," Barnett not wanting to wait for her reply left the squalid room slamming the door behind him.

* * *

At around midday Robert and Del found themselves walking along Whitechapel High Street outside the famous London Hospital. A busy street market stretched from the junction of Bakers Row through to Cambridge Heath Road, the odour of which filled their nostrils as fresh meat, vegetables and flowers blended oddly together and permeated the air. Robert considered that it seemed the standard smell of the East End having lived with it all his life. He wondered if the rest of the world smelt any differently. His peaceful thoughts were suddenly disturbed.

"Oi! Stop thief!" A scruffy working man charged past the two of them bumping shoulders with Del and almost stumbling, but regaining his balance before heading towards Cambridge Heath Road. Both Del and Robert began to give chase tucking their beat helmets under their arms and found themselves with a fruit stall holder in hot pursuit of them.

"He's bleedin' nicked two pocketfuls of apples from my stall," he shouted behind them. Both the constables ignored him focusing on their quarry that Robert recognised as a man he had arrested the previous month for being drunk and disorderly. Michael Kidney was the sometime partner of Elizabeth Stride the station cleaner and had been known to assault her in the past so Robert was always keen to 'square him up' given an opportunity. Kidney was running flat out along the busy thoroughfare knocking into people and sending some of them crashing to the floor, leaving the following police to jump over them or stumble around them. As all of them left chaos and panic in their wake they seemed to be followed along the road by the sound of a choir of aggrieved East Enders. Kidney seeing an opportunity to lose his pursuers ahead ran in amongst some squalid tenement blocks to try to give them the slip. As he disappeared around the corner Robert and Del knowing the area well split up and took different routes, Robert continuing immediately after Kidney whilst Del went straight on to get to the other side of the building

The estate that the tenement was a part of was a warren of gloomy passageways formed by the tall, dark and foreboding brown brick Victorian buildings. Dark and sinister with each of the blocks possessing a deep layer of dirt from the polluted air of the area. Decaying window frames from a lack of maintenance looked out into the passageways like the watery eyes of many of the aging occupants. The nature of this construction allowed the formation of a dark labyrinth of alleys that afforded easy or concealment of the many suspicious goings on normally far away from the prying eyes of the law. It made the conduct of prostitution simplistic too with dingy but private places for the street women to take their clients having plied their trade.

The two policemen had now broken into a walk to allow them to try to spot movement and re-engage their suspect, so no longer were they running with helmets in their hands, but stealthily scouring the entranceways and landings to find Kidney with one hand on their faithful wooden truncheons for self defence and the other ready with their whistles to call for assistance. Each of them trying to keep the noise from their heavy soled boots to a minimum; both all too well aware of the wandering undernourished street dogs that may alert their quarry to the presence of his pursuers. They passed dirty poorly fed children from time to time who were huddled in groups on the stairs whose mothers looked on as they hung their ragged laundry out of the windows.

As Robert passed a stairwell Kidney lunged out at him with a broom he had found to use as a weapon lying around discarded. Swinging the heavy head of the broom he managed to catch Robert in the stomach knocking the wind from him. Kidney then pushed him to the ground and jumped on top of him and started to try to strangle him. Robert, pushing against Kidney's arms, could sense the stench of stale alcohol on his adversary's breath so strong and overpowering it made him wretch. He knocked the arms of his assailant away from his throat and threw a couple of punches into his chest knocking him back.

Robert was suddenly aware of a shadow being cast across the two of them and was relieved to see it was Del, who he could see was swinging his truncheon high above his head ready to launch it down onto the first part of Kidney he could hit. This turned out to be the back of his head and he collapsed in a heap to one side of Robert as the result of the blow from the heavy dark wooden weapon. Robert looked up at Del Lake with a smile of relief and appreciation.

"Thanks, mate," he said looking up at his partner,

"What are friends for?" replied Del with a broad grin on his face.

Del pulled out his whistle as Robert jumped to his feet and placed some handcuffs on Kidney who was now groaning lying on the floor.

"Can I get my apples back now, constable," called the portly and red faced market trader who was now about twenty yards from them.

"Certainly," replied Robert who now pulled the half a dozen green apples from Kidney's two jacket pockets. As he did so the stall holder now extremely out of breath arrived with them, bending double trying to regain his breath puffing heavily and very red in the face. Robert handed him the apples.

"Thank you, constables," said the market trader cheerily. He then handed them an apple each nodded in a courteous fashion and turned away strolling off back through the estate to return to his pitch.

Del cleaned his apple up on his trouser leg and with a loud crunch bit into it and began to chew on its sweet flesh. He winked at Robert and spoke.

"All in a days work eh, son?" Robert looked at his partner smiling and shaking his head at his casualness and followed suit with his own shiny green piece of fruit.

As a result of the blast on the whistle another three constables arrived out of breath and red faced one of which included Taffy Williams who Robert thought looked as if he was about to pass out from physical exertion. He coughed up copious amounts of phlegm on his arrival spitting it out with venom not enjoying so much physical exertion. Swearing and cursing to himself he leant up against a wall and began rolling himself a cigarette.

Soon a 'black Mariah' arrived for the carriage of Kidney to 'The Street' where he could sleep off his drunkenness before facing a charge of drunk and disorderly again and assault on police.

* * *

Wednesday 29th August, 2.40.p.m and Dr Francis Tumblety left the Ritz Hotel for the short walk along Piccadilly and into Green Park to take the afternoon air and sun. The fifty-five year old 'physician' strolled along in his American cavalry uniform displaying colourful medal ribbons on his chest, the uniform itself was tailored around his mature frame and 5'10" stature and was topped off with a deerstalker type hat which cast a shadow over his face down below his large handlebar moustache. He also always walked with a dark wooden cane by his side, frequently swinging it in a garish manner, this particular accoutrement hiding as much of a dark secret as his outward respectable appearance. He had made a rich living as a self proclaimed 'Herb Doctor' or 'Electric Physician' in the United States and with the resulting profits from his patents for miracle tonics such as 'Tumblety's Patented Pimple Remover' he was able to travel extensively and live on a very lavish basis. However, elements of his past had required him to travel frequently on occasions to avoid the authorities.

Francis Tumblety was born in Ireland in 1833 one of eleven children of a poor family that moved to Rochester, in New York State when he was quite young. This Irish American background and his overt Fenian sympathies often brought him to the attention of the police whenever he travelled to London. London had been undergoing a wave of violence mostly in the form of bomb attacks since 1867 when twelve people were killed in Clerkenwell after the Fenian rebels attempted to rescue some of their members. They further conducted a bombing campaign against the Metropolitan Police between 1883 and 1885 including an attack on Scotland Yard. As an uneducated and misguided adolescent he spent his time pedalling pornography to the canal boatmen who worked the waters which ran through Rochester linking it to Buffalo. This fuelled an unhealthy early interest in carnal matters which were exaggerated when he began work in his late teens at the disreputable Lispenard Clinic, a practice which specialised in crude hysterectomies, venereal diseases and other gynaecological matters, again creating unhealthy obsessions early in the young Tumblety's mind.

Around 1850, he left Rochester still an uneducated and under achieving young man to travel the USA and ultimately make his fortune. He set himself up within a couple of years in Detroit as an 'Herb Doctor of international repute'. He had gained education and articulation over the time since he had left Rochester and created falsified qualifications to back his exclusive practice. His potions and tonics succeeded in making him a very wealthy man and from 1854 he lived on a lavish basis. He returned to Rochester in a blaze or publicity and glory hailing himself as a 'Miracle Doctor' and either riding through town on a handsome white horse or walking in a cavalry uniform, to which he had no entitlement, with two greyhounds. The community seemed to have forgotten the un-ambitious and sexually frustrated youth that had left many years before.

He practised his brand of medicine all around the United States and Canada finding himself in Toronto in 1858 where his loathing of women took hold, in a bitter and complete contrast to his earlier and younger obsession with the opposite sex. He met a local woman at his practice some years older than himself but exquisitely attractive and seemingly very cultured and honest. They began courting happily and after around six months they decided to marry having a civil ceremony at a district registry office with just the requisite number of witnesses in attendance.

Now living together, there were some nights of the week when she would go out and Tumblety would stay curiously at home, idolising her so much he dared not ask for fear of harming their seemingly idealic relationship. He was becoming possessive about her in the wake of the romantic and passionate sex life he found them having, something he had lusted for as a young man and with her knowing how to pleasure him at every turn. He felt sexually fulfilled for the first time in his life.

He was so happy in his married status but frightened about losing his wife that he constantly showered her with gifts to express his love for her, culminating in the expensive purchase of a diamond and emerald jewellery set for her. The diamonds being a symbol of eternity and his eternal love for her, and the emeralds to complement her beautiful green eyes.

His paranoia about her movements twice a week with 'friends' pained him so much that he followed her one night, and for once not in his garish uniform to avoid bringing attention to himself and allow him to blend in with the townsfolk, away from their marital home. A walk of ten minutes later found her entering to his shock, disbelief and despair a known brothel, where through a well lit downstairs window he could see her plying her trade and leading clients seductively up stairs.

Emotionally destroyed he ran back to the house sobbing all the way and vowing to distance himself from all woman kind forever, having had his heart broken by his first and only love, a common whore. When she returned in the early hours, Tumblety, his dogs, his horse and all possessions were gone, except for his wedding ring which she found on their dining table. He shut all memories of her from his mind including her name. The wonderful jewellery set, however, remained permanently in his possession as it was his way of maintaining his fortune without depositing in a bank's vaults.

He moved on to St John, New Brunswick to set up a new practice. His bad luck followed him there when within months a patient called Podmore, a locomotive engineer he was treating with 'medicine,' died from poisoning. Tumblety was forced to flee to avoid facing a manslaughter charge and took himself off to Boston, again to set himself up in new surgery but being far more careful with the type of medicine he practised. He specialised in pimple cures and took a real interest in his female patients, secretly now beginning to plot his revenge against whore-kind by getting to know women anatomically. His surgery flourished and he soon had branches across the USA in New York, New Jersey, Pittsburgh and San Francisco. This kept his lifestyle fully funded and he travelled to other US cities such as Chicago, Niagara and Philadelphia as well venturing to Liverpool and London and on to mainland Europe.

It was then that he first began to hear the voices. The emotional trauma he had suffered over the proceeding period had set off a chemical imbalance in his brain causing him to begin to suffer with paranoid schizophrenia. Tumblety would be frequently invaded by loud and disturbing male voices calling for him to distance himself from 'all whores' and to 'wreak revenge amongst them and take trophies to signify his triumphs.' The first initial months he managed to suppress these strange and unknown voices in is mind but as time moved on they became more vociferous and called for him to take action. There was a familiarity in the voice that blindly he could not place. Feeling that the affections of others which had once made him so happy could help him, he decided to take drastic action.

He felt it appropriate to distance himself from women to prevent the voices forcing him to take action, so he now sought sexual satisfaction amongst the company of men, a matter that he kept secret from the American high society within which he mixed. All that some within this peer group knew was that he had developed 'a deep hated and distrust of women'. Despite this hatred, he did not find the company of men brought him any sexual satisfaction merely making him at times feel dominated, so he developed a thought process to a different end. He would indulge in intercourse with common whores bringing about a sense of power and domination, one class over another. However, on occasions he had the habit of disturbing those with whom he discussed the matter, like the New Jersey lawyer Colonel C.A. Dunham.

Dunham a close friend of Tumblety's found it strange when he lost contact with the doctor over a few months. He had felt he had seen a change in his friend after the episode with his wife but put it down very naively to the emotional distress the discovery must have caused. Little did he know how Tumblety's mind had begun to twist or the new obsessions the doctor had developed.

Beginning to kow-tow to the voices, Tumblety lacked the courage to go and kill and physically take trophies, but he felt if he gained a collection of medical specimens and continued to try to sexually dominate women it may suppress their demands. Paying visits to hospitals and medical colleges around the state, Tumblety initiated and expanded his collection of female anatomical specimens. But to his bitter disappointment it merely fuelled the voices to implore him to share their beliefs.

The months had passed and out of the blue Dunham received correspondence from Tumblety requesting him to come for dinner to discuss important matters. Concerned about his friend's absence he agreed and arrived at the Doctor's house one winters evening for dinner. The Colonel was visibly shaken when over dinner that night the matter of his wife's deceit had come up for discussion with Tumblety who had then taken Dunham to his office where in a cupboard he had a large collection on specimen jars in which Tumblety claimed to be collecting examples of the 'uterus of all classes of women'. When Dunham inquired as to why, Tumblety simply answered 'so I can have reference to an object of desire'. Clearly shocked the Colonel decided to cut short his dinner engagement and left Tumblety's house never to see him again. The most disturbing aspect had been the request from Tumblety for him to join him in 'the blood letting of whores'.

In 1887 on his first trip to England whilst being driven by the voices, staying in Liverpool and then before moving on to London, Tumblety met a beautiful young Irish girl called Mary who was very shy and quite defenceless it seemed with her having been widowed at an early age. Amazingly to him, he was so taken with her loveliness that the voices seemed to begin to fade and he now believed that his best therapy was to once again try to forge a relationship and a trust in female kind. If he could achieve this he felt confident from the voices suppression that he could live a calm and fruitful life again.

With her background and her own seemingly emotional frailty, Tumblety got chatting with her on a regular basis in the hotel bar where she worked and he was staying and they eventually had dinner together. He felt she was vindicating womankind to him and his dark ambitions on women definitely began to subside and they started to see each other on a regular basis. There were many years between them but it allowed them to build a protective bond with each other especially when they both discussed their varying emotional pasts, although Tumblety was far from fully truthful.

But for Tumblety the emotional darkness within him began to trouble him after the first time they made love. Coming in to contact with a woman intimately had been a brave new step for him and a fascination to take 'specimens' himself for his collection began to grow within him from the dark subliminal programming the voices had given him, even with this beautiful young Irish girl. He had told her that his profession was that of a physician but he had also taken up art as a relaxing pastime and Mary frequently became his subject set amongst a landscape of the Liverpool coast or Lancastrian hills.

But his stay in Liverpool was interspersed with trips to London where he would stay in the grandest hotels and then skulk off to the East End. There he would engage in filthy street sex with the local whores to satisfy the overwhelming sense of female domination that the voices drove him to achieve. So strong were the demands of the voices, they drove him to consider lodgings in the Spitalfields district to indulge in longer periods of depravation with these women in private. He got to know the geography of the district very well, and it was not uncommon to see men in military uniform there, either on leave or out drinking and debauching, so Tumblety blended in well. As far as Mary was concerned he was always on business. He had also put the word discreetly out amongst the medical fraternity in East London that he wished to purchase particular female specimens to add to his collection.

Months passed with this outrageous and depraved behaviour on one hand and then emotional stability with Mary on the other. He must do something to try to resolve the two halves of his life. Short of Victorian electrotherapy, what could he do? He decided he would go to Paris for some thinking time and see if he could suppress his emotions. But on breaking the news to Mary she insisted on going with him. He tried to talk her out of the idea but with the tears flowing and the stories of her past spilling forth once more, he agreed to take the young Mary Kelly with him. They travelled first class together all the way to Paris settling in a hotel in the fashionable and famously bohemian Monmartre district known for it's artists. They had a suite which consisted of a main living room, a bathroom and two bedrooms as Tumblety respected a lady's privacy and felt that Mary deserved it with the short time they had known each other, despite their intimacy.

Walking the streets of an evening together Tumblety found himself distracted by the sight of dogs being walked, owning his own in the USA much to the annoyance of Mary. For him and his ownership of dogs he understood his deep interest in them; they always offered him unconditional love. Both were fascinated by the portraits they saw of naked models in oils and water colour on the streets and on returning to the hotel Mary made a suggestion to Tumblety.

"Francis, would you like me to pose like the models we've seen?" Thinking cautiously about the matter Tumblety agreed as he felt it might help his delicate emotional state by attacking his obsessions head on and therefore be good therapy.

The next night he opened his art materials bag to get his sketching items out as Mary readied herself. The voices had returned to him slowly but surely since leaving England, to the extent they had driven him to leave the hotel early in the mornings to seek 'trophies from a new continent.' He removed the false bottom he had made just to take a look at the specimen bottles he had recently got from the local hospital

Whitechapel

to see if he could kick the unhealthy obsession. He had slipped out on a couple of occasions early in the mornings to avoid Mary's curiosity to go one of the local hospitals to buy some foreign examples for his collection. These 'trophies,' and the desire for them, were fuelled by the voices that dominated his actions over them and prevented him from discarding them or trying to resist collecting more. He felt sure in few days with the relaxed Paris atmosphere and the seeming love of a good woman his paranoia and the voices would once and for all die and he could throw all this bizarre collection away and make a new start.

Only that very day at 6.a.m he had made his way to the Pasteur Memorial Hospital to visit the pathology department to collect a specimen for which he had negotiated with the mortuary attendant. Having made a request for uterus of an African prostitute, something which he knew he would not get readily in London, the rather dubious mortuary attendant even by Tumblety's standards had obliged very quickly and willingly.

The mortuary attendant was a twenty-two year old Polish fellow who had claimed to have served surgeons apprenticeship in his home town of Nagornak before leaving for the brighter lights of Western Europe. He had told Tumblety of his intention to move to London to settle amongst the Polish community in the East End and was merely passing through Paris. He didn't admit to having been there before and having to leave following an allegation of a serious assault. He felt that a year on the dust would have settled there and he could return, but not to the West India Dock area where he had previously worked as a barber. Young Severin Klosowski had a violent streak within him and an unhealthily high sexual drive and unbeknown to Tumblety he had made for the Bois de Boulogne the notorious forest within the city known for its use by night of women of the prostitute class. With this knowledge he concluded that he could satisfy his sexual and violent desires and receive a fee from the curious Dr Tumblety at the same time.

At 11.40.p.m the night before, he had been scouring the area for his victim when he had come across a black woman who had just finished with a client and spotting Klosowski sealed her own fate by making her way towards him. She smiled revealing a row of even white teeth a legacy of her healthy diet whilst still a native of the French Colonies in Africa and spoke to him in French which he understood to a degree.

"Do you want a good time, young man?" she said seductively whilst walking with an exotic sway towards him. He could feel himself becoming very hot all over and just wanted to indulge in pleasures of the flesh now the chance had been presented to him. He replied to her advances.

"I have a cab waiting, will join me elsewhere?"

"As long as you are paying, my darling, then anywhere." They linked arms and walked around a corner to a waiting cab, to which Klosowski had already given the driver instructions to head to the Pasteur Hospital.

They climbed aboard and the driver whipped the reigns to set the horses off at a trot to make their way through the busy Parisian streets. The footways along the boulevards were crowded with ladies and gentlemen taking the air or enjoying some pavement dining along such famous thoroughfares as the Champs Elysee.

"I'm Monique," she said as she began to unbutton his trousers. He just smiled in return as he felt himself stiffen within his suit trousers and began to unbutton her blouse to reveal her unfettered rounded ebony breasts with large dark brown erect nipples; the shade of them an erotic contrast to the rest of her flawless African skin. She pulled herself across his lap lifting her skirt as she did so, her free hand already working him up and down energetically having freed him. Detecting how hard he now was she allowed herself to sink onto him knowing they would slide together with ease as a result of her last liaison. He grunted loudly burying his head into her bare breasts as she flung her head back and began to pant with excitement lifting her self up and down with her thighs to provide her client with pleasure.

The passionate sounds emanating from within the cab were lost amongst the throng of humanity in the busy streets and the sound of the horse and carriage itself along the cobbled streets. After several minutes of passion their unloving sexual encounter was over, and for Monique so was her life. As Klosowski did up his trousers and she fastened her blouse he pulled his belt from around his trousers. Monique was looking out of the window and speaking to him unaware of his intentions.

"You are my greatest ever lover," looking round to her client for a response the narrow leather belt was flung around her neck and pulled tight before she could even emit a scream. Fighting for her life she lashed out at her assailants face with her long fingernails to try and inflict enough damage for him to stop, but only making a glancing lunge she failed and within thirty seconds of her blood supply cut off to her brain she was unconscious.

Now pulling up outside the hospital, Klosowski casually replaced his belt and leaned out of the cab to pay the driver and said "Look, my friend, could you help me in with her? She's fainted." The driver, curious as to their destination anyway asked no questions so as not to jeopardise his tip. He assisted his fare to the door of the Hospital with the unconscious woman and was rewarded handsomely for his troubles. Now, by himself, Klosowski dragged Monique off to the mortuary. He placed her limp body onto the examination table and began to strip her. He found this dark skinned woman very erotic and once naked he tied her down and gagged her. He wanted one last opportunity with her before she had to be slain. Poised above her, she came round from her temporary coma to find the man who would be her final contact with life upon her and within her. Then he cut her throat.

Klosowski had no concern or remorse as no one in Paris would miss just another colonial whore from the infamous Bois. The only people who could raise any concern were her own kind and the authorities would be unlikely to listen to them. He got to work on the body, after he had made himself a casual cup of coffee, for it to be ready for his client early in the morning.

Tumblety paid Klosowski handsomely for the specimen and hurriedly left from the mortuary to make his way swiftly back to the hotel so as not arouse Mary's curiosity. Klosowski counted his money and smiled to himself. He now had his money for a ticket to cross the channel and realise his ambitions in London.

Chapter Three

Tumblety sat himself in an armchair facing a chaize-longue about ten feet way from him for Mary to pose on. She entered the room in a dressing gown and walked across the room making positive eye contact with her prospective portrait artist. Then standing in front of the chaize-longue she undid the waist tie on the gown allowing it to fall from her shoulders to reveal herself to Tumblety wearing only a seductive smile. He took a deep intake of breath as she did so, still after the time they had known each other taken aback by her beauty. Mary then laid herself out on the couch and got into a comfortable lying position and the 'artist' began his work.

He initiated her portrait with a soft leaded pencil in his shaking hand sketching a basic outline of the furniture and Mary's form lying within it. As he got the detail flowing he worked his way along the outline of the body he had created on his pad filling in detail and shading. Excitement bubbled within him and his quivering nature grew rather than subsided, feeling himself driven by the voices to pay attention to the distinctively female attributes of her body creating what amounted to a female caricature, with emphasis on her breasts with prominent nipples, making them now out of proportion with the rest of the pencil drawn body and the same with her crutch area paying particular detail to it and emphasising it unnecessarily, an area he had become obsessed by. The voices and their various tones then caused him to freeze. From hearing a jumble of pitches he now picked up on and could only sense one specifically speaking to him.

'Coward, take your own trophies, let some whores blood. Who do you think you are, sketching, you should be drawing the life from her.' Finally he recognised it and its familiarity. It was his own voice within what was becoming an ever more tortured mind.

During the sketching process Mary could see from his face that he was becoming more and more troubled by the experience. But why? They seemed to get on well and have an intimate relationship, so why was his expression becoming more stern and tortured? She noted he was beginning to perspire heavily too. The voice raged in his head.

'A whore, she's a whore like them all, you cannot trust her, do your work and take a trophy, you pathetic sexually inadequate fool.'

In his own mind Tumblety was replying 'Leave me I will not succumb to you, she is innocent, she is good, I will not kill her, she is my salvation.'

'She will deceive you and hurt you like all the others.'

'She isn't the others, this is Mary and I love her.'

'Romantic imbecile, what is love; male gullibility born out of female sexual temptation, kill the whore!'

Suddenly he shouted aloud "No I will not!" Tumblety grabbed the paper from his pad, and ran from the room and away down the hotel corridor.

Grabbing her gown Mary pulled it on and ran after him but found him gone and nowhere in sight. Alarmed she returned to the room and stared blankly around. She had observed bizarre behaviour from him before but no outburst such as this. Just as she thought her life was beginning to find it's way again, now this. She noted that the pad was still present but minus the top sheet. However, it had left an imprint on the sheet of paper below it of what Tumblety had been sketching which she began to examine. What she saw bothered her. Aware of the sensuality of her own body she was disturbed by the emphasis that this sketching put on the sexual areas of her body. What was going on in his mind? Where was he going to on those early mornings?

She walked over to the window and stared out across the Paris skyline. On the window ledge was a carafe of red wine, pouring herself a glass she took a refreshing mouthful of the sweet alcohol which she had started to avoid so well, but now felt drawn to. He then reappeared in the room.

"Francis, what the hell is going on?"

"I can't talk now, I need to sleep."

"What? You behave like that, sketching some filth version of me and you need to sleep, what about me?"

"Leave me alone, we'll talk tomorrow."

"Francis, I may not be here tomorrow." The voice in his head interrupted Tumblety's reply, 'You maybe more right than you know.'

"NO!" Tumblety screamed.

"Francis, you're scaring me."

"I promise we'll talk in the morning." Tumblety stormed off shutting himself in the so far unused second of the two bedrooms the suite possessed. Mary pounded on the bedroom door pleading for him to let her in so they could talk. He ignored her calls and laid out on the bed holding his hands over his ears, the only voice that he could hear was the evil sound of himself screaming within to 'Kill all whores!'

The next morning Mary woke to find Tumblety out. She decided to look in his arts materials bag.

* * *

Before returning to Mary from his early morning trip to the mortuary, Tumblety out in the fresh air of the Paris Streets, felt in control of himself again this morning and decided to take action to appease and apologise to Mary. Stopping off along the Champs Elysee he entered a jewellers to purchase a necklace as a gift and an engagement ring, he felt the time maybe right whilst in Paris to ask Mary for her hand in marriage, and the necklace may help smooth over his bizarre behaviour from the night before. Moreover, he felt that such strong emotional actions may help overcome what he now identified as his own dark side.

The sales assistant was a brisk and business like young Parisian smartly turned out with a good command of English and a confident manner. He reminded Tumblety of himself when he first returned to Rochester having found his fortune. His success in generating his wealth had brought with it problems. Following the unfortunate incident when a patient had died under his care, he had had to go on the run to avoid almost certain prosecution. He discovered that keeping money banked was quite restrictive to this end so after that incident he withdrew all his money barring a checking account and invested it in diamonds. Easy to conceal and carry, for a man of his obvious social status a commodity that he could easily exchange for cash. He had invested his fortune wisely and had a collection of two flawless emeralds, the cheaper end of his investment, fifteen high carat value diamonds and one huge flawless diamond about an inch and a half round of an almost immeasurable carat value due to its perfection. It was his main fortune. Casting his mind over the thought of his investments he bought a pretty emerald encrusted necklace which he felt would compliment Mary's eyes and a ring with no stone to carry one of the diamonds from his collection. He would marry the two items together and have them mounted in a few days.

He returned to his carriage which had been perambulating him around the city for the morning's duration and left for the Monmartre Hotel knowing nothing of Mary having fled. Walking up the stairs having claimed his key from reception he felt very positive and upbeat about the new life ahead he would be forging for himself. He seemed to have the love of a good woman, although he realised that the previous night had been tense, and as a result was gaining control of his dark side, which had plagued him ever since that fateful marriage. Although the one bizarre link between these two women who had so invaded his life was that they both had the most striking green eyes he had ever witnessed. How coincidental that he should be drawn to two women with the same physical feature, although Mary's were somewhat bluer. That must have been what had subliminally drawn him into investing in the emeralds and he felt sure that with mind to previous experiences 'lightning could not strike twice.'

He turned the key in the door and called happily "Mary, I'm home," but heard no reply of her gentle Irish brogue. "Mary?" He began pacing around the suite looking for her, but to no avail. Then he spied his artist's bag open on the bed with items strewn from it including the jewellery box. 'My God!' he thought, 'where has she gone, what has she done?' The specimen jars were everywhere, she had discovered his dark obsession, but to top it all, opening the jewellery box he discovered that the main diamond and a handful of the smaller diamonds were gone.

He now stood to be ruined socially by her discovery and also now certainly financially unless he recovered that stone. Rage began to develop and as it did so he heard a familiar voice.

'I told you, you soft centred sentimental fool, she'll destroy you.' But now all he could hear was himself echoing the sentiments of the distant voice which had belittled and driven him to the brink of insanity so far.

'I should have listened, you were right all along. Now that thieving harpee must die, I will not be wronged twice. I shall be down on all Whores....'

When in London he always took a room in the finest hotels such as the Ritz and only indulged his sordid vices in the squalid East End of London, now with more purpose than ever. In so doing he was safe in not besmirching his reputation amongst the well-to-do of London's West End society who knew him. He knew London well having frequented the 'old enemies capital' as he called it on three previous occasions. These trips had given him an intimate knowledge of the Whitechapel area and its surrounding districts and it was here that he suspected that Mary Kelly may well have settled.

Months had passed since the ill fated trip to Paris with Mary and he had developed a new rationale in his thinking. He had succumbed to the voices and would soon start on his work in 'the blood letting of whores'. In creating an agreement with his dark side it allowed him to think without intrusion. This was a logical place for Mary to come. As a simple country girl might think it easiest to get lost there amongst the crowds. He had discovered from enquires in Wales using a private detective that she had spent a time whoring herself there before they had met, which drove the knife into him more deeply. With this in mind, if she was in London she would be perhaps living in the West End if she had decided to trade in the gems, or if she was too stupid to have done anything but keep them, which he hoped she had, she would be working in Whitechapel or Spitalfields. With her looks wherever she was working, if working she was, she would never be short of clients.

He looked at the fine wives and mistresses of the gentlemen who were also taking the air that afternoon. He worked hard to keep his dark carnal thoughts at bay and suppress his murderous urges until he entered Whitechapel. As his thoughts lay elsewhere, he felt a tap on his shoulder and turned around instantly to see who it was, raising his walking cane slightly and tightening his grip on it as he did so. Tumblety turned to be confronted by a handsome English gentleman well dressed in a three piece suit and sporting a bowler hat. He was slender with a smooth complexion and a neatly trimmed typically Victorian gent's moustache. He was very much the image of Queen Victoria's grandson Prince Albert Victor. Montague John Druitt faced Tumblety with an expectant look.

A smile appeared across Tumblety's face and he began to greet Druitt. Grabbing hold of his upper arms with his own he spoke with his distinctive American twang.

"Druitt, old boy how are you, great to see you again." Druitt relaxed his look and smiled himself and relied to this jovial greeting.

"Not bad at all thank you, Doctor, not bad."

The dashing looking Druitt was a successful practising solicitor and noted sportsman especially during his days at Oxford University where he also excelled in the debating society. Not everything he touched turned to gold as his real driving ambition had been to be on the stage, but after poor reviews as Sir Toby Belch in Shakespeare's 'Twelfth Night' as a young man he gave up the idea of a career as a thespian. This pained him still some eleven years later but depression had run in his family from his mother's side and sometimes got the better of him. To console himself he ventured into the East End to indulge in debauchery with street women which increased his own self esteem by allowing him to achieve a sense of sexual conquest. He therefore had much in common with Tumblety, but when the Doctor was not around to keep his spirits boosted following the satisfaction of his urges in Whitechapel, he would fall into a deeper depression for lowering himself so. He would then often find himself by the River Thames in Wapping contemplating death having debauched himself so shamefully in Whitechapel. He knew one day he would have the courage to do it. It was in Spitalfields whilst drinking with some unfortunates in The Ten Bells public house that he had first met Tumblety. A relatively small pub, Druitt had spotted Tumblety across its smoky and always lively bar in his military finery at a table with three women around him, all in various states of age, dress, size and un-attraction. For both he and Tumblety the one common and redeeming feature they both had was a taste for cheap sexual gratification. None of the women or Druitt knew Tumblety's true intentions when he went to the East End. He would now use them to track down Mary Kelly and to fulfil his bloodlust along the way.

"You know, Monty, your resemblance to that damn Grandson to the Queen is uncanny," said Tumblety in his American East coast accent.

"Doctor, would you please address me as Montague. Monty is the preserve of my mother and brother as a name, thank you. And furthermore, the only advantage this look gives me is the occasional free knee trembler from the ugliest bitches thinking they're about to be plucked from obscurity. Because of all these Cleveland Street rumours about the Prince they keep thinking I'm him." It was rumoured that Prince Albert Victor had secretly married a catholic prostitute having fathered a child with her and their liaisons took place in Cleveland Street.

"Sure, cut the doctor crap when we're about town and call me Frank, its better around the ladies," retorted Tumblety. "Now let's grab a cab and get going to Whitechapel, we'll talk along the way."

They strolled from Green Park into Constitution Hill and past the walls of Buckingham Palace down to its front gates. Passing these gates two constables on duty outside tipped their hats to Druitt making the common mistakes that Tumblety had highlighted. Strolling into The Mall Druitt waved down a horse-drawn hansom cab. They both climbed aboard.

"Where to, your Grace?" asked the driver. Smiling broadly and knowingly Druitt replied.

"Whitechapel, my good man. The Ten Bells, Commercial Street."

* * *

Getting on for late afternoon the same day Robert and Del had finished another early shift and had walked from 'The Street' down to The Britannia public house. Some of the other lads off duty had joined them in there with the whole establishment now being a mix of traders, prostitutes, soldiers and policemen. Working in such a tight knit area most of the prostitutes, or 'toms' as they were known by the police, all knew each other. A group of three were sitting together at a table getting progressively drunk, which helped dull the senses when plying their trade later, and beginning to howl with raucous laughter.

Robert was transfixed by Mary Kelly who was sat with forty-six year old Catherine Eddowes, a common prostitute who appeared haggard, drawn and typically looked beyond her years. With her current lifestyle she had done well to live to forty-six. The other woman with them was forty-three year old Mary 'Polly' Nicholls. A native of the area all her life, she had a bloated, ruddy appearance no doubt the result of alcohol abuse and was very plain.

"Oh for God's sake, Rob, she maybe pretty but she's a bloody tom, mate," said Del to Robert trying to break the stare he had fixed on Mary.

"I know, but if could catch her now, before it takes its toll on her maybe we might have a future together, she's quite sophisticated," replied Robert defensively.

"Leave it out, mate, sophisticated? Oh, she must be tomming it around here. Just go and bloody well drag her away from the other two."

"I'm building up to it, Del, I will do it in minute when things are.... right."

"Well in the meantime until things are right, do you want another beer?"

"Too bloody right, that might help bring on the right moment." Shaking his glass at Robert Del said "Well it's your round, the usual please."

Robert turned to Wilf the portly mutton chopped ageing barman to place their order. As he did so The Britannia's doors flung open violently and Long Liz Stride marched in followed by her would be partner Michael Kidney who the two off duty constables had recently arrested . Kidney was some seven years younger than her and quite over protective of her resulting in frequent arguments between them. They were both drunk and shouting violently at each other entering the pub.

"Why don't you go to hell and die, you good for nothing fucking slag!" she screamed to him nearing the bar.

"You fucking slut, plying yourself on the streets for pocket money and titillation, you don't have to yer know."

"What allow you to try to keep me, you're always drunk and never able to get it up as a result, you pathetic weasel, at least someone who can do it gives me something in return my way." Kidney screamed at the top of his voice at her. "Whore, how dare you speak to me like that in public, I'll knock your fucking block off!" He stormed the last few feet up to her where she now rested with her back against the bar and drew his right fist back. She screamed out in terror "NO, NO," as he reigned a heavy blow down onto her left cheek, and then again onto the top of her head as she fell wailing to the floor.

Typically the Victorian clientele in the bar area looked on as if being entertained, some of the burly working men raising a smile. Robert said to Del "I can't let this happen," and rushed from next to his friend over to the aid of Liz still on the floor with Kidney now kicking her. Robert pulled him around by his left shoulder and stared at him standing straight on and said "Okay, big man lets see how tough you are." He got into his pugilist's defensive stance with Kidney immediately throwing a punch at his face. He easily blocked it and then with immense speed and aggression attacked Kidney with a volley of punches to his face, then stomach and then finally an upper cut to his jaw, knocking him to floor. Kidney crumpled like a dead weight with blood beginning to stream from his nose and from one side of his mouth. Del approached them.

"There was never going to be much of a competition really was there? Not with your past hobbies."

"I can't let it go on, not to a woman, mate," replied Robert. In the meantime there was a stunned silence over The Britannia as everyone looked on at him for some seconds and his handiwork. The doors were flung open and a couple of the late duty constables came in having been beckoned by a client who had rushed into the street for help as the fight between Kidney and Stride had started. They were constables Bill Smith and Ernie Thompson. They saw Robert and Del stood over Kidney and Liz sitting against the bar crying intently still and nursing a swollen left cheek.

"Your handiwork then, Rob?" inquired Smith.

"Yes, but totally justified, he'" pointing to the unconscious Kidney "was knocking ten bells of shit out her, excuse the local pun of course," exclaimed Del.

"Oh, it's no problem," said Thompson, "we were just curious." He continued addressing Liz.

"Do you want anything done with this gent, Liz?" asked Ernie Thompson knowing her from the police station.

"No," she replied sobbing, "Please just take him and let him sleep it off."

"No worries, luv," said Smith as they took an arm from Kidney each and dragged him out to await the arrival of a 'black Mariah' to take the unconscious prisoner to the cells at the Street.

Robert helped Liz to her feet by the bar. "You all right Liz?"

"I have felt better, darling, you know, sorry to get you involved."

"It's no problem, wouldn't let that happen to anyone, let alone my best seamstress." This brought a smile to Liz's face and she felt comforted by his words. The only trouble being in reality was that he wasn't always going to be there to help. She had to leave Kidney.

Polly Nicholls came up to the bar and put her arm around Liz to lead her to her table. She spoke to Robert as she did so, "Thanks for looking after her, mate, none of us could have done it." She then continued in a raised voice. "And none of these other so called men would have helped." As she led Liz away her words simply fell on deaf ears.

Del spoke to Robert, "Well after all that excitement I don't rightly know as want another drink in here, I'm off. I shall see you tomorrow, my lad."

"Yeah, maybe you're right I think I'll be going too." As they turned away from the bar having bid Wilf a good evening Mary Kelly confronted Robert pressing a finger into his chest.

"Not so fast, constable, we ladies there have clubbed together to buy you a drink..." Despite her trade, Del saw this as Robert's perfect opportunity and decided to leave. "See ya, mate," nodding and winking to Robert knowingly.

"Yeah, see ya, Del, and thanks mate,'" Robert said appreciatively.

Robert now stood at the bar with the stunning auburn haired Mary Kelly, with her emerald eyes, fair skin, pleasant demeanour and slender face she was everything Robert could ever want in a woman. Wilf approached them and spoke. "Now Ginger, what can I get for you and your gentleman?"

"Well, constable, what will it be?" she smiled at him seductively.

"Mary, to start with, you can cut all that Constable rubbish and call me Robert. Secondly, I'll have a large Scotch, please Wilf"

"And a half of stout for me please, Wilf," asked Mary in her subtle Irish tone.

"That was very brave of you, Robert; he's a nasty man that Kidney, he won't forget you now."

"Mary, I couldn't stand by and watch anyone take a beating, let alone someone I consider a friend."

"Do you consider me a friend then?"

Robert began to feel warm inside talking to the object of his affection so closely now. He tried not to blush as he spoke. "Yes, of course I do, in fact I'd like to ask you if you would come boating with me in Victoria Park this Saturday afternoon?"

"You do know I live with someone now, don't ya, Robert?" Robert immediately felt deflated by her response. "Well no sorry I didn't."

"But I would love to. Where shall we meet and what time?"

"How about outside the London Hospital around one o'clock, I'm off that day."

"That's settled then. I'll see you there, come hell or high water. I love boating, it reminds me of being a child."

They carried on chatting and finished their drinks at the bar over the next half an hour. Secretly they both detected chemistry between them each eagerly looking forward to leisure time away from the crowds in the park at the weekend.

"I must be going now, Robert. I've got to go home."

"Can I walk you there," he asked intuitively.

"Proper gent, aren't you eh? Why of course, but not to the door Joe Barnett will go mad otherwise."

"Where is he now then?"

"Pissed over the road in The Ten Bells I expect."

They left The Britannia arm in arm turning right out of the door towards Millers Court and Mary's dreary home. Robert felt elated as he walked her to the entry of the small tenement block and she kissed him gently on his cheek. She walked away and before turning a corner and disappearing out of sight gave him a seductive smile and a wave. It had been a simple but fantastic last hour or so and he felt excited about the weekend.

Chapter Four

Fate is a fickle mistress, sometimes working for you, but many times against. Tumblety and Druitt had been in Whitechapel for some hours and were now making their way to The Britannia. They were approaching only yards from the north of the pub as Robert and Mary had left to the south. As usual Tumblety was in his military finery but somewhat unusually he now carried a Gladstone bag as an additional accoutrement whilst Druitt was in a smart suit. He had used to go out in a guards uniform he had won in a bet with a guardsman literally off of his back, but had given it up after his last outing with Tumblety as he frequently got dragged into drunken singing and then brawls with other off duty soldiers. This was made especially worse when standing on a street corner waiting for your associate with a stream of drunken servicemen walking past abusing your given regiment.

They entered The Britannia and walked up to the bar and were served a pint of ale each by the ever obliging and ruddy face Wilf. They chatted and surveyed the bar room and saw the group of three women, Liz Stride, Polly Nicholls and Cathy Eddowes sat together laughing and drinking. They knew that these three were of exactly the class they enjoyed and would supply them with what they wanted. They carried on drinking at the bar together watching the East End dwellers come and go. One of the women, Liz, got up and bade her companions a good night; Tumblety immediately noticed that this tall slender hag, although the best of the bunch, had a large swelling on her left cheek obviously from some kind of assault. She had a distinctly different look to her companions with high cheek bones and fair to blonde hair, almost Nordic. This was indeed an accurate observation on Tumblety's part as her parents were both Swedish and Gothenburg was her region of birth. Now the occupants of the table were down to two with, conveniently, two additional chairs. The two apparent 'toffs' decided to make a move and join the remaining women, Eddowes and Nicholls. They approached the table with Druitt introducing them.

"Good evening, ladies, may we join you?" Eddowes and Nicholls looked at each other with Cathy then speaking.

"Of course you can, gentlemen," now waving her glass at them, "and you're welcome to buy us both a drink too."

"With pleasure," responded Druitt taking both their glasses, bowing his head courteously and giving them a flashing smile. He made for the bar whilst Tumblety ingratiated himself upon the two women.

"Well hi, ladies, I'm Frank and that there is my good friend Montague. I'm a doctor and he's a lawyer. We've money and time to spend on a couple of fine ladies like you."

"Oh, ain't you the sweet talker, proper smooth he is, eh Polly," said Cathy Eddowes to Nicholls.

"He certainly is," smiled Polly revealing a set of tarnished and uneven teeth. "But what the bleedin' hell is a lawyer?"

"Oh, I'm sorry ladies we sometimes speak a different language, you might call him a barrister or solicitor. Let's face it we are two nations divided by a common language," Tumblety chuckled at his own humorous observation. Polly and Cathy just stared at each other blankly with his comment passing way above their intellect.

Druitt returned with a tray of drinks, beer all round, there was rarely ever anything sophisticated about these types of women. He had in fact only met one common East End prostitute who drank anything more ladylike. She was a young pretty auburn haired Irish girl known as Ginger. He had spent one evening with her and didn't see her around too often probably because she could afford to charge more due to her good looks and therefore needed to work less. He had certainly never met her when in the company of Tumblety, only on his rare solo forays into the area. He sat down passing the drinks out to everyone and looked around the table and said "Now, where were we?"

"Your mate 'ere says you do law, mister," said Nicholls in a drunken slur.

"Please call me Montague, and that's correct, I do practice law." Eddowes bore her rotten teeth in a halitosis smile and spoke.

"Maybe you can give us your card and you can sort us out at the court or nick," she turned to Polly, "Never know, Poll, we could give 'im a freebie in return!" They both roared with laughter with Tumblety joining in while Druitt looked at all three of them unmoved. He was forced to see their side of it as they continued chortling and slowly he began to laugh with them.

The four of them continued inane conversation, mainly for the gents to placate their one night mistresses until the two women felt compelled to leave The Britannia to earn their doss money. Time had got on, Druitt and Tumblety had had to tolerate the women's unintelligent and often unintelligible drivel for what seemed like several hours, all the while plying them with more alcohol.

"Right then," said Cathy Eddowes, "Whose wiv me?" Being slightly less pox ridden overall in Druitt's perception to the other woman he jumped at the chance and replied "Me, your lady," a weak attempt at unnecessary flattery.

"Off we go then, my fine gentleman," she said grabbing his arm and dragging him out of the pub and off to Red Lion Court, a quite alley where they could indulge in their vices.

Tumblety stood up, offered out his arm for Polly to join him which she did so obligingly knowing this would pay, and together, her a little unsteady on her feet, they left the pub. They headed south along Commercial Street towards Whitechapel High Street. It was around 11.p.m and the East End still seemed to be teeming with people.

'Damn it,' thought Tumblety anticipating his first chance to gain his own trophies tonight, 'we might have to stroll around for a while.' The trouble with that for Tumblety was that her intake of alcohol would wear off eventually out in the open if not kept replenished. The streets were full of people wandering around aimlessly such as drunken toms looking for a quick shilling knee trembler while stoned out of their minds on alcohol, drunken servicemen, street vagabonds looking to pray on the weak but also policemen, the only group with a legal purpose. Polly spoke drunken drivel to Tumblety as they entered

Whitechapel High Street and then took him down George Yard. She fell with her back against the wall and began hitching up her skirt.

"Come on then, fancy Dan, come and give me my doss money and see what you get as change," she carried on a drunken giggle as she revealed herself to him. Tumblety looked around up and down the yard. They were only a few yards from the main road, but at both ends he could see people passing. He spoke to her to try to take her off somewhere else.

"Come on, honey, this is too public, I need somewhere quieter to really help you earn that money, with interest even....What do ya say?" His American drawl tailing off questioningly.

"I ain't got time to walk around, Mister Yankee, it's 'ere or find someone who can." There was impatience in her tone. She was stubbornly drunk and wanted her money. Tumblety could feel rage developing inside him, but last time he was nearly caught out, it must not happen again. He surveyed up and down the alley again. There were some openings he could try to take her to.

"Okay, Polly, lets move up a bit." He took hold of her arm. She didn't like this action and pulled her arm away protesting violently; but Tumblety held on.

"Take your fuckin' hands off of me, you bleeder. Who the fuck do you think you are, manhandling a lady!"

"Some Goddamn lady," Tumblety mistakenly said under his breath.

"Right, get your hands off of me and fuck off!" Polly pulled away from him violently and struck out with her right fist catching the side of his face. He let go and she stormed off back to the High Street, Tumblety turned and gave chase. As they both rounded the corner and he was about to pull her back a constable came in to view from Osbourn Street. It was PC John Thain. She ran up to him yelling.

"Oi, that fucker tried to hurt me, constable, whatcha going to do?" She was pointing back towards Tumblety seemingly frozen to his spot nervous of the intervention of the law.

PC Thain looked her up and down and could immediately smell drink from her. He looked at Tumblety and knew exactly what was going on between them, or so he thought. He spoke to the two of them, gesturing with his finger to Tumblety to approach, which he reluctantly but pragmatically did so as not to court unwanted attention.

"Now then, mister, I know what your here for and I know what she's offering and that's fine. But don't hurt the ladies here plying their trade, or you'll feel the wrong end of my companion," he revealed his truncheon just slightly from underneath his beat duty cloak. "And the two of you if you kick up a fuss will see the wrong side of the cell doors at the nick. Do I make myself understood?"

"Yeah, all right then Thainey, just get him to piss off," said Polly in a low tone.

Tumblety nodded his head in acknowledgement.

"Now watch your tongue, Polly. Now you go that way, and you that way," Thain said, gesturing them to each take the opposite directions along Whitechapel High Street. They both did so, Tumblety somewhat reluctantly, but knowing he would walk around the block and follow her off afterward. He would have to jump her and drag her off.

Tumblety walked around the block north of the High Street and ran parallel through Wentworth Street, Old Montague Street and eventually back down into the High Street near The White Swan pub, one of his haunts, and hopefully one of hers. She would be looking for a client, although it was now getting very late. He stood in a doorway opposite the pub and waited, donning a deerstalker hat from his Gladstone bag to disguise his outline from her a little more in the dark. Over an hour went by and Polly eventually emerged with a rather grubby little man, distinctly foreign looking dressed very shabbily and with somewhat of a hunched and furtive walk.

They headed back along the High Street towards the scene of Tumblety's near disaster. He followed them at a discreet distance. Things were looking up as she was now much more drunk than before. Eventually they were passing Church Lane and laughing and staggering Polly steered her client into the lane and then into the church yard. Tumblety waited outside of the church yard listening and able to gain the occasional glance through some railings which were mainly shrouded with bushes.

He could see her hitching her skirt up and leaning herself back against a gravestone for support. The rather odd looking client approached masturbating violently. Polly looked on and said, "Come here lover and let me do that." The man walked up to her and as she lent forward he ejaculated all over her arm and face as she'd lent down. She pulled herself back, screaming at him, whilst he laughed at her.

"You filthy Jewish, fucker, I pull your bleeding' cock off come 'ere!" Aaron Kosminski backed away from her fastening up his trousers. She very bravely got up and lunged at him scratching his face with her nails deeply across his right cheek.

"Whoring bitch!" he shouted as he slapped her back knocking her to the floor. He went to kick her but Tumblety called out disturbing him. He entered the yard to confront Kosminski.

"Leave her alone, you bastard!" said Tumblety very menacingly. Kosminski turned to face Tumblety looking him up and down. He squinted at the American, hissed at him and spitting at the floor in front of where he stood and then barged past and disappeared into the night. Polly was on the floor sobbing and holding her face. In her drunken state she didn't recognise his form especially with him having changed his outline with the hat to be sure of the deception. Tumblety began to speak to her in quite an accurate English aristocratic accent.

"Come, my dear, let me take you home."

"I haven't got one, sir, just need to go to the doss house."

"I can help you get there, come let us walk together." He held his hand out to her and taking hold of it she brought herself up onto her feet. They walked out of the church yard arm in arm, Tumblety shrewd enough to choose the arm that Kosminski had not soiled. She steered him the direction that she wished to go in which eventually took them along Bakers Row, and then she turned them into Whites Row which in turn led into Bucks Row.

Tumblety couldn't believe his luck, they were in an ultra quiet back street and he had seen no one near them for quite some minutes, and there was no one in view. Almost time to strike, but first some conversation.

"Do you know a girl called Mary, sometimes referred to as Ginger or Fair Emma?" he asked of her.

"Oh, I know a few Ginger's me, sir," Polly answered drunkenly.

"This one is a very pretty Irish girl."

"Yes, I do know her I think, sir; she drinks in the pubs along Commercial Street. Don't know where she dosses mind." Tumblety had suspected as much, but the confirmation helped. "That's very helpful, Polly, thank you."

"How do you know my name then?" this was her last ever question.

"Well, lady, fortune favours the bold," he said in his usual accent.

Before Polly could react he grabbed her by the throat completely restricting her wind pipe, and at the same time dropping his bag and pulling a knife from his coat pocket. He pushed her towards some gates to a yard. In one swift movement he pulled the knife across her throat striking deep into it with such ferocity that he cut her neck right back to the vertebrae of her spine. He pushed her almost immediately lifeless body away from himself to avoid the worst effects of the arterial spray. She fell in a crumpled heap on the cobbles of the street which began to fill with rich red arterial blood; her body resting against the yard gates. Her body shook violently in the last throes of life as she made a hideous sucking noise which was the failing attempts to breathe.

Tumblety, unbeknown to Druitt or anyone else, was wearing a very thin cotton copy of his usual tunic over his main garment to take the worst of the blood flow, which he could then stuff into his Gladstone bag. This was a measure he had learned to take from the last time.

Still no one around; he could comfortably get down to his grisly work undisturbed, this time not making the mistake of waiting but going straight into it. He raised her skirt up to reveal her abdomen and as was often common practice Polly was not wearing any underwear. With the knife in his hand he cut deep into her stomach making a clean incision which plunged into her intestines resulting in a massive blood flow oozing down either side of her body onto the floor rapidly forming an expanding crimson puddle. Tumblety was careful to be squatting on his feet as opposed to kneeling so as not to soak his trousers in her blood. Coupled with the out pouring of blood was the stench of her digestive system now opening up to the elements and with a few more deep slashes across her body quite clearly on display. The smell made Tumblety wretch and he began indiscriminately cutting into her organs and pulling tissue and loose flesh out of his way and placing it on the inside of her upturned skirt upon her chest along with an ever increasing amount of stomach material, frantically cutting and searching for her uterus the prize for which he committed these ghastly crimes.

Being an untrained and self professed doctor his knowledge of anatomy was not particularly precise and he was now frustrated by lots of intestinal matter which seemed to be clouding his quest. He cut more with greater ferocity and purpose ripping her internal organs to pieces and creating more mess to be followed by an attempt to search through with his bare hands. He had been working for quite some minutes now not taking much notice of his surroundings and was startled by distant footsteps as he worked. He looked around taking stock of his environment but could not see anyone. He was growing frustrated and felt he would shortly have to give up, vowing to prepare himself better next time with greater anatomical study prior to embarking on another such quest.

'Damn!' he thought, 'I cannot work any longer without risking certain discovery,' this rational thought wasn't even opposed by his dark alter ego. He began racking the disgorged flesh and other matter back into her now hollowed stomach and pulled her skirt down to somewhat sickeningly cover her modesty; a measure of how his ever increasing twisted mind was working and demonstrating a macabre sense of decency. He pulled off his lightweight tunic and wiped the knife blade and his hands down on its body and stuffed the whole lot somewhat unceremoniously into his Gladstone bag.

Looking the street up and down again and then he made off west along Bucks Row to return to the west of town and his luxurious accommodation at the Ritz. Polly Nicholls was left on the pavement a butchered mess so ending her pitiful life of vice. Her final client simply melted into the night and away from the squalid East End.

Meanwhile Druitt had long since finished being serviced by Cathy Eddowes and knowing what the Doctor was like for somewhat dragging out the nights' debauched events from last time decided to simply return home. He had paid Eddowes her money and despite her typical filthy East End condition had actually received a quite good sexual experience from her and thought about recommending her services to the doctor the next time they forayed into the East End together. He flagged down a hansom cab whilst passing through Whitechapel High Street to take him home to his quarters at Mr Valentine's School, Blackheath where he worked part as a schoolmaster whilst also practising law. He would be cautious about arriving back late as Mr Valentine did not approve of late nights, so he would stop short in the cab and walk into the grounds so as not disturb anyone.

He looked out upon the streets of London wondering what his friend's debauched evening had consisted of. As he did so he began to feel great shame and disgust on himself for his own sexual foray. As they approached the Victorian construction project of the new river crossing to be called 'Tower Bridge' he called to the driver. "Stop the cab!" He did so with Druitt briskly alighting and throwing the fare at the driver whose horse trotted off at his command as Druitt strolled off in the direction of Wapping. He reached the shore side after a brisk walk and stared aimlessly out to the river on the gas lit Thames embankment wondering if he as yet had the courage to end his life so full of failure and immorality. He leant against the embankment wall and looked vertically down to the dark swirling water; he would need to make it quick when he did it, weight his own coat down to sink more deeply and guarantee no escape. He looked around him but there was nothing to use. Tonight wasn't the night after all. If he reduced his time in Whitechapel perhaps that might boost his self esteem. He stood up straight and looked west along the river. London by night was a beautiful city and he felt it was not yet his time to give it up.

As he did so a passing constable on the Wapping beat saw him; having seen the police intelligence regarding such activity he spoke to the well dressed gent on the shore side.

"You all right, sir?"

There was a pause from Druitt before he broke his glazed stare out across the river and spoke "Yes, fine officer, just gathering my thoughts."

"Nothing for me to worry about then, sir, you have been seen here before."

"We all have our little places we like to retreat to, constable, and this is mine."

"No problem, sir, see you again." Druitt was unaware of the officer passing on as he was again staring glassy eyed across the river.

* * *

Three a.m. Michael Ostrog came shuffling along Bucks Row and spotted what he perceived was a flat out drunken tom laying by the gates to what was Franklin's wood yard and thought his luck maybe up. Thinking he could perhaps indulge in a quiet freebie if she was unconsciously drunk and satisfy one of his typically sickening sexual urges he approached her and lifted her skirt in the dark, poorly lit Bucks Row. He bent down about to kneel between her legs when he, aghast, noticed her terrible wounds. The extent of the mutilations shocked even him and fearing he would be held guilty of this attack he disappeared into the shadows and out of the area. His survival instincts kicked in heavily fearing discovery and possible blame he ran as fast as his legs could take him away from the scene and deeper into the East End's warren of slums. This left Nicholls lying with her skirt hitched up as she was discovered just over half an hour later by a couple of local men; Charles Cross and Robert Paul passing through on their way home.

Utterly shocked by their discovery they shouted "Murder, murder!" at the top of their voices disturbing the local residents who looked out of their windows. They were joined in minutes by Constable Thain and then Constable Neil, both of whom were local offciers and knew each other well. They had been walking on separate but adjacent 'beats' which allowed them to arrive within minutes of each other. Thain shone his oil lamp into the prostrate woman's face and looked up at Neil saying in a distressed manner, only having seen her hours earlier "Bloody 'ell John, it's Polly Nicholls!"

It was 3.45.a.m.

Chapter Five

Inspector Frederick Abberline stirred on hearing the sound of his large copper mechanical alarm clock begin to strike at around 6.30.a.m. He rolled over from the cuddled sleeping position he found himself in with his wife Emma and turned it off. He sat up on the side of his bed in the three bedroom terraced house in the leafy east of London suburb of East Ham and rubbed his eyes. He stood up and began shuffling across the bedroom to head out to the bathroom mindful of not stepping on the tail or anything else of his wife's beloved Norwich terrier 'George' sleeping on the landing. He walked into the bathroom and lent on the washbasin and faced into the mirror above it.

Fred Abberline was born in Blandford, Dorset the son of Edward and Hannah and moved to London in 1863 to join the Metropolitan Police. He had worked extensively in the East End during his twenty-five year service spending fourteen of them as an inspector in the area and therefore had an intimate knowledge of the geography and society of that side of London. This would be a profound factor in his selection, as yet unknown to him, in heading the immediate investigation of the two prostitute murders in Whitechapel at 'street level'. He currently worked directly out of the detective department or C.I.D at Scotland Yard and little did he know that the second murder of a local prostitute was about to have a profound effect on the rest of his police career and life.

Staring into the mirror he saw looking back at him a rather greying and becoming marginally paunchy forty-five year old in dire need of a shave. A decade of alcohol abuse during the 1870s the period during which he spent so much time in the East End had taken its toll on him. The stress of being at the inspector level in both uniform and the C.I.D in the area drove most to the solace of a drink after hours, and sometimes even during it, to relieve the tension that dealing with countless rapes, assaults, robberies and occasional murders all with extreme violence created. His face was somewhat lined a little beyond his years hence his propensity for maintaining either a beard or mutton chop moustache to try to break up the weathered look of his skin. He washed his face and ran a comb through his short hair and decided that was enough grooming for this morning, the bonus of currently sporting the beard was the lack of necessity to endure Victorian poor quality razors and the razor burns they inflicted. He dressed in a fairly typical Victorian gentleman type way with a smart three piece single breasted suit, rounded collar white shirt and tie, black brogue shoes and eventually a trilby type hat. He had in fact now been off of the 'demon drink' for the best part of a year since working in the more civilised surroundings of Scotland Yard, little did he know that was to all too imminently to change.

He kissed Emma as she lay slumbering still and then headed off downstairs with George in tow. Opening the back door the dog ran out into the fresh August morning air and came to dead stop in the middle of the garden with his nose held high in the air sniffing the atmosphere intently. He then looked around at Abberline and came running back in doors barking as he came now wanting some breakfast as his master would be preparing his own. Abberline bent down and gave him a good rub on his head and then grabbed a couple of biscuits from a tin marked 'George' and fed them to the little terrier who ate them briskly and enthusiastically and then ran back outside for his own inevitable ablutions.

"Stupid mutt," said Abberline under his breath but smiling and began making himself some tea and toast.

Usually leaving for work around 7.15 and catching the omnibus service along the Romford and the Bow and Whitechapel Roads into central London, he was disturbed when the door knocker sounded around ten past the hour. He strode to the door with the dog barking and strutting along behind him and opened the front door to be greeted by a former colleague beyond whom he could see a hansom cab waiting in the road. It was George Godley a detective sergeant with whom he had worked in the Whitechapel area and who he knew was still posted there.

Godley was a man of a total of eleven years service with the Metropolitan force and aged thirty. He was born and bred in East Grinstead, Sussex so like Abberline not a native of the area and also like Abberline he had immersed himself during his career in the East End and was all too familiar with the nature of its society. He was a strikingly handsome man with short, smart dark hair and a well kept moustache and dressed this morning not dissimilarly to Abberline, almost the standard detective dress of the department.

"Morning, Fred. How are you?" he said in a casual but friendly manner to his old friend and colleague, extending his hand to shake Abberline's.

"I'm bloody well, George, actually old fellow, but what the bloody hell are you doing here at this time of the morning, and on a Thursday to boot?" he took Godley's hand and shook it firmly as they smiled at each other.

"Well to answer your first question, Fred, I am very well and as part of the answer to your second question, I am looking forward to working with you again." Finishing his reply he thrust the morning's edition of 'The Star' newspaper to Abberline with a bold headline.

'SECOND UNFORTUNATE SLAIN IN WHITECHAPEL.'

"Bloody hell, George, what's all this about then? Doesn't normally make the headlines," Abberline said somewhat surprised at the news headline.

"The papers have got hold of it and they think that there's a pattern emerging. The Commissioner is also very unpopular and there is the hype that no one cares for the lower classes."

"All right, George, that doesn't completely tell me what you're doing here," Abberline said with nagging and obvious awareness for Godley's visit.

"Superintendent Arnold is being put in charge of a priority investigation of these murders, and this is all since just after four this morning when the news broke at The Yard that the second woman had been murdered."

"Well with a mind to the fact it's only quarter past seven, they wasted no bleeding time getting on to you and then getting you round here."

"Are you going to ask me in for a cup of tea as because of rushing here first I haven't had one yet, or am I going to keep briefing you getting as dry as leather makers crotch on your bloody doorstep!"

"Sorry, mate, come on in there is more in the pot," he gestured Godley past him to the kitchen where the other George was now jumping up at the back door and barking to be let out. "Shut up you little bleeder," yelled Abberline opening up the door at the same time. Godley ignored this intent on pouring himself a cup of tea from the pot on the gas cooker.

He had been up since 5.a.m when a local inspector, a measure of the importance of the matter, had called at his modest house in Stratford just a few miles further in towards London from Abberline's. The inspector was passing on the orders from Superintendent Arnold to get Abberline immediately and bring him to The Yard for a briefing, and telling Godley that they were both assigned to the case until it was resolved.

"Sorry about the doorstep, George, I was just a little bit stunned to see you. It's been a few years as you know. Bit of a shock to think I'm getting thrown back into the fray of the East End."

"Don't worry, it's good to see you, and I haven't seen you looking so well for ages."

"I'm off the sauce, George, for good."

"That's good to know, I'll keep you to that, come on we'd better go." They climbed aboard the cab and the set off to meet Superintendent Arnold at Scotland Yard. On route Godley briefed in Abberline on the two cases so far.

"Okay, George, so the second one has been butchered somewhat, but the murders of prostitutes especially are not uncommon in Whitechapel, so why all the fuss and why me?"

"Fred, even you must accept that two in just under a month is quite unusual, and you are almost universally known in the East End so the powers that be feel that your presence will help calm the area."

"Well I shall bloody well tell Mr Arnold that he's not transferring me back as a public satisfaction exercise, and that I will run the investigation my way," Abberline spoke with the obvious annoyance over his appointment in his voice.

"Okay, Fred, I'm only the messenger," Godley replied placing his hands in the air in a comic gesture of surrender with a smile. It broke the tension that had began to develop between them, although a tension of only professional minds beginning to focus on the case; they stared out of the carriage windows with the East End flashing by as they continued on their journey to The Yard.

Arriving, they dismounted from the cab and were saluted by a constable posted on the front desk who knew very well who Inspector Abberline was. Godley knew exactly where Superintendent Arnold's office was from the orders he had been given earlier in the day. They knocked on the door and a deep baritone voice called for them to enter.

Sat behind a grand oak and leather desk in a heavily leather padded captains chair was the fifty-three year old superintendent. A good working colleague of Abberline's, he had spent most of his career working in the East End too so Thomas Arnold knew its layout and geography well. Balding and bearded, he wore the traditional high necked senior officer's tunic sporting campaign medals from his spell in the Crimean war, an interlude in his life that divided his police service into two parts. From his vast experience of London's East End and his knowledge of Abberline's crime detecting reputation he knew that he was choosing the right man for the investigation on the street.

"Good to see you, Frederick, and you Sergeant Godley, come on in and take a seat gentleman." He ushered them towards the two conventional oak office chairs positioned in front of his desk.

"As you know the Commissioner has been under pressure to show an interest and fairness to the lower classes since the riots of the last two years at the Lord Mayor's show, Clerkenwell and Trafalgar Square. These vicious murders have begun to stir unrest in the East End already with the local people believing that the government and police don't care about them. There are mutterings of vigilante committees being formed. This has as yet not happened as far as we know but we must nip it in the bud before it does. Frederick, you are popular man there and the locals will believe that something is being done to catch this maniac if you return there."

"Believe, Superintendent?" Abberline asked quizzically.

"Yes, they'll see that something is being done."

"Something will be done if I am to be left to run the investigation with George as I wish to, there is no case of 'believe' if you are putting me back to where I almost drunk myself to an early grave. My job will be to catch this man as quickly as possible and I expect no political hampering in doing so," there was obvious anger in is voice and his direct response. He disliked the term believe and emphasised it in his response because he did not wish to be a political pawn, but an effective policeman looked to with trust and respect by the public. It was something which he had always commanded from the people of Whitechapel and Spitalfields in the years when he worked there. Godley remained diplomatically silent as Arnold responded.

"Absolutely, Fred, this will be your case and you will run it as you wish on the street in order to reassure the local people and to catch this man. I shall oversee it only, but I will need regular updates on progress. Come to me directly for resources. Chief Inspector Donald Swanson will be a nominal figure above you just to comply with the usual command structure of these things. I have already informed the local stations to lend you all possible assistance and they have set aside an incident room at Commercial Street Police Station if you want. You are to liaise directly with Inspector Spratling and Sergeant Kerby."

Godley and Abberline exchanged a knowingly dissatisfied glance hearing the names of the two local officers they were deal with, uniform officers who had made no secret of their dislike of detectives in the past.

"All right then, Superintendent, what do you want me to do first from your perspective before I begin my investigation?" enquired Abberline.

"Your choice, Fred, but I do know that Spratling will be waiting for you either at the scene or at the mortuary right now."

Abberline looked at Godley. "Right then, George, off we go back to the sunny old East End. Thank you, sir."

They exited Arnold's office leaving an uneasy atmosphere. Abberline had not liked the brief intimation of a political posting and had quite obviously made no secret of the fact. He wanted to be doing his job, unhampered for the best results.

"Careful, Fred," said Godley, "You don't want this to end up being a lasting career move due to you old foible; belligerence." They walked out of The Yard and hailed a cab to head off for Bucks Row and the murder scene of Mary Nichols. It was now 10.a.m.

* * *

The morning boat from Boulogne arrived in Dover around the same time that the detectives left The Yard. As it had been entering the breakwater Severin Klosowski had gone on deck and taken a deep breath of the English coastal air. So fresh in its taste it brought about within him the feel for new opportunities within a new country. He had plans to find himself lodgings in the East End of London and find his feet in medicine or if necessary barbering within the Polish community where he could blend in unnoticed. He could see they were nearing the quay side and he was keen to be one the first off so that he could get a good seat on the train to London.

There was a slight bump which unsettled some people on their feet as the boat met its moorings. Klosowski remained steady on his feet and with his air of confidence strode onto the gangplank as soon as it was lowered despite shouts of 'Wait!' from some of the dockside workers and sailors. His command of verbal and written English was good and he ignored their derision and spotted the signs for the station. Having passed through the immigration control he walked with excitement through the streets of Dover taking in the new sights and sounds of England and noting how different in many subtle ways to France and the rest of mainland Europe it was. He observed with great interest the look of English women, their style, their varying types of deportment and, as they passed closely by, their scents. He drew long lingering breaths through his nose so he could fully appreciate the wonderful perfumed scent of the high class women emanating from their soaps, the powders and the perfumes they carefully prepared themselves with.

There was a vastly different odour from the lower class women he passed, most of them trying to disguise poor or non-existent levels of personal hygiene with shockingly fragranced cheap perfumes. Both had their individual merits as far as he was concerned dependent on his mood.

He bought his third class ticket to London and waited on the platform. He could see further along an Arabic looking young girl of about twenty, slim, tidily dressed in clothes which gave her away as having come from France too. He found her alluringly attractive as he had done Monique from the Bois, but had no murderous intentions, purely sexual. The train pulled in to their platform, empty having come from the sidings leaving plenty of space for all. He followed her into the carriage she chose and sat opposite her in a set of four seats, her flowing Victorian bustle encompassing the seats onto which she sat whilst he dominated his seats with his case and overcoat and dark homburg hat to try to discourage anyone else from joining them.

The train set off with the customary jolt but at least with everyone settled in their seats. He could not take his eyes off of this tanned skin beauty as she looked restlessly out of the window trying to avoid his stare. He would either have to wait until the train emptied or follow her off of the train if she was also headed to London. He could feel himself beginning to shake with excitement at the thought of probably being the first man to take her and his palms began to sweat with the anticipation of being able to take part in some debauched sexual act. He noted that she was quite heavily made up and that her Victorian blouse collar seemed to come up very high to under her chin. He did note that as the journey went on that she began more and more to acknowledge his stare and on one occasion stared back at him with the hint of a smile.

Passing out of Ashford continuing to the capital she got up and headed for the carriage door. As she reached it she looked back at him and gestured very subtly with her head for him to follow her. He could not believe that she was willing to partake in sex with him so willingly so he followed eagerly feeling his excitement growing. She found a toilet cubicle in one of the second class carriages and opened the door beckoning him in. He happily followed and found her standing in front of the sink looking at him and licking her lips as she watched him enter. He considered that she might be a prostitute from France looking for new employment in London. He had not intention of paying for anything.

He lifted her onto the enamelled sink and she sighed with excitement as he did so. She was fumbling with the belt and buttons of his trousers to free him as he had his hands around her waist. He ripped open her blouse to reveal wonderfully rounded pert breasts that indicated her level of excitement. He plunged his face into them kissing and sucking on the flesh with lustrous intensity, and at the same time he begin searching within the folds of her bustle to reach her womanhood. Eventually he moved up from her now saliva coated chest to kissing and biting her neck. She began to pant with excitement as he did and pulled hard on him with her right hand whilst her left hand felt for his rectum to give him a quick but massive climax and avoid full intercourse.

Suddenly he discovered two things which caused great horror and for him to immediately pull away from what he thought had been a woman. As he had kissed her neck he became aware of the fact she had an Adams apple and also felt his hand brush an erect penis. She was a hermaphrodite. She too had a look of horror from his discovery as she would normally keep this tucked to one side to avoid detection and looked with fear into the dark eyes of Klosowski wondering what he would do next. He pulled up and buttoned up his trousers and turned away as if he was about to leave. She felt relief as it looked as if he was going to walk away. But before she could react he turned swiftly having taken a surgeons knife from his coat and slashed out at her face gashing it across her cheeks and nose and sweeping twice, once in each direction to maximise the damage. She screamed out in agony and shook as he attacked her, cursing at her "You will never fool another man again as they will never give you a second glance now!" He wiped the blade of the knife with a ragged handkerchief from his pocket and put it back in his coat and opened the cubicle door.

She tried a vengeful lunge with her hands at his face but she was not quick enough, he caught her hands and threw her back onto the sink. He looked cautiously around and saw no one. He pulled her out into the corridor and punched her twice in the face inflicting more damage to her nose and causing her to sob heavily. She began shouting "Au secours!" repeatedly but not for long and to no avail. Klosowski wrenched open one of the carriage doors to the outside world, "Non, NON!" she screamed as he threw her from the train, observing her body tumble over and over as it ended up lifelessly in a field.

Klosowski washed his hands and returned casually to his carriage seat.

Bryan Lightbody

* * *

Abberline and Godley arrived at Bucks Row the murder site of Mary Nichols to be met by a crowd and some uniform constables clearing up the blood from the scene with buckets and stiff brushes on the cobbles. Abberline spotted a paper boy with a dirty looking old collie dog to one side from the rest of the crowd who was watching the actions of the constables intently. The crowd was made up of a few grubby looking working men, a large bunch of what appeared to local prostitutes, assorted children of all ages with a group of constables and a sergeant keeping them all to one side. About half a dozen of the filthy street kids were larking about as if nothing had happened as all the adults talked amongst themselves in hushed voices. Abberline immediately approached the paper boy.

"What's your name, son?" he said as he began stroking the apparently friendly dog's head

"Ralph. You're Inspector Abberline, ain't ya?"

"You know your stuff, young fellow, who told you that them? Him?" he said pointing to the dog and smiling.

"No, I don't think so, mister, 'e's clever but 'e's a dog. It was 'im over there," he said pointing to one of the constables doing the washing down.

Abberline flicked him a penny and said "Well, you keep your ear to the ground and your eyes open and let me know what you see or hear, all right?" Ralph took the money eagerly and replied "Certainly, Mr Abberline, you leave it to me."

Abberline and Godley approached the two constables who were doing the scrubbing. They were both aware of the two detectives heading towards them and they kept their heads down and carried on brushing. One said to the other

"That's bleedin' Abberline, isn't it, Rob?"

"Yeah, it is, but don't know the bloke that he's with, Del."

"Oh, that's George Godley used to work around here, don't you remember?"

"Suits all look the same to me, Del Boy, don't remember him meself."

"So, what the bloody hell do you two think you're doing then?" said Abberline.

"Inspector Spratling's orders, sir. Clear it away now that the body's gone."

"You know what all that is, son?" asked Godley.

"No, sir, I don't," answered Robert Ford.

"Evidence, Constable, and its Sergeant Godley."

"And you're Inspector Abberline," piped up Del.

"Got it in one, lad, where is Inspector Spratling?"

"He's down at the mortuary at Old Montague Street Workhouse Infirmary with the body and Dr Llewellyn, sir."

"Well, George, it's off to there then." As Abberline continued to speak the sergeant from the crowd walked over to them. "Now you, lads, when you've finished get yourselves back to The Street and start tidying up the incident room for me please."

"I don't think so, they're my blokes and I say what they can or can't do. They are going back on patrol," said the bearded sergeant.

"Do you know who I am, sergeant?"

"I expect you are Mr Abberline," he replied arrogantly looking the detectives up and down, "And I am Sergeant Kerby." Abberline stepped up to be face to face with Kerby.

"Well, Sergeant Kerby, if you know who I am then you may well know that you are to lend us all courtesy and help in the swift resolution of these murders. So you, Sergeant, will go with them and clear up that incident room. I expect to find it ready for us first thing on Monday. Now, all your lads, are they the early shift?"

"We are, guv'nor," said a somewhat disgruntled Kerby.

"Well, once you've got it tidied up and ready for us and an eventual squad of detectives you're off. Don't want to hear that the C.I.D never gives you something." Kerby took Rob and Del off to The Street and Abberline and Godley made for the mortuary and the expected showdown that Abberline knew he would have with one of his old working uniform rivals, John Spratling.

They arrived at the Old Montague Street Workhouse Infirmary Mortuary to find Dr Rees Llewellyn, a forty-nine year old General Practitioner and one of the district's Divisional Surgeons, examining the now naked body of Mary Nichols with forty-eight year old stern faced Police Inspector Spratling looking on. Llewellyn was dictating his findings to a constable who was making notes in his pocket book. Abberline and Godley listening as the doctor catalogued her injuries.

"Five teeth missing, a slight laceration to the tongue and bruising on the right lower jaw. All consistent with a blow to the face, or pressure from being held. May or may not be linked to the homicidal injuries. Injuries to the neck, I shall catalogue in more detail but needless to say that the neck wounds are so deep as to go back through all tissues to the vertebrae. No wounds to the upper body cavity but to the abdomen we find several deep slashes, which again I shall elaborate on in my notes, all very jagged and caused by the same instrument being used violently downwards. They appear to have been done left handed, or cutting backhand."

"Well, Doctor, what kind of man do you think might have done this?" said Abberline

"You're the detective, Abberline, why don't you tell us?" responded Spratling aggressively.

"Because I've only just arrived, John, but seeing as how you've been around all day, what do you reckon?"

"I think it's just some local nutter, in fact two nutters as both the eventual states of the bodies are different, don't know why there's all the fuss of getting you Yard boys in."

"Because, my Dear John, we don't make some early shift assumption but look at all the evidence, so I wish to speak to Dr Llewellyn about both the month's murders, so if you'll excuse us John......." Spratling stormed off from the mortuary.

"We'll see him back at The Street no doubt, George. Now then, Doctor, you've examined both bodies, do you see any link between the two?"

"Well, Inspector, obviously only the second victim has such extensive mutilations, but both have had their throats cut deeply cut. Both would appear to have been cut by someone who is left handed as both initial slashes to the neck area are from the victims left to right. Also I suspect that the same or similar knives have been used on both victims judging by how much damage was created; only a powerful and sharp butchery knife could do it."

"Or surgeons, doctor."

"Surgeons save lives, Inspector, not take them."

"But you would agree that a surgeon's knife could do it?"

"I concede only in the weaponry, Inspector."

"Doctor, can I take it you will be available should there be any other victims?"

"If I am on duty Inspector, then yes."

"Well if you're not I might like to call on your services for a continuity of opinion."

"I don't mind, Inspector, but please don't set me against my divisional surgeon colleagues unnecessarily."

"Don't worry, doctor, I shan't be doing that, good day to you." Abberline and Godley left the mortuary.

"Fred, I don't think it's a great idea to try to upset the divisional surgeon."

"I'm not trying to upset him, George, just gain a different view point, not a copper's." They walked briskly and from the mortuary to Commercial Street Police Station a relatively short distance. Abberline hoped that on arrival the incident room would be in the process of being prepared for the case to be launched in earnest the next week.

They were greeted by the desk sergeant as they entered and both walked through the station as if they had never left and found their way directly to the incident room they would be using. The two young constables and Sergeant Kerby had made a good job at making the place usable and presentable, the walls were clear although grubby from previous use and there were several cleared blackboards all set with chalk on their shelves and board wipers. There were several desks and wooden filing cabinets dotted around the room and just about enough chairs to match although not any two of them were the same. The floor had been swept and there were two doors into the room from different corridors. If they needed the space, Abberline thought, they could block off one of the doors. The lighting was from a dim electrical source but there were old gas units spread around the walls ready for use if necessary.

"Only one thing missing, George," Abberline said as they surveyed the room. "Some tea making stuff, we need a little stove in one corner with all the bits, because I'm bloody parched."

"I'll make sure it's done for Monday, Fred, because I feel exactly the same."

At that time Sergeant Kerby stuck his bearded face around the door at them. "Everything all right for you, guv'nor?" He asked almost genuinely with a faint smile.

"Splendid job, Sergeant, but mind you two of your finest cups of tea, for me and George here would top things off." The faint smile disappeared from Kerby's face as he strode off to get refreshment for the detectives. In the meantime they exchanged a wry smile.

Chapter Six

Saturday 1st of September 1888. Robert Ford arrived outside the London Hospital early for his one o'clock date with Mary Kelly. He could see over the road a large crowd gathering for what he understood to be a most unsightly freak show, ironically opposite the place of so many medical breakthroughs and healing. Whilst he was waiting for Mary he listened to the show announcer stood outside on the pavement of the Whitechapel Road.

"Roll up, roll up for the greatest freak show in Europe. You will feel terror, you will feel pity, you will feel amazement, you might well feel sick when you cast your eyes on a man who is quite simply not one thing or the other. His features are that of an unimaginable jungle animal, his skin has the texture of a hide; he does not have the bone structure of a man. Ladies and gentleman, and I must stress NOT boys and girls I invite you to come in for your viewing excitement, for your imagination overload, to enter and meet Mr John Merrick, THE ELEPHANT MAN!"

The crowds swarmed the grubby seedy ticket booth at the entrance to the shop desperate for some cheap thrill or titilation.

Robert looked on disgusted at these people indulging in another's horrific misfortune and tried to put it to the back of his mind to be in a good humour for when Mary arrived. He hoped that she would not have a macabre interest in seeing the poor wretch in the show. Robert looked himself over in a reflection from a window in the London Hospital and was quite pleased with his efforts. He had turned out in his best three piece suit, plain black leather shoes and a wing collar shirt with a tie. He hoped Mary would like what she saw. He straightened his neck tie much to the delight to a couple of passing squaddies who could not help but comment in a falsely high pitched voice "Oo, you look gorgeous, luv," who then chuckled to themselves and walked on in what was obvious to Robert a semi drunken state.

As he turned to view the main road again Mary was stood immediately in front of him, he could do nothing to help his mouth opening and his lower jaw dropping with what he saw. She was not in anything that resembled her working clothes; she was wearing a tight fitting crushed velvet Victorian lady's dress in a deep blue with a cream coloured blouson jacket on top, a blue and cream bonnet to match her outfit with her radiant auburn hair tied back like flowing like the mane of a graceful thoroughbred mare, a lacy parasol and she was wearing high shoes of some kind with the height at which she stood and the way she held herself. He could detect the obvious but subtle scent of perfume which seemed to be of good quality and was pleased he had matched her effort with his own turn out.

"Mary, you look beautiful. I don't know what else to say," Robert could not stop staring at her shaking his head in amazement. He thought she looked lovely everyday when he saw her, but now she appeared both gorgeous and elegant.

"Well, Robert Ford, I must say you look the kind of gent who should be accompanying me, you look marvellous too."

"May I accompany you to the boating lake, madam?" Robert said imitating as best he could an upper class voice.

"Certainly, sir," Mary replied in her normally soft Irish accent which was of a very high class nature from her own attempts to always be more than she was by birth.

He stretched his arm for her to take it and they began walking east along Whitechapel Road in the general directions of Bow and Victoria Park. They walked and talked and turned along Cambridge Heath Road to head to the western end of Victoria Park. It was still quite a way to walk so they paused not far along the road at an omnibus stop. They continued effortlessly chatting as they waited but it was not long before the bus came along. They boarded with Robert eagerly paying the fare for the two of them and they sat themselves on the open top deck as the sun was out and the air was fresh and sweet, as fresh and sweet as it could be for the busy, clogged streets of the East End. In fact as they headed north and gradually further east the nature of the streets and the property that passed significantly improved, especially once they reached the wealthy environs of Hackney and Bow.

The omnibus turned right from Cambridge Heath Road and made its way along Victoria Park Road. 'Vicky Park,' as it was and still is known, stretches from the edge of Hackney east to the outskirts of Bow, nearing the borders with Stratford. A distance of just over a mile. As a result the buses made several stops along their way past the park stopping at the various points of activity or interest ranging from the boating lake to the tea rooms and bandstand or just by some of the quiet rolling areas of grassland or small copses of trees.

Robert and Mary alighted by the boating lake and then walked arm in arm through the ornate wrought iron gates forming just part of the Victorian railings surrounding the entire park. Being the weekend and a day blessed with fine weather the area around the lake and it's various facilities was crowded with much of the East End's populace more finely dressed on the whole enjoying a day out in stead of work, but Robert noticed the crowd was punctuated with some very wealthy types from outside the locality who were obviously enjoying the parks country atmosphere too. He noted the odd rogue around too who had made no attempt to alter their normal working appearance and eyed the people around them cautiously, looking possibly for victims or being wary of the police who also took time to stroll the grounds for their normal patrolling purposes. Robert found it sad that even in this haven people still had to be on their guard.

He noted that Mary's appearance turned many a man's head not only due to her exceptionally fashionable turned out appearance but also too because of her stunning natural beauty. What was she doing involved in such a deplorable trade in the East End? He was determined if some kind of relationship blossomed that he would take her away from this as soon as he could.

They strolled up to the queue for the boating lake chatting comfortably and enjoying a day out like the rest of the world around them and in a short while they were at the head of the line at the ticket desk with Robert handing over the money for their session on the lake.

The ticket entitled them to a row boat for two finished in a somewhat weathered royal blue colour which quite coincidentally off set the shades of blue in Mary's outfit and Robert's suit bizarrely well.

They climbed aboard with the tatty little rowing boat listing characteristically from side to side as they did so, Robert got aboard first and confidently stood offering Mary his hand to help her on. She took it with her parasol swinging off of her forearm as her free hand pulled up her skirt slightly to avoid it snagging on the rough sides of the boat or skimming across the water's surface. They both sat down facing each other with Mary more to the aft of the boat looking forwards and Robert facing backwards more towards the stern comfortably next to the oars.

He confidently took an oar in each hand and the boat keeper cast off their rope securing them to the shore it landing with a thump in the area behind Mary in the boat. With a bias with one oar Robert got them facing to the centre of the lake and he then rowed with languid strokes to not wear himself out to get as far away from any of the banks as possible. He pulled the oars in securing them along the boat's sides and then moved to sit next to Mary.

"So, Miss Kelly, how are you enjoying your day?"

"Very relaxing thank you, Constable Ford."

"Who'd have thought that the East End could look so tranquil and have somewhere that allows you to feel completely at ease and away from it all."

"Reminds me of Ireland, calm inland waters, lush grasslands and swaying trees in colourful blossom. I shall go back there one day, settle and never leave."

"Sounds wonderful, is that alone or do you see a man in your life?" Mary considered her reply carefully. She was very fond of Robert, feeling totally at ease with his company. He would be the kind she pictured this settled life with but was concerned not to scare him off, avoiding a sense of coming on too strongly. She could at least be assured that he was fairly unmoved by her profession or else she doubted he would be here now. "Of course with someone, don't want to be some old maid in Limerick, all talked about behind me back."

"What about Joe?"

"Oh, he's really more of a house-mate than anything else, can't see him being me man to be in Ireland. Anyway, what about you, Robert, what do you want from your future?"

"Well if I'm to marry whilst in the force, I need to move my wife out to the leafy suburbs to live so I can still get to work, but we can raise some kids in a decent environment."

"All on a constable's wage then, eh?"

"Well, if can make sergeant then we could do it at a struggle, but if I make inspector then it's a real ambition."

"I do like a man who plans a future, there's more to you than a pretty face and a nice arse, Robert Ford," she giggled in a suggestive way. All Robert could do was blush and start to laugh too.

"It would be un-gentlemanly to say what I like about you, Mary Kelly." They continued giggling.

They stared into each others eyes as their laughter gradually subsided. After what seemed like an eternity of staring into the emerald pools which were Mary's beautiful eyes Robert moved towards her and gave her gentle kiss on the lips. Mary responded simultaneously with equal pressure against him, he must know that she was developing strong feelings for him. He pulled back following that initial contact to look into her eyes again to gauge her response. She was looking longingly at him so he immediately took her in a passionate embrace in his arms and they began kissing with real intention as lovers do, tongues clashing and wrapping against each other heatedly, each signalling their desire to the other as a result.

After several minutes of this passionate activity Mary pulled away her mouth from his remaining in his arms and whispered "Robert, take me to your lodgings. Now."

* * *

That day during the morning the inquest into Mary Nichols murder was opened presided over by the colourful forty-four year old coroner Wynne Baxter. Abberline and Godley were in attendance at the Whitechapel Working Lads Club and at their request the matter was reconvened for Monday, but ultimately it would not be until later in the month that the police had any real evidence to present.

"Certainly, Inspector Abberline, I shall adjourn matters for it does seem only prudent that we set the ball rolling today and hopefully wrap things up by the end of the month," was Baxter's gambit.

"Thank you, sir, and I hope that we won't end up with several running concurrent."

"What do you mean, Inspector?"

"Well, sir, this is the second prostitute in four weeks, I'm hoping that there's not a pattern as they've been victims of bloody knife attacks."

"Well, I'm sure it's just coincidence, Inspector."

"So do I, sir," said Abberline closing the conversation but feeling that with his drafting into the case maybe things were set to escalate. He hoped it was an unfounded concern.

* * *

About 5.p.m Ralph was walking along Whitechapel High Street with Bruiser on a homemade makeshift rope lead enjoying the rest of the day off from selling papers. He was dressed in his usual scruffy clothes but had no need of his heavy coat on the bright and pleasant day so it lay on the floor of his lodgings at Millers Court along with his prized blankets and his probably comatose mother. They trotted along quite happily watching the world go by as they passed the many stalls making up the Saturday market. They were all winding down and clearing up due to the time but some still had produce and certainly all were flush with their day's takings. Ralph saw coming towards him a furtive figure dressed in what he thought was a vicar's suit, the shape and movement of this person closely resembled that of the man he'd seen dart away on sight of the police a few days previously in Red Lion Court.

Michael Ostrog saw the boy and took little notice of him as he would have little or no ready cash on him. He cast his eyes around the stall holders to try to spy which one might have the most profit for him. He saw a quite short stocky ruddy faced fifty year old man clearing up his poultry stall. These stall holders usually made good money from brisk business throughout the day and if Ostrog caught him unaware he could use a weapon from the stall if necessary, although the keeper didn't look as if he could give him much resistance. Ostrog's only short coming in his plan was that he had not counted on the fact that the boy had casually walked on but had then stopped and was watching him from the shelter of a doorway, curious as to what this shady looking character was up to. Ralph knew he would at least get some information for Constable Ford on this new face to the area.

As were most of the stall holders the poultry man was going about his own business of clearing up with only a little stock left on his display when Ostrog approached the stall. Ostrog had certainly been careful to observe that there were no police around as he passed through a gap and got behind the stall raising his fist in anticipation of his victim turning round. He saw that the stall holder wore a waist pouch which would be holding the day's takings and fastened around his back with only a tied bow to secure it. He grabbed one of the free ends of the bow and pulled it firmly making it untie instantly and it fell to the ground with a clatter from the coins within it. The stall holder spun around clutching the void where once his pouch had hung. Ostrog let fly instantly with a devastating punch with his raised right fist connecting with familiar accuracy onto the nose of the stunned stall holder shattering bone and spraying blood across his face and down the front of his off white cotton apron. He reeled backwards against his butchers block as Ostrog made a darting move to grab the pouch of money lying between them on the cobbled market floor.

Dropping his sight from his victim to look at the pouch, a momentary lapse in Ostrog's usually predatory efficiency, he was oblivious to his victim's reaction of grabbing a ten inch steak boning knife from the block. As Ostrog looked back towards his quarry he saw the knife heading towards the top of his head accompanied by the cry of "You fucking foreign bastard, I'll teach you!" Ostrog threw himself as much from harms way as he could, but his evasive action was not enough. The knife buried itself deep into the muscle of his left shoulder, so much so that as he continued his avoidance move the stall holder was forced to let go of its handle. Ostrog screamed out in agony "Niet! Damned whore's son, may the devil curse you!" Still having hold of his prize but now laying on the floor he swung his legs around violently in a sweeping action catching the stall holder's shins and pitching him forward onto the floor. He landed heavily on his face doing further damage to his jaw and leaving him clutching his face and screaming in pain.

Unable to retaliate any further, Ostrog scrambled to his feet and with head down and moving fast he surged his way through the gathering crowd with the money in his right hand and his left arm hanging limp with the knife embedded in his scrawny shoulder muscle. He ran off along the High Street towards the junction with New Road with Ralph and Bruiser following in pursuit to keep tabs on his escape. Behind him Ralph could hear the varying cries from the gathered and now mobilising crowd in the market ranging from 'Find the Old Bill!' to 'Lets lynch the bastard ourselves, fucking foreigner!'

Ralph watched Ostrog make his way south in New Road and then heard the sound of police whistles coming from the opposite direction of the High Street, he stopped to wave the constables the right way. They approached Ralph and Bruiser now barking with excitement. One of them breathlessly spoke to him.

"What's going on, boy?"

"That bloke going off down there, he's just robbed the poultry man. There's a bloody knife sticking out of his arm too." Ostrog looked round just at the point when Ralph was relaying the information to the police and pointing in his direction.

Like a wounded animal he couldn't stop and risk succumbing to his pursuers and was forced to carrying on running towards Commercial Road knowing in his mind that he would silence that newspaper boy and his geriatric dog. The whistles carried on blowing from behind him as he neared the junction ahead and he was then stunned by the sight of two more police rounding it and now closing him down from the opposite direction. He stopped dead in his tracks with only a second or two to spare to consider his options. He had only one good arm to fight with and he was now being almost surrounded by four policemen but with one line of escape along Nelson Street. He was forced to drop the money so he could defend himself. Then he braced himself with his legs locked firmly out as he stood upright and clutched the handle of the steak knife with his right hand.

The four approaching policemen stopped watching stunned all about fifteen feet from him as they observed the unfolding terrifying display of pain control. Ostrog with a look of defiance had veins standing out prominently in his neck and in the sides of his forehead as he absorbed the pain. He pulled the knife inch by inch out of his shoulder until the whole six inches by which it had been buried were free and now being held up in front of him dripping with blood. He surveyed the aghast faces of his potential captors with the endorphins generated within him from the chase dulling all sensations of pain. He knew that as with the poultry man he would have to make a pre-emptive strike to gain the upper hand and give himself a chance of taking revenge on that boy.

He lunged at the nearest constable with a hard stabbing movement managing to land the knife deep into his right thigh, the officer then dropping instantly to the floor screaming in pain. He made a slashing movement at the next nearest one who stood back to avoid a contact with the third and the fourth now with their truncheons drawn. Having distracted them with his attack he then ran as fast as he could into Nelson Street with two of them still chasing whilst the third tended to his fallen comrade.

The adrenaline carried him swiftly and gave him a good start on the constables. He ducked into the nearest doorway which led him into the maze of one of the tenement blocks. They followed only seconds later but he had already disappeared, melting into the East End slum with the rest of the lost souls scattered around the corridors and stairwells of what was ironically 'Russia House'. Ostrog found himself a bolt-hole beneath some stairs behind piles of festering rubbish which he was prepared to tolerate for long enough to guarantee that his searchers had given up. As he heard footsteps passing above him on the stairwells with the house now swarming with the accursed police, Ostrog's adrenaline levels began to drop and the throbbing pain of his shoulder began to thump louder and more intensely. He would have to go and seek medical attention when the area was safe again. For now he had to suffer in silence.

Back in the High Street Ralph observed intently the constables taking details from the poultry man as Bruiser sat patiently against his leg; the rest of the gathered crowd began to disperse and go about their usual business. As was common place, few had come forward to the officers to give witness accounts so the young boy waited patiently to give his account of events. Whilst he waited he listened to two of the constables who had been the first on scene chatting about the afternoon's excitement.

"Well, that bloody madman has got to be Michael Ostrog from what I've seen of him and what the punters have described him like," said a thin, drawn looking Commercial Street constable.

"Look what he did to Wilf's leg, cut to bloody ribbons it was, take him weeks to walk again," replied his chubbier colleague.

"Mind you, it being a poultry knife it's used to cutting through more meat that what's in his leg!" They both laughed darkly together, a way of surviving the stress of it all for them.

Eventually the furiously scribbling constable who had been taking details from the poultry man turned to Ralph and bent down to speak to him eye to eye, but immediately turned his initial attention to Bruiser.

"Well, my fine furry friend, what did you see then, eh? With them sharp sheep dog eyes of yours?"

"'E saw lots, but 'e can't tell you nothing, 'e's smart but he can't talk, mister." Bruiser gave the constable his paw and looked around him in a rather bored fashion.

"No, of course not, son, but what did you see, you work around here don'tcha."

"Yeah, and you're PC Jonas Mizen, I know you, you've nicked my mum when she's pissed."

"Sorry, lad, its only work you know. Anyway, how do you know my name?"

"'Cos I've seen you in court to give your evidence, ain't I."

"All right enough of that, what did you see then?"

Ralph gave a full account of the violent events in the market with an intricate description of Ostrog. Jonas Mizen was forced to get a second note book from one of the other constables as a result of the sheer volume of the details he had taken from the boy regarding the violent robbery. Once finished they each went their separate ways with Ralph apprehensively considering a return to Millers Court and his drunken, whoring mother.

* * *

Robert's lodgings were empty but for the ever present Bosun. Now awake he greeted the familiar inhabitant and the lovely Mary warmly and after a few minutes of fussing from the pair of them he retreated to his basket and grubby blankets.

"Which way is your parlour then, Robert?" Mary said mischievously.

"The only way is up," he said pointing to the stairs "And keep going to the last room at the top, I have the attic lodgings, with a view," he said mocking society gentlemen. Mary giggled in a devilish fashion sending a wave of excitement through young Ford.

"Then lead the way then, darling."

He took her hand and then led her up the narrow and creaking staircase passing several landing windows which allowed the warm Saturday sunshine to stream welcomingly into the dark Victorian end of terrace house. The door to his room was not locked, that facility long since defunct, and Robert pushed it open to reveal a tidy but Spartan bed sit. Opposite the door was a wall with a small window which looked out north towards Bethnal Green Road. It was bordered either side by a set of heavy black cotton curtains hanging from a somewhat rusted metal pole, devoid of any finials so as a consequence a curtain ring and part of the curtain hung uselessly from the left side limply against the bare grey plastered wall. To the right of the room was an old iron bed with pleasantly clean looking sheets and an Ida down over the top of it, to the left was a pitted wooden chest of draws next to which was a table with a single chair. On the table was neatly laid out a kettle, enamel mug, plate and cutlery. Beyond that in the corner was a butler sink in very worn and chipped enamel while above it hung a mirror Robert used for shaving and hair brushing. Below it was a shelf with very tidily arranged toiletries including an old mug holding and razor, shaving brush and, unusually for working class Victorians, a tooth brush.

Mary shut the door which revealed behind her to the left hand side of the door at the foot of the bed a linen press wardrobe on top of which was a battered leather suitcase. To the right of the door was a small wood burning stove for heat and basic cooking which was vented out through the wall and a shelf above it attached to the wall with some various culinary jars and packets.

"Quite the little home maker aren't you, Robert."

"I do my best, Miss Kelly," he replied removing his suit jacket and laying it over the back of the lone chair.

They stood silent looking into each others eyes for a few seconds that to Robert seemed like an eternity. He then approached her and they embraced kissing wildly and passionately now totally away from any public gaze, they could be totally uninhibited. For the second time today Mary felt like a real woman, not a common whore, kissed, loved and wanted for all the right reasons that any civilised man should want a woman. They frantically began undressing each other, Mary undoing his tie whilst he unbuttoned her cream jacket, then moving closer and reaching around to her back he unfastened the her dress as she undid his waist coat and then his shirt. She pulled it off his shoulders and rubbed her hands firmly over his lean and only lightly haired chest. As she felt her dress become loose she pushed Robert backwards and stepped out of it with the crushed velvet garment falling to the floor, forming a second pile of discarded clothes next to Robert's.

She stood in a fine white Victorian corset that seemed to make her gorgeous hair even more auburn with its lightness, with the undergarment exaggerating her fine figure and with her breasts partially spilling out of the top of it. The dark stockings contoured her legs which had been given an exquisite shape by the lift from her heeled shoes. She pulled Robert's waist belt free from its loops and tore down the button fly of his suit trousers. She could feel his stiffening and pulled it free from his white cotton underwear, kneeling down she eased him gently into her mouth. Robert's head went back in ecstasy and his whole body tensed with exhilaration as she massaged him against her tongue in and out of her mouth. He had never felt such a sensation before with his limited number of sexual experiences, but nonetheless significant in their exploration of carnal pleasures.

He looked down at Mary just as she was looking up and they caught each others eyes, each knowing what the other wanted. She let him fall from her mouth and stood up, turning around and saying to Robert "Undo my corset lace, darling." He did so with somewhat shaking hands whilst Mary undid her stockings and as the corset loosened she pulled it down stepping out of the last of her clothes. She turned around to face him. She was the most stunningly beautiful woman he had ever seen. She had flawless pale skin covering her hourglass figure, her generous breasts were crowned by large erect pink nipples and she completely shaved her body. She went and sat on the corner of the bed as Robert stepped out of his trousers, underwear, socks and shoes. He approached her and dropped to his knees at the edge of the bed in front of her in-between her legs.

They kissed again for several minutes as he ran his hands gently in an almost tickling fashion up and down her thighs and the contours of her torso, then breaking away from the kiss and beginning to gently kiss and caress her breasts and nipples. She began to faintly moan with pleasure as she had never had a man treat her so gently before, loving her instead of grappling and fondling her in a primitive fashion. He moved down to between her legs and as he did so she lay back on the bed and opened her legs wider as he began to pleasure her with his tongue. It darted inside her a couple of times before settling on massaging her causing her to become more and more stimulated.

Within minutes she was experiencing a climax like never before and then she lent up and whispered to him "Robert, please make love to me." He stood as she sat up and lifted her in his arms, laid her out gently along the bed and then climbed onto the bed laying himself tenderly on top of her supporting himself with his arms either side of her chest. She took hold of him and guided him inside her. It penetrated her easily prompting a moan of pleasure and satisfaction and then they rhythmically moved with one another. Both panting and moaning in-between breaths and boughts of hard passionate kissing. He kissed her neck, her breasts and gently ran his hand around her astonishingly pretty face

She wrapped her legs around his waist and pulled him into her as physically close as she could now, moaning loudly and constantly. His brow was sweating and the perspiration running down his back from sustained love making over quite some time and he thrust into her faster and faster. He felt the sensation beginning to change and pushed his last couple of times as deep as he could, throwing his head back and groaning with pleasure as he came deep inside her, she reciprocally yelling loudly as a result of a second deep orgasm. They stayed locked with one another kissing on the bed for several minutes before Robert rolled to one side but still arm in arm.

"Robert, no one has ever treated me like that before." A concerned look came across his face as he lay there, next to a woman he was falling deeply in love with.

"Like what? Did I do something wrong?"

"No," she said nestling up closer to him, "you did everything wonderfully; no one has ever been that tender before. You made me feel like a woman who is loved."

Robert's eyes had welled with tears and the lump in his throat stopped him from replying. He held her tightly and hoped this moment would last forever.

Chapter Seven

Wednesday 5th September 8.a.m and Francis Tumblety now considered it time for himself to find lodgings within the squalid East End to give himself a bolt hole to go to wait for the heat to dissipate if the police found a victim early and began to cordon the area off. He would not then have to worry about getting back immediately to his grand quarters in the west of town. Enjoying the last of his breakfast at the Ritz Hotel he waved to the head waiter to get his attention, smartly dressed in his black dinner suit he came promptly to the Doctor's table to tend to his request.

"Victor, a cab please at reception for the East of the City."

"Certainly, Doctor," replied Victor humbly and hurried off a few steps and then beckoned one of his own minions to run to reception and arrange the request.

Tumblety was beginning to run up a considerable hotel bill and needed to recover his valuable gems to cash one in for money to deal with such matters. If he didn't get them soon the issue of money could become embarrassing. Of the stones that had remained in the box, which wasn't many of the smaller diamonds and the two emeralds, he had already been forced to trade in the diamonds for ready cash. A sum of money now depleted. He felt he could not part with the emeralds until his quest was over. They were a salient reminder of all the things his twisted mind considered to be wrong. So not only would some hovel in fetid Whitechapel or Spitalfields give him a local escape but it would perhaps help keep his living costs down a little. Finishing his breakfast he lifted the fine damask cotton serviette off of his lap and placed it neatly on the finely laid luxury hotel dining table. He already had his cane and hat with him negating any need to go to his room so dressed in his traditional garish civil war based uniform he strode arrogantly out of the breakfast lounge, through the hollowed corridors or the Ritz to the reception area. Spotted immediately by one of the bellboys the main door was swung open for him and a cab was waiting exactly opposite the door, the driver nodded to Tumblety in acknowledgement and the Doctor climbed aboard.

With the crack of a whip the cab lurched off as Tumblety made himself comfortable in the leather quilt-studded seat and looked out surveying the bustling West End streets. The area possessed a very different populace to the filth ridden East all going about their individual days of either toil or leisure. The carriage took as direct a route as possible from the Ritz passing along Piccadilly to the famous Piccadilly Circus, along to Leicester Square, Charing Cross Road, through Holborn into the City of London proper through Poultry having already clipped the top of Old Bailey, passing the Bank of England and on to Cornhill, Leadenhall Street and finally arriving of the conjugation of Commercial Road, Braham Street and The Minories. He still did have a reserve of money for day to day expenses, which to him was a God send to be able to continue his adventures but most importantly his revenge and psychosis fuelled crusade. He proffered the driver the exact money for his fair; frugality would help ensure the maintenance of the crusade.

He had had his 'ear to the ground' as it were to discover the availability of cheap but comfortable lodgings in the various pubs he frequented in the East End and discovered there was a room free at a Mrs Long's house at number 22 Batty Street, Portsoken Ward, Whitechapel. It's proximity to the general area of his quest and other debauched antics was ideal and the five to ten minute walk from were he alighted the cab would help familiarise himself with the South side of the locality.

He watched carefully those passing by him and the unfortunates he in turn passed keenly looking out for Mary and putting an end to his frustrations. In comparison to the flourishing West the air smelt rotten in many places as a result of piles of rubbish and blocked or defective and in some places non existent sewers. Long before the search for Mary he enjoyed abusing the unfortunates of the area sexually in a frustrated attempt to wreak revenge and put closure on his one and only treacherous wife. He derived pleasure from degrading himself associating with these women as did Druitt from the sense of power it developed within them. He could feel these emotions and needs welling up inside him as he roamed the streets that were the home to his sexual prey.

As he rounded the corner of Fairclough Street into Batty Street he cast all thoughts of sexual dysfunction from his mind to get on with checking out the room at 22 Batty Street and then negotiating a price with Mrs Long. From outside the property was a typical squalid looking Victorian two up and two down terraced house. The door was a faded wooden four panelled style with a fan of small glass windows, four in total, above the panels at head height. There was no door knocker and so Tumblety wrapped on the door with handle end of his cane. Paint flaked from the door as the sound of his knocking echoed in the street causing Tumblety to look around in an embarrassed fashion, fearful that he may draw unwanted attention to himself.

After ten to fifteen seconds the door opened; it had seemed like an eternity to Tumblety as a crowd of filthy East End children had gathered following his wrap on the door. They were watching him curiously, delving deep into their noses at the same time with muck covered fingers to relieve their nasal passages of soot having gathered just from breathing the local air. Stood in front of him was a surprisingly clean looking fifty-five year old woman in traditional dress and neatly tied back long grey hair. Her skin was weathered with a creased leathery appearance and her smile, as he introduced himself to her, revealed what was a typically local dental feature; decaying and missing teeth.

"Good morning, Mrs Long, I've come about the room vacancy," said Tumblety in his distinctive American drool.

"Come in, Mister, I'll show you it. Not from round here are you."

"No, just paying a visit to the old country, ma'am."

"Proper polite you are. What you want a room round here for then, eh?"

"Well, ma'am, I'm a doctor involved in social research in deprived areas. I believe you've got to spend some time amongst the people to make a serious study."

"Oh, very privileged 'ere we are then, an intellectual in our midst. Thought you was some kind of Yankee general with all that get up."

"No, not now ma'am, it's the last remnant of my military service during our civil war. And please, if I take up your room, treat me no different to anyone else. That way I can get a true reflection of life here."

During the conversation she had taken them through the house to a set of stairs built centrally, up the stairs and along a short narrow corridor and opened a door into the room which overlooked Batty Street itself. A feature that he considered could prove useful in the future. The room was clean but in a state of decay needing the window replacing as the wood was rotting and the plaster on the walls was crumbling in a few places. The room was only equipped with a bed, a wardrobe and an old dining chair on three good legs and one slightly shorter one. As a place to stop to avoid capture, or to simply retire to until more cabs were running in the foul East End streets it was perfect.

"I'll take it please, Mrs Long. I feel I can be at one with the people here, and really get to know them inside and out. You know what I mean?" he said to her in a quizzical fashion.

"I do, sir. Just one month's rent in advance then please. Four shillings."

Tumblety reached into his pocket and pulled out the change and handed it to a grateful Mrs Long. He bid her good day and left with his keys. She returned to her washing and scrubbing chores in her downstairs scullery with the thought crossing her mind, 'what was his name?'

* * *

2.p.m at Commercial Street Police Station; Abberline and Godley were now comfortably settled in to their incident room with signs of the investigation really taking shape. Information about the two prostitute victims was chalked onto the black boards and plan drawings of the two murder sites pinned to the walls. The board with details of suspects was ominously blank. There were several desks for the investigating officers involved which at the present were only Abberline and Godley and two newly appointed detective constables both around thirty years old, Murphy and Parish. Significantly, where the occupants of the office were concerned, was a table set aside with the facility to make tea for anyone present.

"Bill, old son, get some tea on can you. Might stimulate the old grey matter," Abberline said addressing Murphy. The young DC got the kettle going on the old iron gas stove next to the table and spread out four tarnished and stained enamel mugs. He lifted the lid on an equally weathered looking enamel tea pot and spooned some tea leaves generously into it.

"Fred," began Godley, "You know that Ostrog was spotted the other day and involved in a violent robbery. He also has been suggested for a nasty attack and subsequent sexual assault at a baker's in Brick Lane. Do you think he's a possible?"

"Well, he's certainly worth finding and pulling in. But to do so we're going to have to trawl the doctors, legal and struck off as the poultry man buried a knife good and proper in his shoulder. Now despite the fact he's got some medical background he'll have to get it patched."

"We'll make a start on that if you want, Guv," said Murphy on behalf of himself and Parish.

"Okay, lad, I'll leave that with you two, it'll probably draw a blank but might as well make a start at the London Hospital. Get in with the doctors there and they may know of some loose cannons practising locally and back street as it were. Me and George are going to start looking over the scant alleged witness statements from the murders on the last sightings of the victims, see if we can throw up anything new."

Murphy made them all a steaming cup of tea and they chatted socially for sometime before the two young DCs got their jackets and left, Abberline sat at one of the desks with Godley sat opposite him.

"Right, George, Martha Tabrum, last seen with another prostitute called Mary Ann 'Pearly Poll' Connolly just before midnight with two guardsmen. They split up taking one each and disappeared to make their money. 2.a.m and PC Barrett sees one guardsman waiting in Wentworth Street allegedly 'for a chum' and that is it. Identity parades with the guards have failed to come up with anyone. So, right now, dead end. What about what's on Nichols so far?"

"Well, seen at various times from 11.30.p.m on Thursday the 30th, right through to 2.30.a.m when she was last seen, drunk, by Ellen Holland but on her own having blown her doss money and looking for another punter. No descriptions of anyone. Fred, desperate as it is, we've got to wait for a local copper to come across a murder about to take place or having already happened. We've got nothing to go on."

Abberline got to his feet rubbing his face and approached the suspect's information board. He disliked having so little information available to him regarding the suspect. Usually there was a positive description from someone, or at least consistency in a scant one. "I know, George, I know." In his mind Abberline addressed the empty suspect board. 'Who are you, you bastard, who the hell are you?'

* * *

Friday 6th September 10.30.a.m and Mary Kelly was busy packing her belongings at Millers Court. Since the fabulous boat trip with the new man in her life, a new reason for living and cleaning up, she had decided over the last few days to leave the well meaning Joe Barnett. She had been back to Millers Court since Saturday but only to change her clothes. She had tried to stay with friends or in doss houses to avoid seeing Joe while she made up her mind and plucked up her courage to confront him.

She possessed a very battered leather suit case which she had laid on the bed and was busily packing. As a matter of priority she had placed the case of precious stones in the suitcase first and was neatly folding her clothes on top of it so if Joe came in he would not see it. It would be her and Robert's money to escape London for a new life together. She was mentally preparing herself for the event of Joe arriving home this morning, but when she heard the foot steps in the cobbled passage outside her expected forthright stand she would make to him began to waiver.

Joe barged the door open and stood in the doorway looking in at her. For what seemed like an eternity he stood there staring at her as she had turned and now engaged his eye contact with her piercing greenish blue eyes. In a low and calm controlled voice Joe spoke.

"Mary, what are you doing, girl?"

"I'm leaving you, Joe, I can't' live like this anymore or around here either."

"Have I ever wronged you, Mary?"

"No, Joe, you haven't. It's just I don't love you. I never have and never will. This was an arrangement of convenience among two friends. We don't have a future, Joe." Barnett paused and considered his next line carefully. His eyes he could feel were welling slightly and a lump was beginning to form in his throat. He didn't want to have difficulty expressing himself as a result of emotion so he spoke carefully and slowly.

"Mary, I love you, I've only ever wanted what was right for you. Why do you think I want you off of the streets? Why do you think I have never raised a hand to you when you're drunk unlike other men? Mary, don't go, marry me and I'll make you happy. You'll never have to work again. I've always earned money; we can start a new life somewhere else." Mary felt herself beginning to cry as a result of his impassioned speech. Tears began to roll down her own cheeks as she replied to him, her voice strained with emotion.

"It's too late, Joe, I've made up my mind. I don't see my future with you. I'm sorry." She turned away and carried on packing. Barnett now had to compose himself to accept a situation that broke his heart.

"Mary, leave your things. I'll wait to you're out later and I'll come and clear out. This is your place, always was, I can't stay here with that memory in mind."

She had her back to him as he delivered his last sentence with tears streaming down her face. "Oh, Joe!" she cried and turned to run to him at the door to hug him for one last time, but when she turned he was gone. She ran to the doorway calling, "Joe, Joe!" and looked up and down the passageway but could not see him. She ran through from Millers Court to Whites Row and could still not see him and when she finally made it into Commercial Street she was confronted with the masses of the East End going about their everyday work. He was gone.

* * *

Saturday 7th September, 11.30.p.m. Annie Chapman staggered into the kitchen at Crossingham's doss house, 35 Dorset Street with a black eye and clutching her chest as if in pain. She was a five feet tall, stout with a thick nose prominently adorning her face giving it a somewhat masculine look. Her dark brown wavy hair was a mess and her blue eyes were glazed from alcohol abuse. Timothy Donovan the deputy manager of the doss house spoke to her.

"Annie, what's wrong with you now?" Clutching her chest she replied with heavy in takes of breath and the stench of alcohol on her words.

"That fucking bitch Eliza Cooper she done this to me. If I wasn't so fucking pissed I would have fighted back and then we'd see."

"Annie, why was she fighting you?"

"'Cos I told Harry the Hawker about how she had fiddled him see. Fucking Eliza nicked a florin out of his pocket and replaced it with a ha'penny. I saw her do it so I told him. She's been going on at me alarming the last week and tonight early she fucking done me, ain't she?"

William Stevens a regular at the doss house walked in on them and frowned at Donovan as if to ask what was going on. Donovan looked back at him rolling his eyes and shaking his head in disbelief. Donovan then spoke to Annie again.

"Look, Annie, you know the rules, no money, no bed. You'll have to go or come back later."

"Oh, that's fucking nice; throw an injured woman out on her arse." As she uttered these words she began getting to her feet, unsteadily, and as she stood up she swung a punch at Donovan which was never going to connect and in the process dropped a box of pills she had in her hand that smashed on the floor. She fell to her knees to start to collect them up, then putting them in some scrap paper. She looked up at the two men watching her.

"Bastards, all bastards," she murmured.

"What are they for, Annie?" Donovan asked her.

"They're for me ribs and eye, from the bloody infirmary to ease the pain." She got to her feet and twisted the piece of paper to hold all the pills together.

"Don't you think you should take some?" asked Donovan as she was about to leave the building.

"Oh, fuck off," she slurred as she exited into the East End darkness a little after midnight.

Meanwhile Severin Klosowski had found himself in the East End following an eventful journey from Dover to London. The area suited him as it was a district where a man could melt into the background with complete obscurity amongst a population who in the main were only concerned in their own self interest; survival. He had been drinking lightly in the pubs around Spitalfields to acquaint himself with the area by engaging local men in conversation and all the time observing the general population around him, especially the unfortunates who would make easy targets for brute sexual lust or worse. He walked around sporting a deerstalker hat on many occasions, an untidy but presentable suit and he was distinctive from his piercing eyes and his very dark and thick moustache. It was now around 5.a.m and his appetite for sexual fulfilment was growing after so much time out in the crowds.

Annie Chapman had been back to Crossinghams once already without any doss money and had been ejected by Timothy Donovan when he had discovered her eating a baked potato she had taken from the kitchen.

"Don't let the bed, I'll be back soon," she said staggering off along Dorset Street in the direction of Commercial Street and a prospective client. She made her way past The Ten Bells public house and continued north towards the next junction which was Hanbury Street. In the distance stood on the corner of the two roads was Klosowski directly under a gas street lamp creating the obvious silhouette, even to the drunken Chapman, of a man and therefore prospective doss money.

Walking on the other side of the road was Elizabeth Stride, who sober and with a place to live had decided in the end to not solicit herself that night and was making her way to Commercial Street Police Station for her cleaning job. She saw Chapman on the opposite pavement and decided to cross to speak with her briefly.

On seeing her face closer to she exclaimed to Chapman "Annie, whatever has happened to your face?"

Chapman was too drunk to recognise her friend from the local pubs "Who the fuck are you and what do you care?"

"It's me, 'Long Liz,' who did this to you?"

"Liz?" she paused as her drunken mind began to match the name to the voice in front of her "Oh, Liz! That cow Eliza Cooper, look don't worry love, I'm all right I need some doss money, you got any?"

"I'm sorry, Annie, I got nothing to spare that's why I'm off to work now at the nick."

"At the nick? Bloody coppers, bastards the lot of 'em. If you ain't got nothing, get out of my way, I need him," she drooled then staggering towards the figure under the street light.

She barged past Stride making a direct line on her unsteady feet for Klosowski stood under the light. Stride walked off crossing the road to make her way to The Street looking across at the figure of Klosowski who looked back her with violent eyes. Stride hurried on as a result of his evil stare passing a woman who she knew also as Liz greeting each other as they did so. The other Liz, Elizabeth Darrell, crossed the road and saw the figures of Klosowski and Chapman stood under the street lamp and as she approached they turned and began walking arm in arm along Hanbury Street the very direction that she was intending to head. As they passed number 29 the couple who were still walking slightly ahead of her stopped and as she passed them Darrell heard some lines of their conversation. She could tell that the man had a distinctly foreign accent as he spoke but did not lift his gaze as she passed, his face therefore shielded by his hat so only his slightly bearded chin was visible; Klowsoski had not shaved for several days. He was slightly taller than herself and she heard him ask of the woman, whom she did not know, "Will you?" to which the drunken looking woman replied "Yes." Knowing exactly what was going on she hurried embarrassedly past them. She had not heard the full conversation between Klosowski and Chapman.

"Will you let me fuck you for a shilling?" he asked in his foreign tones.

"For three shillings, I'll let you use all three holes if you want lover."

"Will you?"

"Yes."

There was a passageway which led to the back of the terrace of houses that they were stood outside of that Klosowski took her along to find some privacy. He had little intention for paying for anything, just using her to settle his lusts and if she got violent he always had one of surgeons knifes sheathed within his suit jacket to deal with trouble, it was a little memento he had brought with him from Paris and ready to be used on British soil. They stopped at the end of the passageway just short of the yard at the rear so they maximised their privacy from the main road.

She slide down the wall unsteadily until she was crouching and her head matching the height of his waistband; he looked down on her with a sense of absolute domination. She was much older and uglier than he would have preferred but she would do for tonight he thought as she began to unbutton his trousers. He could feel himself becoming erect as she did so and within seconds his stiffening was pulled free by her and she began to masturbate him. It felt good to him and he began to groan with approval which made her do it a little faster. Looking down he saw her begin to guide him towards her mouth. He shut his eyes in readiness to feel the sweet sensation of her tongue and lips working rhythmically around him, but within seconds he received a great shock. She had entered his penis into her mouth in quite an accomplished manner but in her drunken condition had failed to keep her mouth open sufficiently and on the first stroke of coming back out of her mouth had dragged him against the closing jagged teeth she possessed. It caused a massive sense of pain to Klosowski and drawing blood from a cut as a result.

Now rapidly softening he was not quite free from her mouth and he had to pull it out clenching her jaw open with his hands as he did so to minimise damage. She was almost too drunk to realise what she had done as he slapped her once it was free sobering her up a little. She screamed out and stood up unsteadily against the wall. He grabbed her by the throat with his left hand to stifle her cries and drew the knife from in his jacket, but she reacted quickly used to rough treatment on occasions by her East End clients and she punched down hard on his left arm against the elbow joint forcing him to loosen his grip. It caused a sharp pain in his elbow and at the same time she kicked him in the right shin with her left leg. Unfortunately she was too late to see the knife coming as he slashed it swiftly across her throat cutting deeply and severing her vocal chords among many injuries. She staggered about clutching her neck as he pushed her into the yard at the back of

29 Hanbury Street where she fell to the floor writhing in agony seconds from death.

As she lay there dying very silently, Klosowski looked down at his blood covered penis. It hurt him a great deal as he wrapped it in a handkerchief and placed it back inside his trousers doing them up as he turned, now even more rage filled having examined himself, upon Chapman. Her dying glance looked up at him as he began shaking and curled his lips back to attack her almost lifeless body with the growing pool of blood around her head and shoulders. He dropped to his knees along side of her and stabbed into her neck with a deep deliberate cut which he drew across her throat feeling a slight bit of resistance as the knife passed over the vertebrae of her spin. The blood flow from the neck didn't massively increase as he had already managed to sever the main arteries. Looking at her face he saw the life ebb out of her leaving him to take revenge on her pitiful ravaged body.

He moved down her body and lifted up her dress to reveal her abdomen. He lifted the knife high and cut down hard across her stomach instantly opening the lower abdomen cavity as result of the depth and width of the cut. The smell, normally overwhelming to those not used to working with death, to Klosowski was matter of fact as a result of all the post mortem's he had assisted with in Paris. He cut out her intestinal tract feeling its bloody warmth pulse in his hands and discarded it over her right shoulder to expose the organs contained within the pelvic region. Klosowski turned his pathologic knowledge to his advantage and cut out with one stroke of the knife and removed in their entirety the organs directly in the front of the lower cavity. There was wide open sewer nearby and in revenge for his own injuries he threw the uterus, the upper part of the vagina and most of the bladder into the sewerage hole. His sick and tortured mind worked on the principle that she left this world incomplete she could not enter and function in the next. He sat back on his haunches to survey his work as he began to calm himself. He decided to search for anything worthwhile and then make good his escape. He cut open her pockets and found a twisted piece of paper that he opened to find it held some tablets. Discarding these to one side he searched further and came across a piece of coarse muslin, two combs and two farthings which he place in a pile next to her head. "You need these for the pearly gates," he said under his breath.

Whitechapel

He wiped his hands and knife on her dress and had been fortunate not to contaminate himself with any other blood as a result of some of his old working knowledge from the mortuary. He left the body of Annie Chapman in the yard with a blood sprayed fence close by to her.

Incredibly, no one had seen or heard a thing.

Only a matter of about half an hour later John Davis entered the rear yard of 29 Hanbury Street and saw the body of Chapman laying close to the fence and the rear steps of the house. She was as Klosowski had left her, undignified with her skirt still up exposing her stocking legs and abdomen and the intestines thrown over her shoulder. Davis moved to the sewer retching and was sick as a result of the shock of what he saw. A crowd soon gathered and after 6.a.m and with the assistance of many constables to cordon the area off Inspector Chandler, the morning's duty officer from 'The Street', took charge of the scene to await the arrival of Inspector Abberline and the Scotland Yard Detectives.

Chapter Eight

Sunday 8th September and Abberline and Godley met at their office at The Street before walking across to the murder site at Hanbury Street to join the uniform officers under the command of Inspector Chandler. Also in attendance was the divisional surgeon for the morning Doctor Bagster Phillips. The scene of the crime could almost be observed from the front doors of the Police station and Abberline found it galling that the killer could commit a crime literally right under their noses. The fifty-four year old doctor had arrived on scene at 6.30.a.m and examined the body in situe to establish the provisional 'diagnosis of death', a commonly used glum Victorian expression, before ordering it removed to the Whitechapel Workhouse Mortuary in Eagle Street. He finished his examination around 7.10.a.m as Abberline and Godley arrived fresh from a hot cup of tea at the police station on the crisp September morning as it was. Abberline was surprised by the Doctor's humour and appearance, although he shouldn't have been.

Normally George Bagster Phillips was a dapperly dressed gent with well groomed hair and neatly kept heavily bushed sideburns with highly polished shoes and the pleasant smell of quality men's fragrances. He normally carried with him a broad and jolly demeanour and sense of humour being able to make light of all circumstances, a mechanism for those dealing with such unpleasantness to survive. As a result of a heavy evening of port and cigars following a Masonic lodge meeting, Phillips was severely hung over and wheezing heavily from the harsh abuse to his lungs from rich strong Cuban cigar smoke. He was not in a good humour as the smiling Abberline addressed him

"Morning, Doctor, good to see you so early in the day, although you must have dressed in the dark, sir," noting his unkempt hair, shirt buttons fastened askew and neck tie done up pulling to the right side well off centre.

"Abberline, is there any of your detective loafers in your office over the road?" Abberline noted the stench of his stale breath from his over indulgences and now stood addressing Phillips also noting the lack of use of his fragrances. "Yes, Doctor, head over there and I'll join you shortly, if those loafers as you put it are not there then help yourself to all the stuff."

"Abberline, try to give some of those uniform mannequins some direction, one of them was washing the blood away when I arrived. They do know what evidence is I assume?"

Godley cut in sensing the doctor's abrasiveness could either be a sense of annoyance or amusement to Abberline. He wanted to avoid the former.

"They do, sir, sorry we'll bring it up at the next briefing with this having happened, help yourself to some macaroons when you get your tea, sir."

"It's a bloody Saturday morning, Sergeant; I expect some bacon and eggs too, like I'd be getting now at home. If they're not available at your filthy little office bring some back with you."

Phillips marched off in the direction of The Street whilst Abberline turned to Godley.

"I bought those bloody macaroons, they're ours, George. In fact they're bloody mine."

"Just trying to placate him, Fred."

"Well he'll be eating yours and not bloody mine once we get back there. And don't forget the bacon and eggs for the return."

Working the early turn shift were Robert and Del who were busy trying to clear up the scene with stiff brushes and buckets of water as the two detectives rounded the corner to see what was going on at the scene of the crime.

"Oi! What the bloody hell do you think you're doing again?" barked Abberline at Robert who was scrubbing the roughly cobbled yard whilst Del poured on buckets of cold water to dilute and disperse the blood. Robert didn't bother looking up as he replied to the hostile tones that had addressed him.

"What does it look like; I'm not having tea with the bloody queen am I?"

"Not having tea with the bloody queen, sir, I think is the answer," said Abberline quietly and cynically as he stood before the two young constables who, having both now looked up stood to attention. Being local officers they instantly recognising Abberline and Godley. Del looked across at Robert through the corner of his eyes and waited for his foolishly vocal mate to answer.

"I'm sorry, sir, Inspector Chandler's orders now that the body has gone, sir."

"You know what that was, son, don't you? Bloody evidence that us, the detectives, need to be privy to," replied Godley in an unsympathetic tone. "You newer uniform lads need a bit more savvy drummed into you about scene preservation for evidential purposes. You were doing this before the doctor got here, so he says, washing away vital clues to him and us. What have you got to say, lad?" Godley was now standing directly in front of Robert face to face almost nose to nose looking to intimidate a reply from the boy through his own pent up frustration.

"We stopped when the doctor turned up, Sergeant," chipped in Del.

"Oh, you do speak as opposed to stand there nonchalantly watching your mate do the scrubbing and take a rollicking, eh?"

"Yes, Sergeant, we was just following Inspector Chandler's orders to try to discourage the crowds by giving them less to see."

"Yes, that's it, sarge, it wasn't our choice, honest," added Robert foolishly.

"Sarge, bloody sarge? There's only two kinds of sarge in the Metropolitan Police, sau*sarge* and *sarge* and onion on a Sunday roast, and I'm not bloody either of them so you will address me properly!"

"All right, George, it's obviously not all the lads here's fault, we need to speak to all the duty officers and sergeants to brief the shifts so that if this happens again to leave the scene as they found it and keep the crowds at a good distance away. I mean look, all the blood stained footprints, we've got no idea if any of them belong to the killer now and we don't even know if she's been moved before the doc got here by the ghouls charging a fee to see her and the scene. We have got to establish more control of the scene to ever have a hope of catching the bastard. Where is Inspector Chandler, lads?"

Robert replied "Sorry about all this, sir, he's inside 29 trying to establish witnesses to anything."

"Right, okay lads, I'm intending to be back in the incident room around an hour from now. Come in for a cup of tea and we'll have a chat about how you can find out more at a scene, then you can let your mates know, never know, if things get any worse there could be jobs for you in there."

"Yes, sir," replied Robert.

"Thank you, sir," said Del echoing the sentiments of his now sheepish colleague. They put down their brushes, picked up their beat duty helmets and began to make off towards Commercial Street.

Annie Chapman's body was still in situe having been covered over with some rough hessian sacking by Inspector Chandler who had also been responsible for clearing away and keeping away the gathered crowds with his officers from the early shift. Looking at the body was Abberline and Godley's next gruesome job before speaking with Chandler. The detectives stood one either side of the lifeless sack covered form and each took hold of an edge of the cover at the head end. Looking at each other and with Abberline giving Godley a nod they both pulled it back at the same time revealing the dull open lifeless eyes of Annie Chapman and the gaping neck wound framed by congealed blood but exposing the entire interior of the throat cavity. The wound cut so deep that even them as laymen could see the severed windpipe, the now vacant severed artery ends and the outline of her spine.

They were both grimacing at the sight of the top part of Chapman's remains but it was nothing compared to the sight that was about to shock them as they continued to roll the sacking back down beyond the abdomen. Initially the massive abdominal wound was disguised by her dress but as the rough sacking dragged open part of her ripped skirt with it, the horror of her injuries was revealed. A massive crescent shaped cut extended from above her left hip across the bottom of her stomach and finished above her right hip completely opening it up as if to disembowel the whole of her abdominal cavity. The sight and

Whitechapel

the smell of this hit Abberline and Godley instantly and near enough simultaneously causing both of them to gag and for Godley to pull out a handkerchief to cover his face.

"God almighty, Fred, what sort of monster can do anything like this?"

"I don't know, George," replied Abberline with fury developing inside him as a result of the horrifically violent aftermath of the attack which he saw in front of him, "but if find him he's going to die if not by the gallows then by my hand, old friend." They surveyed the butchered mess of what was left of 'Dark' Annie Chapman and her almost empty stomach cavity and stood for some time surveying the blood sprayed along the fence. Appalled by the lack of dignity that this unfortunate woman had in death Godley covered her over again and stood in silence for a few seconds looking at the sacking with Abberline stood opposite. They looked at their surroundings taking stock of what they had seen and trying impossibly to put some sense to it all.

"All right, George, lets go and find Inspector Chandler and see what he has discovered thus far for us," said Abberline then walking off through the police lines to enter the rear door of 29 Hanbury Street.

Inspector Chandler was inside number 29, a typical slum East End dwelling taking notes from John Davis who had discovered the body as to time, position and state of dress and location of belongings. It was not uncommon for people such as drunks to be robbed in the street either conscious or unconscious by thieves known as 'muchers,' so Chandler was trying to establish if Annie Chapman in death may have been further preyed on by a mucher. He had taken several pages of notes from Davis establishing that he had discovered the scene exactly as it still was barring the cleaning up of the blood. Any mucher may well have been scared off by the sight of the murderous injuries and therefore fled the scene to save being accused of the crime.

Others who had gathered early at the scene were being questioned by other officers from the early shift from The Street as well as by the two new detectives seconded to Abberline. All were within number 29 and all trying to tell their varying accounts over the noise of everyone present talking. They were varying East End types, Henry Holland, James Green, Jim Kent and a local landlady Mrs Handyman all talking with individual officers at once creating a loud chatter. Each conversation was struggling to overcome the constant din and becoming louder as Abberline and Godley entered.

Twenty-nine Hanbury Street was a typical three storey two rooms on each floor Victorian slum terraced property which, once filled on the ground floor with five potential witnesses and four policemen, one of whom was being spoken to by two locals desperate to tell their versions and all trying to elicit information from them, was simply oversubscribed and bursting at its seams. Abberline and Godley stood silent in the doorway for the best part of a minute observing this chaos before individuals quickly noticed them and fell silent, eventually leading to complete silence as Chandler finally spotted the two yard detectives.

Joseph Luniss Chandler was a thirty-eight year old career policeman who had made uniform inspector in fifteen years. He had worked most of his time like Abberline in the East End and in fact they had spent time serving together at Commercial Street when Abberline was a uniform inspector and Chandler was a young sergeant. They had a good professional relationship then and neither would see any reason for it to change. On seeing the detectives at the door Chandler broke away from John Davis and made for Abberline with a warm smile and extending his hand to greet him.

"Fred, how the hell are you, you old sot!" This was a sarcastic greeting from Chandler who also wrestled with a drink problem. They shook hands warmly and vigorously.

"Off the sauce and on the case, Joe. What you got for us?"

"The old boy there," Chandler began pointing to John Davis, "lives on the third floor at the front of the house with his wife and three sons. He was a bit restless and went for a wander in the early hours and found what was left of her." Abberline surveyed the interior of the property as Chandler spoke noting windows. He was grateful for his old friend's efforts so far.

"Right, thanks Joe, we'll go and talk to him. Can you do us a favour, can you give your blokes a brief at your next shift parade about scene preservation, as everyone so far has been a bloody mess. People and coppers walking all around and I'm getting it in the neck from the doctors. We need all the help we can with evidence to catch this bastard." Abberline addressed this as diplomatically as he could.

Chandler appreciated the delivery and the sentiments of what Abberline said. "Fred, no problem, I'll pass it around at The Street and do it first thing tomorrow to my lot. I'll get back into the yard and see what's going on out there and let you sort out Davis. Good to see you again, mate."

"Yeah, you too, see you at The Street." Chandler made his way out as Abberline and Godley approached John Davis.

Davis was a stooped and ageing fifty-three year old carman at Leadenhall Market. He appeared to be a little pensive at being left to these two imposing looking detectives. Abberline wanted to put him at ease. "John, look it's a bit noisy in here can we go upstairs to your place?"

The nervous and prematurely elderly man stammered as he spoke. "Certainly, Mr Abbbbb..erline, you don't mind my wii......fe being there do you?"

"Not at all, you lead the way."

Davis led them up a narrow and rickety wooden stair case that due to its cheap construction creaked on every board. Godley and Abberline noted that the building was surprisingly free of damp or smells for an East End property and that on the whole staircase which ran at the rear of the building there was only one window. Both detectives had noted that all the rooms at the rear did have windows that overlooked the yard. They entered a clean but cramped room which held a double bed, a table and three chairs, a sink and a dilapidated wardrobe. It had one window which overlooked Hanbury Street itself. Mrs Davis sat at the table and immediately got up as the three men entered. Abberline spoke to try to put her at ease immediately and noted she was drinking from a steaming mug, it smelt like fresh tea and he wanted her to enjoy it despite the circumstances.

"Please, don't stand on ceremony for me and George, Mrs Davis, stay at your seat if you wish and enjoy the rest of your tea," said Abberline as amiably as he could. She sat back down and Abberline ushered to John Davis to join his wife. He pulled out a chair and offered the third to Abberline who duly took it with Godley settling himself on the edge of the bed.

Abberline began the questioning as Godley pulled his pocket book out from his suit jacket along with a pencil. "So, John, how long have you been here?"

"About tttt..two weeks."

"Just you and Mrs Davis?"

"Nnnnno, me, Jean and thhhhhhh...three boys, Mr Abberline."

"How do you know me then, John?"

"You ssss..s.orted me out years ago after I got beat up yyyyy......years ago outside The Ttttt....ten Bells."

"Ah, I see," Abberline could not recall him having been to many fights at The Ten Bells. "So what can you tell me?"

"Wwwww......well, I don't ssss.....sleep good sometimes and I'd been a bit dddd...disturbed through the night so I got up for some air about qqqq...quarter to six. Never heard anything all nnnnn....night but came down into the yyyyy....yard and well, it was hhhhhh.....horrible, Mr Abberline. Blood all up the fffff...fence and her all rrrrrr....ripped up."

"So you never saw anything or heard anything. Any neighbours say anything to you this morning?"

"No, nnnnn....nothing, I think most of them are tttttt....tarts or pimps so they was out I think."

Turning to Godley, Abberline remarked "Well that explains a lot I think we'll find, George."

"Your wife or boys see or hear anything?"

"Nah, all asleep."

"Where are the boys now?"

"Out, mmmmm...making a crust, sir, one sells papers, the other two work up chchch.....chimneys."

Abberline took a moment to consider his train of thought. Godley chipped in during the pause. "John, has that body been moved at all or disturbed between the time you found it to the time the police arrived?"

"Well, I wwwwww.....went up to Commercial Ststst....street nick and at the same time JJJJJJ....Jimmy Green and Jim Kent went looking for a copper. Your other blokes are talking to them, they llllll....live next door at the front of their places too. But from what I remember I don't reckon it was touched. Who'd want to touch that, I mean."

Abberline asked a final question. "John, who was charging money to see poor old Annie before the police arrived."

Davis looked pensive and exchanged glances with his wife before answering, "No, I ccccc...can't get involved in no gggggg....grassing Mr Abberline. You'll have to ask sssss....someone else."

"Did, you know Annie, John?" asked Godley.

"No, nnnn...never seen her before, ever."

The two detectives got up to leave. "Thanks for your time, Mr and Mrs Davis, if there is anything else don't hesitate to contact us will you," said Abberline in closing.

Mrs Davis chipped in. "Catch him soon, Mr Abberline; all of us are really scared, day and night."

"We're doing all we can," replied Abberline and then the two of them left to return to the gruesome scene outside.

"Strange sentiment from her, Fred, do you think she works on the street herself?" said Godley as they reached the yard still filled with police and locals most of whom were milling about for no reason. The body they noted had now gone, taken to the Whitechapel Workhouse Infirmary Mortuary.

"Maybe, George, but maybe she's just worried for all women, he might not always choose unfortunates."

The doctor had seen what he needed to see, the photographer had been prior to Annie's move and the junior detectives had sketched the scene and had the rest of the immediate investigation in hand. It was time for Abberline and Godley to return to their office at The Street and confront the difficult Doctor Phillips. They passed out of the yard of 29 Hanbury Street seeing the photographer packing up with Robert Ford and Del nearby stopping any folk just wandering in.

"Frank," said Abberline addressing the photographer, "did you get a picture of the arterial spray on the fence?"

"You what, Guv?"

"The blood on the fence, son!"

"No, Guv'nor, sorry run out of plates."

"Well can't you get some more?"

"I'll try, but it ain't quick, I've got to go to The Yard for them."

"All right, you do that, in the meantime, you," said Abberline pointing to Robert Ford "do a sketch of them in your pocket book, and take your time I want it accurate. Robert and Del had ended up being kept at the scene for crowd control. Robert looked at Del as if for inspiration but really because he'd sooner his friend shouldered the responsibility this time after the earlier error.

"Don't look at him!" yelled Godley "Get on with it, lad!" Robert stepped forward drawing his notebook and pencil whilst Del surreptitiously winked at him and stayed at the yard entrance. He stood back and began cautiously and as accurately as he could to draw.

The photographer took himself off to Scotland Yard for more photographic plates and returned some three hours later to find the scene abandoned by police, the junior detectives thinking all was done. The blood had been washed away innocently by Mrs Davis. He knew there would be hell to play so he told Abberline later that the plates were over exposed and produced no image.

Chapter Nine

A week after the fight with the poultry stall holder and the police, Michael Ostrog was still seeking attention for his deep wound. Murphy and Parish had turned up nothing in relation to his wound having been attended anywhere as a result and it had seemed that they were unlikely too. Late on the night of Sunday 8th September he found himself in 'The Blind Beggar' public house in Whitechapel Road; the bleeding had stopped following him rudimentarily wrapping his wound in an off cut of a cotton sheet he found in the rubbish. There he met John Pizer at the bar, a thirty-eight year old second generation Polish Jewish immigrant working as a boot finisher. He fancied himself as a medical man having worked briefly as a slaughter man, then a butcher and attending many public post mortems. He felt if he could stitch a few wounds on the side it might make him some extra cash. He was known within the neighbourhood in which he worked as 'Leather Apron' due the distinctive apron that he was always seen in. Following discreet enquiries Ostrog had been directed to the pub to seek his help. Pizer noticed the heavy makeshift bandaging Ostrog sported and the pain he appeared to be in and saw the obvious opportunity as he was approached by Ostrog.

"That looks a bit sore that, mate," he said to Ostrog having made eye contact with him at the bar.

"Yes, and what's it to you, friend?" came the reply in a heavy European accent that Pizer could not place.

"Well I do a bit of back street surgery and thought you might need some help."

"How much?" Ostrog growled in a low voice looking around him.

"What d'ya say, couldn't catch it, mate?"

"How much, all things have a price attached?"

"Well, I've got to look at the wound first, might need a bit of cleaning, maybe a stitch, can't give you a price until a consultation."

"Where?" said Ostrog with growing suspicion.

"Mulberry Street, 22, not far. It's for your health mate, just trying to help."

"All right, let's go. You fool with me and I kill you."

"Fucking hell, mate, bit strong. In fact, stuff it find someone else."

Pizer turned to leave to then feel the sharp pointed blade of what he imagined to be an exceptionally large knife in his back. He froze, the stranger it seemed had the next move.

"You take me and fix me and I pay you, you walk away now and I kill you outside for insulting me. I kill before in Russian army." Pizer could feel the formation of sweat induced by fear on his brow, what choice did he now have in this dangerous situation of his own making.

"Follow, me I'll sort you out all right, I won't rip you off neither," he turned to look at Ostrog, ironically continuing. "I am some what at the mercy of the point you have made, sir." They left the pub and made for Mulberry Street.

22 Mulberry Street was a run down old cobblers shop. As a premises it had been in Pizer's family for many years and he could be a little itinerant in his presence there. The main reason he practised illegal medicine as an aside was that it kept money coming in during his absences. Frequent times being closed meant that he was an unreliable business to use affecting his meagre profit margins. Brushes with the law and alcohol were what normally created the unforeseen absences that kept him away. They had walked uncomfortably together from the pub with not a word of conversation between them. Pizer pulled out a door key for number 22 from his leather apron which he almost constantly wore holding normally the tools of his legal trade and money. As they entered together Pizer could detect the faint smell of infection

from Ostrog's wound which indicated to him it was several days old. They made their way through the cobblers section of the shop to the rear where Pizer had a makeshift medical type couch constructed from old wooden crates, cotton wadding and leather.

Ostrog sat himself onto this slowly and indeed painfully grasping his injured arm as he did so to prevent himself knocking it. To Pizer it seemed that he had little strength or use in the arm. Without a word between them Pizer stepped up to the couch and began to slowly to unwrap the make do bandage that Ostrog was wearing. Ostrog made no attempt to resist and just grunted in pain when the bandage it self tore away from the gaping wound in his shoulder and upper arm muscles. The stench of infection that Pizer had suspected now truly hit him as the wound was a festering mess. Dead skin surrounded the deep gash which was various discolouring shades of yellow giving way to a healthier redness the deeper the wound became indicating even to Pizer that the wound was, at least, not beyond repair. Unwrapping the temporary dressing had discoloured Pizer's own clothing with blood and some rotting human tissue.

"Mate, there's two ways I can deal with this," said the would be doctor to his now almost prostrate and grimacing patient, "We can have a go at cutting the dead and infected flesh away, wash it out with spirit and then put in a couple of stitches and job done in a couple of hours. Lot of pain though as I don't do anything with any anaesthetic."

"Yes, I understand, I am Russian military surgeon. Other method is what?"

"Well, see them pots over there marked fish bait," said Pizer pointing to three glass jars with muslin lids tied around their necks, "they're full of maggots. We isolate your wound, add the maggots what then eat all the rotten flesh. Bit of a tickle, takes eight hours or so, so you'd have to rest the night here to get it finished like."

Ostrog knew that a man practising illegal medicine could be dangerous. He might wonder why he was treating such a wound and contact the police to deflect attention from himself. With this in mind and the fact that this 'surgeon' had asked him no questions he would take the quick but painful option. "I will take your first suggestion, have no time to wait around all night, just give me something to bite on to vent the pain."

"No problem, that comes as a standard part of the practice. We'll get started then and when we're finished that'll be six shillings," said Pizer.

"Don't worry, Leather Apron, I will give you something for your trouble," replied Ostrog, trying to disguise menace in his voice. Certainly Pizer was uncomfortable in this man's presence, but any business was business.

Pizer brought a tray to the couch consisting of a large surgeon's knife, three scalpels, scissors and a basic suture kit, all a little old and slightly tarnished but surprisingly clean, especially by the standards of the Russian army Ostrog observed. In addition to this were some gauze pads, a bottle of surgical spirit and some fairly clean looking bandages. Ostrog was determined to watch as the work began and progressed through to the end and to assist in the whole process if necessary. To try to preserve his meagre clothing he removed his coat and two shirts despite the fact they were already damaged. It also gave him a clear view of the surgery being conducted in case he wished to try to interject with points of advice or direction.

Pizer gave Ostrog a thick piece of rubber cosh to place in his mouth to bite on and then set to initially with some gauze and spirit to clean away congealed blood and give him a clear view of what he needed to cut away. Immediately as he applied pressure Ostrog flinched in pain and remained tense with his face grimacing tightly and biting hard on the rubber with as yet no sound as the wound was cleaned. Veins protruded in his neck and along his temples as he strained to take the pain the procedure was so far inducing. Following this action for several minutes Pizer stopped to change implements and the pain for Ostrog temporarily subsided and he relaxed but for only a few moments. Pizer then picked up one of the scalpels to have a go at cutting away the infected skin at Ostrog's request. The Russian shut his eyes and pre-empted the pain by beginning to bite harder on the rubber as he felt the blade begin to slice into the healthy skin just below the dead and infected layers, a process in which there was no choice if this method was to be successful. Tears streamed from Ostrog's face as he felt the scalpel running into the muscle tissues of the upper parts of his tricep, bicep and in the main deltoid muscle. He knew his arm would have to be immobile for sometime and he would have to work slowly to resume strength in it. But if it meant ultimately keeping his arm the short term inconvenience was obviously worth it. Pizer had nothing as clean as a kidney bowl to discard surgical remnants in to, so dead flesh and other bodily deposits he threw to the floor to clear up later.

Ostrog felt the pain subside as Pizer finished cutting and opened his heavily watering eyes to take a look at the work done and also noticed Pizer preparing the suture kit to close the wound up. He was surprisingly pleased with what he saw as the wound although prominent was not as wide as he might have first suspected and the smell from it seemed to have dissipated. As he carried on studying the wound he was hit by the shock of Pizer cleaning the wound out again with some fresh gauze and spirit; it stung immensely as his surgeon unsympathetically wiped it firmly although he appreciated the benefit it should bring prior to suturing. Pizer put the gauze down and picked up the primitive needle and thread from the tray and pierced one side of the wound and passed the needle and thread through it twice before starting to pull the wound together and stitch each side to the other. The pain that this caused was minuscule in comparison to that Ostrog had felt whilst the wound was cleansed. It took about an hour from start to finish for the whole process to be complete and for Ostrog to be pulling his clothing back on and Pizer to be placing his instruments into a bucket to be cleaned later, he also used a coal shovel and dustpan to pick up the flesh from the floor and discarded it into a dustbin in the rear of the room.

Pizer wiped his hands over with some old cotton sheeting but his apron and his shirt were smattered in blood as a result of the process which for the time being he disregarded focusing on getting payment from his client. Ostrog was straightening his clothes looking at himself in a faded mirror on one side of the room scanning the reflected image of the room for potential weapons for himself as he had no intention in paying for the service he had received. His view was that 'Leather Apron' should be grateful for his life.

"Right then, squire, that'll be six shillings."

"Yes, right," said Ostrog falsely searching each of his pockets with his good arm whilst noticing the blood stained coal shovel just a few feet to his left. He felt two loose pennies in his trouser pocket and jangled them together to relax the tense looking Pizer and then dropped them as he withdrew his hand from his pocket ensuring they were landing near the vicinity of the shovel.

His ploy worked perfectly as he could tell that Pizer had completely dropped his guard believing that the Russian was obviously going to pay. He and was looking away from Ostrog towards an old faded clock ticking away indicating the early hour on the wall. Ostrog took a firm grip of the shovel handle as he bent down as if to pick up the money. He was raising himself back up again as Pizer turned to face him. At that very moment in a swift action Ostrog drew the shovel slightly back and then swung it forward heavily striking Pizer right on the top of his head sending him sprawling limp to the floor completely unconscious with a slight gash which began seeping blood down his forehead and onto his face.

Nonchalantly Ostrog now took his time to search the entire premises to see if he could find any money 'Leather Apron' might have stashed away, a common man such as Pizer would not use any form of bank. It took him some time but pacing out the area behind the shop counter carefully he found a particularly squeaky floorboard which by pulling away the hessian matting on the floor and lifting the floor board he found held Pizer's stash of money. There was only about fifteen pounds which he felt although a significant amount of money was probably not all of it. A man as slippery as Pizer must have had more but he didn't want to risk him now coming out of his temporary coma. Pizer was fully able bodied unlike him at present. Although a dangerous man he felt not worthy of murder as it could bring unnecessary attention to himself as a result of having been seen in public with a known local figure.

He took one more look at Pizer still prostrate on the floor in the back room. "Dos vadonya," he said as he walked casually by his victim and out from the rear of the premises, as despite the hour he did not want to draw attention from the front.

Some hours later Pizer came to realising within seconds where he was and what had happened. He rubbed the top of his head which felt damp and received a shooting pain from the bruising he had received and discovered his hand thick with congealing blood from his wound. Immediately he knew he needed to check to see if his patient had ripped him off and discovered his money hide plundered; he moved straight away to his second hide behind a vent brick in his festering outside toilet and to his relief at least found that safe.

His only real chance of revenge against this dangerous man was to make a robbery report with the police and deny any counter allegations about illegal surgery if his assailant was caught. Covered in a significant amount of blood on his apron, shirt and hands, he rushed into Mulberry Street unaware of the night's gruesome murder which had taken place less than five minutes walk from his premises the other side of the Whitechapel Road. The time was now 8.a.m and many folk were out and about their daily business and the news had already spread about the murder.

Pizer staggered into the Whitechapel Road looking for a local constable to report his robbery to but in seconds was being demonised by a prostitute in the street. On seeing him she cried out with a shrill loud scream and pointed to him with manic arm actions, emotions undoubtedly derived from being an associate of Chapman.

"There he is, the fucking murderer, look at the state of him, where's the filth! Look at him, covered in blood someone grab him, him in the leather apron!" Crowds of people turned their attentions to her and to him and he could see that a sense of agreement to her observations was very swiftly developing. Pizer couldn't turn behind him the shortest route to the refuge of the shop because of the following crowd beginning to gather so he had to run towards the City Of London.

A screaming mob began chasing him, clipping at his heels, the shrieking unfortunate amongst them and the most vocal. "Look at the fucker, all covered in poor old Annie's blood, let's get him and tear him limb from limb. Get the leather apron, that'll be justice!" In Whitechapel at the time there was a rumour of an individual who wore a leather apron and a deerstalker hat threatening the prostitutes with a knife demanding money or else he said he would 'Rip them up!' No one had actually seen this man in action to report him to the police but word had spread that, if he existed, he maybe responsible for the murders of Martha Tabrum and Mary Nichols. Pizer may have fuelled this story as a result of his own drunken deeds. Often when drunk he would insult and man handle some of the prostitutes hoping for a 'freebie.' These actions elaborated on by the prostitutes to the police and their pimps may have created the legend of 'Leather Apron'. To this point no one had ever formally identified anyone with this alias but with the current atmosphere of unease in the area coupled with Pizer's bloodied appearance the scare mongering people of the East End needed little provocation to find a foil. This morning, following a third murder and Pizer unwittingly being spotted in the state as he was in the street, the rumour now amongst the populace had a basis in fact. If he didn't get away he was sure to be killed by the mob.

Running, his lungs within seconds were short of breath from physical exertion and fear and Pizer thought he would die innocently in his eyes at the hands of a frenzied mob. He didn't even know another murder had taken place. Up ahead he could see a horse drawn omnibus pulling off from a stop and he was slightly out pacing the crowd. With a desperate spurt of effort and his lungs and leg muscles burning he managed to grab the back of it and begin to make good his escape. The bus was moving off at sufficient speed for it's passengers to be oblivious to the mob.

The bus pulled into Leman Street and Pizer jumped off of it knowing he could make it swiftly back to the rear of Mulberry Street from there and lay low for a few days. This he did so carefully navigating the route from there via Commercial Road having taken off his leather apron and rolled it up to try to detract attention from himself. He was pretty much home free as he turned into Adler Street which led him through to the rear of his shop. Once inside number 22 Mulberry Street Pizer collapsed onto his own couch to recover from his double ordeal. He would have to clean himself up and then find the police.

Meanwhile Police Sergeant Kerby and Constable Thain and made heir way to the commotion in Whitechapel Road and were now surrounded by the shouting mob all trying to tell their stories at once. Kerby lost his patience with the shouting and eventual jostling they were receiving within minutes of arriving; he blew hard on his whistle to silence the crowd so that he could address them.

"Right, shut up the lot of you and we'll get through this one at a time." The unfortunate who started it piped up. "The murderer, he was here, dark haired bleeder with a leather apron all covered in blood. He run off. Dark hair I say and about thirty-five." The officers turned to each other and John Thain spoke first.

"Sarge, sounds like John Pizer, old Leather Apron." A dark featured diminutive ill looking man with a foreign accent spoke with venom from the crowd. He had been seen by Thain first of all scavenging in the gutter.

"That's him. Leather Apron, I saw him too. Covered in blood. Better get him before we do." Aaron Kosminski then melted back into the crowd having shouted his bit. He carried on ferreting in the gutter for food, for his mania did not allow him to eat food given to him by another.

Thain and Kerby spent the next half an hour amassing a story against John Pizer. They would need to pass this information onto the detectives for them to act on. They'd have to do it soon before this 'Leather Apron' ended up the way of Tabrum, Nichols and Chapman. While they collated this evidence William Bates a sensationalist journalist from 'The Star' newspaper arrived on the scene to try to get an exclusive story but in his usual way also whip up the crowd to sell more papers. He was about thirty years old, intelligent, ambitious and well groomed and dressed. He looked like the sort that usually frequented the area at night for business which belied his own humble East End origins not unlike young Ralph's the paper seller. Bates was well known locally having graduated from reporting in low key publications in the area to the big league of journalism and always put a massive human interest slant on all stories, sometimes not only exaggerating actions but downright lying about them. Kerby was not pleased to see him there and instructed Thain to say nothing to him. When they were asked to comment both declined any comment which was subsequently reported the next day as:

'LEATHER APRON EVADES POLICE',

And in a smaller sub text left as

'LOCAL POLICE WITHOUT A CLUE,
THANK GOD FOR ABBERLINE.'

* * *

Back at The Street, Abberline and Godley were in the incident room along with the now significantly mellowed Dr Phillips who had taken on a better humour as a result of a healthy amount of macaroons and several large cups of tea. Godley had been unable to get bacon and eggs on the short walk back to The Street so he had to settle for buying more macaroons, a fortunate purchase as all of the others had been eaten by the doctor. He was now enjoying a large cigar left in his overcoat pocket from the night before and a glass of whiskey which he claimed was as a medicinal 'hair of the dog' from one of the detective's desks. There was an amiable atmosphere in the office but a serious discussion between Abberline, Godley and Phillips about motive and motivation for the murders.

"So, Doctor, what's your take on all this, do you think it's the same man, or co-incidental and conducted by many men?" enquired Abberline.

"Well, Inspector, if you had asked me after number two I would have said two unlinked crimes. But number two and three follow the same hallmarks in many ways so I really don't think anyone can comment accurately. I think you either have to catch one in the act or see what follows, hopefully nothing."

"Do you believe it likely there could be more, sir?" asked Godley

"Undoubtedly, Sergeant Godley, either the same man or men if they are in some macabre competition or perhaps someone who kills to gain the same notoriety."

"How would you go about catching him, Doctor?" asked Abberline.

"Well, you're the policeman but since you ask you do have men in plain clothes? If so why not try a new tack. It's all very well to have men in disguise as men; why not have men in disguise as women. Let's face it none of the unfortunates are generally pretty so disguise is not impossible, I believe the French police use it as a technique and call it 'agent provocateur'."

Abberline and Godley looked at each other and gave a nod indicating they each felt it maybe worth a chance. Volunteers maybe the only problem to dress as a woman. They discussed the case with Phillips for another hour before he decided bed was calling and a hansom was called to take him home. Doctor Phillip's points disturbed the detectives deeply. Could it be the work of several or one? Had he or they finished? Were they three unrelated murders fuelled by money or lust? It would be time to get Doctor Llewellyn's take on the latest murder. At that moment there was a knock at the door and Robert and Del entered. Both keen to get back in the good books of the detectives, they tried speaking over each other and failed dismally to communicate to Abberline until he gestured with his finger for them both to stop, be quiet and then pointed to Robert to speak for them both.

"Sir, just to let you know the crime scene is all finished with, sir. Anything else we can help with, sir?"

Abberline and Godley looked at each other with a knowing glance before the inspector then looked back to the young constables and spoke.

"As it happens, lads, yes. Too many 'sirs' in one sentence, boy. So sit down shut up and listen to a job you two maybe perfect for, Inspector Spratling permitting." They sat down and looked at each other with excited curiosity. Godley went to the tea pot and brought the lads over a fresh piping hot cup each. They received it gratefully, foolishly believing they may have made it into the C.I.D, they were getting close, however. They were about to join the team.

* * *

Monday 9th September 7.15.a.m; Detective Sergeant William Thick, known locally as 'Johnny Upright' due to his physical posture and integrity, along with Detective Constables Parish and Murphy, had been tasked with arresting John 'Leather Apron' Pizer for many reasons. Firstly, as a obvious suspect following the crowd incident of Saturday morning, secondly to eliminate him from enquires, and thirdly for his own safety as on the Sunday whilst the last statements were being taken his lodging house in Holloway, 'Crossman's', had been attacked with bricks and bottles by an East End mob. It was only a matter of hours before the vigilantes would descend on 22 Mulberry Street. The police pounded on the door as Pizer stood in fear in the front room of the premises, the cobblers shop, clutching a heavy leather beating mallet and a working knife ready to defend himself against the mob. He refused to answer the door and stayed silent despite the fact the detectives identified themselves as police.

"Pizer, we know you're in there, open up or we're coming in," shouted Bill Thick. Pizer stood firm. Thick nodded to Parish who shoulder charged the door which gave way immediately. They were all carrying heavy truncheons and Murphy had manacles. A black Mariah was parked with it's uniform driver outside. Pizer stood in the middle of the shop brandishing his weapons with the colour draining from his face. He screamed out in panic to try to ward them off. "Don't come no closer, I'll do ya, I really will."

The detectives held their ground for a moment as Thick spoke to give Pizer a chance to come quietly. "You're just the man I want, come quietly, son, and you won't get hurt, you can see we're coppers, try anything silly and I'll bust your skull open."

"That fucker did that on Saturday night; I don't care, come and take me then!" This was a very unwise move by Pizer, all three moved forward and while Parish drew his attention, with the first attack coming from Murphy who struck at the side of Pizer's right knee. His leg buckled and he went down onto his right side dropping both weapons as Thick struck him across his right upper arm to ensure he was completely disabled. Pizer cried out in pain from the strikes and screamed "All right, I'll come, don't fucking hit me again, you copper bastards!" This was an unwise insult as Murphy deadened his other arm for his troubles. He carried on screaming as they manacled him behind his back. "Murder, murder, get off, you bastards!"

"It will be murder if you don't come with us, Pizer, the mob will be here soon if we don't take you," replied Thick.

He was wrong, as they took Pizer outside to the Mariah a mob was already gathering and as he emerged with the detectives they began jeering and throwing rotting vegetables. He was placed in the Mariah and it set off at speed with Bill Thick leaving the constables to search the house. Fortunately another uniform constable was on hand to stand guard at the front of the house while they did so. Part of the crowd chased the police carriage for a short distance but gave up as it gathered speed. They soon all dispersed as the detectives pulled out the bloodied apron and shirt from Pizer's rubbish. Expecting the visit from the police he had hidden his surgery tools well and they were never found. This was fortunate for him it may have inferred guilt and sent him to the gallows before the reign of terror on Whitechapel had finished.

Unsurprisingly Will Bates was in the crowd as the Mariah pulled off and spotted a group of unfortunates who were screaming and spitting at the Mariah as it passed. Two of them were Cathy Eddowes and Liz Stride, both weeping and screaming with emotion as the police withdrew with Pizer who also had some rotten vegetables which they feebly threw at the police transport as it passed. He approached them sporting his usual appearance; today they were not keen to see any journalists seeking a story in their sober and emotional state.

"Did you know Annie, Annie Chapman, ladies?" He addressed the question wrongly to the tall and statuesque Stride. She looked at him with complete disdain and for once he was caught off guard and left speechless.

"Why don't you just fuck off, you horrible little toff bastard!!" She screamed at him and at the same time punched him firmly on the right cheek knocking him off his feet and landing on his backside on the cold cobbles. He could say nothing. They pelted him with the last of their rotting vegetables and walked away weeping still for the loss of their friend. The next day the headlines very damningly read for Pizer:

'PIZER / LEATHER APRON ONE AND THE SAME.'

And the sub text read;

> 'POLICE PREPARE CASE TO SEND HIM TO THE GALLOWS AMONGST LOCAL HYSTERIA.'

Francis Tumblety when he read this news several days later was not pleased that someone else was killing in Whitechapel as it would undoubtedly lead to a larger police presence in the area.

* * *

That evening George Lusk was getting drunk in The Ten Bells public house in Commercial Street and raising his voice to vent his dissatisfaction in the police and the government following the three murders in the local area in the recent weeks. George Lusk was a forty-nine year old builder who specialised in the restoration of old time musical halls. He was a well know local figure as a result of this building company employing local crafts men to ply his trade. Recently a widower, he had seven children to raise so employed various local girls as guardians so he could work, attend Masonic meetings as a member of the Doric Lodge and go out drinking. He was known at times as a 'rebel rouser' and this night he was calling for action by the people over the murders.

"All you hard working men and women of Whitechapel and Spitalfields, you don't deserve a lack a protection. That's what it is, the politicians making sure that there are plenty of coppers in their areas, the West End, and out in the leafy Hams of the East, but for us real working people we can go hang. They come here to drink our cheaper beer, abuse our women and demand protection from the few bobbies that are here. It's not right, brothers and sisters, we must form up, we must act!"

Much of the pub clapped and cheered as he made his final point with a loud crescendo to his voice, he took another swig of ale as he waved to thank them for their adulation. The land lord was not happy, however, knowing that a visit from one of the local police inspectors like Chandler or Spratling could get him shut down with such behaviour taking place. He approached Lusk at the bar from his own side to have a quiet word in his ear before he continued. He hadn't counted on Lusk's aggression under the influence of drink.

"George, look, mate, can you tone it down a bit or take it outside. If Spratling pays a visit I'll be closed down. I can't live with no licence, or worse still no pub." Lusk looked up from his glass and smiled at him breathing fetid beer smelling breath in his face as he spoke. He looked at the landlord but his voice was addressing the masses.

"Did, you hear that, brothers and sisters, this bourgeoisie dog doesn't want us in here."

"Not them, George, just your ranting," replied the landlord irritated by his accusation. Lusk always walked with a heavy stick, not as an aid but as a weapon. With a swift hard movement he pulled the ageing landlord half way across the bar and held the stick hard against his throat. The landlord was caught totally by surprise and froze in fear of the immediate and impending violence.

"So you don't like me defending the people, you pig, so I shan't ask you if you agree with the formation of a vigilance committee to meet here then, eh?"

"I'm sorry, George, I just don't want no trouble, mate, that's all." Lusk pushed the stick hard against his throat so that his breathing was restricted but speech was impossible. He again addressed the crowd "We're not welcome here people, I propose the formation of a vigilance committee, who is with me, eh?" he shouted with passion. A mass of shouts of support emanated from the drunken crowd.

Lusk threw the unfortunate Ten Bells landlord away from him crashing into bottles against the rear of the bar; he then landed in a heap on the floor, dazed and cut by broken glass. "Follow me brothers and sisters, we're off to The Crown in Mile End Road to form the 'Whitechapel Vigilance Committee!'" Over half the pub stood up to follow him, the remainder were women and off duty policemen who couldn't safely get involved despite their beliefs. The doors of the pub were almost flung off their hinges as Lusk threw them open with considerable force and the crowd followed after him all heading south along the gas lit Commercial Street.

That night at The Crown public house in Mile End Road the Whitechapel Vigilance Committee was formed and Lusk was naturally voted president by the very mob he had roused. As an organisation it would come to give the Police as many problems as the highly illegal Fenian movement operating in London trying to bring freedom to Ulster through terror.

* * *

Friday 20th September. Following a week's intensive training on operating in plain clothes Robert and Del were back at The Street. Murphy and Parish the detectives assigned to the case had taken many statements since the Chapman murder from witnesses who had vague recollections of the movements of her and those of Mary Nichols. The results were not helpful; in fact in the minds of Abberline and Godley they cast doubt on the theory of one lone murderer.

Abberline had eliminated Pizer as a likely suspect through witness statements and those willing to support his alibi, but he was being held still in custody for his own safe keeping until a judge or coroner could give direction of his innocence so it maybe reported in the press. He had made an allegation to the police of assault by a Russian who he had met in a pub and then walked in his direction with him home and attacked Pizer in the street. Pizer explained that the man had pulled a knife on him and forced him to go to his work place to steal money from him. Once inside Pizer claimed to have tried to disarm the man who had fallen on his own knife in the process, hence Pizer himself being covered in blood, and then having failed in his robbery made off leaving Pizer to nurse his own wound in the form of the head injury. Those drinking in The Blind Beggar with Pizer had supported his story about the Russian. The wave of hysteria was diminishing a little as a result of over ten days of no incident but the notion of the lack of anyone having been caught was kept alive but George Lusk and the newly formed Whitechapel Vigilance Committee.

The detectives were assessing and re-assessing the cases so far. Chapman had been seen last with a man with a foreign accent, fuelling theories of a Jewish immigrant suspect, who was 'a little taller than her'. She was only five feet tall so without more specific detail on how much taller it was not much help as most men were noticeably taller. He wore a hat and looked 'dark', referring to hair colouring. Mary Nichols had only been seen in dispute with a 'toff' some hours before she was found dead by PC Thain and this individual was allegedly quite tall around 5'10" well dressed and well spoken, again in some foreign accent, yet despite having been spoken to by a constable there was no further description. Little did the police know that the man who held the key to murder as a witness was already a wanted man; Aaron Kosminski. Details of Martha Tabrum's last movements were available but a worthless identity parade of guardsmen suspects had not found a killer.

Abberline had little to go on with a very diverse chalk board relating to description. It seemed of little or no help at present with too much contradiction, unless there were separate individuals, in which case how do you catch an ever changing killer? It was time to put his two latest recruits to good use. Robert and Del were in the incident room to get a briefing from Abberline on their duties for the next fortnight. He began speaking earnestly.

"All right lads you won't like this but this is how it's going to be. Permanent night shifts as that's when he seems to be striking." Robert and Del looked at each other pulling and uncomfortable but knowing face each. "You're both young fellows but you, Del boy," pointing to him as well to emphasise his point, "have the, how shall I put it, the fairest complexion."

"What's that got to do with anything, Guv?" inquired Del. Godley interjected.

"Well, son, it's like this, you are going to dress up as an unfortunate and he," pointing to Robert "is going to shadow you from a distance at all times, dressed as a vagrant. You've both got to not look out of place and one of you is bait." They both looked at each other sensing they were equally feeling unease.

"The French call it agent revocatoe, that is to set a trap to catch the man," said Abberline.

Robert and Del sat silent thinking about what they were expecting to do when another man in plain clothes entered the room. Abberline spoke and shook hands with this man as he did so to introduce him to those in the room. "This is Inspector Walter Andrews from Special Branch, how are you, Wally?"

"Very well thanks, Fred," he replied warmly.

"This man is the Mets' resident expert on surveillance, which you've had input on anyway, but also more importantly disguise. He's got a carriage full of stuff with him from The Yard which you lads are going to unload into the nick and we're going get you sorted to do your jobs."

Andrews nodded in recognition of Abberline's input and said to the lads "All right, fellows, follow me," and led them from the office to the station yard to his waiting carriage. "Should be a fun afternoon, George, watching them get transformed."

"Let's hope that the trap works, Fred, and we don't create another victim." They stared at each other and then got back to reading some of the gathered statements as they considered Godley's words while they waited for Andrews and the young officers to return. "Oh, and, Fred, its provocateur." Abberline was embarrassed by his obvious error.

"Yeah, I know, I was just testing the lads." Godley nodded knowingly. Even the most renowned detectives can make mistakes.

Chapter Ten

That afternoon, Ralph and Bruiser were enjoying a quiet walk and game in Victoria Park. He had been hard at work selling his quota of papers all morning and the sun was out so he and his oldest pal enjoyed the warmth it gave in the green open spaces. He threw a cheap wooden ball he owned for the ageing dog who trotted and fetched it dutifully and dropped at Ralph's feet. The sun had brought many people to the park and Mary Kelly was walking through there with her friend Cathy Eddowes, both of them enjoying the escape to the safe, daylight, uncluttered area. They sat and watched the boy and dog playing from a distance, Mary recognised young Ralph but did not want to disturb him. After five minutes or so of the game the old dog was getting a little tired so he fetched the ball one last time and then trotted off to the shade cast by a tree. This was only about thirty feet from Mary and Cathy. Ralph ran over to Bruiser speaking as he did so, "Well done, old fella, you deserve a rest." The dog was panting heavily as he lay on the grass and wagged his tail with the words of encouragement as Ralph approached. The newspaper boy then spotted the two women. He only knew Mary though.

"Hello, Mary Kelly, how are you today, my pretty lady?" he said with false juvenile bravado.

"Very well, young man, are you and your fine looking friend all right?"

"Yeah, me and him are fine. Gonna go and scrounge some tea at home or somewhere soon."

"Lovely, you take care and give my best to your ma when you get home, Ralph."

"Thank you. Seen Constable Ford lately?" Mary got a warm feeling inside at the mention of his name, and hadn't worked the streets since their afternoon together. She had decided with all her heart that he was the one; but because of the scare over the murders they had only seen each other in passing when he was on patrol. Although she had packed, she couldn't yet bring herself to move out of Miller's Court.

"No, not really, but if you see him before me give him a kiss from me," she replied jokingly.

"Not bloody likely!" Ralph shouted and then ran off towards Grove Road, Bow with Bruiser trotting on behind carrying the ball.

Ralph ran along Grove Road with the dog in tow towards Mile End Road. He passed the junction with Roman Road watching for traffic for both he and Bruiser as he crossed. Suddenly as he passed a narrow alley way he was grabbed by the back of his shirt and pulled off the main road. The dog trotted on a fraction and then realised his master had turned off and turned round to follow. It was Michael Ostrog who had grabbed the boy having seen him running towards him from a distance. He had hidden to take his revenge. He knew the boy must have shopped him to the police and needed to silence the little runt from any further damage. He was expecting the dog too and although his left shoulder was still weak it had become strong enough over the twelve days since the 'operation' to wield a piece of wood quite efficiently. The dog turned into the alley to be met with a blow to his head. Ostrog struck out as hard as he could with the wood at Bruiser striking him and the growl that the dog had started to present became a yelp and with a second strike the dog collapsed motionless, his head gashed open. He had hold of Ralph the whole time as he did this in the vice like grip of his right arm.

"You fucking bastard, you've killed my dog!" screamed Ralph. Ostrog dropped the wood and threw the struggling youth against a wall knocking the wind out of him and he slumped to the floor. Ostrog grabbed him by his shirt lapels and picked him up. He stood side on now to Ralph so if the boy lashed out he wasn't presenting a vulnerable target. Ostrog hissed at Ralph "You little bastard, you shop me to police. You die!" he took hold of Ralph by the throat and pinned him to a wall. The boy urinated in sheer terror as he tried to speak out and punch Ostrog. He did manage to rein some blows on Ostrog's hip and thigh side on but to no avail. He could not speak for the vice like grip that Ostrog placed on his throat with his rough hands.

Ralph's short life sadly began to pass before his eyes as he felt his head getting lighter and lighter starved of life giving oxygen. He saw his mother, smiling down on him as if he were still a babe in arms; he saw Bruiser as a puppy staring into his face as if seen as an out of body experience as a dog facing a baby; he saw his pitch in Commercial Street selling 'The Star'; he could smell the waft of perfume from Mary Kelly's room; he could taste the mash from the pie and mash shop next to The Ten Bells and could smell the stench of beer from the pub; he saw Constable Ford walking towards him smiling warmly; and he saw Mary and Bruiser in the park. The images began to fade and become very dim and increasingly hard to see. Then for a split second in his consciousness he felt nothing and saw nothing. This was that ultimate moment in human life; death.

The boy's body fell limp in Ostrog's hands and he let it slump to the floor. Looking up and down the narrow street he could see that he was safe; no one had seen him. He walked out of the alleyway leaving the two silent and still bodies behind him and casually strolled towards the park always on the look out for police. He passed a flame haired pretty girl at the gates on the way through with a more haggard looking forty-odd year old and disappeared into the green of the park leaving the urbanised East End behind. Mary couldn't help but be disturbed by this odd looking man dressed in a cleric's type suit, with a blood stained and patched up left shoulder to the jacket. It was the evil satisfied look in his eyes that she didn't like and the fact he was sweating profusely.

Some minutes later Bruiser came around whimpering from the unexplained pain he felt in his head. He sat himself up and could see Ralph. He approached him and nuzzled him to get him to move but got no reaction. He licked his face repeatedly but again with no reaction. Then he settled himself next to Ralph resting his head on one of the boys out stretched arms. He lay like this for about an hour which to the dog seemed like an eternity. He sensed death now as the boy's body was getting colder. He stood up and walked out into the street kicking the wooden ball on the way which rolled into the gutter and came to a rest as lifelessly as Ralph in Grove Road. The dog sat on the pavement by the alley and began howling.

* * *

While Ralph suffered such a violent and sad death at the hands of Ostrog, Robert and Del were unaware of the tragedy as they re-paraded some two hours or so after they had left the incident room having undergone a transformation at the hands of Inspector Andrews. As was the plan hatched within the office, Del had taken on the 'provocateur' role having been dressed and heavily made up to pass as an unfortunate. His fair complexion as expected gave not trace of a shave shadow and his slight build carried the female disguise well. Only the ungainly walk he proffered gave weakness to the deception but with work it could pass as the effects of drink. Robert had been disguised to pass as a vagrant, of which the East End already offered so many. He had been given the filthy clothes from a drunk who had died in police custody to wear that meant there was no need to 'scent him up' for realism. He had purely needed to have been given the unwashed look with a combination of theatrical make-up and real dirt.

The pair breezed into the office fully in character, without Andrews initially, with Del tottering on his low heeled boots and Robert limping heavily and doing so with the aid of a beaten crutch. Abberline, Godley and the other detectives in the office who were variously busy with tasks looked up in astonishment at the audacity of the two street types who had found their way in. Godley shouted to them "Get out, and back to the cells! Who let you out!" and stormed out past them jolting Robert as he passed by striding out to find some uniform officers to take care of them. The pair looked at each and began laughing as the wilier and investigative Abberline approached. He tumbled within seconds of Godley's outburst who it actually was and called out to Godley now ranting in the corridor.

"It's all right, George, they're with us," and he began chuckling. In the corridor Andrews approached the bemused Godley with a knowing smile and said "Fooled you, eh, George?" Godley's initial anger had to break into a smile then a laugh as he realised how he had been almost unintentionally duped. They all gathered in the office. Murphy passed out mugs of tea to everyone as Abberline began a briefing.

"Right, then, we have put out two plants here who are going to work the streets every night seven until three until this bastard or bastards are caught. If it proves too much for them to cope with we'll get another two lads in to help. How it works is this; Del, or should I say 'Delilah'," the room roared at the joke made with the name juxtaposition, "will wander as any unfortunate would but not pick anyone up of course. What we're looking for is someone to attack, but if you get an inclination that you're being lured into something go with it. Rob will keep you in sight at all times and be watching everyone moving around you too. If he thinks there's someone of particular suspicion you should go off with work out some sort of signalling between you. Now Rob's got his whistle and truncheon still and 'Delilah' I've got something for your bag." Abberline went over to his desk and pulled open a drawer. He reached in and took out a small shiny metallic miniature revolver. "If you are in real danger, use it. If you are threatened at least point it, all right, son?" He passed the revolver to Del who stared it for a moment without answering. "I said all right?" repeated Abberline.

"Yes, sir, fine."

"Right then, all of you go and get some grub and start hitting the streets at seven when it's getting dusk. And yes, you will all be on overtime today as we're all on until three as the first night of this methodology." All of them eventually trooped up to the station canteen to enjoy a hot meal and get full bellies for the long night ahead.

* * *

Mary and Cathy had turned along Old Ford Road on leaving the park, and so although having heard Bruiser's howling they never came to realise it was him. A drunken soldier was the first to pass Bruiser who clipped him round his already tender head as he passed. The dog cowered at further attack as the soldier staggered on. PC Jonas Mizen was the next to arrive at the scene following the drunk and again the dog cowered at the approach of another uniform. Mizen, immediately seeing the dog's distress, took his helmet off and approached slowly and spoke gently to calm him extending his hand for the dog to smell. He recognised Bruiser from his time patrolling The Street's ground and wondered where the newspaper boy was he normally saw him with.

"All right, Bruiser, there's a good boy, you're okay now." The dog slowly wagged his tail from the friendly approach; Mizen noticed the injury to the dogs head. "We'll sort you out, lad, where's your boss, eh?" He had the dog's confidence fully now and was able to stroke him along the length of his back, an action that seemed to keep the dog calm. Bruiser then got up and wandered to the entrance to the alley. He stopped and looked back at Mizen a sign that the constable took to mean to follow him. Mizen did so and saw the dog walk just a couple of steps further and start to nuzzle a limp body. Getting closer Mizen saw it was in fact the paper boy he would expect to see with the dog and quickly bent down to his aid. The boy was now barely warm and so Mizen picked him up, brought him into the street, drew his whistle and began blowing furiously for assistance. Not being qualified to say whether or not the boy was dead he vainly wrapped him in his tunic as he waited for another officer to arrive.

He was joined firstly by an out of breath Taffy Evans who on seeing what the situation was flagged down a hansom cab and made a demand of the driver. "This lad here needs hospital treatment now! Take my mate and him to Whitechapel!" Mizen got into the cab clutching the lifeless boy in his arms and with the crack of the driver's crop the cab lurched off to the hospital. Taffy secured the scene and the whole site was eventually dealt with by Inspector Chandler. Such an almost routine death in comparison the prostitutes' murders didn't attract that much attention and it would be some days before Ralph's mother would even know. The death of a child was not considered that out of place with them killed by jealous boyfriend's of their mother's, or because they couldn't be kept properly by their families, or sadly because they had been sexually abused and then killed once their purpose had been served.

Bruiser was taken back to The Street and placed in a dark and damp kennel in the yard. He lay down once inside and had been led there without complaint and lay motionless staring at the kennel door. He didn't even move when two bowls one containing tripe and the other of water where placed in there with him.

* * *

Wednesday 25th September. It hadn't been a very positive few days for Abberline and his team. Five days of plain clothes patrols had produced no leads or entrapped anyone in anyway. It had just left Robert and Del cold and bored and Del on occasions in fear of being severely beaten when he struggled to fend off 'business' when he was pressed. Robert was frustrated as it hadn't seen Mary even in passing over the weekend so decided during the day to go to see her. Wynne Baxter had closed the inquests for both Mary Nichols and Annie Chapman with the verdicts of unlawful killing but had been outspoken at each. At Nichols he criticised the police for not noting her abdominal injuries at the scene, an issue Abberline felt was unfair as fault lay with the initial examination by the divisional surgeon, and at Chapman's inquest expounded an outlandish theory. He stated that the killings were motivated by a request from an American doctor offering large sums of money for uterine specimens to accompany a monograph he was researching. These issues were the very next day splashed across the front pages of all the newspapers, whilst the tragic death of Ralph hadn't even made the first few pages of the papers.

Although not happy with the American theory on the face of it, it did give Abberline another line of enquiry. John Pizer had been cleared of any connection to the murders and was seeking compensation from the police for his detention, so as a result he kept quiet about being robbed. To top off an unhappy day the main C.I.D office at Scotland Yard had received a letter dated the 24th September. It had been couriered to Abberline immediately. It read:

Dear Sir,

I do wish to give myself up I am in misery with nightmare I am the man who committed all these murders in the last six months my name is so and so I am a horse slaughterer and work at...... I have found the woman I wanted that is chapman and I done what called slautered her but if any one comes I will surrender but I am not going to walk to the station by myself so I am yours truly keep the Boro road clear or I might take a trip there. this is the knife that I done these murders with it is a small handle with a large long blade sharp on both sides

Abberline, Godley and Bill Thick were the only ones in the office and passed the letter around each taking a great deal of time to study it before conversation around it began.

"Well, I think it is a load of bollocks," stated Abberline quite categorically

"I must say I think I agree, Fred," said Godley, he continued addressing Bill Thick. "What do you reckon, Bill?"

"Well, by the post mark it is from south of the Thames and it does refer to Borough High Street. It tells us nothing at all. It strikes me it is from a sad attention seeking individual trying to complicate matters further for us."

"Yes, I agree, Bill. George make sure the courier goes back to The Yard with strict instructions not to breathe a word of this to the press. If they do we'll have a rush of these bastard things on our hands. We haven't got time to deal with this kind of rubbish."

Godley left the room to seek out the courier whilst Abberline studied the letter again. Although he considered it a fraud was he missing anything? He pondered the matter of a hot cup of tea.

* * *

Meanwhile Robert had managed to meet Mary at Osgood's Cafe in Lamb Street in the heart of Spitalfields Flower market. It was a homely little East End cafe that essentially catered for the flower market workers but also did a healthy regular trade from those passing through. Robert knew these premises with their characteristic gingham table clothes and steamed up condensated windows. He frequently used it when on his uniform local beat. They knew him too and at this time of the day he wasn't in disguise and sported a clean appearance to meet with Mary. They sat together enjoying tea and eggs and bacon while they talked.

"Robbie, where have you been, I haven't seen you properly since our day on the lake, darlin'?"

"Well, with another murder I've been seconded to the inquiry under Abberline with Del. We've got to do some real bad hours until it's done."

"How come I haven't seen you walking around then?" This response pleased Robert as it meant that there was some mileage in the disguises.

"Look, you've got to keep it a secret, but me and Del are in plain clothes doing a special patrol to try to catch whoever it is so I can't speak to you when I am. Anyway, what are you doing out and about, I thought you was moving in with me?"

"Look, I may not be selling myself 'cos of saving me for you now, but I am allowed to socialise with my friends. So I'm out and about at The Ten Bells and The Britannia to see them that's all. I'm packed to leave so give me the word and a key and I'll be round." Robert dug deep into his pocket and pulled out a door key and passed it to her.

"Here, my landlady is expecting you. Make yourself at home and I'll be in during the early hours. What you doing with Miller's Court?"

"I'm keeping on for my friends for a few weeks; they can use it as a bolt hole if they're stuck."

"All right, but watch it. We don't know who he is, what he looks like and how he fools people to go with him. Tell your friends to be careful and if the have any bad encounters find a copper and report it."

"Robert," she looked down into her tea psyching herself up for a question she didn't really want the answer to, but curiosity had got the better of her to ask it. "What did he do to Mary and Annie? We've heard it was horrible, real savage. Robert paused before answering and looked her in the eye to answer.

"Look, they've said a lot in the papers and much of it is true, but it's like this and this should make all the girls take care so listen as I'm repeating none of it again. He cut their throats, and I mean deep, right to the bone," she looked at him aghast and held her right hand across the top of her chest fingers spread wide. "Then he went to work on them, he cut their stomachs open and pulled out some of their innards and took some as it hasn't been all there once they were examined." He was about to continue but she put her hand up in a clear gesture of not wanting to know any more. She shook her head and was a pulling an expression of sheer revulsion. They sat silent for some minutes him looking out of the window and her staring into her tea as if in shock.

"I will take care; we should leave London though, now, let's go and start afresh." There was emotion in her voice, she needed once for all to go but didn't want him to know how they could afford to go until he agreed to leave because of the origin of her potential wealth. Robert took her hands in his across the table and thought carefully about his answer.

"I promise we will when all this stops, which I hope it already has. This is my community and I want to ensure the police get him, them or whoever before I am prepared to leave. When the job is done we can go and I'll be a constable elsewhere and you can be the mother of my children." She looked him in the eye with tears of happiness, never believing this sort of good fortune may come her way. She respected his words and squeezed his hands in reassurance of his words unable to speak through emotion.

"And when I have the money I shall properly propose with a ring. Now, another tea, love?" She smiled and stroked his hand across the table bringing a contented grin to Robert's face and a warm feeling in his heart. They drank more tea and spent a very easy time together in Osgood's as the safe daylight world passed them by outside.

* * *

Severin Klosowski had settled himself into East End life very quickly having fallen on his feet with a ready made business. He had previously worked in West India Dock Road as a barber and now came across a barber's shop in Cable Street, E.1 which had closed down the week before he arrived. He rented it immediately and moved in to set up and found all the existing hairdressing equipment still there. This meant a significant financial saving to him and a loss to the typically greedy landlord who cared not for the condition of the premises so didn't realise that there had been something left there he could have sold for profit. He had a new sign made up and hung outside to try to attract a variety of clientele and not just the Poles or the Jews. Ironically it read 'George Chapman, Barber.' A sick irony he would choose the surname that was shared by his East End victim. To him the name meant nothing until he later bothered with a copy of 'The Star' and discovered he had chosen the same name as his victim. It would help too in disguising his background and his previous time in the East End. With his limited command of written English he was able to spell it having also now read it.

He found that within days of being open his initial slow start lead to a regular turnover of patrons by the middle of his second week, a factor that was no doubt assisted by his ability to price his services low following his lack of essential capital outlay. The business would help establish him as a respectable member of the local community in time.

* * *

Godley returned to the office not in a good humour. Those in the incident room could see it in his demeanour and the thunderous look of anger on his face. "Fred, you won't bloody believe this."

"Believe what? Surely you must have got him or sent someone to get a message to him?" replied Abberline.

"We didn't know it but this was actually the letter's second port of call, The Yard in their wisdom had decided to send a copy to the Central News Agency too, so tomorrow it's going to be plastered across all the dailies, and we'll end up with a flock of bloody hoax mail everyday!"

Abberline curled his lips and considered a reply carefully and then spoke in a very calculated tone. A very positive slant regarding this development had struck him.

"Yes, George, you're right, but what if it motivates this killer, whoever he maybe to try to goad us publicly. What if he decides to communicate to taunt us by letter? What if in his boldness and arrogance he slips up, hints in the letters, consistent post marks, all things that might come back and haunt him. There could be a positive in this."

Godley looked around the room. Everyone present looked to be carefully considering Abberline's words and began looking at each other and nodding. He could be more right than anyone may ever know.

"Fred, that is a bloody brilliant thought, bloody brilliant. Do you really think it might smoke him out?"

"Only time will tell, George, only time will tell. I don't for one minute believe that the decision made at The Yard had that in mind, but we have to be prepared to make the best of a poor situation. Now we need to plan tonight's plain clothes patrols. Look in lads and listen." Abberline then proceeded to deliver a briefing on where they would post everyone and what new information had come through from the constables on the beat. Robert and Del had now turned up and listened intently to their nights planned activity.

The Central News Agency at number 5 New Bridge Street had been founded by William Saunders MP. He had established it and made it into a limited liability company whose business was quite literally news and, as a result of the reputation it had developed, was always the first to gain the scoop stories to sell off to the newspaper publishers. Their most famous example was when the CNA received the news of the fall of Khartoum and the death of General Gordon twelve hours before anyone else. It telegraphed important events, parliamentary reports, Stock exchange and market reports, law cases, racing results and other news worthy items to newspapers, exchanges clubs and news rooms. Most communications intended for general publication were forwarded to the Central News Agency by messenger or telegraph. Messenger was how they received the news from Scotland Yard of the potential murderer's letter when courier arrived there prior to attending Commercial Street Police Station.

The positive relations between the CNA and the Police were as a direct result of links forged by John Moore the Agency's general manger who had written to police chiefs requesting information on the murders. The police had been happy to oblige hoping that witnesses or persons with information may be encouraged to come forward so they were equally as happy to pass on the text of the letter they had received for the CNA to distribute amongst London's news community. Each of the papers paid handsomely for it but it was inevitability The Star that paid the most so got to publish it exclusively on the morning of the 25th before anyone else; they would all be forced to publish it in their later editions.

8.p.m and the briefing had finished and the plain clothes boys were about to go out on the ground when Robert could hear a faint scratching from the kennel in the yard of The Street and went over to investigate. As he neared he could hear a faint lonely weak pining from the dog that must be inside the kennel and he began to speak to it as he approached to reassure it.

"It's ok, doggie, it's a friend coming to see you, don't fret, we'll get you home. As he looked in he was shocked to see that it was Bruiser who he knew was inseparable from Ralph. "Oh Bruiser, mate, what the hell has happened, what are you doing here? Where the hell is Ralph?" As he looked in the old good natured dog lay still with his head on his paws staring up sadly with his eyes craning upwards with an obvious look of distress. Robert could see the now dried out wound on his head. He pulled a handkerchief from his pocket and rinsed under a tap nearby. He opened the kennel and dog lay still. He gently cleaned the wound reassuring Bruiser as he did so before shutting the door and leaving him there temporarily as he went to make enquiries.

Robert rushed in to the front office where the records of dogs lost would normally be kept and bumped into Taffy Evans as he did so who was about to go off duty, albeit very late. Knowing the old copper had been early shift he asked him if he knew anything about the dog brought in.

"Well, Lad, I do as it happens. I was called down to just off Grove Road by one of the other lads whistling and there was the dog howling like a bastard in the street by an entrance to an alley. Old Mizen was out of the alley itself when I got there with the paperboy pretty lifeless but wrapped in his tunic. I stopped a cab and packed them off to the hospital and stayed at the scene and once all the clearing up was done brought the poor old bugger back to here, pal."

Robert was confused and concerned "Hang on, the dog is here, but what happened to this boy?"

"I told you, the paperboy, he got taken to the hospital and was dead though, bloody pity, nice young lad him, see him everyday normally in Commercial Street with that old dog." Taffy for once seemed genuinely a little moved by the incident.

"Ralph, then," Robert said, stunned and staring into space, "little Ralph, The Star seller," he said in disbelief.

"Yeah, that's him, yeah, nice young lad, bloody shame," said Taffy pulling his tunic on. "Bloody real shame. Sorry mate, got to go, Mrs E got some pie waiting. See you tomorrow, lad." Evans was gone out of the station office door before Robert could think of what to say.

He wandered sadly back over to the kennel and again could hear Bruiser whimpering. Some old rope was tied to the kennel door's upper grill so he took it, opened the door and got a brief tail wag from the dog that recognised him equally. He fastened the makeshift lead gently around the dog's neck who then slowly and stiffly stood up and walked out of the kennel with Robert nuzzling his hand for a bit of affection.

Robert bent down and gently took the dog's head in his hands stroking the sides of his face and spoke gently to him looking him in the eyes.

"Don't worry, old fella, you can walk with me tonight and come home with me later, but we'll have to see Ralph's mum tomorrow, mate, and she might want you." The dog responded by wagging it's tail and lifting one his front paws onto Robert's hand and whining gently.

Del spotted Robert and met him middle of the yard as Robert made his way from the kennel with Bruiser in tow. "What you doing with him?" Del asked quizzically. Robert crouched down by the dog and stroked him reassuringly and was very distant staring at the dog as he spoke, his mind on revenge for the boy's death.

"He's coming with me tonight; he can't stay in there, poor old sod."

"Well, where's Ralph then? It's his bloody dog," said Del curiously and with a hint of impatient puzzlement. Robert paused before answering and then stood up and looked directly and coldly into Del's face.

"Murdered. Now lets get out there, I need to do something decent amongst all this death."

Back inside The Street in the investigation office Abberline and Godley were now drinking tea with Doctor Llewellyn before all of them headed off home for the night, the detectives wanting to get his view on the murders having gained that of Doctor Phillips. In his broad Welsh accent Llewellyn spoke expounding his theories in a booming almost theatrical manner as he sat back with his steaming mug of tea and pipe burning with finest old shag tobacco.

"Well, Abberline, I see it like this. You've now got three of these poor unfortunates who have been ripped up in the same manner and the second two have the same characteristics with the abdominal mutilations. This is quite obviously the work of a madman, a psychopath as we now call them, bent on wanton killing. It would be to me purely co-incidental these murders could be done by more than one person, by that I mean a different person perpetrating each of them. You could possibly, by co-incidence, maybe, have two killers by chance with vastly different motives but the same M.O. But not three. Find one or all of these men and the chances are it will stop, gentlemen."

Abberline and Godley looked at each other saying nothing with Abberline then standing from his desk, mug of tea in hand, and strolling over to the two black boards now together with scant witness information. He drank from his cup as he perused what was written.

'Male, 5'2" to 6', aged 27 through to 50, stocky to medium build, military clothing or smart attire or street ragged clothing, local accent or foreign of some sort seemingly eastern European or some type of colonial lilt, deer stalker hat, peaked working cap, top hat or military working hat, seen with a cane, without a cane and finally believed either to carry a bag, or' just to complete the vague information Abberline was reading, 'no bag.' He stared at the board shaking his head and then turned to speak to Godley and Llewellyn.

"What do you two think of all this information then?"

Godley spoke first "Fred, it's useless, none of these people around any of these incidents have seen either the same person or probably seen anyone connected with it. They are seeking attention and the desire to get their name in the local paper for bit of notoriety."

"Detectives," said the Doctor, "You overlook a very important factor in all these contradictions. Let me ask you, in what condition is the majority of the local populace in the early hours if still on the street?" The two detectives paused, looked at each other then Godley clicked his fingers in true Archimedes type acknowledgement and laughed and then spoke to Abberline.

"Fred, this is all so vague and such a lot of bollocks because most of these so called witnesses are drunk. They don't know what they have seen. The only ones with any credibility are the few sightings of strangers in the area by policemen."

"Well fuck me, George,"

"Sooner not, Fred, but thanks all the same," replied Godley before Abberline could continue which lightened the room as they all laughed at the joke.

"Fellows, we have struck a key point, these testimonies on the whole are bloody useless. We need to dig deeper and further with straight forward enquiries but we also need more than the number of disguised patrols we are using now. Get Spratling to get some more volunteers for that tomorrow, and if he can't get volunteers then forced men. We have to flood it with lucid people to catch this bastard and take him to the gallows."

Little did Abberline know how the events of the coming night would not make it easy to get volunteers for the plain clothes patrols. They all drank their tea passing the remaining minutes before heading home reflecting on the nature of the local people.

Chapter Eleven

Del and Robert headed off into Spitalfields and The Ten Bells along Commercial Street one walking either side of the road as they didn't actually want to be together. On their plain clothes patrols Robert was merely tasked with watching Del's back from a distance with tonight being no different. Del was yet to be approached by anyone other than pitiful penniless local drunks, most of who weren't sober enough to get to the pub door, let alone have sex somewhere beyond it. Del was dressed again as an unfortunate whilst Robert sported a Victorian working man's look with Bruiser in tow on a scrappy piece of rope. Not only could Robert not bear to leave the sad old dog in the kennel but he also he felt that having him with him might help authenticate his cover. It was now close to nine with the evening drawing close and the temperatures holding an autumnal feel; the streets were busy with drunks, prostitutes and policemen dotted around to try to allay public fears and maybe catch the culprit, and there were a few teenage children scurrying about most just playing late with each other but some out to thieve.

Passing Lamb Street, then Hanbury Street the site of the Chapman murder and then Red Lion Court to get to The Ten Bells the picture was almost the same in each of these side streets; the unfortunates selling their wares, stray dogs running around with some of the miscreant children and families on their doorsteps trying to take in the fading light. Robert waited on the opposite side of the road from the pub as he watched Del enter the now over crowded saloon bar with Bruiser sitting and waiting patiently with him, then resigning himself to a laying position on the cold cobbled floor. He took a pipe from his pocket and began to amateurishly light it and draw on it whilst he delayed his own entry to the pub. He stood watching those come and go from the general area and observed passing constables who correctly ignored his presence as they passed by.

He saw two very well dressed gentlemen approach walking north in Commercial Street from the direction of Aldgate which wasn't particularly out of place as well to do gentlemen often came for excitement or debauched entertainment in the area. What attracted Robert was how different they were from each other. One dressed in a top hat and three quarter length steed jacket with a wing collar shirt and cravat, looking remarkably like Prince Albert Victor. The other gent with him sported a large handlebar type moustache and was slightly portly and much older than the first. He wore a military type tunic, though not of English origin, and an American cavalryman's type hat. Both had canes but no bags.

Tumblety and Druitt chatted freely about the merits of alcohol and whoring in Whitechapel as they headed towards the doors of the pub each laughing heartily at the other's observations. Druitt would see a darker side to his colonial associate tonight as drink took its toll, and Tumblety sported no bag as he would try to control his mania and just subtly gather intelligence from locals about the whereabouts of Mary Kelly. As they passed Christ Church and crossed Church Street to reach The Ten Bells, Tumblety glanced a steely look across the road at Robert which the young policeman found unusually piercing. Did this strange man recognise him as a policeman? He certainly hadn't seen the uniformed stranger before, perhaps he read too much into a chance stare. The two gents disappeared into the pub.

Robert remained outside watching the comings and goings when he felt the dog stand from his laying position and step forward towards the kerb and stop as the lead went taut. He looked up to see a furtive looking character passing the pub paying much attention to those around him dressed in a shabby cleric's type suit with dirty dark hair and an unkempt beard. The cleric looked across the road in his suspicious demeanour and saw Robert and the dog stood there. He paid significant attention to Bruiser. As he did so the dog reacted instantly. He began

Whitechapel

to pull hard on the makeshift lead, barking and snarling at the stranger as if about to want to attack him and ready for the fight, even beginning to rear up on his hind legs and shaking at the lead and collar to get free. Bruiser was going mad with uncharacteristic aggression.

Both Robert and the cleric reacted to this. The cleric ran south in Commercial Street almost immediately as he saw Bruiser react. The two behaviours Robert saw were so bizarre that he forgot about the job in hand with Del and reacted by checking the road was clear to cross and give chase with Bruiser almost pulling him along still barking and now snapping savagely to get to the stranger. As he chased the cleric he could see the man had impairment to his left arm which slowed his own speed of foot. Robert already started to wonder if this could be the man who had given police the slip following the attempted robbery in the market. The cleric had got a bit of a start on Robert and the dog and was approaching the junction with Flower and Dean Street having passed Fashion Street, knocking passers-by out of the way with a shoulder barge or a push as he tried to make good his escape. Robert dodged the human debris in his quarry's wake as best as he could with the aging dog seemingly with a new lease of life pulling hard at the lead in front of him and jumping or running straight over previously toppled pedestrians. Robert couldn't believe the irony in the fact that there were no policemen in sight just at the point when he needed them most.

At the junction with Flower and Dean Street a cab was just alighting a passenger who was paying his fare to the driver as the cleric reached them. He punched the passenger in the face, a well to do West London gent, and with his good arm pulled the driver from his seat. He landed heavily on the cobbles of the street as the cleric then jumped onto his perch and grabbed the horses' reins. He whipped them sharply and with a characteristic snort the horse then lurched forward into the start of a gallop. Robert and Bruiser continued their chase initially closing a little on the cab but within seconds it started to make distance on them. As luck would have it another hansom was coming along Flower and Dean Street towards him apparently empty. He flagged it down with driver asking him "Where to then, guv'nor?" Robert ignored the question and with no identity immediately to hand he pulled the driver from seat almost as roughly as the cleric had done. He and the dog jumped onto the cab bench. Again whipping the reins like his quarry he lurched off in pursuit turning into Commercial Street.

"Come back here, you thieving bastard!" cried the cab driver after him as he tried in vein to chase Robert down the road. The cleric had about a hundred and fifty yards on him and was approaching the junction with Whitechapel High Street where he was forced to slow with Robert getting the chance to gain some distance because of the crossing priority stream of traffic.

The cleric saw a gap and lurched forward forcing an omnibus to swerve to a halt and another cab to mount the pavement sending pedestrians scattering. One drunk staggered into another who taking his intentions as hostile punched his believed attacker in the face sending him crashing through a haberdashery shop window. Robert now close behind was able to take advantage of the delay to the cleric and was now only about thirty feet from the lead cab able to follow him through the path he was creating. They sped into Leman Street with both cabs sliding sideways on the cobble stones as they made their hurried and almost out of control turns and then kept heading south towards the river. The dog sat silent on the bench of the cab either stunned into this state through the fear of the ride or in anticipation of capturing what he perceived as prey now in a deadly chase. As they approached the junction with Alie Street, Robert could see policemen ahead who had obviously spotted the speeding cabs. Not realising what was going on, both of them at the junction stepped out to try to flag down the speeding drivers, Robert getting ready to take evading action to avoid injuring his colleagues. He could see one of them was 'Ginger' Tom Wilks a thirty year old local officer who Robert knew vaguely in passing from another shift standing in the carriageway blowing his whistle and raising his arm gesturing the hansom to stop. Foolishly thinking the lead cab's driver would adhere to his instruction he stood his ground slightly to one side of the carriageway as the cab approached and was struck by the side of the carriage and spun violently back onto the footway. Robert could only look on in horror as he saw Ginger land with a massive wound to the side of his face with the other officer now going to his aid.

Robert's blood was now up and his mind wandered back to the murder of young Ralph. Why was this dog acting so deranged towards this individual he was chasing? Could it really be something as obvious as that he was the boy's killer? They passed into Dock Street going through the junction with Cable Street where to one side was a parade of shops that included Chapman's hairdressers. The cleric frantically and frequently looked behind him to discover the proximity of his pursuer and saw that no matter how hard he drove the horse he did not seem able to shake him off. Eventually he turned off of what was to become Tower Bridge Approach and headed down towards the bustling St Katherine's Dock where he might be able to dump the cab and lose himself amongst the deserted fish market stalls. Robert's cab began really closing on the clerics with the dog now sitting bolt upright and focused on watching the cab in front sniffing the air intently. It had not only been the sight of the cleric that Bruiser had picked up on but also the smell. It was etched into the dog's mind now and he could smell revenge, should a dog be able to sense that emotion.

The cleric pulled hard on the reins as he neared St Katherine's Dock and the horse slipped violently on the cobbles as he did so. He needed to lose speed but had left it too late. The horse instinctively sensed this and gave up trying to stop and saw an open area on its left and tried to turn into it. The horse's violent manoeuvre immediately tipped the carriage over with the cleric letting go of the reins as he was thrown onto the cobbles harshly landing on his already damaged shoulder. He cried out in pain and cursed from the hard fall which tore skin from the side of his face as he slid along the cobbles. He struggled to his feet and with the impact injuries weighing him down he began to limp off towards the quayside and its fish stalls. Although empty, they created a maze of cover. Robert had pre-empted the cleric's actions and had managed to stop safely as he saw the loose horse now drag the sideways cab along for a short distance until it stopped through fatigue only several yards along the open entrance. Before he could even drop the reins and dismount the cab, Bruiser was off and running with the intention now of solely stalking down this human nemesis.

"Bruiser, come here!" Robert cried in vein but to no effect as the dog was off and hunting. Although the light had nearly completely faded the gas lamps provided a good substitute and Bruiser could make out a vague shape in amongst the stalls but most importantly he could smell his prey, and it's fear.

The cleric found a rancid smelling stall he thought might be able to use to put the dog off his smell and rolled himself in the tarpaulin that draped the display part of the stall. It was covered in decaying fish remnants; bones, flesh, scales all creating a hideous stench. He then scurried away from it and noted another stall finished with a decorative skirting which he could use to hide behind and under the stall. He rolled under it concealing himself wincing in pain as the moved over his injured shoulder and gagging with the intense smell of the rotting fish.

Bruiser entered the alley among the stalls he had seen the cleric disappear behind and went from a run to a trot having now lost sight of his prey and relying on smell. Robert eventually closed in behind him breathing hard from a fifty yard sprint and spoke softly to the dog. "Good lad, Bruiser, good lad," and watched the dog keenly sniff the air. Having lost sight of the cleric himself too the dog was his best chance of finding him safely and maybe quickly. The quayside fish market was deserted and eerily quiet with only the sound of the Thames lapping nearby and the occasional sound of gulls. The gaslights created a haunting glow. The dog slowly moved from stall to stall sniffing intently all around them, and at the second one stopped and heavily examined its scent. "Well done, Bruiser, good lad, go on, pick him up fellow," encouraged Robert. The dog stopped dead. What had he discovered? Robert became tense and reached inside his jacket to a pocket containing his truncheon. The dog was transfixed it seemed for an eternity on this one spot. He then moved sharply sideways on to it, cocked a leg and urinated on the spot. He trotted on contently stall to stall until again stopping at the one with the foul smelling tarpaulin with its rotting remnants and again began studying it in great detail. He seemed to spend what Robert thought again was an eternity and the policeman was now becoming disillusioned,

"Bruiser, if this just a piss trip then just empty your bladder and let's go."

The dog began to snarl with his sniffing this time and could astutely pick out the cleric's scent from the fish. He trotted on sniffing the ground towards the skirted stall under which the cleric was still cowering and sweating profusely.

Bruiser paused next to it and took a long pause sniffing it up and down while the cleric only feet away under the stall pulled his knife ready to defend himself. He could sense the dog to his side at the front of the stall where he rolled in. Bruiser charged in from the end of stall nearest the cleric's head and bit hard into his scalp repeatedly. The dog kept savaging his head and the shock of the attack had caused the cleric to drop his knife and flail with hands to defend himself which were in turn savaged as his head was.

His legs kicked out from under the skirt near Robert who immediately grabbed one of them and dragged the cleric out and Bruiser along with him attached to his already weakened left arm. Despite the facial injuries from the crash and the dog's attack Robert could now see immediately that it was Michael Ostrog. In his heavy Russian accent he screamed at Robert.

"Get this thing from me, please, please!" The dog proved hard for Robert to control, it was intent on attack as a self defence mechanism. It took him about a minute of pulling Bruiser by the tail and the scruff of his neck to get the dog off. Having done that he took hold of the flailing rope still attached to dog and tied him to a stall. Ostrog misguidedly thought the worst attack was over.

Robert with his truncheon in hand knelt down across the chest of the injured Ostrog and holding the weapon with a hand at each end placed it flat across Ostrog's throat.

"Now then, you fucker, did you kill the boy that owns that dog. Tell me or I will let him finish you off while I hold you down. TELL ME!" Ostrog in pain and fear, two feelings he normally only inflicted rather than received, blurted out his answer almost instantly with the dog snarling and snapping and trying to get to him pulling hard on the rope that bound him and with the pressure Robert was applying slowing increasing on his throat.

"Yes, Yes! I did it, what are you his father you English scum, he's an urchin so what! Just get off my throat!" The screaming of his answer got his breathing working again and the fight or flight emotions began to kick in for Ostrog as the primitive section of his emotional state began to take control. He began to struggle and buck under Robert's weight who had, as a precaution, pinned his arms to his sides as he knelt on him. "Don't bother, Ostrog, it won't work out," Robert said coldly ensuring his weight remained firmly on him. Before the Russian could answer he began pushing down hard with the truncheon cutting off Ostrog's air supply.

Robert's sense of right and wrong over Ralph had taken on a biblical context, an issue which he felt no shame about; only revenge for a young life wasted by someone so evil. Bruiser could sense Ostrog's life ebbing away and began to become calmer as the struggling lessened with Robert's pressure on his quarry's wind pipe. The pressure was so great he heard it crack as it gave way. Within just over a minute the dog was laying on the floor making a gentle whimper with his head resting on his paws as Ostrog lay perfectly still and lifeless. Robert sat back on his haunches to survey what he had done and contemplated his next move. He would not go to the gallows for scum like this.

Robert dragged the body over to the quayside and then untied the dog who also wandered over to quayside and sat peacefully watching his new master. Robert collected about 80 pounds of lead weights used to tie down the stall's awnings. He tied them all to Ostrog and rolled him over into the river with the body dropping limply into the fast flowing water and showing no signs of resurfacing, just a few lone bubbles coming up to the surface. Ostrog's notorious criminal mantle would be taken on by his younger brother. Equally vicious in his own way but living off his brother's reputation, he would spend the rest of his criminal life by claiming to be the noted Michael; although never knowing what had happened to his brother.

Robert sat himself on the quayside gently next to the old dog and began slowly stroking him as he did so. They both stared out into the dark moonlit river and each gave out a big sigh of contentment. Robert pondered his life sat there for some time.

Elsewhere events were unfolding in alarming way which Robert would only discover when it was too late. The murder of a worthless public enemy would soon be expunged from his mind as the investigation into the Whitechapel killings faced a major setback.

* * *

Inside The Ten Bells Del stood quietly at the end of the bar by himself watching the movements of the varied clientele in and out of the pub and around its interior. Although not totally comfortable in disguise even after several tours of duty working in this way, he was at least feeling more at home with the nature of his work. The atmosphere was typically noisy with a high level constant drone of a myriad of conversations with the occasional raised voice or screeching laughter. He saw soldiers drinking with soldiers exchanging battlefield stories, working men discussing the latest demands from their tyrannical employers and a variety of men chatting to the unfortunates to establish a price for their services and a location to go and do business. Looking around the room he had noted two well to do gentlemen enter the pub who were now sat by themselves engrossed in conversation and sipping from tankards of ale. One sported a large handlebar moustache and a military type uniform whilst the other bore a striking resemblance to the Queen's grandson.

Del was too far away to be able to hear the conversation these men were having. Tumblety was an astute observer of human behaviour as a result of his years on the medicine show circuit in America, and as a result of brushes with the law. He prided himself on spotting when people looked out of place or uncomfortable in what they were doing, and now tonight he had seen two individuals that he knew did not blend naturally with the squalid surroundings so well. He had guessed that as a result of his actions and those of the perpetrator of the other murder that the police would have the area under substantial scrutiny. He could curse whoever had killed Annie Chapman as he knew she might have taken him one step further to Mary Kelly; still the prostitutes ran such a close knit community the loss of one out of his hands wouldn't significantly delay his quest. Even so it was one less set of trophies for his sickening collection.

"Montague, have you seen any body that looks out of place to you tonight?" Druitt surveyed the bar for some seconds before returning an answer to the Doctor.

"Well, not really, the lady at the end of the bar" pointing to Del "is a little masculine but not unpleasant, and otherwise we are surrounded by the usual goings on."

"Masculine, huh? Ever thought it could be a man in disguise to catch the murderer? Could be a cop?"

"Well, no, the thought hadn't crossed my mind, old chap. But then why should it?" He looked back at Tumblety quizzically.

"Didn't you see that fellow on the other side of the road tonight as we arrived with the dog? I have never seen a working class man with a pipe handle it so badly and so unnaturally. He wasn't a smoker in normal terms; he was another cop, out in disguise obviously trying to catch the killer. But they also might interfere with our merry making, old friend"

"But why should they, they're not bothered by illicit shagging in the alleys are they? You're bloody paranoid and I don't know why." Druitt looked away and drank from his tankard wondering what this conversation was all about. What difference did it make to them if the police were using disguises?

Tumblety realised he was courting attention to himself on the subject and might draw unwelcome suspicion from his friend. He rapidly changed the subject but thought hard about his next move that night. "Hey, Monty lets go up to the Commercial Street Tavern, I fancy a change of scenery."

"All right, haven't been there for a while. There might actually be some reasonable looking toms in there." They downed their drinks and made their way to the door through the bustling and cajoling crowds of the pub.

Del had been watching these two using the mirror behind the bar to avoid attention from them and just felt an inkling about the uniformed stranger. Thinking back to the briefings for the very first murder of this gruesome series he pondered the uniform connection. As the two gents left through the doors he decided to follow to see where they were going to next. He felt compelled just to watch this man's actions tonight. He couldn't see Robert and assumed he had melted very well into the East End throng tonight and felt sure he would shadow his every move for safety.

The two gents made their way north in Commercial Street towards the police station which stood practically opposite the Commercial Street Tavern public house. As a building it was not dissimilar to the Ten Bells as it stood on a corner plot with its doors opening out from the front corner onto the main street revealing a single saloon bar. He followed at quite some distance dodging lecherous drunks as he did so and felt sure that neither was aware of his presence keeping them under surveillance.

Whitechapel

He was quite right, both Tumblety and Druitt were unaware of his actions as they strolled along the squalid East End thoroughfare happily laughing and joking and planning to get properly drunk in the next venue. Del paid casual attention behind to see if he could spot Robert. His friend had proved such a reliable colleague and good friend over time he felt sure that he must be there but at a very discreet distance. He saw Tumblety and Druitt reach the doors; as they were about to enter a giant of a man burst through them holding on to a scrawny youthful drunk by the collar at the rear of his jacket. He was swarthy with a heavy rough looking cane under one arm as he threw the drunk out on the street. The un-coordinated loose limbed body rolled off the kerb into the gutter and lay there simply groaning and then promptly rolling onto his front and vomiting. Tumblety and Druitt stood back to watch this take place to avoid any soiling of themselves as the swarthy man watched from the open bar doors. A bandy legged brindle coloured English Bull Terrier wandered up to the open doors from inside and stared at the drunk with his narrow slit like eyes and barked at him by what was obviously his master's side.

"When old Harry says you've had enough, then you've had enough. Now fuck off and come back when you've learnt some manners for the bar you little bastard." The dog dutifully barked again at his masters side as the swarthy man brushed his hands, turned on his heel and re-entered the pub.

"Well, we mustn't let that phase us, Montague, the night is young still!" Druitt gave Tumblety an uneasy smile and the pushed their way through the double swing doors. Del stood outside for sometime just watching the general area immediately outside the pub before deciding to enter now beginning to feel a little less certain of his friend's presence somewhere in the vicinity. He crossed the bustling street and as he approached the door two rough looking drunken guardsmen pushed open the double doors to let themselves out and on seeing a lady about to enter dutifully held the door open for Del. He gave them a misguided and not convincing smile as one of them belched some vaguely audible speech at him "My pleasure, darling," and pinched a handful of Del's backside as he passed. "Blimey, luv, that's a firm one, how much?" In as high a pitched voice as possible Del replied "Fuck off, I only shag officers!" The two lowly squaddies saw the funny side of this and strolled off laughing at this reply.

Taking a deep breath he sighed, blowing air out from swollen cheeks and entered the pub. Inside a loud constant drone permeated the air from the many raucous conversations going on and the place was packed out with the working class, off duty soldiers, a smattering of well to do's and many prostitutes. At first glance he couldn't see either of the men he had been observing so he made his way to the bar to buy himself a drink. As he stood there waiting to be served at the busy bar an arm stretched around his waist from behind and he felt the proximity of a face by his right ear from the individual's breath as words were spoken softly into his ear with a refined English accent.

"My friend thinks you're a little masculine, but I think you look worthy of a good shag. Are you offering business?" Del turned slowly to face a man who sporting a fine pencil moustache was the man who resembled the Queen's grandson, Prince Albert Victor. This individual he instantly recognised as one of those he had been following all evening. Where the hell was Robert? Right now he needed to know he was around if he was about to play along with a potential suspect. He would have to accept that Robert must be outside and take the risk of following on this line of enquiry. He took a breath and began to speak imitating as feminine voice as he could to try to nurture this potential lead.

"Well, actually I am and with only fine gentlemen such as yourself, I don't do nothing cheap. For you a couple of shillings for whatever you want." He felt he had carried off the deceit well. His 'client's' response would be the telling result.

"Well, madam, that sounds good, how about a little wander outside to the privacy of an alleyway off of Wheler Street?" Del swallowed hard at this invitation. But where was the other one in the uniform? He assumed that he must be seeking out his own little bit of 'cunny' for the night.

"Well, you lead the way, sir, as long as your money is good I don't care where we go." Druitt offered his arm for Del to take which he did so and they left the pub together under the watchful eye of not the police, but Dr Tumblety.

* * *

Half an hour had past whilst Robert sat on the quayside with Bruiser thinking about what he had just done, thinking much about Mary and poor murdered Ralph and the justice he now felt he had brought. He hoped the boy would rest easy in his pauper's grave. As he contemplated those he cared about Del suddenly came into his mind with a shocking realisation of his neglect of his friend's professional welfare in his hazardous under cover position.

"Fuck it, Bruiser, we've got to run." He jumped up from the quayside with a rapid movement that startled the dog who barked in surprise and then ran with him. The commandeered hansom had gone the horse wandering off of it's own accord so he would have to run; Bruiser kept up which was and arduous task for a dog of his age. They made their way out from the dockside and into the busy streets that led up to Aldgate and Whitechapel High Street. The streets were busy with the people of the night drunk and or lusting after sexual pleasures all of whom frequently seemed to stagger into Robert's way slowing down his progress.

As he ran along the pavement through the junction of Mansell Street and Braham Street he could see two soldiers a little drunk ahead of him blocking the path. He knew he would have to mind his way round them as their demeanour looked as though they were spoiling for a fight. Unfortunately for Robert they had already discussed his approach and as he made to step off of the path to go around them the one nearest to him put out a foot which caught Robert perfectly across the ankles taking him to the floor. The dog stood its ground in front of them and barked furiously snarling to put them off of any further attack. Robert hit the floor heavily winding him and cutting his brow above his right eye causing blood to trickle down his face. The dog's reaction was one the soldiers had not expected; they stood still and one of them aggressively addressed Robert.

"Call your bastard dog off before you both get a kicking."

Robert was on his knees wiping his brow with the back of his hand and noting the blood. He did fancy his chances with these two as being sober he would react more quickly.

"All right, fellows, all right. Bruiser, come here, boy." He signalled to the dog with his hands and the dog stopped its defence and walked to his side.

"Right oh, thanks mate, and don't get on our way again, all right." Robert nodded his head and let them turn away before lashing out quickly and aggressively. He gave a swift punch to the base of the skull to one putting him down instantly, the soldier dropped like a boxer felled in the ring with a knockout punch, the other turned round to face him.

He swung out wildly at Robert who ducked away from the punch and struck his assailant in the stomach with a firm jab as he did so, winding the soldier significantly. He staggered back slightly so Robert stepped forward, as did Bruiser and fired a quick succession of punches at his opponents face. He had adopted a fighter's guard with his fists up but Robert's combination was too fast and aggressive and two caught him firmly on the jaw knocking him to the floor out cold. The dog began tugging at the soldier's trouser leg having snapped at it quickly and now shook the leg violently as if holding a small animal his mouth attempting to break its neck.

"Bruiser, that's enough," he had to pull the dog away to re-enforce his command. Pleased with his handy work he again wiped his brow finding more blood and turned to head north to find Del to discover that he was confronted by two City policemen who were over lapping their patrol into his district. One of them spoke as they approached the other holding his truncheon in one hand and tapping the other hand menacingly with it.

"Right, lad. Stand still, I think you'll be coming with us for all that."

"No, you don't understand, they attacked me I was just defending myself. They knocked me to the floor, look at my head."

"Defending yourself is one thing, knocking them out cold is another. Just keep your hands by your side where I can watch them."

"Look, I'm undercover 'old bill', here's my warrant," he frantically searched his pockets for his police warrant card but in vain. He had lost it during the fight on the quayside. If he could get them to take him to The Street at least it would be in the right direction and they could prove who he was quickly.

"Look, take me to Commercial Street nick and you can confirm who I am."

"Yeah, we'll do that, lad, as you can be charged there too." At that moment one of soldiers came around and saw the police with Robert.

"Look, officer, we don't want no trouble, it's my mate's fault see. Let us go and we'll say nothing if he doesn't," said the soldier pointing at Robert.

"Well then, you lucky lad, that suit you does it I suppose?" said the policeman without the drawn truncheon.

"Yes, very much, can I go then please?" asked Robert.

"No, we still need to verify your copper story at The Street."

"Right, then lets go then, please." The soldier roused his mate and dragged him off down Mansell Street.

"What's the hurry then?" said the policeman.

"I'll tell you when we get there mate, and then I won't have to repeat myself, eh?"

"All right, Mr smart mouth, you lead the way." The two policemen followed Robert and Bruiser north in Commercial Street.

* * *

Druitt led Del boy out of the tavern turning right immediately into Wheler Street, a dark and wretched smelling back street which passed under the Broad Street Line. The dark unlit area underneath the railway lines provided a favourite place for the unfortunates to ply their trade.

"You do have exceptionally fair skin and that's a lovely eau de toilette you are using," said Druitt attempting to charm his way round his 'shag' for the evening.

"Why, thank you, kind sir," Del replied uncomfortably wondering where Robert was and, when to blow his own cover to either put another sex pest off his scent or maybe expose the murderer. He could feel the prospective punter pull his arm against his own body tighter therefore trapping and tightening his arm in an obvious act of sexual interest. As they walked he could see they were entering the darker and darker recesses of the area under the railway bridge. Del was beginning to feel uncomfortable. Trying to avoid his disguised voice cracking he spoke nervously and uncharacteristically for his cover.

"Where are you taking me then, mister?"

"Oh, no need to panic, just for a bit of privacy before we get down to it, are you scared?" he finished his retort with a mischievous smile on his face and an elevated sense of power in his eyes. Del was going to have blow his cover before he would be uncomfortably exposed. He pulled his arm away from Druitt forcefully and stepped back to face him square on.

"Right, chum; I am Police Constable Lake from Commercial Street Police Station under cover on the murder case. I want you to empty your pockets and take off your hat and coat and lay them on the ground."

"You what?" replied an astounded Druitt. "Show me some bloody proof you could be a bloody perverted robber for all I know. I shan't do it!" he finished his outburst indignantly.

Del knew he needed help and managed to draw his whistle from under his jacket and blouse, forgetting about the revolver Abberline had given him. However, as he did so he felt his arms pulled behind his back in a strong wrestler's double arm lock and he was caught completely off guard. The person restraining him spoke with a strange and unfamiliar accent.

"Well, well, Monty, what do we have here? Some sick bastard trying to rob you, huh?" Tumblety kept his arm lock tight on Del.

"No, you fucker, I'm a copper investigating the Whitechapel murders undercover. Now let me go or you'll be fucking sorry!" screamed Del to deter his attacker, struggling in the vice like grip that trapped him.

"Oh, let's just knock the little bastard out and leave him here, he can't hurt both of us, Francis," said Druitt, not really wanting the conflict that Tumblety appeared to be revelling in.

"What? And leave the potential little thieving shit-bag to try and roll someone else? No, he needs a lesson."

"Let me go and you can go on your way," said Del now becoming concerned by the fact he couldn't free himself and facing the potential for a beating.

"Come on, Monty, just a dig or two in the guts, and then I'll have a go. If they don't get taught right and wrong then they'll only do it again," Tumblety seemed to speak with glee towards some impending violence.

"Oh, bloody hell!" Druitt shouted in frustration and swung his cane at Del striking him hard against left cheek. Druitt stood breathing heavily and shaking looking on wide eyed at Del who had turned his face following the blow in pain and now looked forwards again spitting blood as he did so containing some small pieces of chipped tooth. He stared his attacker back in the eyes with complete contempt. Druitt feared the aggression in Del's eyes and screamed with palpable fear in his voice.

"Don't you bloody well look back at me like that you piece of East End dirt! I'm better that you any of you!" He lashed out again with his stick striking his target right on the chin, obviously much less fleshy than the cheek Del could feel a harsh pain travel right up into his head between his eyes. He struggled desperately in once last attempt to break free. He lurched forward taking his assailant slightly off balance and rapidly changed direction charging backwards with all his force sending Tumblety hard into a wall knocking all of his wind out of him causing his arm lock to immediately loosen.

Free, he rushed forward to engaged Druitt who he sensed was the least up for violence, and with the other one maybe only out of the game for a few seconds he knew it best to deal with the weaker opposition first. Druitt swung his cane at him again but Del was equal to this and he caught hold of it with both hands and pulled it from his attackers grasp. He threw in the air to turn it round to now use it to best effect himself. At that moment he had the most bizarre image crossed his mind; of being in a street fight in women's garments and how it wasn't as hard to move around as he may have imagined. Druitt now in mortal fear tried to plead with him.

"Look, I'm sorry old chap, I'm not a violent man, don't hit me. It was him who put me up to this!" He yelled pointing at Tumblety.

"Too fucking late, chum," said Del menacingly drawing the cane back.

"You're a policeman, you can't hit me!"

There was a loud crack as Del connected with the side of Druitt's head and put him down immediately unconscious. He turned swiftly anticipating an encounter with the other so called civilised gent never ever expecting to see what faced him. He was pulling his makeshift weapon back for a strike as he turned and was totally unprepared as his other assailant lunged forward with a large surgical knife in his hand using it in a wild slashing action. It caught him across his left forearm with a cut so deep and sharp into the fleshy part of the arm he never felt it, but within seconds became aware of dampness running along his arm. He swung wildly with the cane but Tumblety well versed in cutlass attack and defence moves from his experiences during the American Civil War ducked neatly avoiding the swing and stabbed Del with speed and accuracy in the lower abdomen.

Del felt the sharp pain of the strike immediately as it penetrated into his stomach and he dropped the cane to clutch his lower torso. He looked down to see the shining black appearance of moonlit blood flowing all over his hands. He dropped to his knees and looked up at his attacker in total surprise of what had happened. In doing so, he saw the swift shining action of the knife drawn to his left and then swing past his front, out of sight below his chin but biting almost painlessly in his state of high endorphin shock into his throat. The wound it opened up ran from his carotid artery to his jugular vein severing both and his wind pipe in the process. He stared for a few seconds speechlessly despite the fact he tried to shout for help at the last human face he would ever see; he was also the first policeman to see the face of the man who would become known as Jack the Ripper. He fell forwards lifelessly bleeding on the floor with an ever growing pool of blood forming around him.

Druitt came around and sat up from his momentary unconsciousness to see Tumblety standing over the prostrate figure in a dress surrounded by a pool of blood.

"My God! What have you done, Francis?

"Just dealing with a Goddamn thief within the Lord's justice," Tumblety said in a flat remorseless manner. He bent down to wipe the blade of his knife on the dress of his unfortunate victim.

"Are you mad? The Lord's justice, an eye for a bloody eye? You're bloody mad, I'm going to have to turn you in, friend or no friend, and he was a bloody copper!" Tumblety looked up at Druitt chillingly and spoke slowly and clearly so that his words would not be misunderstood.

"Listen to me, Monty, you are an accessory to all this, despite what you may plead to the police, so don't fuck with me. Be a good British public schoolboy and keep your fucking mouth shut, if you value using it to breathe."

"You can't scare me, Francis, you can't you know, I will admit being with you but I had no part in the murder you know. You'll see." All

Whitechapel

the time now, Druitt backed away from Tumblety ready to make a run for it knowing his own life was quite obviously in danger. At least he had his stick to defend himself at a distance.

Tumblety stood up and menacingly advanced toward the now shaking and profusely sweating Druitt. "Let me warn you once and for all, Montague, I will kill you right here and right now if you don't give me your word that you'll stay away from the filth. You stiff-assed, public school British are supposed to be good to your word. But, I'll know if you go to the cops subsequent to this, trust me, I will know, and you'll be dead before I'm in one of their stinking cells." He stared hard at his potential victim. "Trust me. I could be looking at a dead man."

Druitt could feel the sweat running down his back and running along the sides of his face and dripping off of his chin. It streaked his necktie and created a dark soaked area plainly visible to his would-be murderer who looked calm and collected with the glinting knife in his hand and relishing the fear he could tell he was striking into Druitt. He swallowed hard and spoke in reply to Tumblety's threat with obvious fear within him.

"All right, have it your way. I shan't go to the police, and shan't tell anyone anything. But don't ever call for me again, if you see me in the street walk away, as I shall. There are no witnesses only you and I, so this unprovoked act of violence will for ever only be known to us, we who are responsible. Now, to use one of your terms, 'fuck off' and leave me alone. I am returning to Blackheath." Druitt turned on his heel and made in the direction of Bethnal Green Road hearing no footsteps following him. A matter for which he was grateful; he did hear Tumblety call after him, however.

"Goodbye, Monty, **our** secret is safe with me, that's for sure. Remember, whatever happens if I get rumbled you're a dead man." The words rang in Druitt's ears again as he had felt them only seconds before as he kept on walking. He heard no footsteps closing on him as he continued walking; when he had made about a hundred and fifity yards he had to look round. Tumblety was gone, all that remained of the extreme violence of minutes before was the lifeless body of a man, possibly a policeman in a heavily blood soaked dress lying in an ever increasing pool of blood. Moments later he entered the approaching midnight bustle of Bethnal Green Road, with images in his mind that would haunt him until his untimely death.

Chapter Twelve

Abberline and Godley were working late at The Street enjoying a steaming cup of tea each having been postulating about suspects, motives and potential victims, the last item being the only certainty within their discussion.

"Fred, we can't do anymore tonight with no new information and God forbid no new victims. We have got to go home and especially you as you've been putting in hours that go beyond the call, old chum." Abberline sat quietly for some moments before replying. He had both hands wrapped around the cup and twiddled his thumbs around its handle, staring as he pondered his reply.

"You're right, old son, absolutely bloody right. George, not you the other George at home, needs me and so does the lovely Emma." Abberline stood placing his mug empty on the desk and grabbed his jacket from behind his chair and swiftly put it on.

Meanwhile it was well after midnight by the time Robert had verified his identity back at The Street and was making his way to The Ten Bells. He rushed in through the double corner facing doors with Bruiser in tow on the same shabby piece of rope. He desperately scanned the bar area. It was fairly quiet now and it was immediately apparent that Del was not in there any longer, but where should he go to next to seek him out? Dragging the poor old dog along with him he made his way back up towards The Street and the Commercial Street Tavern which stood almost opposite the imposing police station. This time it was now around 12.30.a.m and the doors were firmly locked and no one appeared to be inside. "Where the fuck do I go now, Bruiser?"

Only seconds after this vocalised thought a hysterical woman came running out of Wheler Street screaming at the top of her voice "Murder, murder, he's done a bleedin' nother one. Help, help get the fuckin' police!"

'My, God! It was Liz Stride!' Robert thought as he ran past her into Wheler Street to find the next unfortunate victim. As he ran ahead he could see a crumpled heap of woman's clothes ahead under the railway bridge but in the darkness could not distinguish the colours so he would be completely unprepared for the shocking site about to greet him. He let go of the dog so that he could roll the body over and see if he could render any type of medical aid and to see if she was actually dead. He feared she would be on approach as he could see a massive black pool of liquid around the body which was how blood appeared in the moonlit dark.

The body still felt warm as he rolled her over and realised she appeared to have short hair and no hat which he then saw was lying discarded to one side. He stared into the face stained with blood as a result of the deeply slashed throat and saw with sickening reality that the lifeless body he was holding was Del Lake. "No!" he screamed loudly in the air and began to sob, pulling his dead friend in close to him burying his face into the material of his Del's disguise and sobbing with almost no control of his breathing as he coughed and chocked on the tears and mucus generated by his intense and immediate grief. He had several minutes sitting on the cold and blood soaked pavement clutching his dead friend. Dead because he had deserted him to exact revenge for the death of another; dead because the neglect of his duty. The commotion created by Liz Stride drove several of the night duty uniform patrols to the scene of the crime.

He continued to sit with the body of his friend unwilling to let it go in his grief as the crowd around him grew made up of onlookers, police and some press until with the arrival of Dr Llewellyn and Inspector Chandler. Chandler was forced to put his hand firmly on Robert's shoulder but spoke sympathetically to him to persuade him to let go. "You've got to let him go son, got to let him go and let the Doc do his bit, lad." Robert reluctantly and gently laid his fallen colleague back onto the cold cobbles and slowly stood up. He was led away heavily saturated in blood by Bill Thick back to The Street whilst a messenger was sent out to call Abberline to the scene of the latest blood bath.

* * *

3.a.m and Abberline awoke with a harsh wrapping on his door. George began barking violently and by the time Abberline got to the front door the dog was jumping high against the front door ready to ward off the threat he perceived. Abberline gripped the dog under his chest and picked him up tucking him firmly under his right arm and then opened the door. Standing there was a uniformed constable with a black Mariah from the local nick who hurriedly conveyed his message with such urgency that the sleepy and bleary eyed inspector didn't catch a word of it.

"Say that again son so that it's intelligible in this time zone?"

"Mr Abberline, come quick, Wheler Street there's been another one. 'Orrible it is, some copper called Del Lake."

"What do you mean, Lake found it?"

"No, sir, it is bloody Del Lake, butchered he is!"

Within ten minutes Abberline was dressed and in the carriage and on way to the scene. Sitting in the area usually only reserved for prisoners he contemplated the next step in the investigation. Was it safe to continue with such patrols? Perhaps it would be better to draft in more uniform from the City Police or from outer London divisions. He would have to enter discussions with Superintendent Arnold following an exchange of views with Godley. The streets were still dark as the Mariah rattled down the cobbled surface of the Romford Road and into Stratford High Street and beyond and by quarter to four they were at the scene.

The uniform presence under Inspector Chandler had managed to completely clear the crowds leaving only a cordon of what were highly depressed officers at the scene. Their faces told many stories of grief for the loss of a colleague and concern for their own safety, albeit this murder of an officer was in exceptional circumstances. Abberline foresaw the need arising to address the entire manpower of The Street over the next few days. Officers stepped aside to allow him through giving a respectful nod of the head as they did so. The scene was perfectly preserved with Del still in situe as per previous instructions from the detectives for maximum evidential purposes. The sight of the butchered young officer even upset Abberline a hardened campaigner feeling a massive responsibility for his death undercover. He scoured the scene for clues himself of any form as Chandler stepped forward to speak to him.

"Fred, Dr Llewellyn has done an initial examination, pronounced life extinct, etc says he'll see you at the mortuary this afternoon for a full P.M. It'll be the London's for your information. Sorry, mate, you must feel bad."

"Can't help it, John, he volunteered I know but he was part of my team. I feel sorry for his mate, but what the fuck was he doing? I've got to speak to him and find out what the hell has gone on, mate."

"Poor bastard is back at The Street in your office. We've done everything here; do you want us to clear up, mate?"

"Yes, thanks, I'll just have a little walk around while you do."

As officers began gathering implements to clear the blood, a couple of morticians took Del's body away and the whole area was washed down. Abberline began walking around the scene in ever increasing concentric circles one hand behind his back with the other holding a lamp seeing if there was any detail, small object that might have been missed. He must have been scouring the area for about half an hour when eventually on the other side of the road by the gutter he spotted a brass military type button.

It was very clean so he surmised that it could have only have been lost there recently, possibly in the struggle, and took a good look at it. It bore an emblem that he was not familiar with and didn't seem typically British military. The emblem was of two crossed cavalry type cutlasses both curving up to the top of the button. He placed it in his pocket and headed off towards The Street. The button would become a wasted clue in an unsolved murder.

* * *

Meanwhile Tumblety was sipping coffee comfortably in his new and occasional surroundings in Batty Street looking out of his front window viewing the varied human traffic going past. He had already laundered his slightly soiled clothing and was preparing to return early afternoon to the more salubrious comforts of the Ritz Hotel. He felt no remorse for his actions; such feelings had long deserted him in his murderous quest for justice and to expand his horrifying collection. He would have to find Kelly soon as bills needed to be paid. He was more than certain of Druitt's silence but would be prepared to enforce it if necessary. He would leave his drying clothing here and make use of the spares that he had now kept in his bolt hole. He finished his coffee pulled on his plain overcoat to travel more covertly back to the West End as men of his class and look would generally only be seen in the locality at night. Locking the door he made his way along Batty Street to Commercial Road and disappeared into the crowds.

Druitt was down at Wapping Steps smoking furiously and nervously staring into the Thames wondering if long term he could hold his silence. Having witnessed such extreme violence on a scale he had never before encountered either personally or as a witness, his already troubled mind from a life of what he considered to be of failure was in turmoil. He truly feared Dr Tumblety and fully believed that any incriminating action he took would surely bring him to his door. He took comfort in the silence of The Steps as he finished his fourth cigarette of the last quarter of an hour.

* * *

Abberline found Robert Ford with his head in hands, elbows resting on a desk staring bloodshot at the suspect blackboard. The lad was clearly traumatised, but fault had to be established.

"Tea, lad?" Ford didn't look up but answered.

"I'll have one, but don't give me any bollocks about it curing all ills, Guv."

"Now don't be stroppy, boy, seeing as how I need to know where the fuck you were, milk and sugar?"

"Just milk please, Guv."

Abberline finished making the steaming drinks for them both from the permanently boiling kettle and sat down opposite Ford forcing him to therefore converse directly with him.

"Where were you then, Ford?" Robert lifted his face from his hands, sniffed and looked tearfully into the ceiling. He was considering his words and began after some seconds of silence.

"I was following a lead, got distracted. Thought I had seen someone responsible for the murder of the paperboy."

"Who?"

"Ralph, the lad murdered up by the park, his dog went mad when some bloke came by into Commercial Street so I followed him off but he did a runner to St Katherine's and I couldn't find him. Came back and it had all happened. It's my fucking fault. I'm ready for discipline and if you need, I'll jump before being pushed."

"St Katherine's? That's a bloody long way. Who was this person?"

"Ostrog. But I lost him, Guv." Ford expressed these false sentiments without any remorse within him.

"Right. I have no choice, you're suspended from now on, no pay, sorry, but that I know is the standard line. You've got some guilt to carry and deal with, so get away for a while if you can." There was silence between them for sometime while they both sipped tea and obviously each considered the future. Ford finished his mug and stood to address Abberline.

"Boss, I didn't expect any less. I can't get away; I've got to do what I can to help, so I'd appreciate any clues so I can do my bit."

"Sorry, no way, you've got to stay away. Get involved and I'll have you nicked, lad, or we'll both be in the shit." He put his mug down and forced his hands into his pockets and paced through the frustration of Ford's futile request.

"Fuck the job, guv, you'll have to have the boys nick me if I'm in the way then!" Abberline flung his hands out of his pockets to place them on the desk to lean forward menacingly at Ford. As he did so they were both distracted by the fall of the button that landed on the desk. Abberline had accidentally flung it from his pocket as a result of the angry confrontation. Ford immediately grabbed it and looked closely at it.

"Give it back to me now, Constable!"

"Constable? You said I was suspended. Was this found with Del?"

"What if it was? Nothing to do with you now, just give it back." Ford took one last look at the cutlass emblem on the button before tossing it carelessly back at the D.I.

Whitechapel

"Keep it. I've seen it. Very unusual don't you think? You better find who it came from before I do." Ford stormed out before Abberline had time to fully respond. He saw little point shouting after him so would give him time to calm down and go and visit him at his home in a few days, if he hadn't already got himself arrested.

* * *

Several hours later during the afternoon, Tumblety picked up the Wednesday 25th September edition of The Star and read the front page with shock and disbelief:

'Whitechapel Killer taunts Police with Letter.'

He quickly turned the pages to read the re-produced words of the impostor to his crimes, although the possibility struck him that it may have been written by Annie Chapman's killer. Many thoughts crossed his mind: 'How dare someone lay claim? Why the hell make such pretence? If I want publicity directly, *I'll* ask for it. How dare they!' He continued his walk along Piccadilly to return to the Ritz from an afternoon lunch by himself and finished the paper in the lounge bar by reception with a large Bourbon. Having finished both he discarded the paper with some fury in a rubbish bin and abruptly ordered a second drink from a passing waiter.

"Don't you think you could be a little less curt, sir?" asked the offended waiter, foolishly.

"**JUST GET ME THE GODDAMN DRINK!**" raged an angered Tumblety to this, what he considered impertinence. The voices made themselves quite plain and they added within his thoughts 'Write your own letter to set things straight.' The waiter returned with the drink on a tray, Tumblety stood up and faced him, took the glass and shot the Bourbon back in one go, slamming the glass back down on the tray from which he had taken it and hissing at the incredulous waiter "Put it on my tab!" and stormed off to his room. There, at the desk by the window overlooking Green Park he was completely alone with his thoughts twisted by rage and alcohol. His mind was fuelled by the dangerous combination of mental instability and excessive drink consumption.

'Okay, how to write this, Dear? ………..boss, yeah, that's it now time to humiliate and taunt those goddamned cops straight out and that freak the papers reported on 'Leather Apron.' I've gotta mock them and show them I'll make my mark, and keep going 'til **I'm** done. Add in a clue for them to know when I strike again this letter is genuine. Don't want them to know I'm too clever always, few grammar errors and a name? Yeah that'll do, perfect! Enough to spite and intrigue. Me, I'm the one in control!'

He read the letter aloud back to himself once finished.

> Dear Boss,
>
> I keep on hearing the police have caught me but they won't fix me just yet. I have laughed when they look so clever and talk about being on the right track. That joke about Leather Apron gave me real fits. I am down on whores and I shant quit ripping them till I do get buckled Grand work the last job was. I gave the lady no real time to squeal. How can they catch me now. I love my work and want to start again. You will soon hear of me with my funny little games. I saved some of the proper red stuff in a ginger beer bottle over the last job to write with but it went thick like glue and I cant use it. Red ink is fit enough I hope ha.ha. The next job I do I shall clip the lady s ears off and send to the police officers just for jolly wouldn't you. Keep this letter back till I do a bit more work. then give it out straight. My knife's so sharp I want to get to work right away if I get a chance. Good luck.
>
> Yours truly
Jack the Ripper
>
> Don't mind me giving the trade name.

Tumblety then knocked over the red ink he had decided to use messing it all over his hands while he tried to read over the letter with it, but smearing it with the red ink as he did so. It forced him to add:

> "wasn't good enough to post this before I got all the red ink off my hands curse it. No luck yet. They say I'm a doctor now ha ha"

He was pleased with himself; he had even added the 'no time to squeal reference to upset the police more than his other taunts referring to the murder of the policeman in disguise. He felt the name was pure genius and would immortalise the mark he was making on the East End. His natural arrogance and showmanship came through in this bold nom de plum. He dated it 25/9/1888 and posted it to 'The Boss, Central News Office, London City', a very American way of addressing not unlike saying New York City. Was it too much of a clue? His arrogance made him think not, history would be the ultimate judge.

That night Tumblety celebrated with a quiet dinner alone in one of the salons of the Ritz accompanying his meal with an expensive Chateau Neuf du Pape. Whist enjoying this with his chateaubriand he was approached by the hotel manager who had a somewhat stern look on his face.

"Dr Tumblety, I am sorry to intrude, but may I take a moment of your time?"

"Sure, Mr Wilkins, what can I do for you?"

"You are running up somewhat of a high debt for which we would like to take a least part payment, sir, would it be convenient to get a cheque for say £400 in a few days?" Tumblety stopped chewing for a brief second in surprise for needing to come up with so much in such a short time. With the precious stones not yet recovered it would be nearly impossible. He would be forced over the next few nights to try to get information on where Mary Kelly was or actually find her. He regained his composure, gave a small nervous cough to clear his throat and smiled,

"Mr Wilkins, I will have you a cheque on Monday, sir." Wilkins nodded and smiled back replying "Thank you, Doctor, never a chore, sir." He hurried off towards the lobby area. Tumblety was now all too aware of how embarrassing his situation could become but decided to at least enjoy the extravagancies that were before him.

Meanwhile Robert was close to being unconscious in The Ten Bells, mourning his friend and not knowing where his beloved Mary was in his hour of need. His speech had been slurred for at least the last hour but the barman, knowing him well and having heard the news unofficially as a result of local hearsay, was happy to ply Robert with drink to ease the pain. He was barely able to prop himself up sitting on a barstool his hands slipping up the side of his face desperately trying to support his spinning head and keep his eyes open. Eventually his hands were unable to support his swirling head and it crashed to the bar surface as they gave way and in a domino effect he slumped off of the stool and ended up in a heap on the floor of the pub. The landlord let him lay there to sleep it off whilst the pub cleared during the course of the late evening.

At that same time Abberline was at Scotland Yard in conference with Superintendent Arnold and the Commissioner, Sir Charles Warren. Between them they had had to make a startlingly difficult decision.

"Abberline, I fully understand why we must suppress the news about it being a policeman killed, but can't we cover it up as just another unfortunate?"

"Sir Charles, no we can't, sir, because another murder added to his tally will help fuel more fear, panic and news sensationalism in the area. Some of the stories doing the rounds are complete supernatural hokum."

"I must agree with Abberline, Sir Charles, for now we must make as little of this as possible. No adding more to the killer's tally and no letting on that we have officers in any disguise, let alone as women."

"Yes, quite. Tell me, Abberline, will you do another female disguise operation?"

"Not immediately, Sir Charles, we'll do it more conventionally for a while. A second one would break the C.I.D I feel and only give the public more ammo to launch at you, sir."

"Yes, good point. Tom, anything to add?"

"No, sir."

"Well, good evening, gentlemen. Thank you."

Arnold and Abberline left the Commissioner's office. It was getting late.

* * *

The letter was received by the Central News Agency on Thursday 26th September and was initially treated as a joke by all who read it, but it did give a glorious title to the perpetrator of the crimes which would, on the day it was passed to Scotland Yard, be splashed across the front pages and leave the killer with an indelible mark on history. The fulfilment that Tumblety would gain from this coverage and anonymous notoriety was immense when it came. 'Jack the Ripper' would live within the minds of most of the western world forever more. Reaching the hands of Haddaway and Will Bates it would make unbelievable copy for them in almost doubling their circulation when running an exclusive at great expense in return for the rights to it solely for use in The Star. Tumblety's letter was passed to the police on Saturday 28th with the following note hand written by Thomas Bulling a forty year journalist employed by the CNA:

The Editor presents his compliments to Mr Williamson & begs to inform him the enclosed was sent the Central News two days ago, & was treated as a joke.

9.a.m at The Street and Abberline examined the note before opening the main letter and began rubbing his chin as he read the text written in the striking red ink. As he absorbed it's content slowing reading it over line by lurid line the door to the office burst open with Godley sporting a copy of The Star waving it. "Fred, have you seen this fucking rubbish, 'Jack the bloody Ripper' this bastard has had the arrogance to name himself. How the hell do the papers get this sort of stuff before us, the bloody Commissioner or someone should order them to always pass it to us, we decide what sort of evidential stuff should be disclosed, not bloody pencil neck journos." For several seconds he courted no response from Abberline and was unaware of the fact from being preoccupied himself with thumbing through the paper for more sensationalised reporting following his initial outburst.

They looked up at each other at almost the same time, both having read the letter but one original and one the facsimile of it in the press.

"He's an arrogant sick bastard this one, George, mark my words we are far from done. Now we've got to look for our next victim to have had her ears clipped."

"Yeah but, Fred, you are assuming that it's genuine. Who's to say it's not a crank or a journo trying to scare or sell more papers?"

"Would those people taunt us with 'ha,ha'? Would those people ask for the letter to be kept back? No this is from the bastard doing this and we need to find him. He already states that he will kill again by the referral to ears. Catch the bloke who done this, and we catch our adversary 'Jack'." Godley stood nodding his head taking in what had been suggested to him as Abberline passed him the original letter for a look.

"George, this afternoon during the changeover from early to late shift and then tonight from late to nights we have to muster all the blokes at each parade and brief them on this and it's consequences. We want the press there too, Mr Arnold and…."

Abberline was cut short by a young uniformed constable bursting in "Sir, we've got some mob outside calling themselves The Vigilance Committee headed by a fella called Lusk. They're all waving copies of The Star around and screaming for you." Abberline paused, looked at Godley and then spoke to the young constable.

"Well, you tell them I'm coming, and to quieten down before I get there or there will be trouble, they may start it, but we'll finish it." The lad scurried out whilst Abberline and Godley grabbed their suit jackets and made their way to the front of the police station passing Kerby and Spratling on route.

"Want any help, Fred?" Spratling inquired genuinely.

"No, think I'll be all right, but wait in the wings with a few blokes if you can muster some."

As the detectives neared the front of the nick they could hear the shouting and jeering from the crowd. They looked at each other prepared for confrontation and burst out through the front doors into Commercial Street standing on the steps looking down on the waiting mob being stirred up by the ranting of a man Abberline would shortly discover was George Lusk. He listened to this man for a few moments and his trouble-making impassioned speech.

"So what have the police done for you, eh? Or the government? They don't give a monkey's cuss about you or me, the working class, they just readily abuse our women and nick us for drunk and take our money for fines. Far as they are concerned we don't count. Look who's in charge of the investigation here? Some washed up has-been detective inspector! Where's the officer of real rank co-ordinating the action on the streets."

The final comment of Lusk's ranting was heard clearly by Abberline as he emerged into the open air and was enough to launch him into action. Lusk had his back to the police station despite some of the crowd's obvious reaction to something occurring behind him. Abberline strolled purposefully up to Lusk who was wielding his walking stick and grabbed the stick out of his hand and tossed it to one side behind them. The stunned Lusk turned to face him open mouthed and speechless and was immediately spun back round by Abberline to face the crowd and put into an arm lock using Lusk's right arm twisted and placed high up his back in between his shoulder blades. Abberline turned and began forcibly marching him into the police station as the crowd fell silent, aghast at the action unfolding before them. As he was dragged off Lusk struggled, pointlessly, and began to shout to try to whip up the crowd to come to his aid.

"Police brutality! Police brutality! Help me, storm the nick and free me, show how the people can deal with law and order without the police." His last line was barely heard by the crowd as he disappeared into the police station. The crowd were impelled to act and began to rush towards the doors, but inside Godley instructed Spratling, Kerby and a few uniformed officers to head out and disperse the crowd as Abberline wrestled Lusk to the charge room.

Six officers ran from the doors to intercept the crowd waving truncheons aloft to begin to break up the protesters. Punches, bottles, pieces of wood all flew or flailed in the air as despite receiving injuries themselves the police began to beat back the crowd and break up the gathering. At least four others would be joining Lusk inside the bowels of The Street whilst the majority quickly gave up the fight. Spratling had a stark warning.

"Go home! There's enough to do round here without you lot thinking you can do better. We know most of you, gather like this again and we'll crack more heads. Now piss off!" The crowds moaning and cussing under their breath dispersed begrudgingly.

Abberline barged straight past the custody sergeant in the charge room and bundled Lusk into an open cell and let go his grip pushing Lusk forwards hard so he fell onto the wooden bench on the far side of the cell.

"Now then, Lusk you slag, what the fuck do you think you're up to eh?"

"How do you know my name, Abberline?"

"Look here, you pretend middle class Masonic twat, parading around as a man of the working class, I know everything, 'cos the washed up detective in charge has trod these streets for more nights than you've drank port with your apron clad mates."

"Well you ain't doing much about the murders are you, filth."

"I'll tell you, Lusk, and you can tell your mates, we're doing more than you'll ever know, we lost one of our own murdered, probably by this Ripper bastard and he was a working class lad. Now you spout off when you're drunk in the pubs, fine. Bring it into the streets and I'll have you doing more bird in Newgate than you'll know what do with. Do I make myself clear?"

"You can't stop us trying to catch him, Abberline."

"I tell you this, Lusk, do it if you want one of your hooligans with his throat cut and left to drown in his own blood, then carry on. I suggest you do something that doesn't leave you with blood on your hands. I see you again; there'll be more fucking trouble than you'll know how to handle, with your drunken mates and all." Abberline stormed out of the cell slamming the door and paced up to the custody sergeant and barked an order to him.

"In an hours time you drag that fucker out and caution him for incitement to cause violent disorder. Tell him does it again and his world will fall around him and even his ever so helpful Masonic mates will disown him." Abberline left to go back to the incident room to prepare the days briefings.

* * *

Hours later as a result of the excessive alcohol he had drunk the night before, Robert Ford found himself back in his own lodgings with a massive hangover and absolutely no recollection of the events of the evening following the discovery earlier in the day of Del's murder. He was laying face down on the bed with no sign of Mary having been around and wearing no clothes on his top half. He rubbed his bleary eyes and felt the room spinning as he tried to get up off of the bed. Eventually with a great feeling of nausea he managed to find himself sat on the edge of the bed with his head cradled in his hands. With his best friend dead he had to make contact with Mary and get her out of the city, he couldn't bear two tragedies to befall him. He felt she must be sheltering at Millers Court with some of her unfortunate friends to keep them company in a time of such widespread fear. There was a pail of cold water in the room that he managed to shuffle himself over to and found it was luckily three quarters full. He submerged his entire head in the tin bucket for at least 15-20 seconds to try re-vitalising his muzzy head. It worked, and he proceeded to freshen up the rest of himself with it too removing the rest of his clothes to clean away the foul stench of a drunken night from the rest of his lean body before getting changed into some clean clothes to head out to find Mary.

He strolled off along Bakers Row before picking up cut through side streets that brought him out close to Hanbury Street, the location of the murder of Annie Chapman. He made his way past the Spitalfields market from there and eventually stood outside the grotty door of Millers Court, he knocked hard on the door. There was no apparent answer.

* * *

A shuffling tramp walked into George Chapman's hairdressing shop demanding a trim up in broken, mumbled English. Severin Klosowski ordered him to speak up and then demanded that he show that he had money to pay for the cut before actually inviting him to a seat to carry out the task on this filthy street dwelling individual. He took a seat in front of a mirror and Klosowski placed a wrap around his dirty clothes to stop the cut hair sticking to him. He examined Aaron Kosminski's fetid scalp and saw a multitude of very dry skin and some hair ticks crawling.

"My friend, the best thing you can do is to have it all shaved off to stop the onset of any infections beyond what you already have. I must spray you with powder to kill the ticks you have for your sake and mine."

"Do whatever, cut it all off might stop me fucking scratching." Whilst he served his mucky customer Klosowski thought about the fact it had been some time since he had had a street walking woman. Maybe he would venture into Commercial Street tonight and try and seek out the one they call Fair Emma, one of the East End's few pretty prostitutes.

* * *

Druitt sat lonely in his dwellings at the school in Blackheath having told the headmaster he was not well enough today to take classes, which with his outstanding teaching record was massively out of character. He contemplated how to deal with Dr Tumblety. 'Vicious American bastard' he thought, he needed to shop him or set him up in someway, ensuring that it must not lead back to him. He would find it almost impossible to live with the guilt of being party to the murder of a police officer, if he really was, and felt compelled to do something to clear his conscience. Out of character he was drinking a bottle of cheap blended whisky to try to blur the fear from his mind. It helped, after half a bottle he was unconscious and his mind empty albeit for a short time of any of the concerns in his life.

Chapter Thirteen

2.p.m and the parade room at The Street was brimming with everyone going off duty and all those coming on plus the detectives working on the Ripper case, the number of which had now more than doubled just working from this police station. There were also others preparing an incident room at Scotland Yard itself. Members of the local press also were in attendance. Abberline walked in followed by Godley each clutching a wad of information relating to the murders so far; pictures, statements, post mortem reports and scenes of crime plans all to be passed around the officers on parade for them to become fully familiar with what everyone was now dealing with. A hush enveloped the room as Abberline and Godley took to the lecterns at the front of the parade room.

"Good afternoon, gentlemen, and thank you to all who are staying beyond their norm and to those of you having got here early. We shall be brief and to the point as being honest we don't know who we are looking for. As you know most witness statements are from those who were drunk and so we have contradictions in descriptions in height, clothing, facial descriptions and class. But we do know that this person does indulge in the services of prostitutes regularly and seems to want to only kill them. Again as you know this comes from the fact that the only victim outside of that group was Constable Lake, but even he was dressed as a woman of that class. It could be more than one killer working individually; it could be more than one working together. We don't know. DS Godley will pass around details on all we know thus far, so before anyone leaves I want you all to have a good look through the reports to think about venues, maybe the types of men to watch around the local girls; probably anyone, and times of the crimes. This is your community and the people who have confidence in you all are being affected and because of a man called George Lusk they may start to lose faith in you. DS Godley has a picture of this man too. Take his face on board as he could stir things up in front of you or certainly at any crime scene. If things get nasty or you see him gathering a mob get on your whistles and get on them loud. Any questions?"

"Guv'nor, any more plain clothes ops?" asked a contemporary of Del Lake.

"Yes, volunteers only and dressed as local men."

"Mr Abberline, how do you feel about this murderer naming himself, sir?"

"Will Bates, of The Star isn't it?"

"Yes."

"Well, saves you giving a name, unless you know something we don't. It's probably just a local hack who devised the letter."

"I take offence at that."

"Yes, but you can't deny that isn't beyond the realms of possibility? Still, if he is arrogant enough to name himself then he's cocky enough to eventually make a mistake." Bates nodded his head and sagged his lips in apparent agreement.

"Boss, what's the score with the City Police involvement?" asked Kerby.

"They may help with extra patrols, but not yet. Especially as nothing has happened on their ground"

Eventually the questioning fizzled out and the officers of all ranks present passed around the reports and statements among themselves and the members of the press were asked to leave. All were checked as they left to ensure they hadn't tried to take any confidential documents. Godley was on the door supervising the action. A uniformed officer dealt with Bates.

"Bloody police state this, George." Bates addressed Godley.

"No it's not, Bates, it's to ensure you don't spread any more panic. And it's Detective Sergeant Godley."

"You rozzers just don't understand the press. And it's Mr Bates to you, George."

"Hit the road, Bates."

By three o'clock the parade room was empty and the detectives had retired to the incident room, some preparing to walk the streets in the enigmatic quest for Jack the Ripper.

* * *

Sunday 29th September, evening and Robert Ford paced along the Whitechapel Road on his way to check The Ten Bells and The Britannia public houses to see if he could find Mary. He hoped that along the way he may find some of her existing social group to quiz on her whereabouts, although that circle was being depleted by murder or the fear of murder scaring them from the streets. The sites and sounds of the area seemed different now that he walked without police warrant but his loyalty to his community remained strong sensing he would deal with matters that were linked to the crimes of this fiend now given a name. As he passed St Mary's Church on the corner of Church Lane he stood still and dumb founded as he saw an advertising poster for Finius T. Barnums touring European spectacular. On it was a multitude of images that included those of U.S Civil War cavalry types wielding, some of them at least, cutlasses.

So what of the button that he had been shown by Abberline? Did it belong to one of these individuals? The images were hand rendered and did not show that amount of detail. Was this a clue for him to tackle on his own account or information to pass to Abberline to consider, that being if he already hadn't. He decided to seek out Mary first.

Strolling through the doors of The Britannia he scanned the saloon bar area which although early evening was still becoming crowded with the Sunday night revellers. His heart soared as he stared across at a group of women huddled around a table near the bar and saw Liz Stride, Cathy Eddowes and Mary. Stride was the first one to look across and he could see her nudge the others who both looked at him. Mary's face lit up with a beaming smile; she stood and ran over to him throwing her arms around him and hugging him tightly.

"Robert, where have you been?" He looked at her with tears welling in his eyes.

"I could ask you the same question. You haven't been at my lodgings or at yours. Where have you been these past days?"

"We're all scared, darlin', all the girls dead, 'cept Martha, all knew each other and we reckons one of us is next. So we've been moving around from doss to doss. Sorry."

"For God's sake, it won't get any safer than mine!" he sobbed.

"Didn't think you could tolerate us all." She paused at looked at him quizzically as the tears were now streaming heavily down his face. "Robert, what's wrong?" He now fought back the tears to speak and breathe. He paused to take a breath so he could speak coherently.

"Del's dead, Mary, Del's dead." Mary was stunned. It took her several seconds to think and then speak to the almost inconsolable young policeman now weeping in front of her.

"My God, how?"

"The murderer, Jack the Ripper killed him!" She led him over to the table where Liz and Cathy were still sat who both pulled an expression of concern at Mary. She just shook her head back at them to indicate they'd best not interfere. They in fact made their excuses and downed their drinks and left. Mary sat with Robert whose arms were crossed flat on the table with his head buried in them. For quite some time she simply had her arms around him to console him before he finally stopped sobbing and could start rational conversation.

"Robert, there's been no news of this. When did it happen?"

"As I told you we've been doing special patrols for quite some time. The other night we were out, me dressed conventionally for the area and Del in disguise as an unfortunate, oh,er, sorry, lady."

"Don't worry, I don't ply any more."

"I was watching his back around Commercial Street when the dog, Bruiser, he was with me, got really spooked by this bloke. So we followed him off. The dog was really mad, so it had to be to do with Ralph's murder. Well it was. It was a bloke called Ostrog. We chased…"

"We?"

"Me and the dog chased him down to the river."

"Did you arrest him?" There was a huge silence. Robert stared at the table, frozen, unable to speak.

"Well? Did you nick him, or what?" She sensed something terrible troubled Robert.

"No, I killed him." He spoke coldly and distantly without remorse.

"What? You……what?" Mary felt very uncomfortable. She thought she had got to know this man.

"An eye for an eye, Mary. The sense for revenge was too strong in me."

"Robert, that's …..That's…." She looked away from him feeling completely detached with tears gathering in her eyes. She was unable to touch him and pulled her hand away as he tried to take it in his own.

"Mary, you don't understand, that boy was an innocent, and he had as much right as any one to live. Yet some loathsome serial criminal killed him for no good reason. Summary justice, and I tell you this, if I find the fucker who's the so called Ripper I'll do the same to him. I'll protect you at all costs from this bastard." She looked at him troubled.

"You'd kill for me?"

"If I had to, yes."

"You're scaring me, Robert. Let's get away, now this minute. We'll start a fresh, somewhere new." Robert sat silently looking down at the table. "What's the matter with you?"

"I can't, not until this bastard's been caught. He killed my best mate. I owe it to Del to stay until he's found." She considered his words.

"All right, I'll stay off the streets, but I'm staying at Millers Court with me mates 'til it's done."

"Cathy and Liz?"

"Yes, Bowyer doesn't know and he's no need to." Thomas Bowyer was the spend thrift landlord of Millers Court, such a spend thrift that he hadn't replaced a broken pane of glass for some months. Although this aided Mary and her friends to come and go without keys as they could release the internal door latch by reaching through it.

"All right, if you must, but meet me here whenever you need me around nine o'clock, Mary, I'll pop in most nights. I need to make sure you're all right and let you know what's happening." He deliberately omitted being suspended from duty.

Mary looked across at Liz and Cathy at the bar who in turn had been watching the conversation between the two troubled lovers. She beckoned them over and all four sat down and the gin began to flow along with the drunken banshee type laughter. After a time the need to raise some more alcohol and doss money drove out the drunken Eddowes and Stride leaving the troubled lovers together again for a while. Mary and Robert were finding it hard to talk and eventually through sheer frustration she left him staring into a beer glass and perhaps in some way plotting more vengeful acts.

The hours passed through to ten o'clock and Robert left The Britannia for a walk back to his lodgings. Not by a direct route so he could patrol the streets and try to spot some activity. He wouldn't spend long as the fatigue of the recent events coupled with a lack of restful sleep was catching up with him. He passed into Lamb Street along side of the Spitalfields flower market and as he walked along it towards Bishopsgate and the Metropolitan and City Police border, a carriage pulled up alongside of him. The door opened and a deep baritone voice spoke to him.

"Good evening, Constable Ford." He peered in and as he did so the lone occupant leaned forward to see him. He saw a man in his forties, smartly dressed in a bowler hat with a cane propped in front of him on which he rested his hands. Robert looked the man up and down and cynically replied "Yeah, what of it."

"Join me aboard, young man; I have an offer to make you to get you back into the investigation."

"Who are you?" As he asked this question he was bundled onto the coach from behind by two burly but again smartly dressed younger men, who once he was on board slammed the door shut and the carriage moved off. Robert sat opposite facing the dapper stranger.

"I am Detective Chief Inspector Littlechild, Special Branch." Robert was astonished by who this man was and what he wanted with him.

"What do you want with me then, Guv'nor?"

"You're a local boy from what I understand and without a job right now, eh?"

"S'right. What can you do for me then?"

"As a suspended officer we want someone to infiltrate and keep an eye on the Vigilance Committee that has formed in these parts. We have enough problems with the up surge of Fenian attacks in London and we don't want the Irish militants to try to wield this Group for violent purposes. You can get among them as who you are, a suspended policeman, and watch for that sort of activity plus just watch they are up to anyway. Interested?"

"Well, what do I get out of it?"

"Good point, you're not in much of a position to bargain but here goes; you'll be re-instated at the conclusion of the Ripper case and in the meantime we'll ensure that you get paid whilst you work with us. If you change your mind or give up or any other reason I'm not happy with you lose everything. All right?" Such a major consequence was said in such a matter of fact way. Robert paused and thought about Mary's insistence to go, but a short delay could be useful to get some money for a while, it would help him and Mary and avoid them leaving Whitechapel penniless.

"Fair terms, Mr Littlechild, I'm in. How do I start?"

"Good, lad. Get in with the Vigilance Committee and every bit of info you get pass to us via the landlord of the Commercial Street Tavern, he's an ex-copper. If you are in the shit at any time blow your whistle and keep your warrant card on you."

"Ain't got it, Mr Littlechild. Abberline took them." Littlechild pulled both from his pocket and threw them to Robert.

"Problem solved. You'll get your pay through the pub too." The coach pulled up to a halt.

"Right, out you get, lad, we'll speak soon. I'll find you whenever I need to. Goodbye." Littlechild opened the carriage door and Robert alighted into Mitre Square, part of the City's patch. The carriage pulled off rattling across the cobbles and Robert walked out through Church Passage, Dukes Place and into Aldgate High Street and began walking home.

* * *

Mary Kelly returned to 13 Millers Court while Cathy Eddowes and Liz Stride went their separate ways to earn a bit from some punters. Cathy fancied her chances towards the City as Liz made her way along Commercial Street down towards Whitechapel High Street. The streets were still buzzing with activity despite it getting on for twelve. Liz picked up no trade all the way along Commercial Street and had no more luck along the High Street. She eventually walked east along Commercial Road in hope of something. Meanwhile the drunken Cathy Eddowes had got into an alcohol fuelled row in Aldgate High Street and was arrested as a result by Constables Louis Robinson and George Simmons of the City Police and taken to Bishopsgate police station. In the charge room Eddowes was presented to Sergeant Byfield.

"Obviously in for drunkenness lads, name please, lady?"

"Nothing!"

"All right, lads, cell four please let her sleep it off." By nine o'clock she was asleep, contently, drunkenly and safely.

Meanwhile Dr Tumblety had been drinking in a new haunt on the fringes of the East End and the City; 'The Grapes' public house. The Grapes sat on the corner of Aldgate High Street and Mansell Street and tended to be frequented by a better class of prostitute and general clientele due to it's proximity to the financial centre of London and other establishments such as the Sir John Cass college buildings nearby. He also hoped that knowing Mary Kelly was in fact a very attractive girl he may find her here or get some sort of lead as to her whereabouts. His expectations of what The Grapes would bring him were quickly dashed. The pub was busy with many wealthy looking well dressed Jewish merchants who, because of their obvious possession of money, were almost to man surrounded by the best of the unfortunates frequenting The Grapes. The women were all very tactile with these men with their obvious false affection likely to bring them well paying custom. He, on the other hand, was short on cash and had to track down Mary Kelly to recover his fortune. Failing to ignite any conversation, his uniform appearance seemingly working against him in favour of the draw of riches and easy good money from the merchants, in sheer frustration he headed off to a local hot spot for picking up unfortunates; Mitre Square. As he walked briskly and purposefully from the pub he cursed the 'wealth controlling Jews' under his breath. 'I'll make sure they don't get the blame for nothing.' Time was ticking by, it was gone midnight and he suspected sex and the chance of some information may be slim. As he walked the voices returned as it had been sometime since he continued his work and they gave him another notion beyond his precious gems. 'Don't forget, you have not taken a trophy for sometime or done work to keep the streets clean......'

* * *

The International Workingmen's Educational Club was located at 40 Berner Street just off of Commercial Road with Dutfield's Yard located just behind it. Inside much drunken revelry and socialist discussion was taking place to which Aaron Kosminski and Severin Klosowski were party to. A major debate raged amongst a large group of Jewish men regarding the principles of socialism. The debate had been raging for a very heated hour and Kosminski just kept getting drunk whilst Klosowski was losing interest in favour of finding an opportunity for sex before heading home. Kosminski in his stupor having lost track of the debate some time ago turned to Klosowski and tried to focus on him to speak to him.

"You cut hair, eh?" He was mumbling and Klosowski could just about make his words out.

"Yes, what of it?"

"You do mine," he pointed to his scalp. "Very good. Thanks."

"No trouble."

"You not argue any more?"

"Lost interest." He drank some ale from his tankard.

"Why, you seem quite clever."

"Exactly, they bore me. It's Sunday and late and I need a fuck." Kosminski drunkenly chuckled and raised his tankard to his new found friend.

"Me too, let's go split one and get a discount!" He laughed heartily at his own comment and missed his mouth trying to drink pouring it all over himself. Klosowski considered this thought for a moment. This tramp was probably too drunk to get it up anyway and if he was burdening the cost he'd get sex to himself for less money. He'd go with that idea.

"All right, Lipski, lets go."

"Lipski? No, Kosminski."

"Don't worry, it's a term of endearment," Klosowski downed his tankard while Kosminski spilt most of his looking confused. They left the Club together and walked out into Commercial Road towards the City Of London. They could not believe their good fortune to be confronted by an unfortunate plying for trade straight away. She was tall quite slim in her early forties so would probably be a reasonable price. Knowing the state of his accomplice, Klosowski made the response to her offer.

"'Ullo, fine men, fancy something for a shilling each then, eh?"

"As both of our luck should have it, we do, how about a shilling and four pence for the two of us then?"

"I've already offered you a good rate, c'mon don't take the piss." She was right she had actually made quite a good offer. Maybe he'd go first.

"Yeah, all right, how about the privacy of Dutfields Yard, I'm first then he'll see you after."

"C'mon then, darling." She took his hand and led him off to the seclusion of the yard. Kosminski stood opposite the yard to wait his turn in the shadows. He listened in to the activity he was yet to indulge in.

In the darkness of Dutfield's Yard Liz Stride very quickly went to work unbuttoning Klosowski's trouser fly and pulling him free to started to fellate him to get him ready. It didn't take long to get the effect she wanted. "Blimey, you got a big'un ain't ya? Don't take you long neither." She stood up and pulled her bustle skirt up to reveal herself with no obtrusive under garments.

"Turn around; I want to take you from behind."

"As you like, but in my old cunny, no where else." She turned so her back was to him and then leaned forward, wetting herself with spittle on her hand as she did so; she knew it could be painful otherwise. He eased himself in and she gave a genuine cry of pleasurable pain.

Outside Kosminski was listening and had started to abuse himself to be ready to step straight in. Klosowski rhythmically pumped in and out of her leaning forward to caress her breasts. She took his hands and held them still for a moment and spoke.

"Another tuppence and you can have them out as well, lover."

"Well worth it." She undid her jacket and blouse allowed his hands to pull her breasts free. The self-abusing Kosminski pulled harder on himself in anticipation. A few minutes later and she finished Klosowski as she had begun leaving him very satisfied and he happily paid her the price she had demanded not wanting to draw attention to himself now as a local resident. He changed places with the drunken masturbating Kosminski and lit his pipe. Kosminski approached Liz Stride who was back out in the street as Israel Schwartz a local orthodox Jew was passing by giving Stride and Kosminski a filthy look up and down of disgust. He saw the masturbating man grab the woman quite firmly and push her to the floor who shouted in protest at his roughness.

"Oi, oi, oi! Bit more respect please!" Schwartz, concerned, stopped albeit momentarily to watch. Kosminski looked up and saw this and shouted drunkenly at him, thinking of the word he had been called by Klosowski as an alternative to 'mate.'

"Look, fuck off, Lipski!" He helped her up apologising and they disappeared into the yard. The pipe smoking man made a move towards him so Schwartz hurried off.

In the yard Liz went down on her second client and foolishly spoke candidly.

"You're not made like your mate is?" Kosminski grunted in response. "He's quite big."

"What you say?" he replied swaying.

"Oh never mind. How did you want to do it?"

"Don't care." He didn't think he'd make it that far. He was right, she could feel the tension grow in him with her hand and within a couple of seconds he was spent.

"Right, a shilling then, please."

"What?"

"A shilling."

"Oh, yeah," he fumbled for change and couldn't find any only a small knife he kept to ward off muchers. He turned to go but Liz grabbed his arm.

"Oi, you fuckin' owe me, now pay up, you slag!" She bellowed at him aggressively. He always met aggression with violence and pushed her back against a wall and again went to walk away. She grabbed him, spun him round and gauged her nails into his cheeks. He screamed in pain, again pushed her away and drew his knife, which she failed to see. As she lunged at him again he swiped at her with the knife and in lucky act of fate for him, but not for her, connected with her throat and slashed it wide opened. Stunned but with no capability to scream she clutched her throat and fell to her knees. He could hear her breath gurgling as blood and severed airways mixed. She fell to the floor in a ragged heap and within minutes she was dead as Kosminski staggered away, without remorse and unaware of the damage he had inflicted. Klosowski had heard nothing as he was a few hundred yards away having followed Schwartz for a distance to ward him off. When he returned some five minutes or so later he found neither of them in the street so he simply headed home.

Around 1.a.m. Louis Diemschutz a peddler of cheap jewellery pulled into Dutfields Yard with the intention of depositing his cart and his stock with his wife and taking the horse to be stabled at George Yard in Gunthorpe Street. As he drove into the yard the horse shied and pulled to the left and hesitated to go forward. Looking down Diemschutz could see something by one of the gates and prodded it with his long handled whip finding it to be soft. He got off of the cart and lighting a match he saw what appeared to be an unconscious woman who he believed was drunk. He went into the club and related his findings to a couple of the patrons who were good friends, Morris Eagle and Isaacs Kozebrodsky, who both accompanied him outside to try to rouse the drunken woman. To their horror they discovered Liz Stride having bled to death from a slit throat and immediately went in search of a police officer, but only found another club member Edward Spooner. They continued the quest for a policeman and eventually Constables Collins and Lamb arrived, examined the body and blew long and hard on their whistles to summon additional help to secure the crime scene and begin a search of the surrounding area and especially some of the adjacent roads and their premises; such as Batty Street which ran parallel and was the next turning east of Berner Street along Commercial Road.

Chapter Fourteen

"Shut the door behind you please, Cathy," said Constable George Hutt as Eddowes was leaving Bishopsgate Police Station.

"All right. Good night, old cock." Cathy Eddowes left the Police Station in a significantly more sober state some three hours later as it was now approaching 12.30.a.m on Monday morning 30th September. It still took her some time to head down towards Mitre Square where she hoped she would pick up a punter despite the late hour.

Tumblety passed into Mitre Square via Church Passage and entered a dimly lit cobbled open space enclosed by high buildings of a mixed residential and commercial nature. Facing west immediately on his left was one of two buildings that belonged to Kearley and Tonge, the other being on the north side of the square next to which were two houses, one empty the other lived in by a police constable. On his left on the south side was Horner and Co and on the west side was Williams and Co, Mr Taylor's shop and some more empty houses. At this time of night there was no one to observe any activities in the square, be they illicit or illegal. It was around 1.35.a.m as Tumblety stood outside the empty house next to Mr Taylor's shop in the shadows and almost invisible from the east side. The only lights were at the Church Passage entrance and on the north side outside Kearley and Tonge's and he looked across to where he had come from hoping he would see a victim to appear to try glean some information from and perhaps more.

Cathy Eddowes passed along Dukes Place and turned into Church Passage. She had walked by a group of three men who stopped their conversation to see where she went. Joseph Levy, Joseph Lawende and Harry Harris had left the International Workingman's Educational Club about an hour previously and had made their way to this spot via Tubby Isaac's seafood stall. Constable James Harvey emerged from Church Passage and they observed Cathy stop and speak in a very friendly way to him even placing her hand on his chest at one point during their very brief encounter. In the shadows they did not realise it was a policeman as he wasn't wearing his helmet but had it under his arm and was putting out a cigarette. As Cathy left him they saw her go off towards Mitre Square and the constable emerged from the shadows putting on his helmet with the group then realising who he was and all bade each other a polite 'good evening'.

Tumblety couldn't believe his good fortune when he saw a female walk reasonably steadily into sight seemingly having been drinking earlier in the evening. Little known to him potential witnesses were all around not only in the group just out of sight but Kearley and Tonge had a night watchman called George Morris who was asleep. Tumblety was completely concealed from view as she wandered towards him humming gently and looking all around the square while just brushing her hair under her bonnet around the tops of her ears. She got to about twenty feet from him and turned her back towards him, she stopped humming and everything was still. Tumblety on tip toe crept up on her to within arms length.

For no reason she turned briskly to face him quite by chance and brought her hand to her mouth as she took a silent breath in sharply in shock. He tipped his hat and greeted her politely dressed in his usual garb.

"Evening, mam." There was a pause as she moved her hand from her mouth, smiled, coughed and replied.

"Hullo, sir, and what can I do for a fine gent like you?" looking him up and down and sensing the possibility of doss money for a quick service in return.

"I've seen you haven't I, mam, around The Ten Bells or Britannia?"

"You have, sir, haven't seen a fine man like you though. I'd 'member you all right. Real smart you are."

"As a local lady, you don't know a girl almost as pretty as you called Mary, sometimes called Marie-Jeanette or Emma?" Alcohol and keenness to please made Cathy's tongue loose and her naivety took the flattery fully on board too.

"As it happens, I do, sir. She knocks around them pubs too and is courting a local policeman at present. Normally lives round the corner from The Britannia, can't remember the address, know how to get there though. I'm always too pissed when I go there." He shuddered with rage at what she said and also feared the complications of a policeman being involved. If she was courting it would explain a lot about her lack of presence on the streets and that address would be important.

"Does she still work on the street, mam?"

"Nah, proper in love she is. Going to leave this shit hole for pastures new they are from what I can fathom." Tumblety felt the urgency within him to act and he could hear his demons beginning to urge him to as well.

"Only one more question and then perhaps we can do some business together, if you left The Ten Bells, how would you get to Mary's place?"

"Well, you'd cross the road and then go down some little narrow alley. Got a broken window it has, that's all I know love."

The time for talking further was over and Tumblety had gleaned more than on any other encounter. He had begun to carry his Listern knife in a special pouch he had devised on the inside of his right forearm so he could shake it free sliding down and straight into his hand for immediate use with no obvious attention initially drawn to it. During this exchange he had managed to discreetly get into his hand and as he nodded his head in acknowledgment of Cathy's last response he slashed it in a rapid movement across her throat. The blood sprayed unluckily for him almost exclusively in his direction coating his outer clothes and his hat and face heavily. She stood silently and pointlessly raised her hands up to her throat as had all the previous victims, from which she could neither breathe nor speak or scream as if to try to stop the bleeding. She fell forward into the waiting doctor's arms and he dragged her face first into the dark recesses of the south west corner of

Mitre Square. He knew nothing of how little time he had to complete his grisly task make good on his promise to the police to prove his handiwork before he would have to escape quickly via Mitre Street.

He laid her face up on the pavement close to its edge with the cobbles and set to by using the knife to rip open her clothes to gain access to her bare abdomen to start dissecting it to get to the parts his collection demanded. He sunk the knife deeply and harshly into her stomach and ripped fiercely up and down and then across to create a gaping wound in which to work. He pulled out her intestines and threw them across her right shoulder. A small piece still obstructed his work which he cut free completely and discarded by her left arm next to her warm yet lifeless body. He cut into her lower abdomen removing virtually all the womb and most of the uterus, his normal prize, but also took the entire left kidney. This was part of his plan to taunt the authorities even further. His outer clothing, the sleeves of his tunic and his medical bag were covered in warm running blood from the butchering he had just indulged in and even in his psychologically unhinged state he knew he could not afford to be seen before reaching the sanctuary of Batty Street. Having gained his internal prizes he knelt beside the body and looked down on her with absolute contempt for her and her kind. As he stared down at her all he began to be able to see in her face was that of Mary Kelly's. Remembering his taunt to the police he cut off the tips and lobes off of both her ears and then looking at that face again he lashed out fiercely but with design to inflict some very deliberate scars.

He cut 'v' shaped flaps on both her cheeks and a deep cut across the bridge of her nose. He even cut the tip from her nose and then went on to inflict some hideous cuts all around her mouth and across her eyelids. These were vicious actions that served two purposes; firstly to confuse the police with Masonic symbolism and further wreak his revenge on the organisation that had disowned him back in America, and to disfigure her face so that he could no longer see Mary's image looking back at him. His hands and knife were caked in blood and looking at her lifeless form no longer having any use for her torn and stained clothes. He cut off a large piece of her apron from its lower corner to wipe both off. Having done so he realise that the minutes had ticked by and it was now just past 1.45.a.m and he stood to make his escape having just flung loosely into his bag the knife and the vile trophies of the night. He looked up across to Church Passage from where he could hear some foot steps and began to see the shadow of a constable being cast into the square. He ran as briskly as he could into Mitre Street and off towards Aldgate High Street to begin to make good his escape. He was just out of sight as constable Ted Watkins from the City Police entered the square, himself believing that he had heard someone running off.

He had had no choice but to work so thoroughly which now cost him dear making his escape through streets he hoped would be quiet, but within which a man travelling at speed would court attention and especially in his blood soaked condition. As he turned into Aldgate High Street he heard the shrill sound of a whistle being blasted in, from the sound of it, in quite some desperation. The cops had found his handiwork by the direction from which the sound came so soon the area would be swamped. He had to get away briskly and stealthily.

In Mitre Square Constable Watkins had roused the night watchman Morris to help him by sending him off round the locale to the square to see if he could find another officer or a likely assailant. Watkins felt almost physically sick at the gruesome sight that had been presented before him, unable to fathom the psyche of the kind of person to commit such atrocities. Some residents came out of their houses that, apart from the off duty police officer, he directed back into their homes. As a result of Morris's circuit of the area Watkins was joined by Constable Holland who had been patrolling in Aldgate and, as fate would have it, missed crossing Tumblety's path by seconds. He went off to fetch from Jewry Street Dr Sequeira and then informed Inspector Ed Collard at Bishopsgate police station at around 1.55.a.m. Collard sent for the City's divisional surgeon Dr F Gordon Brown before arriving at Mitre Square just after 2.a.m and was surprised by Brown's arrival within minutes of his own. The notoriety and seriousness of the crimes brought Superintendent McWilliams accompanied by Sergeant Foster and even within a short time the acting City Police Commissioner Major Henry Smith.

Tumblety passed the junction with Middlesex Street and ahead he thought he made out the silhouettes of a group of men not more than a hundred yards away. They were walking away from him and by their mode of head dress he guessed them to be local Jewish workers. As he had committed past the junction of Middlesex Street now closing on Goulston Street they must have heard his foot steps as two out of the three turned. Tumblety was directly under a lamp, highlighting the glistening blood on his top coat and bag. One of them shouted.

"You, what's with you? Wait, fellow. Why are you shiny?"

'Damn! My goose could be cooked,' he thought, and he ducked into Goulston Street and ran hard to make some ground on them but began tiring quickly. He had to find somewhere to hide. He made it quite some distance along before he heard another shout from behind; they had now got into the same street. He had got far enough ahead that they probably would not be able to gauge which building he entered to try to lose them. He chose 108-119 Wentworth Model Dwellings and sheltered below a stairwell breathing very hard and sweating profusely from all his physical exertion. He could then hear them talking. They had decided to split up and search the area between them. This would be a real problem because even if not found he would have to be very cautious timing his departure. 'Bastards, if it wasn't enough with the cops on my ass.' He had view of the doorway and saw the silhouette of a figure, one of the Jews, enter. He desperately subdued his breathing but felt his heart beat right through his head, so loud he thought it seemed as if others would be able to hear it and it's beat would give him away and he would be discovered.

His pursuer failed to find him and departed with a very scant search. Lying on the floor he found some sticks of chalk that local children must have left from marking out a 'hops scotch' court. He'd fix both the Jews, for the nights problems they had caused him, and the police with another insulting distraction, this time not by post but by hand on the buildings wall. He had a good knowledge of Freemasonry from a brief involvement in America before his public humiliation in New Brunswick when they failed to stand by him. He knew well the story of Jubelo, Jubelum and Jubela, the 'Juwes' and the crime they committed in the Temple of Solomon. His lodge had disowned him following the death of his patient Mr Podmore and were instrumental in discrediting him. His quick thinking vindictive mind saw another way of distracting attention from himself.

As he stood the piece of apron he had wiped his hands on dropped from his pocket to the floor and he squared up to the corridor wall to write. It didn't take him long. 'That should confuse the trail for sometime' he thought. His deliberate spelling of one word would leave intellectuals and masons wondering if this was ritualistic and laymen simply thinking that the author was slightly illiterate, especially with the double negative. The Jews had made his night difficult in so many ways, and he hadn't found sanctuary yet. He stepped back to see his completed message:

> THE JUWES ARE THE
> MEN THAT WILL
> NOT BE BLAMED
> FOR NOTHING

The deliberate spelling of 'Juwes' would potentially besmirch two groups for which he felt hostility. Now he had to make good his escape. He emerged back into Goulston Street slowly and cautiously and made his way north to avoid contact with the three Jews in case they had not yet resumed their own business. His route towards the sanctuary of Batty Street took him into Wentworth Street, the location during the day of the busy 'Petticoat Lane market' which then led across Commercial Street as he continued towards Brick Lane and Osborn Street. Ever vigilant he had to ensure he passed no one or did it at a massive distance so they could not see his shiny blood stained clothes. There was no point ditching his outer garments as it had soaked through to his white shirt which was then even more obvious to onlookers. His escape route took him past St Mary's Church and into Church Lane the scene of a previous encounter which then spat him out close to safety, or so he believed, into Commercial Road. About to turn left and beginning to let his guard down Batty Street was only three roads up on the right.

Appearing in Commercial Road he turned only fifteen feet from an approaching constable. He quickly ducked back into Church Lane and walked off briskly, but he had been seen.

"Oi, you come here, I need a word." The voice bellowed to him from behind. He briskly strolled a few more feet into the darkness of the poorly lit Church Lane before stopping to confront his potential assailant. With his back turned to the constable he got a knife to hand ready to use to make good his escape. As he heard the foot steps close and another question directed at him he turned ready to strike.

"When I say stop, I want a word, mister, I bloody mean it. Now...." His words were cut short as the Listern knife flashed rapidly across in front of him deep into his face slicing across his left cheek, his mouth and into his right cheek. The attack opened up his face almost literally ear to ear leaving a massive open wound that including his mouth was nearly ten inches across. He helplessly grabbed his face as the blood poured over his hands and he couldn't form his lips to issue a scream or a cry for help. He fell to his knees helplessly in front of Tumblety who then pushed the kneeling constable over leaving him fighting for breath on the cold pavement, desperately trying to call for assistance. He ran back up to Commercial Road and peered round the corner looking east and west to see if he could continue his escape. It appeared clear so he ran across the road still sweating profusely and continued east towards his safe haven. As he neared Gowers Walk he could see two blocks up a mass of police around the top end of Berner Street with Batty Street being only just beyond; but it might as well be on another continent with all that police presence and his overall bloodied condition. He had to get there; he couldn't turn up at the Ritz in this state. He had to find a way round.

He felt a hand on his shoulder as he stood using the building line for some cover from view looking east. He whirled round to see another cop and without time to draw his knife again and noting the officer with his truncheon in hand he punched out as hard as he could at the man's windpipe. He fell like a rag doll as Tumblety then kicked him in the jaw as hard as he could and then took his truncheon about to strike again but pausing with a sudden thought.

The officer lying in front of his feet was a sergeant drafted in with some of his subordinates from another division on the outskirts of East London. He was actually unconscious as a result of the blow he had received and looking at him Tumblety noticed that he was of a very similar build to him. He bodily dragged him with great effort and nearing exhaustion deep into Gowers Walk out of sight to execute his plan. He began shedding all of his own top clothes throwing them in

Whitechapel

a pile and as soon as he had discarded them all on the cobbles he set to work with stripping the sergeant of his uniform. He was out cold and it was difficult to manoeuvre his dead weight. Once stripped of his uniform he stood bent double for a minute or so trying to get his breath listening intently for footsteps or sign of police or anyone nearing him. Having got his breath with only the sound of the gathering crowd from Berner Street in the distance, the occasional dog bark or carriage passing on the main road, he managed to struggle into the uniform complete with helmet and truncheon. He bundled up his own clothes and headed south in Gowers Walk finding a large tin dustbin to stuff them in. Leaving the lid off he lit a match and got them burning and hid his bag deep in a alcove between buildings further down and would fetch it back in the morning. He stood ensuring the fire took hold and then made his way through an alley into Back Church Lane to then try to wend his way into the bottom end of Batty Street via Ellen Street and Providence Street which would lead directly to it.

Officers from neighbouring districts had been drafted in, a fact he knew from the newspaper reporting, so provided he could carry off a vague anglicised accent he should make it home almost incident free now. The streets he had to enter to get home to number 22 were now teeming with local people disturbed by the police that were also frequenting them creating noise searching the locale in depth. He hoped it wouldn't extend to Gowers Walk and so lose his bag. As he walked along the street a young officer addressed him, breaking away from his search.

"Here, sarge, how far out is this searching supposed to extend?" enquired a young constable of him with others turning to listen in Providence Street. He paused and then coughed preparing to give it his best shot at an English accent. He was fortunate to have travelled extensively and studied the various dialects and accents he had encountered.

"Just as far as two streets parallel, either side." There was silence the officers around all looked at each other. He felt uncomfortable.

"All right, ta, sarge." They all resumed what they were doing, moving dustbins, checking doors and dark corners while he casually wandered on within spitting distance of his lodgings.

He turned into Batty Street to see the road buzzing with activity; some residents on the streets gossiping and making their own conclusions as to what had happened, but mainly police pacing the street looking for clues. Strolling towards him was an inspector, unknown to Tumblety it was John Spratling who had been in on the case from the start. He needed to ensure that he did not engage with this man in any conversation so he deliberately crossed the road and seized upon an opportunity to berate a young looking constable searching around some rubbish piled up in the street.

"What are you doing, man?" demanded the would-be sergeant in an ever more convincing English accent. The young constable stopped what he was doing and looked Tumblety up and down noting his outer district collar number, a more rural district further out to the east.

"With respect, sarge, you not being a local bloke and therefore only providing patrols, what the fuck is it to you?" Inter-district rivalry and cynicism would be something Tumblety knew nothing about. He stood open mouthed aghast that a sergeant could be spoken to like this as the young but obviously opinionated and tenacious constable stared back at him.

"Well, sarge, what you got to say to that? Looking for fucking clues ain't I?" Tumblety looked round nervously and shaken by the response. Fortunately for him the inspector had now passed by so he cleared his throat stared back at the constable simply scowling and pointing a finger to him and strolled off towards number 22.

"Fucking country district wankers." The constable resumed his searching.

Tumblety got to 22 and stood with his back to the door looking up and down before putting his key in and entering when he felt no one was watching. He was lucky no one had seen him go in. He dashed to his room and quickly got the uniform off and stuffed it under the bed. He ripped his shirt off which was still blood stained and threw it in the sink and ran cold water onto it. He then watched the activities outside cautiously from his window and began to calm himself down having reached a reasonable safe haven. Had the police called yet, however, to speak to all the residents? He hadn't seen Mrs Long as he'd come in which meant he had no inclination of whether there had been any enquires made of the house. He would have to sit and wait. He rang the shirt out and threw it under the bed joining the uniform and then began to wash to wipe away any possible clues for if the law came calling. Having cleaned himself up and hidden incriminating evidence for now, he lay down on his cheap bed began to relax and waited for sleep to arrive to recharge his now exhausted constitution.

* * *

Abberline wasn't sure of where to go first having again had a cab turn up this time in the early hours at his home to bring him urgently into work. By the reports he was being given by Murphy and Parish who had both come to fetch him it seemed prudent to attend Mitre Square first owing to its ferocity. What he couldn't believe was that the killer had struck twice in one night, or had he? With the marked difference between the two attacks he felt convinced of two possibilities; perhaps the killer had been disturbed at Berner Street or they were two completely unrelated incidents. One other motivation had driven Abberline to go to Mitre Square first; the City Police Commissioner was in attendance with another high ranking City officer so it would only be good protocol for the investigating officer at ground level on the Metropolitan District to attend, liaise and advise.

3.a.m Mitre Square had been completely closed off to any traffic either vehicular or pedestrian on the orders of Major Smith with constables from the City keeping a cordon closed around the murder scene and others performing roving patrols within a half mile radius. Abberline entered the square via Dukes Passage to see a crowd gathered on the opposite side of the square to him who appeared to be looking at or working around something on the floor. He walked over and as he got closer he recognised Major Smith present, several other ranking City officers who Abberline did not know and Dr F Gordon Brown the City's divisional surgeon. Brown was on his knees next to the corpse. In the light and at his initial distance Abberline gained no grasp of the horrific injuries she had sustained. The full extent of the savagery of the attack hit the detective inspector as he was about to engage Major Smith in conversation and he couldn't help but express his shock at it.

"Jesus Christ. The fucking bastard. Sorry, Commissioner, good morning, sir"

"Morning, Abberline. Quite understandable given the nature of the attack, worse than the others, eh?"

"Yes, sir, considerably so. I understand that the other one has only had her throat cut."

"Quite so, Abberline. So where do we go from here then?"

"Well, sir, once the doctor has done his initial examination here perhaps she'll go to the local mortuary…." Smith cut in over Abberline.

"Golden Lane, then." Not ideal for Abberline as it was on the North West side of the City's patch, past the area known as the Barbican.

"And then be fully examined in the morning. A post mortem I will attend with my number two, Sergeant Godley. Before that, get some pictures taken if we can, all the witness statements available to us and I'll go off to Berner Street if one of your ranking chaps can supervise all that please, sir."

"Thank you, Inspector; I shall put Superintendent McWilliam in charge of that."

At that point both men were interrupted by Police Sergeant Jones who had been relayed some news by a constable who had just ran into Mitre Square.

"Sir, something very significant has turned up round the corner. Local copper Alfie Long had found some writings in Goulston Street, Wentworth Model Dwellings, reckon they might be linked. And a blood soaked bit of torn apron." Dr Brown cut in at that moment.

"Torn apron? Could be very significant gentlemen, look," he indicated to Eddowes mutilated body. Abberline, Smith, McWilliams and some of the other officers gathered were overtaken by a sudden silence as they all looked down at Eddowes clothing that Doctor Brown was drawing their attention to. Her massively blood stained apron was in tatters with a large proportion of it missing; they now had discovered the killers escape route.

"Right, take us there," said Abberline in a decisive manner "And the rest of you get this bloody scene photographed, drawn and fully documented, long hand too. Nothing must be left unturned and unaccounted." He stormed off grabbing the young constable who had delivered the message by the arm pushing him forward to lead the quickest why to the graffito and the blood stained remnant of apron.

Whitechapel

Godley rounded the corner into Dukes Passage as Abberline was exiting on an obvious mission. He looked tired and depressed being back in to work so soon; he looked at his friend and superior who so obviously lived now to solve this case and appeared totally focused. Before he could speak Abberline launched a multitude of orders in his direction.

"George, get over to Berner Street and make sure it gets sorted out proper, I want everything. I can't believe this fucker has struck twice in one night. I'll tie the gallows's rope me self if we find him." Godley stood aghast about to reply but was cut off.

"Don't just stand there; take a quick look over there and then fuck off!" Abberline disappeared off with the young Constable heading east, to where Godley had no idea. Godley immediately recognised all those ranking officers around Cathy Eddowes as he took a look at the scene. There was something that seemed unsaid around these men as he surveyed what was going on and what hideous event had taken place. As he wandered around that part of the square, McWilliams then spoke.

"Sergeant, perhaps you could remind Inspector Abberline to address those superior to him with a just a little more respect. Perhaps asking us or suggesting a course of action instead of just telling us."

Godley continued looking at the carnage around him giving some instructions to the Police photographer who had just arrived. Then before he turned to leave, Godley addressed the question.

"Well, I'll pass that on, sir, but just so you know he does address his *superiors* with respect." Godley walked off out of the square leaving the City officers fuming amongst themselves. He exited via Mitre Street to make use of a cab that had been hired since his arrival to carry the detectives between scenes. Sinking into the quilted leather seat he sat back purposely letting out a huge sigh and looking at his watch. Sleep seemed to be commodity kept in short supply whilst this man 'Jack the Ripper' was still out there.

Abberline came across quite a gathering in Goulston Street mainly formed by a variety of police officers. Stood within the crowd were Constable Alfie Long, Detective Constable Halse and another young Metropolitan Detective Constable called Walter Dew. Alfie Long was interviewing a group of Jewish working men who Abberline assumed must be witnesses. Dew saw Abberline approaching and stood to attention awaiting directions or questions.

"Morning, sir." He greeted the noted detective.

"Morning, Wally, what's going here then? I hope it ain't all been trampled over?"

"No, sir, writing and apron bit are still as they were found. Photographer is on his way." He paused and Abberline was about to enter the Model Dwellings, "And Mr Arnold is on his way, with Sir Charles, sir." Abberline stopped in his tracks before entering the building and paused before giving Dew an answer. The seriousness and notoriety of this case was growing massively day by day and a visit by these two individuals in the middle of the night was a measure of its magnitude.

"When they get here, son, make sure you make plenty of noise out here to alert me before they fuck things up." Dew was somewhat taken aback by the detective inspector's response and swallowed heavily before replying.

"Right ho, sir, will do. Just a loud 'good morning' or something do?"

"That'll be fine, just make sure you add their names too. What's that lot that Long is talking to all about?"

"Oh, reckon they saw some bloke with a big moustache all covered in blood disappear in here."

"Interesting, make sure you get decent statements." Abberline walked into the tenement block, the entrance to which was glowing from all the additional candle light that had been brought in. Halse had already entered and had a note book out and was copying down the chalked words. This Abberline quietly observed and he also noticed a uniformed Met constable stood further in the entrance way almost lost in the shadows; he was very upright, smart and holding a military 'stand easy' pose and nodded in acknowledgment to Abberline and spoke.

"All correct, sir."

"Far from it, lad, or else we wouldn't be here. You got all that written down then?"

"Every word, sir, the detail, the layout, the spelling. Bit odd, goes to show whoever's doing this ain't bright. Don't spell Jews like that, does you?" Keeping thoughts about it actually not being an error to himself, Abberline responded to the obviously tired officer, a condition with which he fully sympathised.

"Absolutely. Who's been put in charge here right now?"

"Inspector Chandler, sir. He's just out there," pointing to a yard area at the rear of the premises."

"Right tell him the Commissioner and Mr Arnold are on way so we need to look lively over this, getting it all recorded." He hadn't heard anything and he could see Long looking beyond him to the direction of Goulston Street and the entrance to the dwellings. He heard a voice that he knew would mean interference and he felt his whole demeanour change knowing he was about to be bossed about in his own back yard.

"Ah, Abberline. Glad you're here, Sir Charles has decided to join us," said Superintendent Arnold. Abberline turned round reluctantly to greet them both.

"Good morning, sirs, early start for you?"

"No need for flippancy, Abberline, what have we here?" replied Warren as he stepped into the passageway of the dwellings and began inspecting the graffiti with Arnold immediately behind him also peering in curiously.

"Well, seems it could be some sort of clue but with an odd command of English, sir." Warren read it out loud in a slow, laborious manner and immediately drew an aggressive and rushed conclusion quite deliberately; in his own mind he knew exactly what the key miss-spelt word could refer to.

"It's a load of anti-Semitic rubbish, Abberline and I want it cleaned off now." Abberline looked horrified and stumbled over his reply.

"Sir Charles, this must at least for now be considered a significant clue. It must be photographed and fully documented before we clear it."

"Abberline, we have enough problems with racial tensions in this area and this could cause a pogrom if it's left up. This could clearly be interpreted as the murders being committed by a Jew and we'd have the streets running with Hebrew blood. Clean it off now." Warren turned to a City police inspector and spoke to him seeing that Abberline was about to cross his authority.

"Inspector, clean that off now. It's an order, it's on my ground."

"Wait, Sir Charles I at least need that noted before it goes. But I warn you, history will judge you harshly, sir."

"Detective Inspector, do not ever cross me publicly again. Now get out of the damned way and let's have it cleaned."

"Long, note it down now and quickly," and turning to the City DC Abberline spoke further. "And you get it written down and all." Halse and Long both noted it down, and as history would also discover, in two different versions. Abberline stormed out back into Goulston Street to compose the rage that was developing within him. Having watched the graffiti cleared Warren and Arnold strolled nonchalantly into the street giving Abberline no break from them.

Arnold initiated the conversation in a condescending tone.

"Now then, Inspector, no more nonsense over all this, we need a result. Rowing with the highest ranking officer will not get us that."

"Well, Superintendent, I'm glad you give a shit. Although if you really did you may have liked to consider that also in there," Abberline pointed back to inside the dwellings "is the torn blood soaked section of Cathy Eddowes apron." They both looked at Abberline aghast and in silence. "Oh, didn't you know that? Well that'll teach you to interfere with real coppers. Do correct me, Superintendent, but Sir Charles is not and has never been a warranted police officer, and you haven't worked the streets for over five years." They continued to stand in silence, incredulous to this verbal attack they were receiving. Abberline concluded his rant. "Now with that being the case, fuck off and leave it to the police to deal with this. You'll get your result, and I will get it for you without interference." Warren was unable to reply, Arnold did in a veiled menacing way.

"Very well, we hear you. But let me tell you Abberline, no matter how this repulsive case is resolved, be assured that you will never rise beyond chief inspector."

"Well, sir, that's the best news I've had all day. At least that way I always get to work for a living." They stood silent as Abberline returned to the hallway of the dwellings to examine the apron and ponder its significance. This was the hottest trail they had followed so far. He passed the now just chalk stained wall and felt sick to his stomach.

* * *

Godley arrived at Dutfields Yard to find the usual crowd of local people gathered being kept outside the yard by a large contingent of uniformed police. He entered the yard and saw a body lying just slightly past the gate with an old blanket draped over the upper part from head down to above the knees. A pool of blood had spread well beyond the confines of this blanket and it appeared glistening and black as always in the moonlight. Godley could see a portly bearded Jewish working man stood in quite a distressed state with some local officers one of who was taking notes from this man. He walked over to this small gathering and introduced himself to the constable taking notes.

"Morning, DS Godley, Whitechapel incident room. What's going on here?" Before the policeman could reply the distressed Jewish man who Godley would later discover was Louis Diemschutz butted straight in.

"What's going on!!? Why have you not caught this killer? Whitechapel women are dying and what are the police bloody well doing?"

"Sir, your name please?" Godley replied. As the constable was about to answer he was shouted over by Diemschutz again.

"Louis Diemschutz, I am a local salesman. I have a wife; she won't go out after dark. Why have you not yet caught him? Why!!"

"Mr Diemschutz, we're doing our best. We have many lines of inquiry which we can only expand based on news from the public. Have you seen anything, sir?" Godley was trying to empathise.

"I turn up in the early hours to leave my cart and the horse gets very spooked and rears slightly. I steady him and get off the cart and find what I thought was a drunken woman, but she is dead, another victim of this Ripper, why you have not caught this man!?"

"Mr Diemschutz, did you see anyone around at all who could have been involved, leaving or trying to hide?"

"No, I see no one, if I did I'd kill him myself to stop all this."

"Thank you, sir, but I don't think that would be the way forward."

Godley left Diemschutz with Constable Collins the officer who was first with him to complete his statement while he went to see the immediate crime scene. The victim was still there along with Dr Bagster Phillips and the evening's divisional surgeon Dr Blackwell. As he walked over he and Doctor Phillips acknowledged each other and one of the constables pulled back the sheet covering the victim's body. He could see that the victim had her throat cut and the wound had bled heavily, looking up to her face he instantly recognised her. Rubbing his forehead and running his hand down his face over his mouth to chin Godley was taken aback by this realisation.

"Liz the cleaner, Liz Stride, I can't believe it." Phillips was quick to reply.

"Yes, indeed, Sergeant, a bit of a bloody shock to you and your lads I know as she'd worked at The Street for a while. Do you notice anything unusual to the others so far though, Sergeant?" Godley bent down and looked around Liz and lifted some of her lower clothing, noting almost instantly she seemed to have no further injuries.

"Well, Doc, if I'm right, she's only had her throat cut."

"That's right. What about the Mitre Square victim? What was her condition, eh?"

"Absolutely butchered, Doctor, no comparison to this. What are you suggesting?"

"Simply that before anyone gets the melodramatic idea that the same man did both, consider that two murders have occurred co-incidentally in the same night."

"Well, that's true, but what if he'd been disturbed here and then gone looking for a victim elsewhere. I mean we know he likes to take trophies."

"Well, that's something for you detectives to decide based all your evidence from tonight and so far. If you'd be so kind now, Sergeant, can she now be taken away to the mortuary and I'll be doing the P.M later on in the day. This 'double event' will certainly court some press and interest at the inquests."

"The 'Double Event', or 'Jack's Double Event'. What a headline for Monday morning, gents." Godley and Bagster Phillips looked around to see Will Bates stood there notebook in hand keenly scribbling as much as he could of the conversation he had crept up upon.

"Bates, how the hell did you get in here?"

"Freedom of the press, Sergeant. The public have a right to know."

"Be careful of what you publish. There's enough scaremongering as it is."

"Well do the police want to comment then?"

"Inspector Abberline will publish a statement for you later, Bates."

Looking beyond Bates to the yard entrance and Berner Street he could see George Lusk and some working men gathered. There was a heated conversation taking place between Lusk and the duty inspector, who Godley did not know, with Lusk feeling obviously brave with his mob in tow. Godley began to walk over to intervene. At that moment a hansom cab pulled up in Berner Street and Abberline jumped out with the look of a man on a mission and strolled briskly straight up to Lusk. Grabbing him by the lapels of his overcoat he squared up to him nose to nose launching into a bellowed verbal tirade with a fearsome grimace on his face.

"I've told you once, Lusk, and now this is the last fucking time. This is a police investigation not mob rule, I will run you in for riot and sedition if you challenge the authority of the Queens office of constable. My men will crack heads and your reputation will be so besmirched that you won't get a reference to sweep the streets. Now, there are enough experts in and out of the police telling me what to do, so just fuck off and if you see me so much as in the same postal district I suggest you turn tail. I will take you down from your over inflated local and Masonic position. Read the headlines in the next few days carefully as some of your brethren may not be so fucking righteous after all." Abberline threw him to the ground and turned on his heels into Dutfield's Yard with Godley walking towards him. "Turn round, George and walk back in we'll talk later."

"Inspector Abberline, what did you mean by all that?" Asked the scandal hungry Bates.

"Not now, later, Bates, much later," replied Godley fending him off with a push to his chest.

Outside amongst the crowd Robert Ford watched those around him intently for reactions to Abberline's confrontation with Lusk, he hadn't seen the last one but observed nothing within the crowd. With no knowledge of such things as Freemasonry the 'brethren' comment had gone completely over his head. He watched Lusk stand up, put his bowler hat straight and dust himself down. He could see there was nothing Lusk could say to the gathered Vigilance Committee to regain any face. They all drifted off into the dawn light as Constable Collins, now that the body had gone, washed down the crime scene. It was around 5.30.a.m.

Chapter Fifteen

Tuesday 1st October early morning; Dr Tumblety was back in the West End and bought a copy of The Star from the newspaper boy just outside the Ritz. Cash was a major problem and he knew that they would discover his cheque could not be drawn on in another few days time. Unless he considered taking a loan he'd be forced to live in Whitechapel until recovering his wealth from Mary Kelly. He stared at the headlines and read the text;

JACK'S DOUBLE EVENT HORROR

William Bates Exclusive

Sunday into Monday morning saw the most horrific events yet with the murder of two innocent Whitechapel women butchered for no apparent reason other than to fuel the mad Ripper's killing spree. Elizabeth Stride was found with her throat cut in Dutfield's Yard and within the hour the mutilated body of Cathy Eddowes was found in Mitre Square with, by all accounts, horrific injuries yet to be disclosed. Jack the Ripper's

blood lust obviously not yet satisfied, the Police lead by the confrontational Inspector Abberline still refuse the help of local Philanthropist George Lusk and the Whitechapel Vigilance Committee. When will it all end? Four women murdered, law and order in turmoil, the police apparently stumped and the local community snubbed by the authorities…….'

The article went on both to the fury of Frederick Abberline and Francis Tumblety who were simultaneously reading it but in very different circumstances. Tumblety's massively troubled mind raced.

'Vigilance Committee, want to help do they, I'll get them involved, and the kindly Mr Lusk can receive some post then. Then he'll decide to leave it to the dumb cops. Those bastards just don't know where to turn next I'll bet, masons, mad men, who is it, ha! Guess I'll take credit for both just to exaggerate that fear they all have for dear old Jack. I'll put Mr Lusk on my mailing list with a gentle introduction but first I must write to the Dear Old Boss.'

Buying a plain post card later that morning Tumblety sat down in the Café Royal and began scribing a message to the Central News Agency:

'I was'nt codding dear old Boss when I gave you the tip. You'll hear about saucy Jacky's work tomorrow double event this time number one squealed a bit and couldn't finish straight off. Had not time to get ears for police thanks for keeping last letter back till I got to work again.

Jack the Ripper.'

Putting the post card into a post box after leaving the Café Royal Dr Tumblety felt very pleased with himself, knowing that the true extent of the horrors on Sunday night would make the newspapers over the next couple of days following the inquests into the two murders. He returned to the Ritz and packed a travelling carpet bag to lie low at Batty Street until his money situation was resolved. As he passed the hotel reception later that day he tipped them an acknowledgement but did not check out as he left the building.

The Central News Agency received the postcard later that very day and immediately contacted Scotland Yard and passed it to them. But, not before they had their headlines ready the next day to sell to the newspapers. They would report the sensational story of how Jack the Ripper had already contacted them to acknowledge his work and continue to create great fear within the eastern part of the capital.

That evening Robert had decided to cut free for an evening from the Vigilance Committee and visit the American Circus he had seen advertised and had persuaded Mary to go with him. It was based in Victoria Park and had only recently opened in its East London venue having played prior to this in Hounslow on the very western edge of the capital. As they approached they saw the massive traditional red and white big top marquee and the multitude of travelling vehicles around it caging all sorts of wild beasts. Also to one side of the big top was a 'Red' or Native Indian encampment with several tepee tents all belching smoke from their funnel shaped tops. They queued up at the booking trailer, a Wild West stage coach, and watched many of the performers passing by; very quickly Robert realised that this could be a fruitless expedition by him on his own. Everyone in an American military uniform seemed to have buttons like the one he had seen in Abberline's office and certainly more than the odd individual had buttons missing. He resigned himself to the fact that would have to purely enjoy the spectacle of the show and without a mass enquiry of the entire circus staff the police would achieve nothing in tracing leads here. At least he could pass that idea on to Littlechild as an aside to his normal role.

They bought their tickets and walked towards the main entrance to the big top which was staffed by some fearsome looking bare-chested Mohawk Indians. They were taking the tickets from the hands of the audience and ushering them inside with scowling contempt, hissing at the smaller children on occasions just to heighten their sense of trepidation. As Mary and Robert got to the head of the queue one of the Mohawks gave her a good look up and down and nodded his head in appreciation of her form to Robert, the action making Mary feel quite uncomfortable. She grabbed for his hand and stormed inside the tent where they were met by the noise of the crowd, the roar and smells of some of the animals and the bellowing voice of Barnum himself.

"Roll up, roll up for the greatest show on Earth!" They disappeared into the seated masses.

* * *

Wednesday 2nd October; Robert James Lees ate breakfast in the conservatory of his fashionable Peckham Rye home at around 8.a.m having been troubled for some weeks by visions of the Whitechapel killer. Lees was born in Birmingham in 1849 and subsequently brought up in Hinckley in Leicestershire. At thirteen it had become apparent that he was gifted with clairvoyance; at aged twenty-two he was married and then as a result of his talents he worked in a well paid position with the Manchester Guardian. By 1888 he was living in Peckham overlooking the fashionable Rye, or village green, and had become a noted philanthropist and radical friend of the workers politician Keir Hardie. He was well known as a Christian spiritualist and had written several books on the subject. But it was his work as a medium that had brought him into Royal circles having conducted a séance for Queen Victoria in which her late and beloved husband Albert the Prince Consort had spoken with her.

Finishing his breakfast he summoned his valet to flag down a carriage for him to make the journey to the innermost part of the East End of London. Dressed in Victorian finery he kissed his wife goodbye and with his cane and top hat left the smart town house he owned outright and mounted the carriage. The driver set off with the crack of the whip and made his way north to cross the Thames via London Bridge over which he turned right to follow Lower Thames Street into St Dunstans Hill, Mincing Lane, Fenchurch Street and then into Aldgate High Street and finally Commercial Street pulling up outside the doors of the police station.

He had chosen a bad day to decide to attend The Street and speak with Inspector Abberline. With the events of the previous weekend the detective inspector was currently operating with little patience for anything other than hard facts or evidence. He was under pressure despite his contempt for his senior officers to apprehend a suspect; they would not care whether he was either actual or just credible. With each murder that took place there seemed to be less clues to follow and to top it all he now had the prospect of a funeral imminently for Del Lake. This brave officer was not even permitted a service funeral for fear of courting further negative press. That morning, whilst Abberline was in the incident room on his own first thing, he had begun drinking again. It gave him an escape from the rigours of this high profile and tenuous investigation. He savoured the burning and bitter taste of half a tumbler of a particularly coarse single malt whiskey. Having not touched a drop for sometime, it sent his head spinning for a short while before downing a cup of tea and some buttered bread for breakfast.

Lees instructed the carriage to wait. Money was of little concern to him and paying for the driver's 'dead' time without a fare was archetypal of the financial advantaged that he held. He passed through the double doors of The Street's main entrance and was confronted by Kerby, the days station sergeant who looked up with casual disdain at the apparent 'dandy' who had just walked in. In his polished well clipped accent Lees addressed him.

"Sergeant, good morning to you. I wish to speak with Inspector Abberline please." Kerby looked him up and down before responding.

"What is the nature of your business, sir?"

"That is none of your's, Sergeant, but purely his." Kerby was certainly taken aback by this reply and became a little belligerent.

"I see, sir, you are Mr...."

"Lees, Robert James Lees."

"The Queen's spiritual adviser, sir?" Lees was taken by surprise this common officer should know such a thing.

"That is right. Would you kindly tell him I am here, I don't think you now need to glean any further information from me, Sergeant." This comment further wounded Kerby somewhat but he was astute enough to realise he was dealing with a man of influence. He decided leaving this to Abberline was quite the correct thing to do.

"I'll just get him for you, sir."

Kerby made his way through to the incident room to find Abberline sat with his head in his hands staring at statements strewn across his desk while Godley was chalking up information onto a wall mounted board. Parish and Murphy, the two detective constables assigned to the case early on, were studying a map indicating the murder sites which was spread across the wall opposite the office door. They all appeared in deep concentration and following the weekend's events Kerby decided to politely knock to gain attention as opposed to his usual brash bowling into the room unannounced. The detectives all looked round in his direction.

"Sorry to disturb, gents, got a Mr Robert Lees at the front counter for Mr Abberline." There was a pause as they all looked to each other.

"Show him in, Kerby, me and George will have a chat with him," said Abberline.

"Very good, sir," Kerby left while Abberline addressed the others.

"Right then, George stay here with me; you lads get yourselves out on whatever enquiries you have. I don't want a crowd in here to discuss what this bloke has to say. He's got a reputation but it means little to me as he does nothing on hard facts."

Parish and Murphy left making their way off for opening at The Ten Bells as Abberline and Godley put their jackets on and straightened their ties. There was another knock; Kerby walked away and Lees stood in the office doorway. Abberline spoke first approaching Lees with an outstretched hand.

"Good day, Mr Lees, I am Inspector Abberline," they shook hands, Abberline firmly but Lees somewhat limply. "And this is Detective Sergeant Godley. Won't you take a seat, sir?" Lees shook hands with Godley who directed him to a seat at one of the desks while Abberline retreated to his own. Godley placed fresh tea in front of everyone and then sat down as the conversation began.

"Mr Lees," said Abberline, "you are a noted medium and spiritual advisor to the Royal family, what is your business with us, sir?"

"Well, Inspector, I have been troubled by visions regarding this case over the last fortnight and each time the images are nearly always the same. My visions in the past have been of use to many walks of life." Abberline and Godley looked at each other before Godley interjected.

"Mr Lees, it is not usual practice for the police to solve crimes on a spiritual basis, so you must excuse deep questioning and any hint of cynicism. What exactly have you seen, sir?"

Lees closed his eyes and cupped his hands together in a prayer like fashion over his nose and mouth, gently rubbing them over the bridge of his nose, and sat silently for a few moments. Again the detectives looked at each other this time somewhat incredulously.

"I see a woman late at night in a dark and unlit part of the East End. She is drunk and unaware of her surroundings, unaware of being watched by a brooding figure. The figure is only one man but he has two humours. Charming and polite, but then a crazed savage capable of unspeakable acts, but never outwardly showing this side to anyone but the dead. He speaks in a foreign tongue but by demeanour and appearance he could fit in anywhere." The room fell quiet for a few moments. Abberline spoke.

"Mr Lees, trying to put a cold police interpretation on what you have said, are you telling me that this man by day would not stand out and could be anyone from any background, but by night could be spotted by the savagery of his behaviour?"

"No, Inspector, not at all. This man appears to be of good class, not a common worker, and until he strikes you would never spot him in crowd."

"And what about the foreign tongue?"

"That, Inspector is one of the vagaries; all I know is that he is not a native of this land." Godley sat silent and pensive about this, drawing attention to himself as a result.

"What you thinking, George?"

"Fred, the nearest physical interpretation I can put on what Mr Lees has said is that fellow Richard Mansfield, the American actor playing 'Jekyll and Hyde' at the Lyceum."

"That is a very good interpretation of my vision, Sergeant."

"Mr Lees, can you tell us more about the victims, so we could know who to protect?"

"Inspector, not easily, not until quite late very often."

"Mr Lees, that would not be terribly helpful if it's too late. Did you know anything of the last victims?"

"Victims? No, this man certainly killed at least one of those women, you see. He was in a dark alley entering a square with religious significance when he saw his victim. He attacked with extreme violence a woman in her mid forties with an apron who had already been in police custody." He paused before finishing his description of his visions. "And he mutilated her. Didn't he?" Abberline and Godley sat silent looking at each other. They were yet to attend the post mortem for Cathy Eddowes and knew nothing of the mutilations in full. Godley spoke first.

"What mutilations did she suffer then?"

"Hideous injuries to her abdomen, but you'd guessed that, but she has ritualistic cuts to her face. They are either in the shape of the compass or the set square, however you choose look at them."

"What? You're trying to say they're Masonic symbols are you?" Abberline scowled dropping his head in an obvious cynical demeanour.

"No, I say nothing, Inspector."

"Some would say you are now making the mutterings of a fool or a lunatic, sir."

"Really, Inspector? Then answer me this, had she had her 'ears clipped off just for jolly'?" They all sat silently as Lees calmly finished his tea. The detectives had been stunned by this last statement and had not yet seen the body.

"How did you know that, Mr Lees?" asked Godley. Lees stood up.

"Gentlemen, please do not underestimate what I can do to help. Contact me when you have seen the body." He breezed out of the office, passing Kerby at the front counter and left in his waiting cab.

Abberline and Godley sat stunned for a couple of minutes before speaking, simply looking around the photographs, letters and statements in the office. They had begun to receive a lot of what could be immediately considered to be hoax mail.

"Fred, he knew about the letter."

"I know, George that bothers me. He knows so much. How the fuck, does he know so much?"

"He's got the Queen's ear. Maybe he does truly have a gift. I don't think the quip about fools or lunatics was wise."

"I know. Sorry, that was the whisky and that bastard Sir Charles talking having spited me at the weekend. Let's get down to the City's mortuary at Golden Lane and have a look. If it's true what he says then this fucker really is taking the piss out of us. Torn aprons, chalked on walls and letters."

"Fred, what's with the Masonic thing you mentioned?"

"Right, the chalking had the word 'Juwes'. That is not a misspelling that is this bastard trying to lay a second scent, a suspicion confirmed to me by this talk of the symbolic mutilations. He mentioned compasses and set squares, the principle images of freemasonry. The Juwes were three individuals who murdered Hiram Abiff in the Temple of Soloman and their names were Jubelo, Jubela and Jubelum hence the term 'Juwes' and they are the basis for Masonic ritual. We need to get down the mortuary and see if he's right."

They grabbed their top coats and hats and left the office having written a note on the chalk board as to where they were for anyone looking. As they left Godley made one final observation, "And the thing about the site of religious significance, that really got me."

"Mitre Square?"

"You got it, Fred. How the hell did he know that?"

* * *

'Christ!' thought Tumblety. He couldn't find the blood stained shirt he had left in his room at Batty Street and he still hadn't collected his bag from Gowers Walk. Mrs Long wasn't in so he'd have to try to trace the shirt later but he had to get that bag, he couldn't afford to let anyone else find it with his trophies. He'd decided to spend a few days dressing down like a local man to avoid attention which would also make it easy for him to rummage around the area when he eventually got to Gowers Walk to find his belongings. Only a few days on from the murders and the streets had returned to normal with street urchins playing in the gutter and on the pavements, men selling their wares and bustling traffic along the Commercial Road. As he neared Gowers Walk there was an organ grinder with his monkey making his way up into Central London. The beast aboard the organ being pushed by a tired looking grinder stared down with a heavy scowl at Tumblety. It gave the eerie appearance of a presiding magistrate delivering a stiff sentence. He walked south along Gowers Walk having turned in from the main road to find the street fairly deserted with just a few children running up and down along the cobbles. He could see the small alcove among the buildings as he progressed and as luck would have it there was no one close to it. He got to its mouth a turned to look down and spot the bag to find a pack of three street dogs around it sniffing intently with one frantically pawing at it and beginning to have some luck at getting it open driven by the scent of flesh inside.

"Get away from that, you bastards!" Tumblety shouted forgetting that he would immediately draw attention. The dogs persisted; looking around he found a broken broom handle. He grabbed it and began hitting the wretched animals to drive them away. The two smaller collie types ran off with tails between their legs yelping with the shock of the blows but he main dog attacking the bag was a dirty black and white German shepherd cross-bred dog who turned to retaliate at it's attacker. Tumblety tried to strike out with the stick but the dog caught it in its mouth pulling it out of his hand and becoming more enraged by his success and the persistent attack. Tumblety was forced to back off and as he did so he wrapped his coat around his left arm to use to defend himself if necessary. The dog slowly edged towards him with its head down looking up at him through the tops of his eyes and bearing its teeth making a low and menacing snarling sound. Knowing dogs well he knew this animal had little fear of him and in being so quiet no doubt possessed a high level of aggression and tenacity.

He desperately looked about him for something else he could use for defence let alone attack to retrieve his property but could see nothing of use. He continued backing off feeling that the mission to collect his bag was lost when he tumbled over a set of dustbins behind him and fell knocking them everywhere and releasing a deluge of rats running from them; all equally as stunned as him. The rats distracted the dog who sensed fresh game to be had and immediately chased off the largest of them catching it within a few bounds and beginning to crunch down on it very satisfied as the rat made a couple of futile squeals before dying. Tumblety lunged across the road for his bag which he successfully retrieved and ran off south away from some onlookers who had begun taking an interest in the commotion he had created. He ran through and alley way into the bottom end of Leman Street not seeing that the pavement at this point had a very restricted width. He lurched straight into the main carriageway to face an oncoming omnibus and receive a glancing blow to his left arm and shoulder as he desperately tried to avoid a collision. Tumblety was knocked back onto the narrow pavement; the bus driver unaware of what had happened and fell to floor clutching his arm having dropped the bag in the impact. He knew something was broken. Standing up, he grabbed the bag while in exceptional pain clutching his left arm with the right also now holding his precious luggage and made off north in Leman Street managing to then catch a bus back along Commercial Road getting off near Batty Street.

Walking back to number 22 close to collapse with the pain he could see Mrs Long on the door. 'Christ! The shirt,' was the thought that sprung into his mind. He approached her and she was immediately surprised by his mode of dress, a far cry from his normal military finery.

"'ere, what's with the working blokes get up then, you?"

"Mrs Long, you know how I said I wanted to reflect life here, it's just all part of it you see." He was sweating profusely with pain.

"What's wrong with your fuckin' arm then, en all?"

"Mrs Long, I have just had an accident, the victim of a careless omnibus driver. Please let me get to my room to rest."

"What's with that blood stained shirt in your room the night after the double murder then, mister?" Tumblety had a pause before replying.

"Mrs Long, you know that I am doctor by trade and occasionally I still practice. I was out that night when a man was attacked with a broken bottle in The Ten Bells pub. I stripped down to my shirt to administer some first aid and do some makeshift surgery to stem the blood flow. I saved the man's life, so please don't treat me as a murder suspect for Gods sake." She eyed him up suspiciously. He could tell she wasn't totally convinced but it seemed to placate her for now.

She let him pass and then he staggered grimacing with pain up to his room where he dropped the bag and collapsed onto the bed and very quickly passed out, breathing heavily with the physical exertion of the mornings events.

* * *

Robert Ford went into the Commercial Street Tavern that lunchtime and spoke to the barman to pass on his only piece of intelligence so far.

"He'll probably know, but Lusk lost a lot a face with Abberline for a second time the other night, some of the men are raising disquiet. He's all wind and no rain they say. But I'll tell you this; there is absolutely no Irish influence so far."

"Right ho, 'eres some wedge for you, keep your ear to the ground Littlechild says." Robert was compelled to mention one more thing.

"One other thing, I went to the Barnum show last night, loads of cowboys and Indians, Abberline had an American military button he found at a scene, don't know if it's worth looking at."

"I'll pass it on, lad. Take care now."

Robert walked out into the fresher feeling air of Commercial Street and looked south to where he used to see young Ralph selling his papers. He sadly reminisced at what a short time ago it was he and Del strolled the beat happily before this evil struck the area, when they readily won the trust of many of the local community. He now walked as a man apart from the societies he knew. He was segregated from his work friends by suspension and potential disgrace for having left his partner to indulge a personal vendetta, and in many respects he felt apart from the local community as he had to view almost all with suspicion. He made his way towards his lodgings to take the aging Bruiser out for a walk and to wait until dark to meet up with members of the Vigilance Committee at The Blind Beggar pub.

Mary Kelly, on the other hand, was at Millers Court lifting the floor boards to check that her stolen jewellery was still there safe and sound, her and Robert's future together. She pondered Tumbleby for some minutes. Was it co-incidental that all of those killed except for Martha had been good acquaintances of hers? Was he stalking her in the shadows about to strike at any moment getting closer and closer with each victim? She knew he had behavioural problems but could it run to murder? Had she known about the exact missing body parts of her friends she would have put the two issues together and told Robert immediately. She decided to take the jewels and hide them at Robert's lodging where she believed they would be safe until they left once the killer had been brought to justice.

She left Millers Court with a bag and passed a brooding looking man in Dorset Street who viewed her with obvious lust. A foreboding looking fellow only, she guessed, in his early twenties he sported a grand moustache and was reasonably smartly dressed but obviously a local working man. She walked on as Severin Klosowski eyed her up and down. Would she be one who plied the streets later? He hoped so, she would make a change to the wizened older women he had had to recently settle for. She may even be the noted 'Fair Emma.'

Meanwhile Abberline and Godley had arrived at the Golden Lane Mortuary in time to speak to Dr Gordon Brown who had completed his post mortem on Cathy Eddowes.

"Hello, Doc, mind if we take a quick look before we speak, sir"

"Help yourself, Inspector, but as you know it's not a pretty sight, especially now I've finished," said Brown wiping his hands having just washed them. They walked through to the examination table and threw back the cover over her body. The sight and the smell never got any better. Just like an abattoir or a butcher's shop, very cold with the scent of death and an air of surrealism not quite being able to come to terms with seeing human bodies cut wide open and empty inside like a hanging beef carcass. They both knew they would have to discuss the internal wounds in depth with Brown but could readily inspect the face, so prominently discussed with Lees and taunted about in the last Ripper letter.

Sure enough there on Eddowes' face were what looked like upturned 'V's on her cheeks and very similar cuts to her eyelids exactly as Lees had described, but also and most alarmingly the top parts of her ears were missing. Godley was outraged by the killer's cruel actions.

"Fuck it, Fred, fuck it! I can't believe he's fucking done IT!"

"I…." Abberline was shaking his head in disbelief, "I can't believe it me self. What is this bastard's game?"

"Quite obviously sick and ritualistic," said Brown.

"Doc, how do we stop man like this? How do we find him?"

"Inspector, he will find you. He will go too far in his efforts, take too long and expose himself. Each crime is worse than the one before so he has become more depraved. He will find you through his own failings." Abberline considered the doctor's words very carefully and spoke.

"I think I follow. Doctor, what were the other injuries, and is anything missing?"

"Well, the wound to the throat was almost standard, dare I say such a thing, for these crimes; down to the bone severing through all the major soft tissue and arteries. You've seen the extreme facial mutilations to the eyes, nose cheeks and ears especially, driven by what I don't know. The torso, well the front was laid open from the breast bone to the pubic area and from there it diverted to the right carrying on past the vagina to just past the rectum, the extent of this cut served no purpose for what was taken or damaged. The intestines had been largely detached and about two feet of the colon had been cut away. The left kidney had been removed and the left renal artery cut through and the care that this operation was done with indicated anatomical knowledge to me. The lining of the uterus was cut through and most of the womb along with that kidney had been removed. That is a very abridged version of what I found on Sunday, you'll have come to the inquest, today was just to confirm my findings. You do realise that no one knows these murders are taking place as the cut to the throat is so quick and deep that it gives no opportunity for the victim to cry out, Inspector?"

Abberline paused before replying, that notion had not occurred to him before and it did answer a lot of questions regarding the lack of witnesses.

"Doctor, do you believe that the killer has medical knowledge?"

"Inspector, basic mammalian anatomical knowledge is all that is required. One could get this from text books not just as a result of being within the medical profession. Don't make such suggestions in front of the coroner, although you are of course aware from the Chapman inquest that he believes there maybe a link between these murders and some American doctor offering money for specimens of uterus in London?"

"What do you know of that story, Doctor?" asked Godley, having not been present at the Chapman inquest, but knowing Abberline had been. Was his friend and colleague back into the habit of drinking, effecting him in simplest ways having not yet shared this information with him?

"Sergeant, all I know of it is this; there is a chap here who boasts of a collection of such viscera. I have never met him and only know of him through a friend in the United States who had written to me for advice regarding a friend of his who had this hideous collection and ranted on about a hatred of women. He wanted to know if he should take any action, obviously concerned about how his friend obtained and maintained such a collection. By the time I responded by letter he had sent me a telegram stating his friend had travelled to England."

"Who is your friend? More importantly, who is this other individual?"

"Well, he wouldn't name him through a sense of discretion, but the third party is a lawyer called Colonel C.A Dunham."

"Thank you, Doctor, we shall be in touch," said Abberline turning on his heels and leaving the mortuary with no word to Godley who nodded to Brown and followed Abberline out.

Outside he spoke to his friend concerned about the information he had heard discussed at the Chapman inquest.

"Fred, did you know that stuff about the American Doctor then?"

"George, with three murders having taken place at that point and only two with mutilations; I didn't give it a lot of credence. But, following this weekends events we must pursue it as a serious line."

"Sorry, mate a fair point. But you could have told me."

They were both beginning to feel a massive amount of pressure weighing on them following the 'double event'. They walked into Golden Lane which then led them into the main thoroughfare of Old Street where Godley waved down a smart looking cab.

"Gentlemen, where to," said the driver looking at Godley.

"Commercial Street nick please, driver." The driver then looked at Abberline, instantly recognising him.

"Mr Abberline, ain't it?" He said as the police inspector entered the cab.

"Yes, it is. And you might be?"

"John Netley, carriage driver. I am actually just helping a mate me self today. Normally I'm driving a carriage, often for the Royal Mews you know."

"Really, how do you know me then?"

"Your famous, guv'nor, aren't ya. You're the bloke who's going to catch Jack the Ripper. I could help you know."

"Oh, yeah," sighed Abberline cynically, looking at Godley, "How's that then?"

"Well, I've done a bit of training to be a doctor me self, see. I drive a carriage, I could come round with you, driving you like, and then help with the pest mortem and help with motive ideas and things, see."

"You mean post mortem, don't you?"

"Well, yeah. I know all about how the body works."

"I'll bet you do. Tell you what, when you drop us off, give me your card and we may well think about it," suggested Abberline.

"Yeah, lovely, I'll do that, ta."

Godley and Abberline looked at each other with obvious cynicism and watched the world go by on the rest of their journey while Netley gabbled on about which surgeons he had carried and who was who in the Royal family. After a while they did listen intently just to see if there was any value in his conversation.

Chapter Sixteen

Wednesday 9th October 11.a.m; Tumblety was very pleased with himself despite sporting a sling for his damaged arm, he left Cootes Bank in The Strand having secured a £2000 loan for himself all of which he had as cash in a leather brief case. He returned to the Ritz immediately by cab having been absent from there for a week and settled his outstanding bill, much to the satisfaction of the management. An extra bribe ensured they disposed of all traces of his stay. He had kept the cab on outside driven by a man who appeared very keen to please especially when he had asked Tumblety about his profession. Named Netley, he boasted of his own medical prowess and how he had influence with the Royal family, the medical profession an even the police. This man, kept within his employ for a small retainer could be a valuable asset.

An hour later arriving at Batty Street he asked Netley to stop in Commercial Road while he walked down to attend to his business.

Since his return injured to the lodgings he had persistently been eyed with suspicion by Mrs Long and now felt it was time to make good a move to elsewhere with his new funds. He opened the door to be immediately confronted by his irritating land lady.

"Moving out yet, are you, mister?"

"Actually, Mrs Long, I am which will be good news for you and great news for me."

"Listen, I've spoken to my friend Mrs Diemschutz about you. She says I should have called the coppers by now. She says **a foreign bleeder** like you is probably Jack the Ripper, specially with that blood stained shirt. What you got to say to that then, eh?" He approached her, arm in sling, but still in a menacing fashion which made her cower and swallow hard, lowering her head.

"Well I'll tell you this. If was Jack the Ripper do you think I'd let you live for over a week since you first pestered me about my laundry, incidentally soiled innocently, eh?" She paused before replying, with his 5'11" frame now towering over her.

"S'pose not, really. Ya gonna pay me ain't you?" She held her breath as he reached into his pocket. He pulled out some crisp fresh English banknotes for her, guessing a healthy bribe would buy her silence.

"Have you still got my shirt?"

"Nah, couldn't get it clean again. Chucked it."

"Will that cover my arrears, Mrs Long?"

"Er, yes, sir, very much."

"Good," he then held the handle of his cane up to the side of her face. "Excellent in fact. Now don't ever threaten me in anyway again. I promise I'd be back for you before you'd find they get to me, you piece of East End crap."

She sobbed with fear as he collected all his belongings and made his way from the house, throwing her the key and wishing her a 'good day, mam'. When he was gone it took her some time to regain her composure. The traces of the mysterious lodger would lie heavy on her mind for sometime. She retired to her kitchen and began sorting through a pile of dirty bed clothes, amongst which she knew full well she had thrown the shirt.

* * *

Regents Park 1.p.m and a prestigious gathering was taking place of police and home office staff and dignitaries. So much pressure was mounting on the establishment action had to be taken to try to employ new methods to help in detection and bring about a swift resolution to the Ripper case. To this end a trial of bloodhounds was taking place being show cased by the Commissioner himself Sir Charles Warren in the hope that should another murder take place they could be brought in to follow off a fresh scent and catch the killer. Barnaby and Burgho had been brought to London by their noted breeder Mr Brough from

Scarborough and he stood proudly with them slightly separate from the main crowd where Sir Charles was preparing a scent trail for them to attempt. Superintendent Arnold stood within the crowd along with Major Henry Smith, Henry Matthews the Home Secretary, Dr Robert Anderson the head of the Metropolitan C.I.D and a dozen other police inspectors, sergeants and civil servants. The press too had been allowed to gather on a minimal basis to report the event to bring back some public confidence and highlight the efforts being made in the hunt for Jack the Ripper. Will Bates attended as reporter for The Star being prepared with great enthusiasm for another bumbling police failure. The afternoon's weather was closing in on a particularly dark and cloudy basis and a mist or light fog was beginning to rise.

The first hour was spent with Sir Charles initially setting simplistic scent trails. Meat to be traced by the dogs, then clothing and then a person, with the dogs being given a scent of their clothing as a lure to commence. Bates looked on cynically watching these somewhat simplistic tests before the entire crowd was offered tea and cake at the open air theatre café within the Queen Mary's Gardens part of the park within the inner circle. The general socialising and back slapping session of their tests so far was taking sometime and the increasingly bored Bates decided to tackle Superintendent Arnold on the subject.

"Tell me, sir, how do you propose to catch the killer with these dogs then, eh?" He got his note book ready to record the interview.

"Well, Mr Bates, we shall take the dogs to any scene at the earliest possible opportunity and allow them to detect a scent from the victim or the general immediate area of the crime, be it murder or assault and then follow it off accordingly. Sir Charles with his varied career experience in the past and having observed the use of these hounds ensures us that it is the most efficient course of action."

"I see. And do you believe him?"

"Of course I do! Sir Charles has taken on the duties of Commissioner at one of the most difficult times in London. Fenian terror activity, social unrest in the East End and now the murders, if a man who is tackling all these issues says the dogs are our best hope, then I believe him."

"But the last Fenian attack was the year before he became Commissioner, can't credit him with that."

"On the contrary, Mr Bates, perhaps it's down to his use of resources that there have been no more attacks."

"And the formation of a 'Special Branch' within the police, eh?"

"There's no such thing, and if there were I couldn't comment."

"What's going on here, Tom?" Sir Charles himself interjected having begun to overhear the increasingly heated conversation.

"Mr Bates here from The Star is de-crying the use of the dogs, sir."

"Really, in what way then, Mr Bates?"

"Haven't seen them track at a proper long distance yet, Sir Charles."

"Right, then, teas gone on long enough, we'll see to this, I shall conduct the experiment myself."

Everyone left the confines of the theatre café to find that beyond the Inner Circle of the park encouraged by a drop in the temperature through the afternoon and the proximity of the boating lake the light fog had thickened.

"Right, then," said Sir Charles, "ladies toilets just over there. I shall go in and rub my jacket well around the basins and towels and then Mr Brough can set the dogs to work on a proper man hunt. Ensure you allow me at least ten minutes before you start and we'll prove their worth." At this point the dogs were asleep on the café floor and the muttering amongst the sergeants and inspectors was 'no change there, the Boss rubbing himself in the ladies bogs.'

Bates keenly watched the Commissioner enter and a few minutes later exit the toilets and make off to the foggy north of the park; the direction of the zoo, probably not a great idea but Sir Charles knew best. As soon as the requisite ten minutes had gone by the dogs, fortunately now awake, were taken into the ladies toilets by Mr Brough and allowed a chance for a good sniff round, both keenly picking up a scent from the affected surfaces. He released the dogs from their leads leaving the building and they began trotting off, Bates observed that they headed in exactly the right direction. A promising start.

Sir Charles got himself to the south edge of the zoo passing both an enclosure for the wolves and one further along it's perimeter for baboons. Reaching the Outer Circle he turned southbound and arrived at Winfield house where he waited in the porch.

The speed at which the dogs were picking up the track was impressive to all gathered, but all struggled to keep up with their trot across the open ground of Regents Park. By the time they got to the southern edge of the zoo, for a period the track was of no consequence to Barnaby and Burgho who entered into aggressive banter with the wolves who were incensed in their enclosure by the proximity of the dogs. The enraged bloodhounds eventually vented their anger at the wolves by fighting with each other as the wolves fell silent watching and wagging their tales slowly at the spectacle. Mr Brough and some of the sergeants got them separated at some personal cost and they were placed on individual leads to calm down.

They passed the baboon enclosure; the primates in turn erupted into aggression. The males beginning to destroy loose sections of their enclosure 'furniture' in a show of strength to the hounds, who reciprocally played up with their owners and having passed the enclosure reached the Outer Circle and lost the scent completely. Some minutes had to pass until both dogs again became animated with a scent and began to follow it. Unfortunately Burgho went north away from Winfield House while Barnaby picked the correct trail to the south.

Burgho eventually found out a courting couple in the bushes near Gloucester Gate, the lady had been wearing exceptionally strong Cologne she had sprayed in the café toilets earlier. Sir Charles having got prematurely bored left Winfield House and headed off back into the depths of the park. Barnaby picking up so keen a scent, and now far from the zoo and his brother, was let from the lead again and suddenly took a sprint off into the mists of the parkland. Losing sight of the animal Mr Brough called repeatedly to the dog to no avail. Having given chase the gathered crowd moved around in silence for quite some time until they all heard what was initially a chilling cry;

"You bastard hound get back, get back….argh!" followed by a brief dog snarl and then only the cry of Sir Charles Warren as the dog bit him once and then circled him howling and snapping waiting to do more. The chuckling Bates turned to Arnold.

"Well, I think we'll mark that down as eventually successful, despite both of them getting lost in the fog."

For the time being it was decided to keep them on in London as a police resource for the Ripper case.

* * *

Simultaneously that afternoon the funeral of Del Lake was taking place on a low key basis at the City of London Cemetery in Aldersbrook Road, Wanstead. Due to the massive need for manpower on the streets of Whitechapel, more officers had been drafted in from the outer districts to cover patrols within the Ripper's apparent area to allow officers from Commercial Street and the rest of 'H' division to attend Lake's funeral. Suspended from duty as far as everyone knew, it hurt Robert Ford to not be allowed under Superintendent Arnold's orders to be part of the bearer party for his friend. At least Arnold was elsewhere this afternoon so there was no chance of the increasingly grief stricken Ford of retaliating. He didn't begrudge the other choices, they were good men, such as Inspector Spratling leading the party, Sergeant Kerby, Taffy Evans, Jonas Mizen, John Thain, Johnny Neil and a new constable called Bobby Spicer, who in truth was taking Ford's place. Abberline was there with Bill Murphy. Mary was there with Ford to offer her support and as a mark of respect to Del Lake who she knew well from his presence in the area as a local copper. There was about fifty-five to sixty other uniform officers from 'H' division in attendance, some who knew Del well, some as a remark of respect and symbol of police solidarity. Chief Inspector Littlechild looked on at the proceedings from a distance, not in distrust of Ford but to see if the low key funeral of a local officer brought anyone significant to his department's remit out into the open.

It surprised both him and Ford when George Lusk turned up, although commendably on his own without the usual mob in tow and very smartly dressed. All things considered he was a local business leader so he was in truth not an unusual member of the community to attend. Abberline eyed him suspiciously wondering if he was out to regain some face within his mob by showing unity with the police in a 'common cause'. He would address him later at the wake at 'The Three Rabbits' public house in Romford Road, Manor Park. With the difficult circumstances of Del's death no one had been asked to deliver a eulogy, although Del's brother would be doing a reading, so only the priest's words and the formal service would be heard.

For Mary Kelly it was an increasingly all too familiar ritual. She had been to four funerals in the last six weeks, more than she had ever been to in her life; Cathy Eddowes had been buried the day before at the nearby Little Ilford cemetery, Liz Stride had been buried during the previous week, on the 14th September Annie Chapman had also been buried in Manor park and before that at Little Ilford on the 6th September Polly Nicholls had been laid to rest. All of them her friends and as she had highlighted to Robert, but why were they killed?

No church service, the service of remembrance for Lake was held at one of the chapels at the cemetery. The gathered congregation all sat in silence with organ music playing gently in the background as they waited for the service to commence. In the last few minutes before the coffin arrived from the undertakers by horse drawn hearse, the members of Del's family arrived; two younger sisters, a brother and their mother, a smart and proud woman in her late fifties. They walked down the aisle of the chapel and sat at the front, the sisters sobbing with the brother and mother seemingly composed. Everyone heard the doors open one more time and the organ changed its tune to the funeral march signifying the entrance of the priest and the bearer party. With the change of music everyone had stood up and a chill ran down Robert's spine and tears began to roll down his cheeks as he turned to see the coffin passing with the sombre faced members of the bearer party slowing marching Del on his final journey. He looked around the gathered congregation to see many different reactions; Mary was crying silently, Abberline was stone faced and unemotional, Bill Murphy gently wiped a tear from his eye, the Lake sisters sobbed and Mrs Lake and the brother still kept their solemn composure. The slow march down to the front of the chapel to then place the coffin on trestles under the direction of Inspector Spratling, who was carrying Del's beat duty helmet, seemed to take an eternity until it was finally resting serenely at the front of the congregation. Spratling placed the helmet upon the coffin and the bearer party took their seats at the rear of the chapel marching smartly in step back along the aisle.

The priest, Father James Donald, the priest from Christchurch in Commercial Street who dealt with police spiritual needs in Whitechapel took to the lectern, opened his bible and began to speak.

"Good afternoon, to you all. We are here today to celebrate the life and passing of our dear colleague, friend, son and brother Derek Lake. Let us start by first of all singing hymn number 706 in your books in front of you 'The Lord is my Shepherd.'" Everyone stood and thumbed through the hymn books laid out in front of them as the organ began the introductory bars of music. Father Donald led the singing at the appropriate note, his voice booming and rich to try to lift everyone as their singing took on initial sombre quality. It took a couple of minutes to sing the hymn through before the congregation then sat again and the priest completed a first reading.

"Dearly beloved the first reading I give to you is from the first letter of St Paul to the Thessalonians; we shall stay with the Lord for ever.

'We want you to be quite certain, brothers, about those who have died, to make quite sure that you do not grieve about them, like other people who have no hope. We believe that Jesus died and rose again, and that it will be the same for those who have died in Jesus: God will bring them with him. We can tell you this from the Lord's own teaching, that any of us who are left alive until the Lord's coming will not have any advantage over those who have died. At the trumpet of God, the voice of the archangel will call out the command and the Lord himself will come down from heaven; those who have died in Christ will be the first to rise, and then those of us who are still alive will be taken up in the clouds, together with them, to meet the Lord in the air. So we shall stay with the Lord for ever. With such thoughts like these you should comfort one another.' This is the word of the Lord"

Still Mrs Lake and Del's brother sat silent, around the chapel there was some faint sobbing, tears were rolling heavily from Robert's eyes. A prayer followed dedicated to Del and all policemen doing their duty in the face of great danger then based on his interactions with the Lake family Father Donald spoke of him.

"Today we mourn the passing of Derek and celebrate his short but rich life. It is sad to lose a young man so in his prime in his early twenties but Derek or Del died in the service of the job he loved greatly, protecting the public and catching wrong-doers. He was highly regarded by peers, senior officers and his community, a testament to this is the police turnout and I thank Mr George Lusk for his presence and for his major contribution to these proceedings. His beloved family sit here sad that he is gone but grateful for his life and comforted by the knowledge he sits at the Lord's side waiting for them to one day all be re-united, as do dear friends both in and outside of the police force. His brother, Bert, has asked to complete a reading in dedication to Del and one he knew was Del's favourite from their time at Sunday teachings together. Bert, Please join me." Bert got to his feet and took his place at the lectern as the priest stepped to one side.

"This is from John 14: 1-6, There are many rooms in my fathers House." He coughed to clear his throat and paused looking around before starting.

"Jesus said to his disciples 'Do not let your hearts be troubled Trust in God still, and trust in me. There are many rooms in my Fathers house; if there were not, I should have told you. I am going to prepare a place for you, and after I have gone and prepared you a place, I shall return to take you with me; so that where I am you may be too. You know the way to the place where I am going.' Thomas said 'Lord, we do not know where you are going, so how can we know the way?' Jesus said 'I am the Way, the Truth and the Life; No one can come to the Father except through me.' This is the Gospel of the Lord." Quietly and with great composure Bert took his seat.

Father Donald returned to the lectern and led the congregation in the Lord's Prayer. When they finished the bearer party got up and again under the supervision of Inspector Spratling they lifted the coffin, the trestles were moved and the priest led them out, Spratling leading carrying the beat duty helmet that had been on the top of the coffin, the bearer party and the mourners joined on to form a procession behind which filed out following all the way to graveside for the burial.

It was ultimately at the graveside under the final religious rights that Mrs Lake and Bert were both over come by emotion and sobbed heavily, all four of the family members present holding each other. Robert stood with tears streaming down his face as did Mary who stood next to him clutching his hand tightly. There were virtually no dry eyes except for those of Abberline and Lusk. The family all cast earth into the grave using a small trowel left by the side for just this purpose, as did a few closer friends including Robert. He spoke as he did so, his voice breaking with emotion.

"I shall miss you so much, mucker. If I could trade with you and change it all I would. I am so sorry, mate." Mary put her arm round him and led him away following the stream of people as they walked off from the cemetery in the direction of Rabbits Road and the wake at the pub.

Abberline caught up with Lusk and walked with him.

"All right, Mr Lusk, no fights today, what brings you here then?"

"Abberline, for all my dislike of the way the police are handling this case, I still respect the job the lowly constable does, especially one so dangerous and pioneering. It was for the likes of me and my community, for that I can salute that individual as a community leader and be philanthropic if I wish. Fair enough?"

"Yes, fair enough, but keep your men out of the way of the police investigation. We will get him, and I can assure you that if I do, personally that is, I will happily tie the noose and pull the trap door lever without hesitation. Lusk, don't forget this is my community too."

"Then think about how to give them a sense of hope then, Abberline, they need to believe in you again." Lusk broke away from Abberline by quickening his walk to catch up with the Lake family.

Inside The Three Rabbits pub Robert could bring himself to do nothing except prop up the bar with Mary sitting quietly beside him on a bar chair. He was staring into his pint of beer as he felt a tap on his shoulder. He turned to see Bert Lake stood tearfully in front of him swallowing hard to speak.

"Rob, what happened? Just tell me what went so wrong, eh?"

"I left him," Robert stared into space tearfully "just for a few minutes it seemed I left him. When I found him he was gone."

"But why, mate? WHY!"

"Because a local boy had been murdered and thought I had a lead. I messed up. But I tell you this, if I find who did it, I'll kill them."

"That won't bring him back." Bert stared in him in the eye for a few seconds and walked away. Robert watched him return to a table with his family where Lusk was chatting with them; as he sat down Mrs Lake got up and came over to him. He prepared for the worst.

"Robert, he loved you, you know, like a brother. I know you didn't mean to leave him, I've known you too long for that from meeting you and from what Del used to tell us. I believe you would only do it for good reason, but promise this, you'll get the man who did this to the gallows."

"Yes, Mrs Lake I will, I promise you and him that."

Late afternoon Robert and Mary left the wake following on from most of the others from the police community. Abberline had already gone but most of the bearer party were still getting drunk and all of Del's family were still there still engaged in conversation with Lusk. Walking into the Romford Road they headed west with the intention to take the cooler air for a while before hailing a cab back to Whitechapel. A carriage drew alongside them, the door opened and leaning out Littlechild spoke.

"Get in, you on your own, not with her."

"No fucking way, where I go she goes, Guv'nor, like it or not." Littlechild was taken aback by this forthrightness but didn't want to loiter.

"All right, get in both of you, quickly." Robert helped Mary in then jumped up briskly himself as the carriage pulled off with the door slamming itself shut with the motion.

"Right then, who was there and who is she?"

"This is Mary Kelly a local girl, and my girlfriend, she's to be trusted right? Lusk was there, Abberline and Murphy from the murder team, loads of the uniform boys, Del's family and a few others."

"Lusk, eh? Who did he associate with?"

"Abberline and the Lakes."

"All right, any Irish there?"

"Couple of coppers, Taffy Evans, he's an Irishman that couldn't swim."

"Very funny. Where do you want to go?"

"Well, back to Whitechapel."

"Right, get in The Blind Beggar tonight with her, she's good cover, and see what's going on with Lusk's mob. Don't report anything until you got something decent, know what I mean?"

"All right, Guv. I need some money please."

"Here's £20. MAKE IT LAST!"

Littlechild stopped the carriage in Stratford to avoid being seen letting them out in Whitechapel where he didn't wish for people police or otherwise to notice his presence.

* * *

6.p.m. and Godley walked into the foyer of the Lyceum theatre.

"I'm sorry we're closed, sir," said an effeminate male member of the front of house staff, "doors open at 7.15, sir." Godley held up his warrant card.

"Detective Sergeant Godley, of Scotland Yard. I need to speak to Mr Mansfield please."

"I don't know about that, officer, he's preparing for his performance."

"Right, tell him the police are here regarding the Whitechapel murders, and he can either have a polite conversation with me here now or I'll drag him and you down to Commercial Street nick and do this very formally. Now do you want to warn the understudy or let me in?" The steward bent his head uneasily to one side and said "This way, sir."

They arrived outside a dressing room with garish star on the door and the steward knocked lightly. There was an American voiced response.

"Will you fuck off, at this time I am preparing." Godley pushed the steward to one side and opened the door bowling into the room and holding up his warrant card for Mansfield to see.

"Detective Sergeant Godley, Scotland Yard. I need to ask you some simple questions, Mr Mansfield."

"Oh, yeah? Get a fucking warrant and I'll get my lawyer, cop."

"Sir, please don't take that line with me or there'll be no show tonight. Some simple questions for just a few minutes." Mansfield stood up looking confrontational. He was thirty-four, with thinning hair and a square jaw. He stood silent, considering his options and his somewhat brash words. He offered Godley a seat and sat back down again himself.

"Bourbon, officer?"

"No thank you, sir, I'm on duty. How long has your show been on, sir?"

"Well, bizarrely since just before the second murder."

"Honest, that's good. You have a reputation of being the best in the world in the transformation of one person to another. Is it purely physical?"

Whitechapel

"Well, as with all acting you have to put yourself into a mind set beyond your own and become the person you wish to portray to make it convincing. But I don't carry that away from here with me."

"If I gave you dates, would you be able to tell me where you were for us to eliminate you from our inquiries?"

"Why am I in you enquiries anyway?"

"It has been suggested to us that the murders have been committed by a man with two natures, as does your 'Jekyll and Hyde'."

"Oh, come on. This is a theatrical character not real life."

"But it could occur in real life?"

"Sergeant, yes the play is about the dark side of human nature. That's it. Don't accuse me of murder because I have theatrical talent. If it gets you off my back, come back with your dates, but at my convenience. Now good day to you, I have a play to prepare for."

"Fair enough, Mr Mansfield, we'll meet later. Thank you for your time."

Godley left the theatre via the foyer again to be spotted by Will Bates who was collecting complementary tickets for a performance for The Star to review. The presence of the police aroused his journalistic nature and he felt a headline already emerging.

That evening witnessed a low key gathering of the Vigilance Committee at The Blind Beggar with Lusk actually discussing with his gathered members rationally the important role of the policemen on the beat in the area but the misdirection of the investigation by sources, in fact, beyond the well known Abberline. He urged his members to keep patrols low key and if they witnessed any unlawful actions to keep watch and find a policeman to keep them within the law. Robert listened intently and chatted with Mary from time to time over what Lusk was discussing who responded in her broad Limerick accent. It was this that attracted the attention of a stranger they had not seen before in the pub.

"Couldn't help but hear a welcome accent," said a short thick set stranger in a strong Ulster accent. "It maybe over the boarder but at least it's close to home. My name is Sean Miller; may I ask who you and your fella are?" Mary and Robert looked at each other and he gave her an encouraging look before she decided to respond.

"Mary Kelly, and this is my fiancé Robert Ford," they all shook hands vigorously in a friendly manner.

"What brings you here, Mr Miller?" asked Robert casually.

"Been labouring over here for a while but just moved into the area so trying to find a friendly pub and social group. What do you make of this vigilance thing?"

"Seems like people power at work," said Robert "but thuggery must not see out the rule of law."

"Aye depends if you think if the police are on your side or just a pawn of the government." A very political response to a stranger felt Robert.

"Don't know about your neck of the woods, mate, but over here we police by the consent of society." Miller laughed in a friendly manner.

"Good point, Robert. Now what are you both drinking, eh?" They whiled away the evening discussing politics within the echo of Lusk addressing those gathered in the pub; Robert wary of the fact that this could be Fenians trying to infiltrate.

Elsewhere in the pub John Netley listened intently to Lusk and his suggestions to improve police community relations and make effective use of the Vigilance Committee in conjunction with the police. Being the idle gossip that he was and always keen to pass on his slant on the world to his clients he stored away all he heard to brag to others in the vein attempt he always made to improve his credibility. As the evening went on he lost concentration on the subject through his alcohol consumption to the point that the landlord actually refused to serve him. He staggered into the gentlemen's toilets and fell asleep as he knelt in a cubicle having vomited heavily into the bowl.

Chapter Seventeen

Friday 11th October 8.p.m; the Masonic Hall, Great Queen Street, West Central London and a gathering of a group of unusually linked freemasons had been called by the Grand Inspector General, The Duke of Kent. They had one purpose; to discuss the Jack the Ripper murders. The gathering was not large but highly significant and took place away from any Temples within the halls in a private committee room, away from the earshot of those it did not concern. The Duke chaired the meeting with the following individuals present: the Prime Minister Mr William Gladstone, Sir Charles Warren, Major Henry Smith, the Home Secretary Mr Henry Matthews, the Queens Physician Sir William Gull, Dr Wynne Baxter the London Coroner and George Lusk. The Duke stood up at the head of the table addressing everyone and began the meeting.

"Gentlemen, we gather here today in advance of an impending constitutional crisis the like of which we have never seen potentially rising from some isolated area and its people. We know that the Queen has been concerned with slum conditions for many years and the potential for social unrest it can harbour. Now we have concentrated in one part of the Metropolis not only slum conditions but civil unrest brewing as a result of series of grisly murders with little apparent motivation or sign of abating with two occurring in one night. You all have your role in resolving this and all have responsibility for the failings within society that fuel this. Lusk, I shall start with you. What was this foolish notion to try to take the law into the hands of a group of thugs and undermine the natural authority of the police?" All eyes focused on Lusk and he moved uncomfortably in his seat and took a deep breath before rising to speak.

"I can only apologise for my conduct. I was wrong to do such a thing forming effectively a mob and should have offered simple vigilance by the local community to assist the police."

"So, what are you going to do now to resolve this mess you have created, this divide that some must see within the East End that you have driven between police and community," demanded the Duke.

"I shall call a meeting of the Vigilance Committee and offer a new approach supporting the police, a process that I have in fact already touched upon and further enforcing it I hope will reduce tension."

"Good," said the Duke. "All right, before we talk about police resources I wish to call upon Sir William to speak about what may motivate these murders and how that may effect the policing of this matter."

Sir William Gull unsteadily and slowly got to his feet as Lusk sat back down. A man of seventy-two, he had suffered a stroke the year before which had left him partially paralysed along his right side; but his mind was as sharp as it ever had been and he had some strong views on these crimes.

"Brethren," addressing the group on a Masonic basis, "I have observed these ghastly events with great interest over the entire period upon which they have occurred because homicide is not a natural human act. It is driven by an unbalanced and irrational emotional state fuelled by trauma in an individuals life or and imbalance of chemicals within the working of the brain that reverses the sense of right and wrong within that persons mind, this must be especially so when such horrors are committed. The police must therefore seek out a man who has been so badly wronged and seeking revenge that he is driven to act in such a manner; or a man who has undergone this chemical change within his brain, something that at face value would be impossible to detect. But of course, a new theory I have developed since these murders have taken place is one that follows on further from the one involving chemical imbalances. This 'Jack the Ripper' taunts us with letters and mutilates women for no apparent reason but to steal parts of their bodies for reasons we cannot fathom, so sick as to be beyond the comprehension of normal men. He kills in a succession or series, always striking the same way with, importantly, the same victims; and we cannot say if he will ever stop of his own accord so we must catch him. I am developing a theory called the 'succession' or 'serial' murderer as this truly is a freak occurrence, yet if we can understand it we maybe able to stop him or prevent it in the future.

"I must complement the police in their innovative and yet ultimately tragic use of the officer in disguise. You are unwittingly playing into this man's mind, unwittingly understanding how he operates so trying to entice him to play what he may see as his game. I have to advocate that this could be the only way to come close to catching this man, highly dangerous but ultimately the only way to resolve these repulsive crimes." He sat, wiping his slightly moist brow the result of standing and talking in his now generally weakened condition.

Remaining seated Gladstone asked a very un-Victorian question.

"Sir William, tell me you talk in the masculine all the time regarding these crimes. Is not a possibility that this 'Jack' is indeed 'Jill' and sends letters in the masculine to fool us, so the police never look upon women as potential suspects?" Gull remained seated but replied academically.

"A very valid point, Prime Minister, but personally flawed for several reasons. First off, women do not train in medicine or butchery and therefore would be unlikely to have the at least basic anatomical knowledge this individual has. Second, few women possess the physical strength that is required to conduct these unspeakable acts with the speed and ferocity in which they are conducted. Thirdly, my years of medical research with the mentally ill and dissections of the dead have led me to believe that the lobes within the brains of men and women work differently with different chemical balances, and I frankly don't think women are capable of such acts."

"Thank you Sir William," said the Duke, "now I would like to call upon Sir Charles to talk about the future strategy of the police."

Sir Charles Warren, tall and thin with his large droopy Victorian moustache and spectacled face stood nervously to address the group.

"Brothers, I am feeling the pressure of what has become an onerous task being the Commissioner of the Metropolitan force at this time. I will tell you now that if the Ripper strikes once more I shall tender my resignation. However, I shall move the service forward thus; we will keep the uniform patrols at their current doubled levels, increased plain patrols by half and re-employ a limited number of decoys but highly supervised. I will ensure a closer relationship with the community by the use of occasional police briefings publicly for the local people to know about any progress."

"Is there any progress, Commissioner?" asked Henry Matthews the Home Secretary. Warren was forced to pause and swallow hard.

"No, too many conflicting descriptions, most witnesses are drunk and no one has ever even heard an attack taking place. All we know is that he is always striking at old toms."

"This is exactly my point, you must maintain a vigil on the unfortunates, you see. Dress decoys up as them," interjected Gull.

"Decoys are dangerous, but if we must persist then as I said we will."

"And what about Abberline, here we are two months on from Tabrum and we have no result," continued Matthews.

"I dislike him, he is disrespectful and common, but he is a good detective by reputation and he has the support of his men and the community, so I am compelled to leave him in charge on the ground."

A steward arrived with a tray of large brandy glasses all generously filled with brandy and a box of expensive cigars. Wynne Baxter noticed their arrival and as Warren sat and before the Duke could stand he stood up himself to address the group.

"I sense that we are drawing to a close on today's business, but before we do there is a crucial observation I must make. At the Chapman inquest I passed on a snippet of information that I had heard within the medical circle. It may be poppycock fuelled by the crimes for no reason at all and spread as an old wives tale, I just don't know, but Sir Charles you must compel Abberline to act on it. I have heard that there is an American in London, doctor or otherwise who it is claimed is paying money for examples of female uteri. If this is true it is an obvious motivation for some sick and misguided killer, please look into this matter and let me know for my own peace of mind."

"Certainly, Mr Coroner sir, I will," Warren replied respectfully with the coroner's court being the highest court in the land.

"Now, brethren," said the Duke, "let us enjoy a brandy and a quality smoke and discuss more 'off duty' issues, eh?" The gathered crowd chanted a uniformed 'here, here' and helped themselves to what was on the tray.

* * *

Sunday 13th October and the next round of decoy patrols began. Abberline had felt no choice but to re-introduce them as a result of the double event without any pressure from above, although he had been summoned to meet Commissioner Warren and Superintendent Arnold the next morning. Two more experience detective sergeants had been drafted in to conduct the next round of operations, one named Robinson who walked out in full female costume but including a veil this time, with the other, Mather, in regular plain clothes. The evening's events for the pair were really not very encouraging as a result of one incident. They had a man under observation acting in a strange manner with a woman who was an obvious common prostitute. The suspect was a well dressed man wearing a bowler hat, suit, smart shoes and carrying a Gladstone type bag. The officers were concerned this may conceal the implements for wrong doing. Keeping their distance they were approached by a passing cab washer named William Jarvis concerned at their voyeurism who challenged them.

"Wot ya doing muckin' about 'ere for?" Presenting his warrant card Mather replied to the challenge.

"Detective Sergeant Mather, Scotland Yard C.I.D, fuck off and leave us to do our job, he might be the Ripper over there."

"Oh, a rozzer,eh? He a rozzer too?" He lifted Robinson's veil to see it was a man underneath. "Sick bastards!" and punched Robinson in the face. A considerable melee ensued as they arrested Jarvis for assault on police and interfering with an official investigation. They lost sight of the couple who made off on hearing their ruckus never to be seen again. Not a good result and Abberline wouldn't get to hear about it until he had seen Sir Charles.

Meanwhile on the advice of John Netley, Tumblety had found himself smart new lodgings in Graham Road in Hackney which allowed him to be comfortably in distance of Whitechapel, but he was forced not to act as a result of his injury. He had heard from Netley of a new co-operation developing between the police and the Vigilance Committee in Whitechapel a matter which concerned him. There was only one way to fuel further unrest and dissent and that was to write to Lusk directly and shock him deeply. He opened the murderous bag he carried so frequently with him and looked at the jars of specimens from his last foray a fortnight earlier. The idea struck him instantly and with the gift of ambidexterity he sat down at the desk in his room to write another chilling letter albeit in not as good a handwriting and with no red ink left to use. He marked it from a chilling address.

> From hell
> Mr Lusk
> Sir
> I send you half the
> Kidne I took from one woman
> Preserved it for you, tother piece I
> Fried and ate it was very nise. I
> May send you the bloody knife that
> Took it out if you only wate a whil
> Longer.
> signed Catch me when
> you can
> Mishter Lusk

As a well known local community leader it was very easy to know where to send the letter and a parcel too and adding the hint of cannibalism was designed to shock and outrage the staid Victorian society even further. He picked out the specimen jar that contained the kidney he had removed from Cathy Eddowes and opened the lid allowing the smell of formaldehyde to emanate from it into the room. Using a set of surgical tweezers he lifted it out of the jar and placed it on the desk and then swapped the tweezers for a large surgical knife, the one he most commonly used the Listern, and cut it longitudinally in half. It oozed stale blood as he did so and placed half of it with part of the renal artery attached in a small cardboard box and folded the letter up placing it on top of the kidney and closed and sealed up the gruesome package.

He addressed the box and satisfied with his work tidied away the mess he had created and placed the other half of the kidney back in the jar. In so doing with his cannibalistic comment in the letter he paused as he replaced the lid wondering how it would taste, after all lambs kidney was rather tasty....

* * *

The Sunday evening performance at the Lyceum theatre of Robert Louis Stevenson's 'Jekyll and Hyde' was under way with the audience in virtual trance by the mesmerising evil and convincingly transformed Mr Hyde portrayed Richard Mansfield. The rest of the cast, including the noted Agnes Carew and Gabriel Utterson, despite sterling performances, were overshadowed by the masterful and terrifying Mansfield. It was during the transformation scene in the second act that it occurred to Will Bates in the audience exactly why Godley must have been there days earlier. The play was built around the premise that every human being has a demon imprisoned within them and that the right concoction of chemicals could release it on society to gorge itself in an orgy of debauchery and violence. During the play the evil dark side portrayed by the transformation into Mr Hyde commits a violent murder showing that this uncontrolled demon is capable of any unspeakable act. It occurred to Bates that Mansfield must either be a suspect or had been consulted over his knowledge of this form of behaviour. From a headline perspective it made much exciting press to write story about Mansfield as a suspect and the bonus for him, Bates naively considered obsessed by the next big story, was that this sort of press could get people flooding in to see the play. The evening's production finished to a standing ovation with Mansfield and his cast enjoying a total of three curtain calls.

* * *

Monday 14th October and Abberline was surprised by the news the Commissioner broke to him feeling pleased he had pre-empted his major suggestion.

"Abberline, the truth is I don't like you and I don't like your ways but you are popular in the environment where you work with both police and public alike. Apart from the resolution of the decoy patrols, which I am pleased you have begun, you must forge greater links with the Vigilance Committee and Mr Lusk in particular as he could be a valuable ally in the investigation. Meet with him and his people and anyone else from the community who wish to attend at a suitable venue and let them know what is going on, everything except the decoys. Do you understand?"

"Yes, Commissioner, absolutely. I will see to those issues as a priority. May I ask, sir, will you deploy anymore resources?"

"Yes, I am assigning more detectives to boost your plain patrols by half and maintaining the high level of uniform presence."

"Thank you, sir, will there be anything else?"

"Abberline, my reputation lies heavily with this matter. I have tendered to the Prime Minister and the Home Secretary that they can have my resignation should this fiend strike again, so keep on it, urgently."

"Yes, sir. We are all doing our best." As Abberline was about to leave, Sir Charles spoke once more.

"One more thing, Inspector, will you send someone to follow up on this story about the specimen collecting American. The whole thing has been put to me again by Wynne Baxter."

"Oh, when was this, sir?" Warren paused before answering.

"Er," thinking hard not to give away his Masonic connection "Um, by ….post. A letter I received yesterday."

"Certainly, sir, we'll get right onto it." Abberline took his leave of the Commissioner knowing full well the story of the letter from Baxter was a lie and left The Yard to hail a cab to take him back to The Street.

He stood at the pavement side looking for an empty cab to hail when an empty Royal Mews carriage pulled up beside him and the driver spoke.

"Mr Abberline, looking for lift, sir? I am not busy for a little while if I can help." Abberline looked at his watch and considered the fact he had never ridden in a Royal carriage before.

"That's very kind, Mr Netley; I think I will. Commercial Street nick please." He jumped on board and luxuriated himself on the quilted leather seat.

"Anything new then, Mr Abberline?"

"Well, not really but you might be able to help me. You said you move in medical circles, do you know anything about some American looking for anatomical specimens at all."

"I know about two American blokes in the City at present. One is a bloke with a broken arm who I have helped move out to Hackney, keeps his self to his self though, ex-Yankee army bloke or something. The other of course is Richard Mansfield, the actor. Driven him in my mate's cab to the East End, likes a good tom and things see, but now he's in the shit 'cos of you lot it would seem."

"What? We haven't nicked him or accused him; George Godley went to have an informal chat with him."

"The Star says on its headline 'American Actor accused of Ripper Murders!' Bloody all over the billboards it is. Thought it was down to you, like."

"But they didn't even know we were talking to him."

"Well old Will Bates says in his story he saw your Sergeant Godley leaving the theatre after a long and protracted interview. Don't reckon Mansfield can be too pleased."

"Right, change of plan; take me straight to The Star's offices."

Within twenty minutes they had pulled up outside the offices of The Star.

"I can't wait, Mr Abberline."

"All right, thanks for the ride, come and see me about that other bloke if you get to know anymore." With that Abberline strode purposefully inside and was met as luck would have it by Bates who was just leaving.

"Inspector..." He was cut short as the fiery tempered Abberline pinned him against one of the walls of the entrance way.

"You shit stirring, hack bastard! What the hell is today's story about!"

"Oi, oi! Off the suit, copper, else you'll be headlining tomorrow." Abberline reluctantly relaxed his grip but still forced Bates to be close to the wall.

"Fair game. I saw your bloke Godley at the theatre when I was getting my complementary tickets and put two and two together. Foreigner in town, with an uncanny ability of disguise and to become a monster? Seemed like a natural line of enquiry."

"You had no business printing that, Bates, he knocks at our door for slander we'll point him to you. Do this sort of thing again and I'll make sure the edition is seized you will run up a big debt for your bosses." Abberline pushed him in the chest back against the wall and stormed out.

Across town ironically in a sumptuous town house just outside Regents Park, Richard Mansfield had just been brought the morning edition of The Star by his dresser, an effeminate middle aged balding man called Dennis Biggleswade.

"I don't fucking believe this, I'll be ruined! We've run for six weeks with rave reviews and now this! I will be lambasted by all and no one will come thinking I'm the Goddamn Ripper. This is the fucking cops' fault, wait until I've seen the ambassador! Then they'll pay."

"What about the press? Surely the fault lies with them?" said Biggleswade.

"I'll see to those bastards too. Get me my grey suit ready I'm going to Scotland Yard and call me a cab!"

Within the hour Mansfield had been to Scotland Yard and had received a full apology from Sir Charles with an assurance things would not be so indiscreet in the future, but advised the fault for the story lay fairly and squarely with The Star and its staff. The Commissioner advised him to speak to Abberline as a further and next course of action if he wasn't satisfied with his personal and highest assurances. Mansfield made for Commercial Street Police Station arriving to add to the Ripper investigation's list of troubles. Abberline, who was sat in discussion with Godley, Mather and Robinson over the events of the day before with the latest decoy patrol, was called to the front counter to speak to him. Godley joined him to assist with a police perspective on it.

"Oh I'm glad you brought your little fucking terrier with you, Abberline, perhaps you could learn to keep him on a tighter leash and not spread gossip about me as a murder suspect."

"Mr Mansfield first off let me assure you we did not contact the newspapers and we conducted the enquiry at an off peak time basis to be discreet."

"Well funny how Will Bates didn't seem to think so. What you got to say then, Godley?"

"Mr Mansfield, I'm sorry but I never saw Bates around the theatre," replied Godley.

"No I guess you fucking didn't," sarcastically replied the indignant Mansfield.

"Mr Mansfield, I'll tell you what happened, Bates was at the box office as George was leaving. He made an unjustified assumption and ran with it making the rest up as a headline. Now I think to be fair you owe us an apology, and believe you me I will becoming to speak to you further as your name has come up in our enquiry. Now, keep your sarcasm and profanities to yourself and take your beef to the press. Come in here again and I'll run you in for disorderly conduct in a police station. Do we understand each other?" Mansfield stood stunned for a moment to have been played and justifiably so at his own game and considered his words.

"Very well, Inspector, but I expect enquires by you to be absolutely by the book and I shall request that my lawyer is present."

"Very well, Mansfield, good day." And with that final response Abberline followed by Godley turned and left the station's front counter heading off along the dimly lit Victorian corridor. Mansfield was opened mouthed at the lack of opportunity to address Abberline for calling him by his surname only; for once feeling beaten at his own game of absolute rudeness he wandered back outside into Commercial Street. It was a little early in the day but without a matinee on a Monday he went into the Commercial Street Tavern for a drink and some company.

Chapter Eighteen

Tuesday 15th October. George Lusk was enjoying a late breakfast with his children whom he cared for in conjunction with a professional nanny, Eleanor, since the death of his wife earlier in the year. Living in Tollit Street, just off Alderney Road East in the Globe Road area, he and his family of seven had only recently come to terms with the loss of a wife and mother. Fortunately his business was doing well and his brother masons had been very supportive in his grief. His formation of the Vigilance Committee was significantly fuelled by the knowledge that the loss of a wife or mother was very hard to bear.

It was around half past nine and there was an uncharacteristic knock on the door. He received post but rarely any that warranted hand delivery; rising from the breakfast table he made his way along the hall to the front door. Opening it he was handed a small three inch square box wrapped in brown paper tied around with twine to secure it. He thanked the postman kindly and shut the door somewhat puzzled and walked back towards the living room and the breakfast gathering. The box seemed to emit an odd preservative type of smell and so he instantly changed his mind and made for the privacy of the kitchen scullery where he knew he could keep the children out and open it in private. As he passed the living room door his youngest daughter spoke to him with obvious curiosity.

"What is it, papa?"

"Oh, nothing, just something for work, Catherine. Stay in there with Eleanor and your brothers and sisters, I need to look at this in private." He closed the kitchen door behind him and took hold of a pair of scissors and cut the twine to pull it away. He carefully undid the brown paper and as he pulled it away the great sense of the curious smell hit him; it was that of formaldehyde. He could see that the box inside the paper was blood stained. Hands now shaking he opened the box slowly and cautiously to reveal a folded up letter. Lifting it away finding it blood stained, he wretched when he saw what was underneath and dropped the letter in a flinch reaction. As a layman, he did not know if the organ he could see was animal or human or even what it was. He could hear Catherine at the door, with his voice breaking he warned her away.

"Don't come in, darling, papa is just preparing something." She heeded his words and stayed out. He composed himself and picked up the blood soaked letter and began to read it. When he noted the senders sick address he struggled to read any further.

Only someone with a mindset 'from hell' could orchestrate such a thing. He had to get to Abberline.

* * *

Montague Druitt woke up in his school lodgings with a splitting headache from the alcoholic excesses of the previous night that consisted of absinthe mixed with a drop of laudanum on a flaming sugar cube. The cube would sit on a spoon across the top of a glass of absinthe and then be dropped into the distinctive green alcohol and all mixed together. He rarely frequented Whitechapel anymore preferring to indulge his vices in seedier areas of South London for fear of bumping into Tumblety. The murder of the policeman still weighed heavily on his mind but he was fearful of approaching the police as anonymity could be an issue. Druitt also sensed that his former associate could be the man responsible for the unspeakable murders in Whitechapel knowing of his bizarre anatomical collection. He was considering a safe course of action for him would be to make contact with the Whitechapel Vigilance Committee who would be unlikely to be interested him or who he was but keen to pursue a suspect in the case. He was aware that this organisation met in The Blind Beggar on the edge of the ill fated district and decided he would go there, not in his normal dress, but donning working man's clothing to court even less attention. He wasn't required in class today so he could afford to leave himself unshaven, so he cut short his morning ablutions and drank several cups of tea briskly to try to rehydrate and take away the bitter-sweet aniseed taste of the absinthe. With post alcohol induced shaking hands he lit and smoked a succession of cigarettes too while staring blankly from his window across the expanse of Blackheath.

Simultaneously at The Street Abberline was in conference with some of the other detectives discussing the public briefing he had planned at Toynbee Hall for the next evening, and the need for the American specimen collector story to be pursued. He despatched Bill Murphy to visit the London Hospital as a start to investigate the matter, hoping that at least from there the staff may direct them to local anatomy specialists. They were disturbed by a knock on the door and Taffy Evans who was working at the front desk walked in.

"Sorry to disturb you all, but George Lusk is at the counter in a terrible state, you see, demanding to see you, Mr Abberline. He says it's very urgent and a very distressing matter. He's well shook up."

"All right, Taff, send him through please," replied Abberline. Taffy left the office with a lively discussion starting amongst the detectives as to what could have shaken up the normally uncompromising George Lusk so much.

He walked in ashen white and still shaking from the shock of the package he had received with Abberline surprised to see such a confrontational man in such a withdrawn and shocked condition.

"Mr Lusk," said Abberline, "take a seat and tell us what's happened." Lusk slowly sat himself at Godley's desk and stared at the package he placed on the table in front of him, re-wrapped in the brown paper disguising its true nature.

"Abberline, I received this through the morning post," said Lusk pointing to the box. "I can't look at it again; you must see the horror of it for yourself."

"What is, sir?" asked Godley. Lusk sat head now in hands and mumbled,

"It's from one of the victims." The detectives all looked at each other knowing as a group this must be some gruesome human remains. Abberline walked over to the table and opened the box, confidently but with care and caution. He pulled the letter out to reveal what he could recognise as part of a kidney; disturbed he unfolded the letter and read. The others crowded round the desk with many different mixed shocked reactions as Abberline read the letter out loud.

"Sent 'from hell'. 'Mr Lusk sir I send you half the kidney I took from one woman preserved it for you, tother piece I fried and ate it was very nice. I may send you the bloody knife that took it out if you only wait a while longer. Signed catch me if you can Mr Lusk'." Abberline paused and looked up from the letter to those in the room. "The fucking bastard. The sheer gall of him. When we get him I will, I swear personally pull the trap door of the gallows." He passed the letter around the others who in turn read it.

"Mr Lusk, I'm sorry he has dragged you further into this affair and thank you for coming straight to us. I shall get the police surgeon to examine this to confirm if it is human and I will be in touch. Do you wish a police guard on your home, sir?" said Abberline. Lusk stood and composed himself before replying.

"No thank you, Inspector, I don't wish to cause my children undue alarm at present. I shan't hesitate to be in touch if I need your assistance. I will see you tomorrow at Toynbee hall." He left the office and returned home ensuring on way that one of the committee got word to Will Bates.

"George, we need to take this to Dr Brown right away. The rest of you get on with doing whatever." Abberline and Godley grabbed their coats and left for Golden Lane mortuary.

During that afternoon Mary Kelly and Robert were at home at his lodgings with a very uncomfortable silence between them. To Robert, Mary seemed massively pre-occupied and with the events of the previous weeks and rightly so, but he felt they had to talk.

"Mary, you know that when this thing is done then we'll leave here and start a new life. What's wrong? Why are you so quiet?" She sat silent just staring out of the window at the view across the rear of the house in Bakers Row. "Mary, please talk to me. Tell me what's wrong!" They again sat in silence for what seemed like an eternity until she broke it.

"Robert, I think I know who is doing this and why." Robert sat aghast at this statement made out of the blue that he certainly wasn't expecting.

"You swear to not get angry or arrest me because it involves a theft on my part which will secure our future." He sat silent, but thinking of his own very delicate position. He was hardly one to be able to cast judgement upon her.

"All right, go on I promise that everything now is for us."

"I met a man called Francis. An American. We were together for a while and travelled together, went to France. But it was there I found out how odd he was, and not the gentleman I thought he was at all. We were in Monmartre in Paris and he said he liked art so I said he could sketch me. When he was finished it was horrid, a sick representation of womanhood. He went out and I found a collection of preserved human specimens, I think all from women, in his arts bag so I knew I had to leave him. But I also found that he had this expensive looking collection of jewels. I was scared, I had no money so I ran with most of them back here, but I don't know what to do with them all, I thought I'd be conned out of them if I wasn't careful, but with you, they can be our future."

Robert was stunned he didn't know what to say, he stood up and began pacing the room and started crying, which rendered him unable to speak for quite a few minutes. He managed to compose himself and speak.

"So you questioned me when I admitted to killing a murderer through sheer rage and a sense of revenge, an act that potentially had no consequence to society other than to benefit it." He took a breath pausing and considering his further words carefully. "And you steal from a man who is a lunatic, goes on a killing spree fuelled by your theft quite possibly which leads to my best friend dying! How I am I supposed to respond?"

"But you love me!"

"Yes, I do, but I'm hurt by the fact you were so shocked by my honesty and all this time you failed to tell me this. We could have stopped these murders weeks ago if you had been honest. Del would still be here!"

"Del would still be here if you hadn't gone on your crusade for revenge. How do you think I feel? What about Cathy and Liz and Mary and Annie? I have to carry the guilt for their deaths too!" A long silence again was cast over the room. Robert more composed broke it.

"What's his name? How old is he?"

"Francis Tumblety, early 50s, wears a uniform a lot, all the time really. Big moustache, tall, not fat but not thin." A silence fell again for a long time between them until it was eventually again broken by Robert picking up his coat. Angrily he said "I'm going out."

"Where?"

"Out I need some air and a drink." He walked out slamming the door behind him. Mary went to the window and crossed her arms in front of her, stared out and began to cry.

Robert took himself off to The Blind Beggar to have a drink and to try to gain some perspective on this earth shattering news. As he neared the pub passing a dark alleyway in Whitechapel Road he got pulled harshly into it by a huge figure of a man and pinned up against one side of it. He instantly recognised a voice that spoke to him from one side close to his ear as he was held firmly against the wall by the giant with seemingly limitless strength.

"Robbie boy, I hear that you are one of the filth, is that right now, eh?" said Sean Miller in his broad Ulster accent. Robert was unsure how he should reply.

"I have it on real good authority. Now while didn't you tell me this the other night in the pub now, eh?"

"It's not true; some one is stringing you along. I'm a bricky."

"My Fenian friends at The Yard don't think so. Patrick, do him." Miller stepped to one side as the huge Irish man let go with his right hand and landed a massive blow into Robert's nose. He felt it shatter and the warmth of blood spread across his face and run down onto his chin. More blows struck his body as he fell to his knees and received a series of upper cut punches devastating the area around his eyes. For a split second he felt the assailant release his grip; he fell on to all fours and as if out of a sprinters position he launched himself to his feet and ran clear back into the main road but heavily dazed from the beating so far. It caused him to lose his sense of direction and spatial awareness and he ran into the busy road carriageway, heavy with moving traffic. He ran into the path of a carriage drawn by two horses and got knocked to the ground by the harness running between them, falling into the path of the nearest horse. He was instantly concussed and knocked unconscious then trampled on by a horse breaking his left arm and then tossed under the carriage. His head made a further heavy glancing impact with the nearside wheels taking off skin across the right side of his forehead with his limp body eventually coming to land in the gutter.

The carriage driver pulled up instantly and jumped from his perch running back to see if the pedestrian was alive or dead. Miller and his thug looked on leaving him for what looked like dead and walked off away from the scene along the alleyway. A crowd gathered around the lifeless looking body of Robert Ford as a pair of patrolling constables ran to the scene one of them being Jonas Mizen who barely recognised his young colleague with his injuries. He spoke to the carriage drive sternly.

"Didn't you see him, you dozy bastard?"

"He ran from nowhere, mate, I couldn't miss him," replied the driver

"Your carriage empty?" demanded Mizen.

"Yes, it is."

"Right, let's get him on board and over to the hospital, he's hardly breathing."

* * *

Wednesday 16th October; Abberline and Godley had had a wasted journey the day before to the Golden Lane mortuary as they couldn't see Dr Brown until today due to the fact he'd been out of London. Today, however, they saw Dr Thomas Openshaw at the London Hospital who gave the kidney a thorough investigation and made a significant conclusion for them.

"Inspector, based on the fact that there was two inches of renal artery left within the victim Eddowes and this piece possesses one inch, the two would match to create the correct length for this blood vessel. The kidney itself is in state of decay driven by alcohol abuse and I could confirm that it is consistent with that of a kidney from a forty five year old, or thereabouts aged, woman with an alcohol abuse problem. This is most definitely from your last victim, gentlemen, no doubt about it."

"Doctor Openshaw," began Abberline, "do you know anything of an American who is in the business of obtaining female anatomical specimens?"

"Your man came here yesterday asking the same thing. The story seems to have developed from a student doctor who spent sometime in Paris in the last year or two and heard from an odd mortuary attendant there of an American who wanted specimens and paid handsomely for them. His story seems to have been subject to the old 'Chinese whispers' attention and it's now told as here. I can tell you, I know of no one doing this, approaching us or approaching any of my immediate colleagues. I'm sure as you know the only person engaged in this is the Ripper and none of us know who he is of course."

"Thank you, Doctor, you've been most helpful. Could we leave the specimen with you for now for safe keeping?"

"Certainly, more the merrier here!" He said humorously. "Good day, Gents."

"Thanks again, Doctor, good bye." Abberline and Godley left taking to the familiar streets of Whitechapel ready to go to Toynbee hall that evening for the public meeting.

The Press headlines that day were not good; especially by no surprise to the police were those on the front page of The Star. The newspaper billboards carried the headline which was re-enforced by the paper sellers:

'Cannibal in London, Ripper eats Kidney'

It was a subject that would weigh heavily on the public meeting that night. This headline disturbed Mary Kelly more than any other as she walked out along Bethnal Green Road with Bruiser having had a night with no sleep worrying about why Robert had not returned to his lodgings. Imparting her sorry tale to him with his furious reaction to her having not told the truth sooner, she was concerned that going to the police now might implicate her in a theft and some issue of withholding information. If her suspicions around the identity of the murderer were true then perhaps now her only course of action was to try to find and confront Tumblety herself. She would have to make herself high profile again on the streets to try to draw him out and in the hope that she would also find Robert again. The matter of him missing was not one she wished to take to the police either knowing he was currently in disgrace over the murder of Del Lake. She continued walking impervious to the sights, sounds and smells of her surroundings except for that of the sound of the newspaper sellers calls ringing in her ears.

"Cannibal in London, Ripper eats Victims Kidney. Panic on the streets, read all about it!"

8.p.m; Toynbee Hall was bustling with the local community taking up every seat and standing along the sides of the auditorium with a conservative police presence spread throughout. On the stage to deliver the police briefing and to field questions from the audience were Abberline, Godley and Inspector Spratling all faces familiar to nearly all of those having gathered. A loud and steady buzz of conversation filled the room as people seemed to compete with each others conversation to be heard. Two minutes past and Abberline stood and drew a silence across the room as he began.

"Ladies and gentleman, good evening and welcome to this first community briefing. I am joined on stage as most of you will know by Detective Sergeant Godley and Inspector Spratling. I will discuss the investigation so far and all of us will field questions from you at the end. I would appreciate if members of the press did not monopolise this session. First of all, I would like to express my deepest regret that these events are taking place. I know better than anyone that Whitechapel is never the most genteel of districts but it has never been the hot bed of violent motiveless butchery. Rest assured we are doing all we can to combat this. Since the Chapman murder we have doubled the number of uniform patrols and have posted regular plain patrols which since the so called 'double event' have been increased further by half. To that end I make no apology if the more coppers out there means you get caught doing things you shouldn't, then tough.

"Personally I don't believe all of these crimes are linked. I don't think the same man struck twice on the night of the 29th and 30th September but I do think he was most likely responsible for Cathy Eddowes death and all the others before. We have no decent description, height, age, clothing and social status; descriptions all vary wildly and I urge you all to perhaps have 'one less for the road' in the evenings so you can all be a little more alert. Some people have noted a man with a large moustache, but let's face it that is not an uncommon feature for many.

Please come forward still with your concerns and with what you see that you don't like, but to members of the Vigilance Committee I say this; thank you for becoming more co-operative and please continue to refrain from taking the law into your own hands. Mr Lusk has decided not to be here tonight as all of you will undoubtedly know why, and I send my good wishes to him. The floor is now open to all of you to ask us what you will please." Abberline sat down as the hall fell into silence momentarily before the first question was presented.

"Mr Abberline, do you think all women should fear or only the unfortunates?" asked a woman in the front row.

"Personally I feel all women in the area should be on their guard, but those who do persist in being out late should pay special attention to who they see, speak to or go off with. Let someone know if possible where you are," replied Abberline.

"Sergeant Godley, why do you reckon this is happening?" asked a publican sat towards the rear of the hall.

"Sir, if we truly knew that, we'd have a better chance of catching this person. We have no clear motive as yet to follow other than he maybe suffering from melancholia or some other mental health problem and is driven to do so as a result."

The publican continued "but ain't it true he takes bits?"

"He has removed some parts of the victims which we believe may fuel his dementia and may give him a reason. It doesn't help us know who he may target."

"Mr Spratling," said a local shopkeeper "is it right you've got coppers here from other places then?"

"Yes, to help boost the patrol numbers," he replied.

"Thought so," said the shop keeper "most of them seem bleeding lost!" A wave of laughter went round the hall.

An hour long question and answer session continued from the local community until the people seemed to be satisfied and their curiosity had been exhausted. Then Will Bates chipped in.

"Gentlemen, just one last simple matter, when do you think you might catch him?" This was an impossible point to answer but Abberline knew he had to respond, wanting to put Bates equally on the spot.

"With public vigilance and support, our officers continuing to work hard together, but most importantly with your help and that of the Press as a whole, especially avoiding the spread of unnecessary fear, then I would suggest at anytime now." Bates didn't like the answer as the room turned to look at him and turning red with embarrassment he was forced to reply.

"Thank you, Mr Abberline." The hall quickly emptied and everyone, except the uniformed officers, with people returning home for the night.

* * *

A week later on Wednesday 23rd October, Mary was frantic with worry about not having seen Robert for over a week and there was no sign of him having been back to his lodgings either. Still reluctant to go to the police, she decided to go to the London Hospital to see if he had been hurt in some way and had been taken there. Walking through the arched portico and up the grand steps at the front of the building she walked up to the reception desk and spoke to a smartly dressed nurse.

"Excuse me, but I'm worried that my fiancé might be here having been hurt in someway." The nurse looked at her oddly.

"Hurt in someway? Don't you know for sure that he has been and so that he is here?"

"No, he went missing a few days ago over an argument and I think he could be here."

"Have you reported this to the police?"

"No, not yet, please, could you just check, I'm really worried about him."

The nurse looked her up and down and then spoke having empathised with her plight. "All right, I'll just check the ward register, what's his name?"

"Robert Ford."

She spent quite some time leafing through a large leather bound register until she came up with an answer, "He's here in Albert Ward, first floor on the east wing."

"Thank you, thank you very much," she gave a slight smile in appreciation but now very worried about his condition and went off to the ward.

She arrived and checked with the staff on the entrance to the ward at the nurses station. A sister in her blue uniform led her slowly down to Robert's bed and told her of his condition. The ward smelt clinical and it was austere by its plain and functional brightness.

"He's been here just over a week. Still breathing, his body is functioning fine but he is in what we call a 'coma' having gone under the wheels of a carriage. He has a serious head wound with a large section of skin missing from his forehead skinned almost to the skull, his face isn't as swollen now but he had a lot of facial injuries including a broken nose. He's got a broken left forearm so that's set in plaster. He's been in the wars this one." As she finished speaking they reached the foot of this bed.

Mary was shocked by his condition and already with thoughts of remorse for their argument going through her mind; she wished she explained things more rationally if she could have. She almost missed the sister speaking to her who had to repeat herself to get Mary's attention.

"I'll leave you with him for a little while, it might do him good."

"Thank you," said Mary sitting to the right of the bed taking hold of Robert's warm right hand and gently caressing it. He actually looked quite peaceful but his nose had suffered a terrible break and the scarring across his forehead was deep and ugly. His left arm had been set in plaster and was suspended by a wire from a traction unit above the bed and she noted he was breathing very normally and gave the appearance of being in a deep sleep. She spoke to him quietly and gently.

"Robert, darling, I'm so sorry. Please forgive me and let's just go from here from all this pain and death that seems to hold a grip over everyone we know and everything we do. I really do love you more than you'll ever know and want to be with you somewhere far from here. You don't have to wait around here for justice to be done; it'll happen with or without you. I just want you to wake so we can go away to the middle of nowhere together." She sat with him for half of an hour before the sister came back to ask her to leave him until another day. Mary reluctantly did so and made her way sombrely into the High Street in Whitechapel and headed towards Commercial Street and her old haunts with the intention to actively seek out Tumblety and settle the matter.

* * *

That evening Druitt walked into The Blind Beggar pub for the third time having finally plucked up the courage to execute his plan regarding Tumblety. He was nervous to be back in the area and at entering such a working man's drinking establishment with few women around. The pub was crowded and he could see a man he assumed, from press coverage, to be George Lusk holding court with a group of about a dozen local men. He stood at the bar having bought a pint of beer and listened intently to what he could hear Lusk saying to these men.

"Fellows, it has been nearly three weeks since the last Ripper attack so perhaps Abberline's patrol tactics are working. With this in mind we have been out on a moderate basis forming local watches of our own around the neighbourhoods and none of our members have seen anything out of the ordinary. We can't allow ourselves to relax our guard, however, so this level of vigilance must be maintained to catch him or prevent him striking." There was a rousing 'here, here' from the crowd at that point when Druitt also noticed a young lad of about sixteen being chatted to intently by a well dressed man of forty at the other end of the bar. Money exchanged hands between them and the boy left the pub to be followed a few minutes later by the well dressed man. Curious, Druitt followed him out and saw him go round the corner into Cambridge Heath Road; as he did so himself he saw the man disappear into a small area of ornamental garden behind some bushes. He walked closing himself to a point where he could hear some very distinctive sounds, the first was that of the well dressed older man grunting and the other was of the lad gasping and then speaking, "Slowly, sir, just to start with it's painful at first." The older man then stopped grunting and aggressively replied.

"Don't worry, lad, few good first thrusts and you'll be well used to it."

Druitt was stunned by what he was hearing but it instantly formed a better plan in his head. He scurried back into the pub not wanting to be caught as a voyeur of the homosexual couple and waited for the return of the boy. It took some time so he continued listening to Lusk and his followers until the boy came back in walking very awkwardly and painfully and returned to the bar. He looked to be in obvious physical distress so Druitt left it for some while before he approached him.

"Excuse me, young man, but I couldn't help noticing you leave the pub followed by that older fellow," said Druitt.

"Look, it will be the same for you as him, £1 and no less."

"No, not for me, but I have a business proposition for you, worth £10 with no pain whatsoever, just a little bit of fibbing. Half now and half once you've done the job."

"Oh, yeah, what is it then?"

"Can we discuss it elsewhere?" The lad looked around.

"Like where? You ain't gonna much me, I ain't drunk."

"No, I'll get a cab outside, you join me and while we go for a ride I'll tell you." The lad paused looking around and then down at his feet for a while chewing his bottom lip.

"Its £10 is it?"

"Yes, half now and half later."

"All right, I'll see you outside in a few minutes in a cab then, mister."

Druitt left and hailed down a passing a hansom and spoke to the driver.

"I'm waiting for a passenger and then take me off towards Commercial Street Police Station." The driver nodded his head in response. The young lad came out and jumped in the cab.

"What's your name, lad?"

"Fred Churchyard."

"Right then, Fred, here's the job. I need you to go into Commercial Street nick and say you've been attacked and buggered by an American who I will tell you about. This has occurred on at least two occasions, and that he's attacked you and some of your mates who are too scared to come forward. You can make up the dates, but the important thing is that you describe him and you see it through to court too, it's worth £10, that's a lot of money." Fred sat silent for two or three minutes looking out of the window as they travelled repeating phrases like 'I don't know' and 'I don't want no trouble', 'you're asking a lot'. So Druitt cut in once more.

"All right, £15 but no more. Five now and the other ten later."

"Yeah, deal, give us the money and tell me what he's like." Through the rest of the journey Druitt described him down to a fine detail and dropped Fred off at the door of The Street. He gave him £5 and said

"See me on Friday at The Ten Bells with proof from the police that you've done what I've asked and you'll get the rest." Fred jumped out of the cab and made his way into the police station.

Inspector Chandler was stood at the front desk when Fred entered and spoke to the desk sergeant. "I want to make a complaint of assault by an American toff in the area." Chandler looked him up and down suspiciously giving little weight to what the lad had just said.

"Oh, yeah? So where and when did this happen then?" said Chandler.

"Well, recent like, to me and a couple of me mates. It was 'orrible, abused us right good and proper. Too ashamed to speak here."

"Tell you what, you come back with your mates and we'll take the complaint from all of you together." Fred felt distinctly uncomfortable trying to make up an assault complaint on behalf of someone else and was losing his nerve. He stood silent before replying for some time considering the money and considering the reaction of leaving now from the man who might still be waiting outside. He decided he had to leave and come back.

"All right, I'll come by later on."

"Right oh," replied Chandler nonchalantly as Fred turned and left to face Druitt.

"You didn't do it did you?" demanded Druitt

"Nah, I couldn't. I need time to think. Bring me back next week and I promise I will do it." Druitt had started along a path he must end.

"Right," he responded reluctantly. "We'll come here next week or no money and I'll shop you for male prostitution." Fred was forced to concede.

Chapter Nineteen

Thursday 24th October 5.a.m; Abberline walked all around the back streets of Spitalfields now officially off duty in sheer hope of finding the perpetrator committing these hideous crimes that occupied all of his waking hours. His wife and dog, his only dependants, had seen little of him for weeks as he chose to spend so much official and unofficial time in Whitechapel, and now again he found himself wandering the deserted district this time in gloomy Gun Street. As he headed towards Bishopsgate, a young constable rounded a corner ahead and walked towards him and recognising Abberline instantly. He pulled himself upright to address him as they neared. It was Constable Bob Spicer.

"All correct, sir," he said nodding his head respectfully.

"Thank you, Spicer. Seen much tonight then?"

"No, very quiet it seems tonight, sir. Hardly anyone about at all."

"Good, stay vigilant."

"Sir, you know this area well, what's the story with the name Spitalfields then?"

"Goes back to when the area here was the site of a hospital and its grounds and the name is from the bastardisation of 'hospital fields'."

"Oh, blimey. What about the 'Houndsditch' just off our bit then?"

"What, do you want, a bleeding tour or something, son?"

"No, just I get asked that's all, sir."

"Last question, comes from the Roman times, when the wall of the city that ran along that bit was the place where the people would throw their dead dogs over the wall to outside of the city, hence the 'hounds ditch'. Now get on with your patrols, you cheeky young bugger!" said Abberline with a smirk on his face.

"Yes, sir. Thanks for the tips. Take care with your patrol, sir." Spicer walked off towards Christchurch and Commercial Street.

It amused Abberline that this lad saw nothing strange in seeing him out on the ground at such an ungodly hour; a fact that he could only put down to everyone being so pre-occupied with the murders, as he was. He walked alone into a near deserted Middlesex Street and turned back towards Aldgate stopping periodically to try to catch the sounds of footsteps from the alleyways. He pulled a hip flask of whiskey from inside his suit and took a generous swig and continued his wandering for another hour before returning to The Street. He found an empty cell which the custody sergeant allowed him to restlessly sleep in for a couple of hours before the next working day began.

* * *

Sunday 27th October; Mary again sat at Robert's bedside clasping his hands in her own having long since given up on talking to him some thirty minutes earlier in her two hour long visit so far. She sat silently hoping he would soon wake up; there had been no change in his condition other than the swelling to his face having subsided and apart from his nose he was beginning to look like himself again. As she sat quietly she became aware of a presence behind her that made her feel quite uncomfortable and knew that it wasn't one of the nursing staff. She turned to see a foreboding looking man she recognised; John Littlechild.

"So what happened to him then?" He asked seemingly to lack any genuine concern.

"He was hit by a carriage in the High Street," replied Mary mournfully.

"Too bad, wonder if it was an accident or if he'd found something out and got pushed?" pondered Littlechild.

"Who would do that? He's only come across decent local people; others that aren't local are decent too."

"Oh, yes, like who then? Who's not local then?"

"Well, just one chap, a nice young Irish lad called Sean Miller."

"Nice Irish chap, eh? You would think that. Did he know what Robert does?"

"No, most people don't take any notice of us in the pubs, and we certainly didn't tell him anything."

"Yes, but gossip, my dear. If he is a new man in the area and some local says 'watch him he's a copper', if your friend Mr Miller is a Fenian activist he will stop at nothing to not be found out. Do you know where he lives then?"

"No, but he drinks in The Blind Beggar."

"Right, I'll get my lads to go and visit him. Now tell me, what does he look like then?" Reluctantly she described Miller to Littlechild concerned about his motives but feeling threatened and vulnerable without Robert conscious and able bodied.

"When he wakes up let the bar keeper at the Commercial Street Tavern know, if you need to get me for anything else speak to him." Arrogantly Littlechild walked off leaving Mary more troubled than ever. She decided to leave for a late afternoon drink at The Britannia.

Mary strolled through the doors of the pub on the corner of Dorset Street and Commercial Street just after 5.p.m; it was quiet with only a few hardened drinkers inside none of whom she recognised. She got herself a tankard of ale and sat alone in a corner staring at the frosted glass that separated her from the outside world wondering when Francis might appear in her life, knowing she would now face this potential peril by herself. Over the next quarter of an hour the pub began to fill up with other women, soldiers, locals in their Sunday best and a regular face she knew; that of the pianist who would liven the place up for the evenings.

He began with a rendition of 'Who will buy my pretty flowers' after a request from one of the local well dressed men whose teenage daughter stood up to sing a solo version in accompaniment. The girl was very tuneful with a soothing quality to her voice and Mary watched her resting her chin on her hand propped by her elbow on the rough bar table lost in the sound of the song reminding her of her late childhood of only ten years previously. She was staring at the pianist and the girl singing with her gaze totally fixed so that she was unaware of movement in the immediate foreground; unaware of the smartly but conservatively dressed figure that now approached her with an arm in a sling. She only acknowledged the individual sporting the large moustache with cold alarm as he sat opposite her and spoke in a very distinctive accent.

"Well, well, Mary Jane. Hello. You don't know how much I've missed you and how long I've been looking for you." Mary was frozen with fear unable to manage a reply, trying but with her mouth moving helplessly incapable of forming any words or even the merest sound as a result of her throat drying up completely.

"Now, there, that's no good, you must be able to say something to your dear old Francis after all this time, eh? I mean you stole every goddamn cent I own near enough when you took my jewels, and look at you living like a whore in the East End of London. Or are you actually a whore? Hmmm?" She took a deep breath and coughed and managed to begin to engage him in a conversation.

"I didn't mean to. I was scared. Your behaviour, your horrible jars. I had no money I had to escape. I can give it all back to you. Just leave me alone, leave Whitechapel alone." She was trying hard to keep tears at bay and maintain her composure with this fearful man in front of her staring at her with eyes that seemed to penetrate her very soul.

"What do you mean? Leave Whitechapel alone? Who do you think I am, eh? Do you think I'm this 'Jack' fellow?" As she listened to him the rage over what he had done was welling up inside her and giving her strength to deal with him on equal terms, a strength which walking the streets of Whitechapel she had been forced to develop.

"If I scream now the whole of this pub will lynch you if I so much indicate who you might be and you'll get nothing except the street hangman's noose. A foreign man accused, your jars when they find them, you're not even denying it. Did you kill those women to get to me? Is there anything that you are not capable of?"

"Yes, never loving a whoring woman again," he replied, lowering his head and snarling through his teeth, "All they have brought me is heartache and pain, and what I do and I take unburdens the heart break that my soul continually seems to live with. Yes I did kill some of those women, not all of them, but by god I wish I had, to rid the streets of filthy whores leaching off innocent and foolish men. Now, where are my jewels?"

"Why? You going to kill me too? If you do you'll never find out. Right now I am worth too much to you alive." She had a point, despite the voices driving his blood lust to be satisfied, he couldn't afford to kill her before time. He sat back staring at her with total contempt before speaking again, contemplating how he could out do her treachery.

"All right, what do you want for us to go our separate ways safely?"

"I'll give you the jewels in exchange for some money to leave. If you do this I won't shop you I'll disappear forever with your secret. If you don't or try anything before we exchange, I'll shop you." He paused.

"How much?"

"How much are the jewels worth?"

"Oh no, no way. Just give me a price." She was ignorant of the vast value of the jewels and had to think about a figure substantial to her.

"I want £3000 and no less. You buy my silence and I leave this country for home." It was a significant amount of money but with the return of the jewels easily attainable and worth it.

"Deal. Where and when?"

"Victoria Park, by the boating lake kiosk in two days time, one o'clock."

"I'll be there, make sure you are alone, because I will find you, believe me." He got up and left The Britannia her eyes following him as he walked across the pub and pushed his way out of the double doors. She began to shake uncontrollably and sob dropping her arms folded onto the table and burying her face into them. Should she allow a man who had just confessed to being Jack the Ripper walk free? She would never realise that at that very time he was unable to physically attack her as a result of his injured arm and was probably at his weakest.

* * *

That evening Richard Mansfield sat back in an arm chair in his dressing room as he listened to Robert Lees reading the results of Tarot cards to him that he had lain out on the counter in front of the mirrors. Since the negative publicity courtesy of The Star, 'Jekyll and Hyde' had been playing to ever reducing audiences every night and the owners of the Lyceum had decided to terminate its run early as a result. Getting to a point where less than half of the house was occupied meant that heavy financial losses were beginning to be sustained. Knowing Robert Lees reputation, Mansfield had called upon his services to find out what the future held for him and if there was a hint of what maybe a good production to develop.

"So, Robert, what do you see?"

"Well, I have drawn the cards three times and each time they are turning up the same. Not all of it will be pleasing to you."

"Lets face it, I'm used to bad news so go ahead and tell me," he slurped from a large bulbous brandy glass as he spoke.

"You will have no further success here. You will have to return to America where you must perform something classical to regain success and notoriety. This show will end imminently."

"Yes, well I know that, tell me something I don't. The rest of it sounds promising, getting away from this shitty forever pissing with rain gothic hell of a city. Anything else?" Lees paused as he stared at the last of the cards he had turned. He knew that they indicated that Mansfield's life would not be long, but he could not tell him this. He paused and lied.

"You will never be successful in love," he thought of this quickly on the spur of the moment knowing that Mansfield was not averse to paying for sex, and never treated any women with much respect.

"Like I said, tell me something I don't know, Robert." He drained the last of the generously filled brandy glass and swapped places with Lees to begin to prepare for the nights show in his final week of performances. Lees politely left, not wishing to spend too much longer at the theatre as crowds sometimes bothered him and he found the subject matter of the play somewhat distasteful.

* * *

Tumblety went from The Britannia to The Ten Bells to get himself a drink before returning to Graham Road. He stood at the bar waiting to order when he became aware of a dark haired, moustached young man with piercing eyes staring at him from the other end of the bar. He looked this individual up and down and realised why he seemed familiar. It was the rather odd mortuary attendant from the Louis Pasteur Hospital in Paris who had gained him a specimen. He didn't know his name and was surprised to see the young man who began to approach him. Tumblety offered his hand and spoke to introduce himself.

"I believe we've met but never been introduced. My Name is Frank Townsend; I'm the American from Paris." Klosowski took his hand and shook it firmly speaking in a heavy accent replying.

"George Chapman. Yes I remember you. Odd collection. How is it then? Need anymore?" He couldn't recall the American's name, but Townsend didn't sound familiar.

"As a doctor you can never have too many, helps with diagnosis you see. How did you get that last one for me, it seemed to be from a very young woman?"

"Just a prostitute brought in dead from the Bois de Boulogne. You paid the money; I get the specimen, if you understand." Tumblety was making eye contact as they spoke and could sense malevolence in this individual. It was an evil that he very well understood so he spoke to try to draw some more detail from Chapman.

"So if I wanted something specifically you could get it for me." Chapman knew he was talking to someone on equal terms and replied with confidence to this question.

"For the right price, all is possible. Tell me what you want and I give you a price." Tumblety now sensed the perfect opportunity.

"I am meeting a woman in two days time in Victoria Park. She is from a specific class and ethnic background. I'd like her specimen if you understand? Plus something else."

"Speak, and tell you if possible and if I am interested."

"I want her heart, it has sentimental value, you see."

"You talk of murder. Price is high. £500 and I get you what you want."

"You can't do it that day, it must be subsequently. She will have a lot of money in her possession which you must find too. Now this is who it is."

Tumblety took a tattered photograph out of his suit pocket of Mary Kelly that he had never drawn from his pocket or shown anyone before. It had been taken in their golden time together in the north of England and was a beautiful sepia portrait of her. Chapman studied the picture and gave it back. He downed his drink and spoke to Tumblety sternly.

"I have seen her around here. She lives around here. I meet you here in four days for the money after I watch the two of you in the park."

"It's a deal," they shook hands as Tumblety spoke further. "Now what are you drinking, George?"

* * *

Tuesday 29th October 1.p.m; Mary Kelly loitered nervously around the boating kiosk but at least took comfort in the fact he had agreed to meet her somewhere public leaving her feeling he would be unlikely to strike at her there. It was a bright day considering the lateness of the month but there was a distinct chill in the air forcing all those out and about in the park to wrap up against the coldness it brought. She pulled her shawl tighter around her shoulders to try to warm herself while keeping a tight hold with her arm on the small case that held the precious stones in a cheap leather bag. She wore it slung by its handles over her shoulder but resting under her arm out of sight. She eyed all those that were coming and going desperately trying to ensure she saw him approaching at the earliest opportunity so as not to give him any element of surprise. Becoming more and more restless on her feet she noted a wooden bench that was placed with its back to the boating kiosk and with the security that offered with its mainly frontal views she sat down on it.

Watching the forever changing but reduced midweek throng of humanity in front of her she initially paid no attention to a police sergeant walking in her direction. As he neared and she felt his eyes constantly falling on her, she gave him a good stare back in return which was when she noted the large flamboyant moustache he was sporting and studied the face of the sergeant in depth. In doing so she was struck with the shocking realisation that it was Tumblety. A few feet away from her he spoke, out of earshot of anyone passing by as she stood to face him.

"Hello, Mary you seemed surprised to see me," he said with arrogance.

"Well, there's no end to your resourcefulness. How did you get that? Did you kill him for it? Did you kill Del Lake?"

"First question, no I just gave the owner of this uniform a good beating, second question, yes I did. The son of a bitch tried to fool my friend and me as a woman. I thought he was a robber."

"You, bastard. He was so young, doing his job and you butchered him. Now you come here like that. You are sick. I should shop you anyway."

"Take stock, my dear. However you choose to stir things up now people will just think you are a mad woman being carted off by the local police. You could end up in one of the canals or anywhere really." Mary could not comprehend how cunning this man really was and knew that he had her at a massive disadvantage; she resigned herself to completing their transaction.

"Show me the money then," she demanded.

"With pleasure, madam," he replied smugly undoing a couple of buttons on the chest of his tunic and pulling out a plain white envelope marked 'Cootes Bank'. "You put me to a lot of trouble. Twice I have had to go to the bank to borrow money and both times because of you, so give me the goddamn jewels so I can close the loans they have made to me." She pulled the bag from under her arm and removed the jewellery case from inside it. They stood facing each other with a mutual need between them and for a moment Tumblety felt a wave of affection wash over him for this beautiful young woman. She was genuinely different to the others he had chosen to kill with a true innocence to her and so much tragedy in her life. Some of the humanity left within him could understand her departure from Paris. The voices that so frequently troubled his mind were silent as they both reached forward to exchange their respective packages and he felt her soft touch as she took the envelope from his hand. He still had only limited use of his broken arm which was quite obvious to her as they made the exchange. She wondered what injury he had suffered. Feeling his hand she did not receive the same sensation and only had a massive feeling of fear and resentment for all the blood shed and heart ache this man had brought. Tumblety felt compelled to voice some of his feelings for her to ease some of the burden of guilt he carried and to try to verbalise the sensation of the epiphany he had just felt.

"Mary, live a long and happy life and be free," his feelings of compassion now face to face with the second love of his life had washed away all recollection of the evil pattern of events he had set in place.

Mary was stunned by the show of humanity from someone she had come to despise and the shock of it drew her breath away leaving her unable to speak. She turned and walked briskly away from Tumblety leaving him stood alone by the boating kiosk as she made for Grove Road to get back to the heart of the East End and keep the money safe. She ripped the envelope open as she walked to find it full of the promised money which brought a sense of achievement and hope to her for the future with Robert. Reaching the exit to the park she hailed a cab and instructed the driver to take her to the London Hospital.

Tumblety still in his police uniform sat on the bench vacated by Mary and cautiously looked around him before opening the jewellery case. He undid its catch and slowly lifted the lid to expose the large diamond flanked by the surrounding smaller diamonds which brought a visible smile to his face. Two of the diamonds would be enough to settle his debts and wipe out any dependence on anything but himself. He closed the case down and strolled briskly from the park to return to Graham Road and discard his disguise having little more use for it. He was still experiencing the feeling of absolution as he walked when suddenly a cold realisation washed through his entire body as he recalled the meeting with Chapman and the agreement which they had made. He would have to pay him off at their next meeting to prevent him from taking Mary's life now that the voices seemed to have gone and he felt in full control of his actions. His only fear was that Chapman knew what Mary looked like already and Tumblety knew too Chapman also had knowledge of Mary being in possession of money. He had to find this man urgently and stop the evil mission he had set him upon.

Tumblety had failed to see Chapman loitering outside of the park's railings watching the exchange take place through a battered telescope. He now knew exactly what this woman that he was to kill looked like. He assumed now for certain that she must possess something of value judging by the meeting that had just taken place and the price the American was willing to pay. He would not bother seeking him out again; he would go and deal with her and take whatever she owned for himself.

Whitechapel

* * *

Thursday 1st November 6.p.m; Robert Lees entered Commercial Street Police Station for the second time and spoke to the desk sergeant with a sense of urgency.

"I must speak with Inspector Abberline, please it's very urgent. Please tell him it's Robert Lees." The sergeant was aware of who he was and immediately sent a young constable to get Abberline from his office. Godley came into the front office and spoke to Lees.

"Evening, Mr Lees, I'm sorry Inspector Abberline isn't here he's out on patrol around the pubs in Commercial Street."

"Sergeant, please take me to him now I have had a terrible premonition."

Godley could sense the fear and apprehension within Lees and fetched his top coat and walked straight out with the noted psychic into Commercial Street and headed south towards The Ten Bells and The Britannia.

They walked into The Ten Bells to see Abberline in deep conversation with two cleaner looking unfortunates at a table near to the bar. With his usual policeman's manner of looking at anyone who entered he glanced across at the door as Godley and Lees, looking uncomfortable with the surroundings, entered. He stood up from the two women, not yet the worse for alcohol, and ushered Lees to an empty table as Godley went to the bar. Lees called across to Godley as Abberline sat him down.

"No alcohol for me, thank you." Abberline began the conversation.

"Mr Lees, there's obviously something troubling you to come here again."

"Inspector, two nights on the trot I have had the same vision in my sleep and each time it becomes more and more vivid, I fear I will see more but must tell you of my premonition so far." Abberline nodded his head slowly in response and encouraged Lees to continue.

"You must first of all find a woman with wealth in this area. She is the next to be killed. She is not a local woman but has travelled. She won't die in the street but alone by a fireside at the hands of a dark and foreboding man who will delight in what he does."

"Mr Lees, this is interesting but vague. There are no women who have travelled and have wealth in the East End. If they fitted that bill they would not live here." Godley returned with small tankards of beer for himself an Abberline and a glass of tonic water for Lees. Abberline asked Lees to repeat what he had said for Godley's benefit.

"Interesting, Mr Lees," said Godley "will you see more in the future?"

"It's possible, I may see more and I may be able to discover where and when it may happen." Vague information didn't help Abberline's cause.

"Mr Lees, I deal in facts and what people actually see in the real world. Premonitions are all very well but I need more to go on to catch the killer or prevent a crime. If I go to the Commissioner with what you tell me he will dismiss me and you as fools or lunatics like I said to you before. I'd like to spare a constable to sit at your house each morning for when you wake but I can't. So..." Lees angrily interrupted.

"Inspector! I am a medium I see only spiritual clues or symbolic events. I am neither a lunatic nor a fool and you will regret refusing my help when the killer strikes again." Abberline quickly responded to the interruption.

"Mr Lees, we are not refusing your help but we can't scour the East End looking for your psychic circumstances to match those on the street," replied an agitated Abberline.

"Mr Lees, all we ask is your patience in this matter for us to start to find the circumstances of which you speak as you perceive more detail," added Godley. Lees realised his sudden unreasonableness and spoke.

"Gentleman, I'm sorry I don't appreciate your pressure. When I see more I shall let you know at the earliest opportunity." Lees finished his drink and hurried outside and hailed a cab to take him home as the detectives finished their small ales and resumed a patrol of the area.

John Netley was again helping his friend out driving his hansom as he picked up the fare in Commercial Street outside The Britannia recognising instantly who it was and engaging him in conversation.

"Nice to see you, Mr Lees. Been doing anything interesting then?" Lees despite his gift of clairvoyance was often naïve to the corruption of the greater world and spoke freely to Netley.

"Just trying to help the police with these awful murders, but they seem cynical to what I have to tell them."

"Oh, really?" Replied an interested Netley for his own ends and managed to glean from Lees his entire involvement with the case on the journey to Peckham. He gratefully received the fare and tip from Lees on arrival and was subconsciously even more grateful for Lees' loose tongue; the information from it was worth a few quid to his contact at The Star, Will Bates.

* * *

Friday 2nd November 8.p.m; it was the third night in a row that Tumblety had trawled the pubs in Commercial Street in a desperate hunt for the man named Chapman. He maintained his caution by going out in smart civilian clothes so as not to draw the attention to himself that the American uniforms usually courted. He had enquired of all the bar keepers but despite all of them knowing of this man by description none of them were sure of his name, though some thought he sounded more like a man with an Eastern European name. No one had seen him in the area for several days. Neither had he seen Mary Kelly on his visits daily to the area and feared speaking to anyone else over the matter in case he drew some suspicion upon himself. He still felt euphorically absolved after his meeting with her and had no urge to pursue his previously wanton and blood thirsty path. He settled down in The Britannia for the next couple of hours enjoying a quart of port to himself and hoping beyond hope that either of them would walk in door. His wishes for the night would go unanswered as he had arranged for a carriage driven by the obliging John Netley to collect him at 10.p.m which he heard draw up outside promptly. Reluctantly he walked out and took the journey home which was more eventful and stressful than he had imagined.

"How are you then, doctor?" politely asked John Netley.

"Fine thank you, Netley, get me to Graham Road as soon as you can."

"You heard the latest then on this Ripper case?" asked Netley knowingly, although he did not realise that his passenger had not seen the papers over the last few days. He earnt himself a pretty penny from

Bates at The Star for his information from Lees. The headlines had been splashed across news stand boards as well as the papers:

'Royal Psychic Helps Police'

With subtext expanding with a description.

'Sought: brooding foreign doctor type with a thick moustache'.

Netley explained these latest newspaper headlines to his fare.

"So what do you reckon about all that then?" He asked cockily as they pulled up outside Tumblety's Hackney lodgings. "Who knows, with that description it could be you, sir. Know what I mean?" he said threateningly. Tumblety was alighting as these last words were spoken. He passed his cane from his good to his weak arm and reached up as if to pay Netley with his good arm, as he did so he took hold of Netley's sleeve and pulled him off of his carriage perch and onto the pavement on which he landed heavily. He passed his stick back across to his strong hand and stepped with one foot heavily onto Netley's chest and jabbed the stick into his throat. He began choking as Tumblety spoke in an ominously calm manner to him prostrate on the floor.

"Are you threatening me, coachman? I sincerely hope not because very few people would miss your passing." Netley struggled to reply.

"I only meant that they might think you were a suspect, I didn't mean nothing by it, honest." Tumblety maintained the pressure on him.

"Good, let me tell you, I find anyone looking for me and I will find you before they find me." Netley was close to passing out and in extreme pain as Tumblety dropped the fare money onto his chest and let go of his choke hold and walked up the steps into his lodgings. Netley had to lie where he was for a half a minute or so to gain his breath, strength and composure before getting to his feet. He looked on ruefully at the building to which Tumblety had just entered and then mounted his carriage rubbing his neck and rode off.

10.15.p.m; Fred Churchyard walked back into Commercial Street to earn his money from Druitt with his falsehood which would keep him off the streets selling himself at least for a short while. Detective Sergeant Bill Thick happened to be in the front office as he entered and made his complaint.

"I want to report a series of sexual assaults on me and on one of my mates."

"Where's your mate then?" asked Thick.

"He's too scared to come in 'cos the bloke what did it is real nasty but I've got a make a stand," replied Churchyard. With the wave of hysteria for all types of violent crime in the area Thick took him into a separate interview room to record details of his complaint.

"Right, lad, your name and address and then lets hear what's gone on."

"Fred Churchyard of 67 Cable Street, Stepney. This American bloke has repeatedly attacked me but only once has he managed to get his way and it was fucking evil. He forced me down, threatened me with a fuck off sword and buggered me senseless. He done it to my mate too months before and he's tried it on with me twice in the bogs of The Britannia."

"You've taken your time. When did these attacks happen then?" asked Thick somewhat curious about the motivation for these allegations.

"He tried it on with me first on the 27th July, then my mate on the 31st August, he had ago at me again on the 14th of October and then buggered me yesterday. I had to do something or else he'll kill someone." Thick was somewhat suspicious of Churchyard's story but listened on. "My mate," thinking of an imaginary name, "Bill Wogan, he's too scared to come forward, thinks the bloke will kill him. This geezer had him at knife point he did." Thick took a full detailed statement regarding the assaults, all of which involved a high or low level of indecency according to Churchyard and then went on to establish the assailants identity and description.

"He's about 5'10", a medium built bloke with dark hair and a big dark moustache, often wears some fancy uniform or otherwise smart clothes. He's about fifty years of age, but the key thing is that he's an American. He's got a funny name too, Tombs, Tongue, Tumbles, Tumblety or something." In his pressured condition to fabricate the story for money he had struggled to remember the American's name.

Bill Thick witnessed the signatures Churchyard provided on each statement sheet and then went on to explain the legal procedure.

"Right, once this bloke is nicked we will need you to attend court as a witness and give this evidence. You going to turn up and do that then?"

Churchyard finished signing the sheets and looked up towards Thick but couldn't look him in the eye and spoke with somewhat false commitment.

"Course I will, Sergeant, I want this man in jail."

Thick showed Churchyard out of the police station and walked through The Street's corridors to Abberline's office. Churchyard walked across the road and straight into the Commercial Street Tavern where Druitt was waiting at the bar for him. The young man walked up to him but could not look at him and stared at the opticals behind the bar as they spoke.

"Well, is it done then?" asked Druitt nervously of the lad who he could see was sweating and clearly disturbed.

"Yeah, got the rest of the money then, mister?" Druitt pulled out his wallet and withdrew some notes to pay the lad the balance for his planned revenge. He felt sick to the pit of his stomach for setting down this course of action and proffered the money to the boy. He snatched it from Druitt's hand and turned to leave, stopping to make a closing comment.

"Don't look for me again; don't talk to me if you do." With that Churchyard ran from the pub and made his way back to his usual area around The Blind Beggar. Druitt casually finished his drink not wishing to draw attention to himself and left sometime later.

DS Bill Thick in the meantime had made his way round to the incident room to confront Abberline with the statement he had just taken as the description of the individual involved could be of significance to the investigation. He walked in to find Abberline and Godley in the familiar routine of being head in hands reading through statements and reports from officers on foot patrols in the area, both uniform and plain clothed.

"Guv'nor, I've got something you might find of interest bearing in mind some of the consistent parts of the descriptions you've had." Abberline looked up from his reading and stretched with a big yawn as he spoke.

"What you got then, it's getting late. Will it excite me?"

"Well I don't know about that but it might be something or nothing. You've had a couple of consistent things in the descriptions. Big moustache and a foreign accent. I've just taken a complaint of buggery from a young fella by an American with a big moustache, and occasionally in uniform." Godley and Abberline looked at each other and listened intently. "I know it don't mean some bullying queer is Jack the Ripper but he's got to be worth finding and pulling in."

"Got an address from your complainant for this bloke?" said Godley.

"No, but he hangs out in all the pubs in Commercial Street, I thought one of our plain patrols would pick him easily, he would stick out a bit after all."

"Good work, mate," said Abberline, "put it in the brief for everyone and as soon as we have a result and he's in let me know." Bill Thick gave the statement to Abberline as he left with a parting "Goodnight, fellas."

Chapter Twenty

Tuesday 6th November. Everyday since the exchange with Tumblety Mary had kept a bedside vigil from midday to six in the evening hoping Robert would awake. He had stirred and become physically restless several times which she was assured was a good sign, but he had not regained consciousness or opened his eyes. Mary had deposited the money from Tumblety in the wardrobe at Robert's lodgings knowing that it would be safe there and now at around 6.30.p.m she found herself depressed and wandering Commercial Street. She entered The Ten Bells and approached the bar where she saw Julia Styles another street worker who she hadn't seen for some while but knew quite well. She was not dissimilar to Mary in height and build and had the same long auburn hair but was not as pretty as the younger girl. Certainly like Mary she could be considered out of place for working the streets of Whitechapel.

"Well, well, the fair Mary Kelly. How are you darling? Ain't seen you for a while? Where you been?" They kissed and hugged with Julia then ordering the drinks from the amiable barkeeper.

"Two double gins please, Pikey," she said.

"Thank you, Julia love, I've tried to get me self off the streets having found a new man and with these murders taking place."

"New man, eh? Very nice, must be special if you ain't working anymore."

"He is. He's had an accident though and is in the London Hospital. Once he's out we're leaving London."

"Got some money then, have you? What does he do then?"

"He's a copper, but he's giving it up and we've managed to save a bit," Mary was never going to admit where the money to leave had come from.

"Well good for you. Want to know where I've been?" said Julia with obvious pride in a recent achievement.

"Yeah, go on then. What you been up to."

"Met this American," Mary went cold for a moment. "Famous actor, Richard Mansfield, shags like a fucking buck rabbit and pays well too. He's had me going to his place all tarted up in me best for last six weeks paying handsomely. Trouble is I'm back here now as he's leaving with that bloody Ripper and The Star having helped close his play." They had both downed their drinks and with the ebullient mood that Julia was in Mary could see it was time for another. Seeing her old friend had lifted her own spirits and the first double put her in the mood for more. It had been a long time it seemed since she had enjoyed a merry evening.

"Want another one then, love?" she asked Julia.

"Does a cat climb a tree, darling. Course. Same again, eh?"

'Pikey', the barman obligingly served Mary another pair of double gins and the two women settled themselves into a relaxing drinking session.

* * *

Francis Tumblety alighted from his cab in Whitechapel High Street to have a walk before trawling the pubs to find Mary and warn her away. He was oblivious to the fact that he was a wanted man as he paid the driver and began strolling from the Aldgate end of the High Street towards Commercial Street. Ahead he could see a patrolling constable, Joe Cartwright, walking towards him in the now dimly gas lit streets of seven in the evening. The officer gave him a good look up and down and politely spoke to him which relaxed Tumblety's initial tension.

"Good evening, sir," he said to the well dressed moustached gent he was about to pass, obviously not a local man.

"Good evening to you, constable," replied Tumblety politely in his distinctive American drawl. The officer's guard immediately came up as he casually walked on past and kept going to create a little distance between the two of them so he could keep Tumblety under observation. He also knew it would give him a chance to meet another policeman to deal with the suspect together. He had listened intently to the briefing that day regarding the man wanted for indecent assault on four counts and knew that the individual he had just spotted would be a strong suspect.

With about sixty yards between them he turned and followed Tumblety in the dim light and as he had anticipated he met another officer emerging from Colchester Street and he beckoned him over. It was Sergeant Eli Caunter, known to his colleagues as 'Tommy Roundhead', who crossed the road to meet Cartwright.

"Sorry, sarge, didn't know it was you. That bloke up there by Commercial Street matches the description of the one involved in those assaults on them lads. Thought it might be better to approach him together to nick him." Caunter looked up to see the figure of a well dressed man turning into Commercial Street. He nodded to Cartwright and they began walking in the same direction.

"Good thinking, lad, let's go and have a chat with him." Caunter spoke in a quiet voice to avoid any attention.

They eventually caught up to confront Tumblety up by the junction with Middlesex Street, so just short of where the busiest pubs all lay.

"Excuse me, sir, can we have a word please," said Caunter with Tumblety stopping in his tracks. Both the policemen had their truncheons to hand. The American turned around slowly and prepared himself to speak. He knew he could not physically confront anyone because of his damaged arm so he had to front out what the officers wanted of him. The thoughts raced through his mind as to why they were confronting him. 'Was his time up? Had he been seen at some point during or after a crime? Had his old acquaintance found the courage to go to the police?'

"Officers, what can I do to help?" Tumblety calmly replied. Caunter continued with the conversation while Cartwright watched intently.

"Sir, can you tell me your name please?"

"Yes, Frank Townsend. I'm sure you've guessed I'm a visitor to your shores."

"Indeed, Mr Townsend. What brings you to Whitechapel in particular? It's not the most scenic part of London. Hardly pretty one might say."

"You're quite right. I am a doctor researching a book on diseases in lower class areas of population; I'm on a field trip you could say."

"Really? Discovered much then?" said Caunter cynically.

"Yes, the area suffers in the same way as deprived parts of New York."

Caunter looked at Cartwright with a knowing glance before speaking again.

"Mr Townsend, I have to ask you to come to the local police station with me as you match the description of an American man involved in four cases of indecent assault." Tumblety could see both officers were ready to strike with their truncheons if necessary and could see little value in resisting with only one strong arm. At least he wasn't being arrested on suspicion of being the Ripper.

"Officer's, I will gladly help but I can assure you that you have the wrong man." Cartwright produced some handcuffs in his left hand. "They won't be necessary, constable, I will come quietly. Commercial Street I presume?" Cartwright put the cuffs away but Caunter took Tumblety's walking cane before he replied again. "Sir, I'll need to secure this please," Caunter held the cane in a good grasp, "and you are correct we are going to The Street." The group of three headed off with a brisk walk north towards the police station with Tumblety again frustrated that he would not find Mary for another night. Ironically he passed within yards of her as they strolled quickly by The Ten Bells on their way to the custody office and further questioning.

Mary Kelly staggered from The Ten Bells arm in arm with Julia Styles at about eleven o'clock wandering straight across the road to head towards Dorset Street and Millers Court. Watching from the shadows of the pillars at the front of Christchurch was Severin Klosowski, also known as George Chapman, noting exactly where the two drunken women had gone to. As they disappeared from sight he ran across the road to try to keep observation on them. He saw them turn into the dark recess of Millers Court and listened to their drunken conversation echoing back along the dim passageway.

"Mary, can I doss with you tonight to save the journey to Bethnal Green, love?" Julia's voice was slurring its words heavily.

"Course you can, I shan't be getting this drunk on Thursday you know," said Mary in a chirpy manner. A snippet of information that Klosowski would use to his advantage in couple of days time as he hatched a plan to gain this woman's wealth. It must be considerable based on what the man called Townsend had asked him to do.

* * *

Abberline had been called back in to The Street from home as a result of the arrest of the American suspect. He had also told the officers who called on him late on that Tuesday night to get Godley in too as he wanted the pair of them present to interview this man. On the journey he sat in a rattling hansom cab. He couldn't believe they had someone in custody who bore the few consistent hallmarks of the vague descriptions given regarding the Whitechapel murders. He really didn't care about the homosexual assault allegations, they could be co-incidental, and he would let Bill Thick deal with them, but he would interview this man intently over the Ripper's crimes and take samples of handwriting from him.

It was a cold November night around eleven o'clock when he arrived outside Commercial Street Police Station his breath visible as he alighted from the cab with an officer on the door of the nick about to leave who held it open for the noted detective. He strolled purposefully to the incident room dumping his top coat, hat and scarf on his desk and made straight for the custody office. Inside he met Bill Thick and Kerby who was the night shift custody sergeant.

"Is George on his way?" he asked of Thick

"Yes, Guv, a cab's been sent to bring him in."

"Right, tell me all about this bloke then, Kerby, and get one of your lads to get me a decent cup of tea." A young constable was despatched to get tea for all those present.

"His name he says is Frank Townsend, a doctor allegedly in the area to do some research on diseases in poorer areas. Reckons it is his first time here in the East End although he did say he's been in London for a few weeks. He's fifty so he says, born in New York to an Irish immigrant family, a doctor and he seems a very calm character. He hasn't been fazed by being here so far. Says he recovering from a broken arm he's had for at least a month."

"All right Bill, good stuff we might have to get the divisional surgeon to have a look at that to confirm it, with that in mind does that rule him out of your case?"

"If it's true, technically yes because two of the alleged assaults were in the last month."

The young, thin, pasty looking probationary constable walked back in with a tray of steaming cups of tea which the gathered group looked at enthusiastically each taking a cup for themselves.

"Well done, lad," said Abberline having a small slurp from his cup. "That's handsome."

"One for me then?" said Godley entering the office from behind the heavy wooden door leading from the main corridor. The young constable was somewhat disappointed when Godley took the remaining tea from the tray that he had ear marked for himself. Dejectedly he walked back into the depths of the custody office from whence he came to make another for himself.

"Right tell George what you have told me, Bill, while I just go and have a look at him through the cell door spy hole."

Abberline sipping his tea wandered down the corridor of cells which were unusually quiet as he began to go and take a look at Townsend. His footsteps were obviously heard by some of the evening's inmates and the noise and shouting began.

"You fucking filth bastards, let me out of here, or I'll do the lot of you!" came a drunken shout from the first cell on the right accompanied by banging on the cell door. Abberline in his calm style paid it no heed and carried on walking and drinking. As he passed a cell two doors down on the left the wicket was open and he heard a hissing sound coming from it and then some hateful speech.

"Abberline, you slag! I remember you when you were a shit bag DS, you sent me down to Newgate for eight months and I ain't forgot." Abberline stopped and bent slightly keeping his distance from the wicket to face his abuser who he recognised instantly from the past in Whitechapel.

"Well, well, Michael Kidney. Nice to see you. Obviously a crap thief still if you're still being caught," Abberline slammed the wicket leaving Kidney to pointlessly shout more abuse after him.

He came to cell number eight the 'accommodation' as it was sometimes called that Townsend had been given. The wicket was shut so Abberline was able to stand square in front of the door unnoticed and peer through the spy hole above the wicket and look at the suspect. He could see a well dressed medium built man of around fifty with the bushy moustache sat very calmly on the bed of the cell with his hands resting on his lap, his cane in the possession of the custody sergeant. For a man who it seemed unlikely to have been incarcerated before he was remarkably calm. He may well be prepared for an interview, although he would not be expecting an interview regarding the Ripper murders. Abberline returned to the main office deep in thought and spoke to the trio of sergeants.

"Right, George, go and prepare the interview room, make it look nice and comfortable non-confrontational. Kerby get ready to do the custody records when Bill brings him out. Bill, bring him up, offer him a tea and then show him in to us. Will you charge him over your assaults today?"

"Depends what he says, Guv, I'd like to trace this other lad before charging him really. If I can't we'll charge in a few days time, giving him a drop of bail to return," replied Thick.

"Right," said Abberline, "give me a couple of minutes and bring him through"

Abberline joined Godley in the interview room. They were keen to try to lull the calm looking Townsend into a false sense of relaxation and drop his guard. The desk was pushed to one side with a single chair for Godley to sit at and make a contemporaneous record of the interview, two other chairs were arranged centrally near enough facing each other with only a slight angle to them to take them off true about six feet apart. Abberline was keen to create an air of informality and having no barriers between them to break any sense of advocacy. Godley took a seat behind the desk with sheets of official statement paper in front of him in a pile and two pens with ink pots to hand. There was a rap at the door so Abberline remained standing as he called for the parties outside to enter.

The door was opened from the outside by Thick who showed Townsend into the interview room remaining outside himself. Abberline beckoned him in.

"Good evening, Doctor Townsend please take a seat." He showed him to the seat facing the door and therefore facing him and Godley. Tumblety, or to them Townsend, was taken by surprise at the high level of courtesy showed to him by these officers and sat in a slow dignified fashion.

"Thank you, gentlemen," he said calmly taking his seat. Abberline closed the door acknowledging Thick and sat himself down facing him.

"Sorry for the discomfort and inconvenience of being brought here, Doctor, but as I'm sure you appreciate these are routine enquiries. I am Inspector Abberline and this is Sergeant Godley of Scotland Yard, we are investigating the crimes of the man who has branded himself 'Jack the Ripper'." Tumblety who had been suspicious of their kind treatment to this point immediately felt himself becoming more defensive.

"I've heard of you, Mr Abberline, but I was arrested on an enquiry regarding assault on young men. It seems that you wish to question me on the Ripper killings. With that in mind am I not entitled to legal representation?" Tumblety spoke hoping to put the detectives on the back foot. Abberline was completely unfazed and Godley kept writing with his head down as if the other two didn't exist.

"Doctor, it is doctor isn't it?"

"Yes," he replied arrogantly

"You are quite right, however, if it is deemed prejudicial to the investigation of a serious arrestable offence, which I am sure you would agree five murders are, then I can begin or continue the interview whilst waiting for that representation to arrive. Now do you wish for the presence of a solicitor?" Abberline maintained a relaxed matter-of-fact manner which made Tumblety feel uncomfortable. He could recognise the old detective's wily skill and experience in such matters.

"Thank you for that legal explanation, Mr Abberline. I won't require a solicitor at present."

"Doctor Townsend, can you illuminate me on whether you have been in England since the start of August?"

"I have, yes."

"And in all that time have you been in London or the greater London area?" Tumblety knew he could lie and say he had been in Liverpool as he knew the city well, but he had no alibi. He knew he would have to try re-kindle a relationship with Druitt to forge a decent alibi regarding his movements in London.

"I have been in your capital since that time, Mr Abberline, and have been for most of August enjoying the sites of the city and the hospitality of the Ritz Hotel. You check with them as to whether or not I have been a guest."

"Indeed we will, sir, but it wouldn't stop you frequenting Whitechapel would it?

"No it wouldn't, Inspector, but I don't think the proprietor's of the Ritz would take too kindly to me returning covered in blood would they?"

"Who said anything about returning covered in blood?"

"But you said that you were investigating the Rippers crimes, right?"

"Yes, doesn't mean I was necessarily accusing you of being him though, does it?" said Abberline watching Townsend shift a little in his seat.

"So, do you have an interest in anatomical specimens?" asked Abberline.

"As a doctor I obviously do."

"Do you own a collection of any specimens?"

"I do have a few here and there, yes for diagnostic and teaching purposes."

"Ever been to Paris, Dr Townsend?"

"What's that got to do with Jack the Ripper?" He said with mock confusion knowing where Abberline maybe going with his questions.

"Just asking because of a story I heard doing the rounds in medical circles." Abberline spoke nonchalantly.

"Well, I don't know what this story is but whether I've been to Paris or not is none of your business, Inspector, I thought your jurisdiction was in London."

"London, the rest of England and Wales actually if necessary," Abberline quipped, he did enjoy the banter of challenging interviews.

"So, were you frequenting the East End on the 6th and 7th of August?"

"I doubt it, I hadn't long arrived. I was probably enjoying a good Chateau Neuf du Pape and Chateau Briand at the Ritz with some company."

"Anyone who can confirm that then?" replied Abberline briskly.

"Probably."

"What about the 31st of August, where were you then?"

"Inspector, I don't keep a diary in my head."

"And the 7th September, and the 30th?"

"I may have been in the East End from time to time beginning my research, I just don't know."

"Who could confirm your movements?"

"That's my business right now not yours," Tumblety was getting fazed.

"Is that so you can prime them first is it?" sniped Abberline.

"HOW DARE YOU!" Tumblety got to his feet.

"Sit down, sir; we are only trying to establish your movements and motivation for being in the East End. Now, what sort of doctor are you?"

"Inspector, this is outrageous. I demand representation or to see a senior officer now."

"I am the most senior on duty, and you can have a 'brief' but it won't stop the interview. What sort of doctor are you?" Tumblety took a deep breath and answered with knowledge he could support.

"I am a former combat surgeon with the confederate army and I now practice herbal medicine and research its benefits to all. I am quite renowned in the States." 'Christ!' he thought, he had just left himself open. He was renown in New Jersey, New England and New York State but not as Frank Townsend.

"So I could look up your reputation with the embassy then?"

"No, I doubt they'd know me."

"But they could put me on to someone who does?" asked Abberline. Tumblety had dug a hole for himself and he felt it becoming bottomless.

"They may do, I am only known in a few small towns in each state."

"So, being a surgeon you would have good anatomical knowledge then?"

"Yes, but any good butcher could do what your Ripper has done." Abberline took a long pause, he stood up and walked around the back of his chair and then turned to face Townsend leaning on the back of the seat he had vacated.

"You are quite right but why would a butcher take parts of a human body away. A doctor might have a use for them?"

"A butcher or whoever might want to eat them."

"Yes, I could understand that with a kidney, drawing the comparison with an animal. But what about uteri?" Tumblety had to consider his answer.

"The product of a sick mind of what is being considered in some circles as psychopathic behaviour."

"Are you the man who calls himself Jack the Ripper?"

"No. Were you hoping I would break down and give you a confession?"

"Not necessarily but it's worth a try. Some will confess."

"Do you have any further *real* questions for me, Inspector?"

"Yes, just bear with us a moment." Abberline turned to Godley to see him finish some writing. "Well done, George. Doctor would you just sign our contemporaneous record for us?" Tumblety looked at the desk and the statement sheets a little ruffled by the interview and replied.

"Yes, of course if it gets me out."

"Don't forget our colleague wishes to speak to you, but it should do."

Godley passed across the papers to the edge of the desk nearest Tumblety who willing signed each of the five sheets put in front of him. As he signed the third he realised the consequences of his actions and paused half way through.

"What's the matter then, Doctor?" asked Abberline with knowing victory in his voice. Tumblety didn't look up but continued, it was too late.

"Nothing, Inspector. Just had a flash in my mind of things to do tomorrow." He finished signing the papers and sat back in his chair looking at the partially smiling Abberline with contempt.

"Right, me and George will leave you to DS Thick. Thank you, Doctor. Goodnight." The two of them left the room closing the door behind them, Abberline deliberately containing his glee until the two of them were alone back in the incident room.

"All right, Bill, he's all yours now," said Abberline.

"Thanks, Guv. I'll let you know when we're done with him. You happy to let me bail him?"

"Yes, provided he puts up surety. If not I want him remanded. He is our best line so far." Abberline and Godley went back to their office leaving Thick to interview Townsend over his complaint.

Back in the incident room Abberline pulled out a drawer in his desk and grabbed a bottle of malt whiskey from it.

"George, I know you don't approved but indulge me this once. We have a major break-through."

"All right, Fred, granted. It's his writing isn't it?"

"You'll have my job yet. He realised when it was too late that we have his hand writing. We need it analysed as soon as, so first thing send someone off with it to The Yard to Anderson's office to get approval from him for it's comparison to the 'Dear Boss' and 'from Hell' letters. He may have just signed his own execution order, my friend." He poured large tumblers of drink for them both and continued. "Keep this bit low key. Don't want any undue fuss early on."

"Fine. This," said Godley indicating to the glasses "is a rare treat I hope you realise?"

"I do, **Dad**, I do," replied Abberline sarcastically. They chinked their glasses together and laughed for the first time in weeks.

* * *

Wednesday 7th November. With the late night from interviewing the man they knew as Townsend, Abberline and Godley didn't arrive back at work until midday. Walking into their office Bill Thick was there to meet them; he didn't look good. He was asleep slumped over a desk head in his arms folded on the table looking as if he had not been home. Abberline approached him and gently rocked him by the right shoulder an action which caused him to slowly wake up.

"Oh fuck me, Guv'nor, am I pleased to see you," said an obviously drained Thick. "Been here all night with that fucker in the end."

Whitechapel

"Did he not make the surety then?" asked Godley.

"No, didn't get that far. After a persistent argument about addresses and absolute denials to being involved in the assaults, turns out he lied about his name. He's called Francis Tumblety, still an American doctor but he came clean as that was the name I was given and he claims the whole thing is a falsehood to tarnish his name."

"Bloody hell. Bit of a story then. Is he still in his cell then?" asked Abberline.

"Yeah. He's been charged over some of the assaults but we kept him here for you to talk to him again and to wait for daytime to secure the surety money. The bank was due to answer at anytime."

"Which bank?" asked Godley.

"Cootes. Says he's got deposits and a credit facility with them."

Abberline looked through the spy hole and seeing that this Dr Tumblety was lying on his bed he signalled to the custody sergeant to open the cell door and he went in. Tumblety sat up to face him.

"So, Dr Tumblety, tell me why we shouldn't put you on remand right now? Tell me why you should be granted any sort of bail then. You lied to me last night," said Abberline coldly.

"The only thing that wasn't true was my name. The rest was right. I should be granted bail because I can afford it, Inspector."

"Right £1500. Can you afford that then?"

"Yes, just send a messenger to Cootes and they will give you the letter of surety."

"Right, you stay in here until we have that letter. Once it's here then we expect you back in nine days to answer enquiries on my investigation and one more issue on Detective Sergeant Thick's case too. Do you understand?"

"Yes, sir, I do."

"What's you're address then?"

"17 Graham Road, Hackney," said Tumblety knowing he would have to look for somewhere else or be ready to move immediately.

"You don't turn up when you are expected then I will personally put your door in." With that Abberline left slamming the door behind him. By 3.p.m Tumblety had lawfully left the police station. Exhausted from a sleepless night, he caught a cab to Graham Road and slept through to Friday morning.

Late that afternoon Abberline and Godley had heard from the main C.I.D office at Scotland Yard that it would take up to ten days for the handwriting to be analysed and inference of guilt satisfied.

"Why the hell does it take so long, George?" asked a frustrated Abberline.

"Because the Mets' one and only expert in a line that rarely has to be pursued is on holiday in France and doesn't get back until the 19th," replied an equally irritated Godley, both men desperate not to let a good suspect slip through their fingers. They could take comfort in the fact that he would now know that he was an obvious suspect and if it was him he would think heavily as to whether he would strike on bail. However, another dramatic twist was about to influence the direction of the investigation yet again.

Robert Lees had not slept from about 3.a.m until day break as a result of the most startling clear vision he had ever had. Having experienced no sleep, subsequently he had meticulously written down a record of what he had seen in his most vivid vision of the next potential or actual Ripper crime. Despite reservations of hostility from Abberline he knew he had to see him to allow his conscience at least to be at rest if nothing else. He knew it would be sometime before the horrors of the murder he had psychologically witnessed would fade. He arrived at Commercial Street Police Station at 5.p.m by stylish carriage which waited for him outside while he went in to conduct his traumatic business. He spoke to the front desk sergeant who sent off a constable to fetch Abberline, a routine he was now accustomed to. Within minutes he was guided by Godley to the incident room where he was invited to sit by Abberline.

"Mr Lees, without wishing to sound cynical or ungrateful, I do hope you have some new information from your visions for us," said Abberline.

"Inspector, I spent the night awake from 3.a.m until dawn as a result of what I witnessed in my last vision. A crime so horrible is imminent that it will shock the core of society and the police service and will scar the memories of all who witness it. I will not be wasting your time."

"Mr Lees, most importantly can you tell me when and where it will happen?" asked Abberline keen to cut to the chase.

"Mr Abberline, my visions as I have said are mainly and mostly entirely symbolic, but..." Abberline cut in with impatience and irritation.

"We have just made a significant break through potentially, Mr Lees, now get on with it and tell me something I need to know!"

"Damn your godless impatience, Abberline! Listen! There must be something from what I am about to tell you that will help you catch him. In the next week a woman not from this country will be the next victim. She will die alone in her own home as a result of a crime fuelled by greed. The killer will be a foreign man dressed smartly with knowledge of what he is doing, with dark evil eyes set behind a face covered by a moustache. They will meet in a building that is named after a figure head of sorts. When she is found she will be unrecognisable."

"Fred, The Britannia. Tumblety matches the description and all we need to do is watch any girls in there that maybe from abroad," said Godley interpreting the vision instantly. Abberline was still cynical.

"Right. You tell no one of this, Lees. There must be no chance of the man being tipped off. Do you understand?"

"I do, Inspector. Tell me when this over and I am proved right, any chance of a simple apology or a thank you?" Abberline ignored him totally.

"Show him out, George."

"May God be your judge, Abberline, you are the most soulless man I have ever met."

"Get out. Yes, your visions are accurate and they tell us much but this is the first time they have given us anything close to a clue before the crime. Problem is Whitechapel is full of foreign men and women, some are smartly dressed, many of both have moustaches and we won't be able to follow everyone to their homes, so don't flatter yourself that you think you might of solved these crimes, if you do, then truly you might be considered a fool and a lunatic. But thank you, don't come back unless you are asked." Lees stormed out too humiliated to reply with Godley looking a little stunned by the outbursts from both.

"George, don't get me wrong, it all helps but consider the logistics of what I have just described."

"But we've got to try, Fred."

"I know. I fucking know more than anyone. Big briefing tomorrow at six, two and ten and get Mather and Robinson on watch for Tumblety."

The worst fact for the two of them was that it was now imminent a murder was coming, there was no doubt of that based on Lees' previous information and that's what hurt and troubled them most, knowing it was coming.

Chapter Twenty-One

Thursday 8th November 2.p.m. For the second time that day Abberline had given the following briefing to all patrols.

"No one takes time off during the next week and everyone will be paid to do an extra four hours after their normal shift. We are looking for a foreign man with a dark appearance, deep set 'evil' eyes and a moustache. He may well be smartly dressed and could be a medical practitioner. Our man Tumblety is already under observation so pay attention to others. He may well, from information provided by Mr Lees, pick someone up in The Britannia and go home with them. Potential victims to be looked at are also of foreign origin with somewhere of their own to go to so there could be a lot of following people off at a discreet distance. Everyone has got to be vigilant because the one thing that is certain is that he will strike. We need to stop or catch him and hopefully both. No questions? Then get out there and find him. I will be out too in-between the briefings." The parade room emptied of all it's occupants who filed out of the police station to hopefully bring about an end to these crimes.

Severin Klosowski was keen to have the money to pay the new world a visit and be able to return if he didn't like it. The task that he had been requested to do by the odd fellow Townsend fuelled his sense of opportunity. If this man had offered him £500 to kill a woman then she must be in possession of more money driving him to act alone and not bother to contact Townsend further. He pondered these issues as he cropped his hair and moustache to venture out to The Ten

Bells that night. The newspapers had been full of information about descriptions of the Ripper and the sporting of a moustache seemed a key element, so keeping it short cropped might allow him to go un-noticed. He wished to pass unobtrusively and changing his appearance should help. He would dress in very average clothes for the area again to be unexceptional. He recalled the picture of Mary Kelly in his minds eye as he contemplated his task for the evening. He had seen her about as he had told Townsend and she was indeed unusually attractive for the normal unfortunates of Whitechapel. He would take delight in her form before killing her. His shop was closed for the day so that he could get into Commercial Street at the earliest opportunity.

Meanwhile Tumbleby had left his lodgings in Hackney to head down to the East End in the hope of finally finding Mary to warn her off. Almost instantly having only walked for some ten minutes to take the air he was aware of a curious man and woman who seemed to be going at a distance to wherever he was going. He guessed it wouldn't affect him trying to find her, but would they intercept him as soon as he did and may prevent him from being able to warn her.

Sir Charles Warren was in his office with a tailor trying out the final fitting of his Commissioners dress uniform prior to the Lord Mayor's parade the next day, 9th November. Used to military dress uniforms the nature of the outfit was not unfamiliar to him although he did feel that there were a few too many feathers in the dress hat. Superintendent Arnold was present in the office and they were chatting about the Whitechapel case.

"Tom, you are aware of my fragile position in relation to this whole affair?"

"Indeed I am, Sir Charles. Abberline seems to have been presented with his greatest opportunity yet to catch the killer. They have one suspect under observation who is on bail for a string of indecent homosexual assaults and information from Robert Lees that a murder will take place in the locale this week. They've flooded it with patrols and watching all foreign men and women as a result. I don't think your resignation will be necessary. I think he will be caught in the act this very week."

"I wish I could share you optimism, Tom. I can't seem to remember a time when this grisly affair wasn't taking place."

Whitechapel

"Don't worry, Commissioner, as soon as this is over then no one will ever remember the whole ghastly affair." Arnold would never really know the irony of his words.

During the afternoon Mary visited Robert in hospital to find a miracle had taken place; he was awake, out of the coma. He was sat in bed when she arrived and chatting happily to a nurse but appeared to have little use of his left arm at present. She ran to his side sobbing and flung her arms around him, with him only able to respond with his right arm.

"Oh, Robert, darling! You're alive, oh I love you so much!" she kissed him and spoke to the nurse before he could reply. "When can he be released?"

Robert interjected before the nurse had an opportunity to answer.

"They say I have to have a couple of days under observation to make sure there's no complications but then I can go, the arm will apparently regain movement gradually as the break heals," replied Robert.

"I'll leave you two to it," said the nurse smiling. Mary settled into the chair next to him holding his right hand in both of hers and earnestly addressed him.

"So, what the hell happened to you?"

"I'm sorry I stormed out, we've got to put our pasts behind us."

"I agree, now what happened."

"After I left you I went for a walk to clear my head. I got dragged into an alley off of Whitechapel Road by that Sean Miller and one of his mates, the biggest bloke I've ever seen. He had some how discovered I was a copper and they laid into me good and proper. There was no way I could beat him so I managed to get free before they killed me and ran. Trouble was I was a bit concussed by them and ran straight into the roadway and got knocked down big time by a cab. That's it, everything went black after that."

"My, God. That bloke Littlechild has been in to see you. He said to let him know through the bar keeper at the Commercial Street Tavern when you woke up. I'll try and get there later."

"Well what you doing tonight?" asked Robert.

"I'm having a drink with an old friend in The Ten Bells. I'll certainly be having one to celebrate darling," she smiled holding his hand.

"Be careful. Have they caught him yet?"

"No. They……."
"What?"
"Nothing. I don't know what they are doing. When are we going to leave London?"
"As soon as I'm out I can tell you. I've had enough. Let's go to Ireland, eh?" He spoke now sensing that life was too precious to hold on to and he had to leave his personal vendetta behind. They spent a very happy couple of hours together in the hospital chatting about the future before Mary had to leave to go and meet Julia. Neither of them knew that it would be last time they ever saw each other.

* * *

Tumblety strolled south in Commercial Street now completely aware of being under constant observation. In a way it didn't matter, he intended to kill no one; he just needed to warn Mary. He had passed The Britannia and was heading towards the High Street when he noticed an auburn haired girl coming towards him in the distance. It was her. They neared and she saw him too and instantly turned off into Middlesex Street and quickened her pace. He picked up his own and looked over his shoulder at his pursuers and could see their alarm at him speeding up. He rounded the corner himself to see her running. He had to call after her.

"Mary! Wait, I've got to tell you something, and now!" She screamed back a reply the pitch of which got people watching them and started Mather and Robinson into a sprint after Tumblety.

"Leave me alone, you killer!"

"Stop, police!" he heard from behind. He stopped to avoid her calling something else incriminating and he felt himself pushed to the ground by the two disguised cops, the one dressed as a woman now veil and hatless and looking very odd. They spoke harshly as they handcuffed him.

"Francis Tumblety, you are under arrest on suspicion of attempted murder!"

"You dim wit's! I'm trying to warn her."

"Oh yeah, heard that before," said Mather. He continued talking to Robinson. "Better go and get her and find out what all this is about." Robinson looked up but couldn't see the auburn haired girl in the street any longer. He ran in her direction looking left and right into doorways and side turnings but she was gone.

"Warn her about what then, eh?" Tumblety fell silent. If he spoke now he would incriminate himself at the very least in a conspiracy to commit murder. He did not know what to say. He began to sob. Robinson returned and helped lift Tumblety off the floor having had his arms handcuffed behind his back. They walked him to the junction with Commercial Street where Mather blew his whistle. Six uniform officers were with them in seconds and what they were actually waiting for turned up within a minute; a black Mariah to transport Tumblety to The Street.

"Is Abberline still in the nick?" Mather asked the Mariah driver.

"Yeah, I think so," he replied.

"Well looks like we might have his man for him then," Mather said with a sense of pride. He and Robinson rode with Tumblety in the Mariah whilst the other uniform officers who had come to the scene wandered off, with their guards now a little down.

Mary made her way up to The Ten Bells via the back streets which had eventually brought her into Church Street leading directly to the pub. She was a little shaken and needed a drink to calm her nerves and was not disappointed to find Julia already at the bar who she spoke to instantly.

"Get me a double G, love."

"My God, Mary, you're bloody shaking. What's up then?"

"Oh I just saw a strange bloke I used to know who gave me a fright. I'll be all right in moment with a good drink inside me."

"Too bloody right, love." The bar keeper served them their drinks which they chinked together to toast themselves and knocked back in one.

"Another of the same please, 'barky'," said Mary getting some coins from her small purse to pay him.

"Blimey, kid, you're in a rush ain't you?" said Julia a little surprised.

"Yes, I've got a lot to forget about," she smiled and looked into her friends eyes "And a lot to celebrate. Robert's woken up and I have a lot to look forward to. This time next week I reckon we'll be our way to a country life in Limerick."

"Well good luck you. Here's to you and your Rob." Julia raised her glass to toast her friend's future. Mary smiled and knocked the drink back again very quickly, this time with her eyes beginning to roll from its intoxicating effect, but getting ready for another. "Bloody hell, Mary, you do want a party dontcha?"

Mary simply nodded her head as she tried to catch her breath. They ordered another double gin each.

All of this was being keenly observed by Severin Klosowski sat in a corner of the pub quietly enjoying a pint of ale and a pipeful of tobacco biding his time watching his intended target who he had been waiting for to arrive. He planned to follow her off close to her home and strike in the privacy of the interior of it. He carried a box inside of which he had sharp bladed butchers gutting knife, a gag and a folded leather sack. He was optimistic by the drinking he had witnessed so far that she would be quite easy to deal with later on, mostly likely being too drunk to offer any real resistance.

* * *

Tumblety had been sat in a cell with his handcuffs removed and had regained his composure during the short journey to the police station and had prepared himself psychologically for another grilling from Abberline.

It wasn't long before the door to his cell opened and Abberline was stood there with his same sidekick again, Godley.

"Hello, Doctor. About to strike again were you?" asked Abberline.

"Is this an interview, cop?" said Tumblety abrasively.

"Just answer the question." Tumblety looked around the cell before speaking and swallowed looking down before looking at Abberline.

"Actually, no. I thought the auburn haired girl was someone else. So it doesn't matter really. Your men over-reacted of course, it's not like I didn't know they were there so it's unlikely, don't you think, that I would commit a murder whilst knowingly being watched. Hmm?" Abberline wasn't going to allow Tumblety any form of moral victory in his mind so he took his time to give a considered reply.

"Well, Tumblety, lets examine where we are at tonight. You are in here and that potential victim is still out there. I reckon if we can go the next seven days without another murder then that starts to give us a healthy case against you."

"What? Keep me here for a week? You can't do that, Abberline." The cell door was slammed shut leaving him alone. He stood and rushed to the door and shouted through the closed wicket.

"ABBERLINE, COME HERE!" He found himself alone with no one taking any notice of him.

Back at The Ten Bells a little before nine o'clock neither Julia nor Mary could make intelligible conversation and both of them were quite unsteady on their feet. They both realised that they had had enough and it was time to wander the short distance around the corner to home and sleep off the effects of alcohol abuse until the morning. The morning was a time that neither were looking forward to with the realisation of how much gin they had consumed. Klosowski watched carefully and could see that they were about to move. They both got to their feet slowly ultimately holding each other up to keep themselves steady and maintain some semblance of balance.

"Come on, Mary love, lets stagger ourselves home and sleep it all off with our imaginary prince charming!" Julia dribbled as she slurred.

"My god, I can't remember the last time I couldn't feel my legs."

"Probably sometime after your fancy Rob filled you up with your legs around your chest!" They both burst into fits of laughter. They struggled towards the door together arm in arm and were about to be hit by the effects of the fresh air and their alcohol induced state.

Klosowski waited for them to get through the door before he stood slowly returning his glass to the bar to give them a bit of a head start and then exited The Ten Bells himself. They hadn't got far when he got outside. The massively drunken state that Mary Kelly was in was even more of a bonus than he could have wished for; the opportunity to resist would be minimal. The two laughing and staggering women had to stop after only a very short distance as the fresh cool evening air had mixed with the alcohol in their heads sending them even further into howls of laughter and shrieks of humorous regret.

"I'm never doing this again," said Mary holding her forehead. 'No you're quite right you won't' thought Klosowski as he kept an eye on them from a distance. He knew their journey home knowing it was nearby from when he had seen Mary Kelly around so he casually stood and lit another pipe for himself.

He felt quite invisible to those around him having removed his moustache temporarily and cropped his hair as no one gave him a second glance with even a pair of patrolling constables paying him no heed whatsoever as they strolled past. His smart but modest attire for the area seemed to help and he had worn a hat to be able to shield his face a little. The efforts to change his usual appearance with the hype surrounding the type of man the police were looking for had been worth it. The women eventually got themselves across to the other side of Commercial Street and turned off into Millers Court, the dark, drab bricked home of some many underprivileged East End people. Its alleyways were featureless brick thoroughfares which smelt of urine and rotting food, as did so many of the slum developments immediately off the main roads. Again he waited for them to get out of sight into the entrance passage and crossed the road himself. He peered around the archway where they had gone to see them further down in a drunken friendly embrace wishing each other a goodnight.

"Thanks, Mary, that was a real laugh. See you over the weekend, eh?"

"Goodnight. Sleep well now and lock your door," replied Mary as she turned away from her friend and towards a window on the corner of what Klosowski assumed must be her rented room. He saw her reach through what he concluded was a broken pane of glass, pull her arm free again and then walk unsteadily round the corner, open the door and enter. The other woman had walked further down pulled out a key and then entered a room conventionally.

Now that they were both in he walked down Millers Court to see where Kelly had gone to. It was number 13 and he could see the broken pane of glass; he concluded to himself that with it's proximity to the door on the other corner she must have lent in and released the door lock. His opportunity was getting easier and easier and he decided to come back in an hour when she would be deeply asleep and strike. He walked back out of Millers Court and went over to The Ten Bells and had another leisurely pint of ale to while away the hour he had to 'kill'.

Mary took off her outer clothes and left them in a heap in one corner of the damp room and got onto the bed pulling a rough and dirty blanket over her and huddled underneath it. There was no fire lit, she hadn't been there for a couple of days and no food or drink in the room either as a result. She had only been laying there for a few minutes when suddenly even in her drunken state she realised she had lost her favoured winter shawl somewhere between the pub and home, or had perhaps left it in The Ten Bells. She quickly got dressed and left her room and made her way slowly and unsteadily back towards Commercial Street. She scanned the floor as she went with blurred and uncertain drunken vision looking for the crochet garment she had lost and finally finding herself back in the pub. She entered and went over to the table where she had been sat and found the shawl draped over her chair. The bar keeper called across to her having seen her enter so unsteadily.

"You ain't having any more, Mary. Look at you; you can't even remember to dress."

"Oh, fuck off and leave me alone!" She slurred beginning to feel a little nauseous.

She left the pub back into the cold night air and sat herself on an empty barrel outside to try to regain some composure. She began taking deep breaths to attempt to over come the feeling of wanting to vomit. All of this was being acutely watched by Klosowski who was somewhat perturbed that she had got up again and the time now was getting well passed midnight. She seemed to sit on this barrel head in hands for an eternity; there was no choice he would have to try and take some inconspicuous action to get her off the street. As he decided to leave the pub bar and approach her she got up and began wandering south towards Thrawl Street appearing a little disorientated and heading away from Millers Court. She continued south then meeting a man coming in the opposite direction to whom she spoke, she seemed to know him.

"Here, Hutchinson, lend me sixpence to get a cab home."

"You only live over there, besides, I've spent all me money going to Romford," the man called Hutchinson replied. Klosowski kept himself next to building line as he watched. She turned and walked north again so he decided to meet her head on and try to 'charm' her off the streets offering to get her home safely. She was staggering towards him with her head down as he tapped her on the shoulder and spoke very simply to her.

"Are you all right, my lady?" She paused and had to think before replying.

"My lady?" she said quizzically and then burst out laughing, to which he responded by laughing to put her ease.

"Do you want me to get you home then?" He asked her putting his arm around her shoulders. She was too drunk to remember the current danger on the streets of Whitechapel and having worked them so long was unmoved by his physical contact with her. She mumbled a just about intelligible reply.

"Mmm, all right."

"You'll be all right, as I have told you," replied Klosowski and walked her off in the direction of Millers Court. All of this had been seen and heard by George Hutchison who knowing Mary's normal status within Whitechapel thought little of it and assumed she had agreed to safely make her normal type of wage. They came past him with Klosowski dipping his head using the brim of his hat to avoid being seen, but Hutchison bent down to look at him. Klosowski stared with hate and aggression back at him looking with his head still down and eyes looking up and just for a moment Hutchison thought he looked a bit like the barber from Cable Street but clean shaven.

He watched them cross over to Dorset Street and loiter speaking for a few minutes, he couldn't quite pick up on all of the conversation but saw her give him a small kiss in apparent gratitude on the cheek and they exchanged handkerchiefs. He then saw them both enter Millers Court and not come back out. He stood around for nearly three quarters of an hour before giving up and walking off.

Klosowski saw her to her door and noted she had left it unlocked.

"That was very kind," said Mary as she opened the door.

"Not at all. You just sleep well; maybe you can buy me a drink sometime." She smiled and went in and closed the door. He waited outside but decided to return to The Ten Bells to allow her to settle, knowing he could get in easily once she was asleep. Mary undressed stripping down to her light chemise piling her clothes carefully at the foot of the bed. She settled down to a restful sleep and very quickly began to drift off with pleasant thoughts of visiting Robert the next day knowing he would be discharged soon.

In The Ten Bells they were still serving after hours as was quite normal on occasions. With little else to do but smoke and drink, Klosowski listened into an inane conversation between the landlord and one of his regulars.

"Here, I thought you was going to change the name of this place?" said the drunken customer slouching across the bar.

"No, you didn't hear me right. I said it used to be called something else years ago before it became The Ten Bells."

"Oh, right. What was that then?"

"The Henry the Eighth. Thing is everyone regular now knows it as the Bells, so what's the point in upsetting them all."

Every time the door to the pub opened Klosowski had a good look to make sure that neither of the women had come back and three times during that next hour there were visits from the police looking around at all who were present in there. The authorities accepted that the more people were out and about perhaps the less chance the Ripper had to strike for fear of being seen. Little did he know that over in The Britannia the police had a plain clothes presence all night based on Robert Lees information; Lees wasn't infalable. When the tedious hour was up he walked back outside and before disappearing along the passage for Millers Court he had a good look up and down Commercial Street. Good, there was no one around to see him. He went straight to number 13 to find the broken glass had been padded out with some old rags, to stop the draughts he guessed, so he carefully removed them and looked in. He could see Kelly asleep in her bed with one arm draped over her body and her face turned away from him. Klosowski slowly and carefully reached in and unlocked the door; he walked around the corner opening the door slowly and quietly and went in, closing it carefully behind him and locking it again. He stuffed the rags back into the window to ensure that no one had the view he just had without specific action to gain it. He walked up to the bed and looked down over the sleeping pretty Irish girl. She was particularly lovely so maybe he might be able to have his way with her before demanding the money and killing her to buy her silence. He emptied the box of his implements and the gag he stuffed it into a lump in his right hand ready to use it, despite being drunk she would still be able to make a lot of noise. The knife he placed in a pocket. It was now between three and four in the morning. He grabbed her throat so hard she was unable to make a noise and as she woke opening her mouth to try to scream he stuffed it with the rolled up gag. She struggled wildly in absolute fear of her life and almost started to get herself off of the bed so he threw himself on stop of her pinning her down with his own body weight. She started trying to kick but without success as she felt his hot tobacco and ale scented breath on her. Was this Jack the Ripper or just a rapist? She would know but only for a few harrowing minutes, if that.

With the hand that had held the gag he pinned both of her arms above her head and with the hand that previously held her throat she could feel him reaching down and hitching her petticoat chemise up to get access to her for the purpose of rape. Having promised herself to Robert she was never going to let another man defile her and with a supreme effort she yanked her arms free of his grasp and punched and scratched him in the face. He yelled in pain and with his body arching slightly she managed to also strike him with one of knees in his groin which forced him off the bed landing heavily on the floor. She got up to get to the door pulling the gag from her mouth and made a loud scream of 'murder, help, murder!' But, her assailant was fast too. He was up from the floor and pinned her against the door with a hand over her mouth before she could open it and drew the glistening bladed knife on her. As he went to swing it towards her face she flayed out with her hands which took a massive amount of knife injury. Her palms and undersides of her fingers and forearms received terrible deep wounds as she tried to defend herself knowing this was the face of death. The incredible pain this created very quickly became numb but it had caused her to drop her guard which was when she felt a cold deep sensation across the front of her neck. Within a split second she discovered she couldn't breathe and felt a warm fluid gushing over her torso; she also felt it draining into her severed windpipe filling her lungs already desperate for air; she felt herself suddenly becoming very faint.

Still conscious he grabbed her by the arms, Mary now without any strength to resist, and dragged her over to the bed where he flung her down before striking again. She looked into his face; she had scarred it heavily with her nails and could see the gashes were deep which must have driven this evil mans vengeance. That was the last thing she saw. Mercifully she lost consciousness and died from the massive blood loss of the throat wound just before he savagely attacked her face and entire body in revenge for her retaliation. He struck at her once beautiful face repeatedly with the knife with slashing and stabbing motions until within seconds there was no face; he cut off her ears and nose. He moved down to her lower body and stabbed deep into her sternum and ripped down with the knife opening up her entire chest and abdominal cavity; he furiously stabbed and slashed at the internals of these areas tearing out her heart and entrails, placing the latter on the bedside table. He cut off her breasts and discarded them at either end of the bed. The more he attacked the greater his fury became as he slashed and stabbed into her thighs eventually skinning them down to the bone and leaving piles of flesh around her lifeless and unrecognisable body. After several minutes of prolonged attack he had inflicted a massive and hideous amount of damage to most of her body, face and limbs. He stood back from the bed breathless and covered in blood to observe his handiwork; as a former mortuary attendant he was pleased with the speed of his work and looked at the blood soaked knife.

The deep red blood dripped heavily off of it and glistened in the faint candle light that lit the room. It looked quite black, almost like some sort of molasses; it fascinated him and he slowly lifted the knife to his face and smelt the blood. Human blood had a quality to it he could not quite discern from other types and finally, after all the years he had indulged in it he was driven to taste it. He licked the blade slowly and with a sense of wonderment at the taste of so much of another human's blood. It drove him on further.

Forgetting the original financial motivation of the crime he turned to the fire place. There was a kettle hanging over the lifeless fire grate which still held some water, into this he placed Mary's heart and a portion of the flesh he had cut from her thigh. He swung it back over the grate and lit a fire from a pile of wood and kindling that sat to one side of the fireplace. He sat on the edge of the bed and looked at what had been the face of Mary Kelly. Her forehead was mostly unscarred and he gently stroked the auburn hair from her face area back over her forehead and onto her scalp, and then just caressed her forehead and scalp gently while the kettle boiled over the fire that had taken a good hold in the grate.

He felt an odd connection to this latest victim of his infrequent blood lusts. Previously there had seemed no chance of failure or being caught because the resistance of his victims had not really been that great. This one had fought back fiercely and almost rendered the chance of her escaping and him being caught a reality; it was a rush that had driven him on and on in the attack and now she gave him the chance to taste human flesh. None of this had happened to him before, and despite the fact he would kill again it would never be with the same sense of excitement. He piled the warm flesh and organs he had removed in a bizarrely ordered fashion.

The cooking human flesh and tissue made a particular smell as the water began to reach boiling point and the lid of the kettle began to vibrate a little. He swung the kettle out from the fire and lifted the lid and looked inside at the red discoloured water. The items weren't quite visible so he reached in with his knife and fished out the piece of her thigh. In the strange fire lit room he couldn't make out its true colour; as he examined it, turning the knife in his hand before he bit into it. He chewed it as he would any conventional meat but couldn't liken the taste to anything he had ever eaten previously. He paused before trying to find her heart in the kettle now unsure of what he was doing. He had gone over the edge of what even he described as humanity or normal human behaviour and did not know how much further he dare to venture. Staring for sometime into the boiling pot he became transfixed by the bubbling water. Eventually he plunged the knife into the kettle and fished the steaming dripping heart out and bit into it quickly and savagely. He enjoyed the taste. He ravenously finished it and fled the room and the unrecognisable corpse of Mary Kelly slamming the door behind him running to the Crispin Street end of Millers Court. In a dark alley he forced himself to vomit heavily emptying the evil unnatural contents of his stomach and stripped off his outer blood soiled coat and discarded it. He ran as fast as he could to Cable Street to the safety of his shop.

Once there he tore off the rest of his clothes and burnt them; he got several buckets of cold water and scrubbed his entire body and poured the icy water over himself almost in a form a penance in his enclosed yard before wrapping himself in a heavy blanket and downing half a bottle of some rough port that he had on a shelf. The alcohol helped dim the obvious sins chasing around in his mind and was a vain attempt to remove the unforgettable taste of human flesh.

Chapter Twenty-Two

Friday 9th November 10.45.a.m. Thomas Bowyer, known to his friends as 'Indian Harry' as he was an Indian army pensioner, was a rent collector working on behalf of property owner John McCarthy. It was a little job he had been doing for many years since he had left the army and helped top up his meagre pension. Mary Kelly was one of the regular addresses on his monthly round and he frequently had problems rousing her or finding her to pay the rent. As a result McCarthy had refused to fix the broken window pane at number 13 Millers Court, something that had occurred as a result of a heated argument between Mary and her former lover Joe Barnett when she had thrown a picture frame at him and missed. It was a dry and bright morning considering the time of year when he knocked on the door and got no answer. He knocked again and called to her as well.

"Come on, Mary, you've got to pay this month or you're out love," he said walking round to the broken window pane. He knew he could have a look through or reach through and open the door up and then go and rouse her in her bed.

He pushed the stuffed rags out of the way to gain a view into the room but was not prepared for the sight that he saw, he moved his hand so quickly in shock that he cut it on the jagged broken glass and screamed out. He stood up and rested stiffly his back against the wall in shock and began sobbing with the sheer horror of the site that he observed. McCarthy was also in Millers Court collecting rents to speed the process up with Bowyer and heard his shriek. He ran to his employee's aid thinking he had been attacked for any money he may have. He was appalled to discover him and his almost catatonic state of shock and couldn't get a word out of him. Eventually still sobbing he pointed at the broken pane and managed a brief and barely audible warning.

"There, she's dead! Ripped up! Don't look!" Those last two words always spoken to deter, undoubtedly drive people to look and McCarthy trying to establish the origin of Bowyer's mental state had to have a look for himself. With just a glance through, he immediately looked away and was sick. They called the police and left the room locked.

Abberline and Godley had gone home at around 4.a.m and with the sheer horror and confusion of the event were late in being called to Millers Court. Superintendent Arnold arrived at around 1.30.p.m and took control of a scene that had been secured by the local duty officer, Inspector Walter Beck and his men. It had not been entered on the direction from senior officers to wait for the bloodhounds to arrive. The divisional surgeon, Dr Phillips, was there ready and waiting with a large group of police officers who were there to keep the scene secured and begin the investigation. He had looked through the broken window and could see that there was no need to be concerned with administering medical attention. While they waited the police photographer took a picture through this window. Amongst the police present was young Walter Dew one of the new 'H' division detective constables who had become known as 'Blue Serge' because of a suit that he habitually wore. Arnold arrived with the news that the dogs were not available and would not be coming at all. He spoke to McCarthy about the premises prior to entry.

"You own this do you?" He asked dismissively.

"Yes I do. What do you want me to do? I can't go in there, not having seen the state of her," replied a still much shaken landlord.

"Just break it down. We'll go in there's no need for you to enter." There was no need to do much to get in. The door was slightly stuck from where the killer had slammed it shut but McCarthy shouldered it firmly and turned the door handle and it open instantly.

He couldn't help but catch a glance of the carnage inside and the smell that is normally carried by a butchers shop with fresh meat in stock. He ran from the door bent over with his right hand clasped over his mouth retching heavily; within a few moments of this starting he vomited through his fingers having stopped and propped himself against a wall. The gathered police kept the crowds back and stopped anyone peering through the window for fear of the distress the scene may cause, avoiding blood thirsty publicity and to offer the murdered woman some dignity and respect. Arnold was one of the first through the door along with Walter Dew, Dr Phillips and the recently arrived Dr Thomas Bond. All were scarred by what they saw and Arnold despite his many years of policing the East End was forced to leave within seconds holding his mouth in shock and disbelief. Dew, despite having slipped on the floor soaked with congealed blood, stayed in with Phillips and Bond as the latter doctor began an examination and pronounced life extinct as soon as he entered the room. Phillips considered this an academic point. Bond's report on the murder scene would make gruesome reading later on for many involved in the investigation that didn't see the site as well as the grainy photographs that the police photographer was setting up and about to take.

Abberline arrived within a few minutes of this initial entry being made along with Godley. They walked in as Dew was in fact going out who spoke to them.

"Boss, that is just bloody awful, awful. I'll never forget what I've seen today. It's nothing but the most harrowing moment in my police career. If I was you, I'd only go in if I had to."

"Wally, you know I've got no choice. George, stay here if you wish."

"No, Fred, I've got to come in. I need to know what we are up against," replied a forthright Godley. The two walked into the room where the doctor had stood to one side to allow the photographer to do his work. Both were speechless by what they saw and Godley's eyes welled up with tears with the sheer frustration of having not been able to stop this unforgettable crime and with the thought of the terror Mary Kelly had undoubtedly faced.

Mary Kelly's body was two thirds of the way across the bed, and appeared so massively mutilated she could have been a victim of having been hit by a train carriage and dragged underneath. The Ripper had hacked off her ears and her nose; her face had been de-fleshed down to the bone; her only recognisable feature was her hair. Blood had soaked through the bed and had pooled on the floor and those that had entered couldn't help but to have trodden in it. Abberline looked around the room and saw that most of her clothing had been burned in the fireplace, and the fire had been so intense as to have melted the spout of the kettle. Godley looked on at her corpse in disbelief; the Ripper had hacked into her body so intensely that her genitalia had been reduced to a pulp; her breasts had been removed and arranged with her liver on the bedside table. Her entrails were also heaped on this table with every organ in her body except her brain having been removed. Her right thigh was so flayed and de-fleshed as to expose a gleaming white femur.

Godley left the room very suddenly and stood outside in the fresh air taking deep breaths it seemed almost on the verge of hyper-ventilating with the shock of taking the entire scene in. Abberline continued looking around the room as well as being consistently drawn to look at the horror of Mary's remains. There was no question it was her; Bowyer had recognised her remains as had McCarthy and both stated it was her lodgings. The clothing left intact in the room was soon identified as hers too by Julia Styles who had been drawn to the scene and wept as she was shown the garments by Dew. Abberline and Godley could both see it was her by the remote parts of her natural human form that remained.

Two more officers arrived at Millers Court one expected and one unexpected especially by those working the investigation; Sir Charles Warren and Chief Inspector John Littlechild. By this time Abberline had left the room and was stood consoling Godley, just about able to keep his own composure.

"Well, Fred, he's done it again I assume?" said Littlechild.

"Yes. He has." Abberline paused looking at his distressed colleague and placing an arm on his shoulder to comfort him. "I thought we had him banged up. I'd got word our chief suspect was inside last night, but obviously not," replied a still reeling Abberline to Littlechild's casual questioning. Littlechild went inside.

"Well, Abberline I have given my letter of resignation to the home secretary before coming here. My position as I'm sure you aware is now untenable," said Warren trying to maintain some dignity but in truth feeling deeply disappointed, especially with such a ferocious attack.

"I'm sorry to hear that, Commissioner, truly I am. I am also baffled as to what the hell is happening. I am lost in truth. I thought we had him."

"I know you and your men have been doing your best. Keep it up, Frederick." Sir Charles grabbed his shoulder with his hand, gave it a fatherly squeeze and walked out of Millers Court.

"Wally," said Abberline "Go and release our man Dr Tumblety on Sergeant Thick's bail. We know it wasn't him tonight. But be sure to tell him he is still under investigation and is still on bail."

"Yes, sir. Straight away." Dew made off for Commercial Street Police Station as Littlechild left the room ignoring all those present and left the scene at an almost frenetic pace. He, unknown to everyone else, had to break the sickening news to someone at the London hospital.

Dew passed the message on to a stunned Sergeant Thick to release Tumblety on bail for his indecency offences and nothing else. Opening the cell door Thick was confronted by the American doctor sitting on the cell's bench staring at him with contempt. He spoke before the policeman.

"Well? You sons of bitches going to let me go?" Begrudgingly Thick replied knowing that he had come to suspect this man as much as anyone; he still may have some responsibility in these crimes pending the analysis of the handwriting sample. He had Tumblety's cane in his hand.

"Yes, Doctor Tumblety you are free to leave, but, as you understand, on bail and I expect you to return here on the sixteenth." Tumblety got up and walked up to Thick and was handed his cane.

"Tell me, why are you letting me go if you think I am Jack the Ripper?" Thick was unsure as to answer; but knowing that the news of the latest murder would have already swept through the area like wild fire he decided to be truthful.

"Because last night he struck again. More horrific than ever, so right now you are off the hook. For now." Tumblety felt a cold chill pass through him not really wanting to ask the next question.

"Er......... who was it?" This may not be wise to ask, he knew he would not be the sort of person who should want to know about an East End murder. He'd have to have a reason. Thick eyed him suspiciously.

"Why would a fine gent like you want to know about a murder of a two bob bangtail, eh?" Tumblety had to be casually concise with an answer.

"Don't know why I asked really. Sorry, it doesn't matter. The papers will carry it anyway."

"Did you want to know in case you had used her services then?" quizzed Thick now deeply interested in the American's enquiry.

"Like I say, it doesn't matter. My tastes don't run to the gutter." If it was her, Mary, then he would have to not show any reaction anyway. Thick showed him out into the custody office where he signed a sheet on his custody record for his bail, still with the surety hanging over him, and was allowed to leave. Paperwork that overtime would disappear at the hand of an establishment led conspiracy to cover up his implication in the killings. He dared not ask any further questions so decided to head south in Commercial Street to see what he could discover from the locals.

Within minutes of leaving The Street and with a brisk stroll he had got the crowd around the entrance to Millers Court in sight; he knew by the composition of police and public that this must be the scene of the crime. The site of where the elusive George Chapman had undoubtedly struck. He knew that it must be Mary who was dead with the witnessing of this gathered crowd and he felt cold, empty and sick. He had set off a chain of events with his own depraved schizophrenic actions and his lack of moral fortitude in dealing with her himself until it was too late and he had asked someone else. He should have delayed making the decision about taking revenge on her until that second meeting with her when he recovered his gems; he had felt compassion and forgiveness. Had he done that, she would not be dead. He wandered into carriageway to cross the road narrowly avoiding being hit by an oncoming omnibus receiving a verbal tirade from the driver as it passed by. He stood on the east pavement and hailed the first hansom that passed; the driver asking politely where he wished to go.

"Just drive," Tumblety replied "I'll decide later. Just drive on."

* * *

At 4.p.m when Littlechild arrived at the London Hospital Robert was wide awake having not long been served a cup of tea. He looked puzzled at Littlechild's arrival, but then recalled that he hadn't yet spoken to him about what he had fallen foul of.

"Guv'nor. How are you then?" said Robert chirpily. He'd given no regard to Littlechild's sad and troubled look as he always appeared that way whenever they met. Littlechild made no reply straight away; with the pause Robert sensed that something awful had happened.

"Guv'nor, what's happened? We haven't lost another bloke have we?"

"Rob, I can't believe I'm here to tell you this, I am so sorry that I am." Robert's heart sank. He realised with cold shock what he was about to be told. It had to be Mary. The world he knew was about to collapse.

"It's Mary, isn't it?" the tears welled in his eyes, he knew he was about to lose the ability to speak has his throat tensed and tightened.

"Rob, I am truly sorry. She was killed at Millers Court by we assume the Ripper by the murder's nature. There's nothing else to say really. Obviously it's all hands to the pumps. I'm supplying extra detectives to get this bastard." It took him quite a few minutes of sobbing and silence between them before he could muster some vocal strength to speak again.

"Was it quick? Did it look like she suffered? Can I see her?"

"I don't think you better hear that now, mate. Read the reports when you get out."

"FUCKING TELL ME! I NEED TO KNOW!" He broke down in tears curling into a foetal possession as he sobbed loudly and was now inconsolable. Littlechild sat on the side of the bed and put his arm round him; an action to which Robert responded to by grabbing Littlechild's jacket and pulling himself into it in a scared child like fashion.

"I'm sorry lad. Let it all out. There's nothing to be ashamed of. Don't go and see her when you get out. Remember her as she was."

"I don't even have a picture of her. Did she suffer?" he asked with tears streaming down his face and mucus pouring from his nose. His face was swollen and puffed out.

"Look. She did have her throat cut. Not as deep from what the doc said. The rest of it is very much the same. Maybe a bit more aggressive."

"Why shouldn't I see her?" He asked needing desperately to know.

"She....she has had her face disfigured. You wouldn't know her."

"Like Eddowes?" Littlechild knew he was forced to be honest.

"Much worse. Robert, she hasn't got a face anymore. I'm sorry, really I am. You wanted to know and you'd find out anyway."

Robert was again unable to speak and Littlechild stayed with him for several hours with his subordinate coming in to see him and receive orders to go and carry out. Littlechild knew with what this young man had suffered this was not a time for him to be left alone. He sent instructions to The Street for an officer to be with him at all times for the foreseeable future, ideally a close colleague from his shift.

Abberline and Godley returned to The Street to personally take the initial description from a man called George Hutchinson, who they would later call back for further complete details of the night's events in statement form, of a potential suspect to pursue. With the assistance of a local artist, a radical idea of Abberline's to try to gain a physical picture early on of a potential suspect; they sat Hutchinson down and gained a useful description to immediately circulate to the police patrolling on the streets and eventually to the general public.

'A man of a respectable Jewish appearance wearing a long dark coat with an astrakhan collar and cuffs, a dark jacket and trousers, light waistcoat, dark felt hat turned down in the middle like a homburg or trilby, button boots a black tie with a horseshoe shaped pin and a thick gold chain. He was around thirty-four and about 5'6". He had a pale complexion, dark cropped hair, and a very slight moustache.'

The accompanying picture was considered very useful by the patrol officers who used it to at least have a basis of suspects to stop and speak to. Arnold addressed Abberline over this radical idea.

"Now then, Abberline, you have shown remarkable initiative in doing this picture thing, try to capitalise on any results it may bring, eh?"

"Yes, Superintendent, we will. I want to see the noose for this 'Ripper' making money for old rope in the traditional sense more than anyone."

"Good. Keep me informed. I have several interviews with the press to deal with. I shall be at The Yard." With that he left leaving Abberline to plan a new tack perhaps to stop any further bloodshed by hopefully apprehending the suspect.

* * *

Tuesday 13th November; Robert Ford turned up at Commercial Street Police Station not with any hope of returning to work but to see Abberline to discover the truth behind Mary's murder. He had now hardened himself to any further out pouring of emotion and took a cold view of the world around him. His dream of settled happiness had gone along with any aspirations for the future. He had resigned himself to one mission and one mission only; to avenge the deaths of the two dearest people to him who had been cruelly taken.

He went straight through to the incident room with his left arm still in a light plaster cast where he met Abberline and Godley. They were sat at their desks pawing over piles of statements, many of them useless, to see if they picked up something new, some vital clue so far overlooked, that would lead them to the killer or killers. They both looked up when they saw him.

"Young Robert. Come and take a seat, lad," said Abberline.

"Thank you, sir. I'd like to read the pathologists statement regarding the injuries to her please." Godley and Abberline looked at each other both considering his request very carefully; they did not know he was coming and two pictures from the crime scene of Mary's murder formed part of a gruesome display of victims pictures which adorned one of the walls. Before they could do anything Robert had spotted them and walked straight over to the display and stood transfixed staring at the awful photographic evidence of his love's horrific end. Abberline looked at Godley both of them remaining silent with no idea of what to say to try to consol him. He studied them for over a minute before turning and facing the detectives who were surprised by the lack of emotion in his face.

"Do you have that report, sir?" Robert asked again of Abberline.

"Yes," he passed it to him. "Here it is. I have no doubt having seen those pictures that I need not warn you it does not make pleasant reading."

"I accept that, Guv. Before I start there is little for me to live for beyond work. I appreciate that I may be subject to a discipline inquiry still but I'd like to get back to work as soon as I can."

"Good, I'm sorry to learn of your motivation for returning but I am glad you wish to. I'll discuss the matter with Mr Arnold and see what he says."

"I appreciate that, Mr Abberline," said Robert nodding his head and straightening his lips briefly in appreciative acknowledgment. He then settled down to read the report on Mary's injuries made by Dr Thomas Bond; he would find it quite comprehensive.

The position of the body
The body was lying naked in the middle of the bed, the shoulders, but the axis of the body inclined to the left side of the bed. The head was turned on the left cheek. The left arm was close to the body with the forearm flexed at a right angle and lying across the abdomen. The right arm was slightly adducted from the body and rested on the mattress, the elbow bent and the forearm supine with the fingers clenched. The legs were wide apart, the left thigh at right angles to the trunk and the right forming an obtuse angle with the pubes.

The whole of the surface of the abdomen and thighs was removed and the abdominal cavity emptied of the viscera. The breasts were cut off, the arms mutilated by several jagged wounds and the face hacked beyond recognition of the features. The tissues of the neck were severed all round down to the bone.

The viscera were found in various parts viz: the uterus and the kidneys with one breast under the head, the other breast by the right foot, the liver between the feet, the intestines by the right side and the spleen by the left side of the body. The flaps removed from the abdomen and the thighs were on the table.

The bed clothing at the right corner was saturated with blood, and on the floor beneath was a pool of blood covering about two feet square. The wall by the right side of the bed and in line with the neck was marked by blood which had struck it in a number of separate slashes.

Post-mortem examination
The face was gashed in all directions the nose, the cheeks, eyebrows and ears being partly removed. The lips were blanched and cut by

several incisions running obliquely down to the chin. There were also numerous cuts extending irregularly across all the features.

The neck was cut through the skin and other tissues right down to the vertebrae the 4th and 5th being deeply notched. The skin cuts in the front of the neck showed distinct ecchymosis.

The air passage was cut at the lower part of the larynx through the cricoid cartilage.

Both breasts were removed by more or less circular incisions, the muscles down to the ribs being attached to the breasts. The intercostals between the 4th and 5th and 6th ribs were cut through and the contents of the thorax visible through the openings.

The skin and tissues of the abdomen from the costal arch to the pubes were removed in three large flaps. The right thigh was denuded in front to the bone, the flap of skin, including the external organs of generation and part of the right buttock. The left thigh was stripped of skin, fascia and muscles as far as the knee.

The left calf showed along gash through skin and tissues to the deep muscles and reaching from the knee to five inches above the ankle.

Both arms and forearms had extensive and jagged wounds.

The right thumb showed a small superficial incision about one inch long, with extravasations of blood in the skin and there were several abrasions on the back of the hand moreover showing the same condition.

On opening the thorax it was found that the right lung was minimally adherent by old firm adhesions. The lower part of the lung was broken and torn away.

The left lung was intact: it was adherent at the apex and there were a few adhesions over the side. In the substances of the lung were several nodules of consolidation.

A closing paragraph covered the remains of food in Mary's stomach and intestines. Robert already horrified inwardly by the pictures on the wall could not believe from this report the savagery with which she had been attacked, and just hoped that she had died quickly before the killer began his mutilations. Re-instated to the police or not he would find the man responsible for these crimes and kill him. He remained silent with Abberline noting that he had finished reading.

"You all right, son?" he asked with fatherly concern.

"No. Not really. I don't believe I ever will be. I'd like to ask that if I am re-instated I'd like to join your team, sir."

"Yes. A bloke that has shown the resilience you have deserves to be on board."

"Thanks. I'll be off home now gentlemen." Robert got up from the desk and left the office to make his way back to his lodgings in Bakers Row.

He arrived home within around half an hour to find the landlady had kindly looked after Bruiser. He took the dog upstairs with him and sat down on his bed. His world was still in turmoil and his plans no longer of any relevance. He decided as best he could one handed to tidy up his room beginning with the mess of clothes that were strewn around the room on top of the table, chair and littering the bed. He pulled at a jacket hanging over the back of the chair which began to pull the chair backwards. He attempted to stop it falling but with only one hand just dropped everything. He walked frustrated backwards to the bed and dropped himself back onto it. He began to sob with frustration and heartbreak; Bruiser jumped onto the bed and cuddled up next to him with his head resting on his paws all too aware of the emotions in the room.

* * *

That evening Sean Miller was walking along Sidney Street towards Commercial Road on his own with thoughts in mind of how he could persuade members of the Vigilance Committee to turn against the authorities following this most recent atrocity. So deep in thought was he that he was unaware of the carriage pulling up alongside and keeping pace with him. After a few seconds he looked across at it aware of it only when the door opened towards him. As he looked inside he was grabbed by his lapels and dragged into the interior by a huge portly suited man sporting a large beard that sat him down and slapped some manacles onto his wrists. He had tried to struggle but somewhat pointlessly against his colossal strength. He then became aware of a smart older suited man sat in front of him in the darkness of the interior. He lent forward allowing the street lighting to highlight his features and spoke menacingly.

"So, Mr Miller. I think you maybe responsible for hurting a good friend of mine. What gives you the right to do that eh?"

"He was a fucking pig spying on an innocent man and other working men," Miller replied aggressively.

"Really? Well, well, we fucking pigs have to stick together, you Fenian bastard. You are plotting seditious activities. For that we must ensure you leave the country," said the man sitting back into the dark.

"Oh, yeah? And how are you going to do that then, pig?"

"Quite simply. We can help you on you're way." The bearded man held tightly onto Miller and gagged him as the well dressed man tied some large lead weights to Millers legs that were sitting on the floor of the carriage. Miller looked out of the window to see that they were alongside the Regents Canal Dock, now known as the Limehouse Basin, a large expanse of inland water linking to the Thames. Miller began struggling and making muffled sounds of protest that then broke into pleading as the carriage stopped along side of the water.

"Like we said, Mr Miller we'll help you leave the country." The driver got down from his perch and with the large bearded man they pulled the bucking and screaming Miller from the carriage with his weights and carried him to the edge of the dockside. The smartly dressed man joined them and looked into the black water lapping against the harbour side.

"Hopefully your countrymen will get the message when they forever wonder what happened to poor old Sean Miller. Way you go chaps."

The two men swung him sideways a couple of times to gain some momentum before letting go and tossing Miller into the dock and watched him instantly sink, leaving only a trail of bubbles.

"Well done, chaps, a job well done," replied the smartly dressed John Littlechild as he pulled a handkerchief out of his pocket to wipe his hands that had been soiled by the tying of the weights. They all got back onto or into the carriage and rode off.

* * *

Friday 16th November; Tumblety returned to Commercial Street Police Station to be charged with all four counts of indecent assaults investigated by Detective Sergeant Thick. Abberline and Godley knew he was there but had still not had a result on the handwriting analysis. It was a great personal frustration and setback to them to watch impassively as he came and went from the police station over the other matters. Tumblety's bail date to appear at the Central Criminal Court or 'Old Bailey' was set to be the following Tuesday, the 20th. The Ripper investigation team could only hope to have a result by then. He strolled out from the front entrance of The Street with an air of unconcern as he knew he would challenge these allegations at court and his social standing against, it would seem a callow youth making the claims, would win him the day.

Four days later at the court the case was being heard with Tumblety and the youth, Fred Churchyard, finally coming face to face. The lad looked terrified appearing in a public forum and seeing the man he was so superficially lying about. Druitt sat in the back of the court out of sight in the public gallery from either party. Unbeknown to him within the crowd were Abberline and Godley. Tumblety was representing himself and sat quietly as the prosecuting council made their case and then called Churchyard to come to the witness box and give his evidence.

Unsteadily he was led through his account of what had happened with an obvious air of nervousness in what he said and the questions he answered when put by the prosecuting counsel. Tumblety had sat impassively through this waiting for his chance to destroy and discredit this obviously false witness. Judge Joseph Reed spoke to him; his chance had come.

"Dr Tumblety, do wish to cross examine the witness?" Tumblety stood.

"Yes, your Honour, I do." He turned away from the judge to the slightly shaking Churchyard and smiled gently at him and began to speak.

"Young man, have you really seen me before?"

"Yes, of course I have. You're the one what buggered me."

"Really? All right. I put it to you, you are lying."

"Nah, I'm not. You assaulted me and my mate."

"I don't think so. I put it to you; you are lying for some personal or financial gain. I also put it to you that we have never met before and you were never assaulted." The boy paused and swallowed before answering.

"That's not true. You assaulted me and that's it."

"No. You are lying and stand to perjure yourself. You were not assaulted and certainly at least not by me. You are a false witness."

"I'm not!"

"You are, young man."

"I'm fucking not!" The judge interjected.

"No swearing in the court or you'll be in contempt."

"You are an inveterate liar who for money would try to slur anyone's good character." The boy was sweating and shaking and now looked at his feet before speaking, his voice breaking a little. He had finally been intimidated to tell the truth; his resolve was simply not strong enough to take anymore cross examination from the American whose steely glare seemed to intrude into his very soul.

"All right!" He shouted emotionally, "I was never assaulted. My mate don't exist. He's right I was put up to it by some posh bloke from South London." The court suddenly went into a constant hum as everyone turned to each to speak with the shock of this announcement. Churchyard carried on shakily telling the truth.

"Some posh bloke who looks like the queen's grandson, works in a school or something by all accounts, told me to do this to get back at this fellow."

"And why was that then?" asked Tumblety.

"Don't know, he just wanted to get back at you it seemed."

"Was his name Druitt, a South London school master?"

"Yeah, I think so. I only did it for twenty quid." The court went into uproar as the judge began to speak.

"Order, order! I hereby dismiss this case as a false and malicious allegation. The complainant is sentenced to thirty days in Newgate, I also issue a warrant for this man Druitt for conspiracy to pervert the course of justice. Dr Tumblety is herby acquitted, with twenty pounds costs awarded from the prosecution."

Thick was furious that he had been taken for a ride by this young liar as the prosecuting counsel packed up his brief. In the public gallery Druitt made a swift exit as Abberline stood and spoke to address the judge.

"Your Honour, I am Inspector Abberline. I must request you keep this man subject to court or police bail as he is a suspect in the Ripper case and I am still waiting for the results of a handwriting analysis. The result of this test could mean that this man is charged with the crimes. There is currently a surety in force for his bail, and I ask you set a date to return to court as he can, if necessary, be charged in your presence or released." The judge considered this application as Tumblety looked around in horror at Abberline's presence and his request. He felt the net closing in and he must now be prepared to sacrifice the surety money. The judge spoke.

"I grant your application, Inspector, the Doctor must return here on the 10th of December for the hearing you have requested and the bail with surety remains in force to that date and to here."

"Thank you, your Honour," said Abberline making eye contact with a hateful Tumblety as he sat back down.

"Do you understand, Dr Tumblety?" asked the judge.

"Yes, sir, I do," replied Tumblety, standing to do so. He approached the bench and extended his hand to Judge Reed. He spoke catching the Judge off guard who autonomously offered his own hand in a handshake in response, never to realise Tumblety's dishonest intentions.

"Your Honour, I must thank you for this great service you have done, I will not let you down, sir," said a very sincere Tumblety. Calculating as ever in his actions he clasped Reed's hand in a Masonic grip; having spent much time since making his fortune mixing with the wealthier echelons of American society the Doctor had become well versed in Masonic customs and traditions from his brief membership of the Brotherhood. He knew that by making this implication, if he was right about the judge being a mason himself, he would set the wheels in motion for the 'Brotherhood' to protect 'one of their own'. It would be Reed's duty to ensure that Tumblety not be convicted or fall into harm's way as he was a brother mason. He clasped the judge's hand in a kind of half grip against that of a conventional handshake and then ensured that he applied pressure with his thumb to the knuckle of the middle finger to convey membership of an organisation who declared 'they were not a secret society, but a society with secrets'. The identity of the true perpetrator of the majority of the Ripper crimes would become one of their greatest secrets, and falsely too. This was just another example of the charlatan Tumblety duping those around him to his own ends to ensure he could make good his escape. No one knew the irony in the actions that Judge Reed would take in immediately contacting Sir Henry Matthews, the Home Secretary, when he left the court. Tumblety disguising himself in the eyes of the brotherhood as a member of such an upright social order knew the deception would be a way for him to seek immunity. They would never betray their own. It was a gamble that would pay dividends to Tumblety but would deliver one of the greatest injustices in the British legal system.

The court emptied, Churchyard was taken down to the court's cells to be transferred to the next door Newgate prison. Tumblety left knowing he now had to prepare to leave in the next few days. He knew that Abberline would come looking for him before the 10th with his address having now been made public in open court. On the steps of the court he was unfortunate enough to come face to face with Abberline, the man that had now become his own nemesis.

"Well, doctor. Don't go too far. You know we haven't eliminated you from our enquiries." He spoke looking the American doctor in the eye. Tumblety saw an opportunity to buy himself some time and incriminate the man he had failed to stop, having set him on a destructive trail.

"Abberline, I have one thing for you to consider, I have heard the name Chapman connected with this matter, perhaps this is someone who you should be looking for," replied Tumblety walking away bumping shoulder to shoulder with Abberline as he did so. Abberline turned to Godley having watched Tumblety walk away and spoke.

"Well, we know he didn't do the last one, but he's no way in the clear. We need to look up that name though, can't afford to assume it's a red herring after six murders."

"I'll get on it Fred when we get back to The Street."

Chapter Twenty-Three

Monday 19th November; John Netley was waiting outside Tumblety's Graham Road lodgings to take his American client off to one of the Central London stations. He had already brought one trunk out that Netley had loaded onto the rear of the carriage and Tumblety now came out for one last time carrying a medium size suitcase, his cane and a gladstone bag. He was smartly dressed as previously but looked unusually flustered. This sense of panic to flee the country had caused Tumblety to bolt without making the clearest of preparations, a massively unusual circumstance for him to find himself in. His sense of thoroughness which had always helped his sense of self preservation would not return until he found himself on route for America, and the port of New York. Tumblety had quite deliberately left his arts bag with its gruesome contents out of sight in the coal bunker at the lodgings in case he had received a visit from the police. In his flight from London he had forgotten about it.

He clambered aboard the carriage and told Netley to set off for Waterloo Station, the terminus well known for travel to France. He was making for Le Havre where he was to board a French steamer bound for his homeland. His familiar cab driver tried to initiate conversation.

"Leaving us for a while then, Doctor?" asked Netley.

"None of your business, driver," replied a cold and abrupt Tumblety. The carriage set off and it was to be a long, slow and silent journey free of conversation for both through the busy Monday morning streets.

The premises were under observation by two of the Ripper detectives, Sergeants Mather and Robinson who were not expecting to see a rapid departure by Tumblety. The two of them desperately tried to hail a cab to follow their suspect off and were fortunate in finding one travelling in the right direction whilst Tumblety's carriage was still in sight. They jumped aboard relieved that their quarry wasn't about to escape and instructed the driver to follow the carriage in the distance; however this mild euphoria was short lived. After only a few minutes, they saw the carriage driven by Netley turn into Mare Street and begin to head south, so for a split second it moved out of sight past the building line. As they approached the junction a group of children, who had been playing foolish games on the street corner, ran into the road after some quoits that one of them had just thrown forcing the cab driver to attempt to pull up his horse quickly and he veered harshly to the left to avoid a collision. The pavement side wheel of the cab shattered as it impacted with the kerb snapping several spokes and causing it to lurch downwards on the left hand side heavily, throwing the two policemen into a heap on top of each other within the cab.

"Fuck it, FUCK IT!" Screamed Mather as he scrambled out of the cab from under Robinson onto the pavement to see the carriage with the subject of their surveillance disappearing. Robinson got out and stood next to him to witness the same sight. They looked across at the group of children who were in shock themselves, and as the cab driver jumped out to approach them. They all ran off not wanting to be scolded.

"Well, that's that then. He's bloody well gone," said a fed up Mather.

"Abberline ain't going to be pleased, mate," replied Robinson.

"No, but at least it ain't completely our fault." The two of them eventually hailed an alternative cab which took them to Commercial Street to face the music in the incident room.

They were quite right in their anticipation of Abberline's reaction; he went into a verbal fury in reply to their news, although within it he did accept that it was circumstances beyond their control. He quickly formulated a plan of action to be put into place to try to catch the obviously guilty Tumblety.

"Right, we need all ports watched at the earliest opportunity and his details circulated to all surrounding forces. We can't let him escape."

"But, guv'nor, don't you need permission from above for all that? They might be resistant without the handwriting analysis coming back," said Godley. Abberline seemed agitated by this information.

"George, I fucking know that, just get it done!" His fury wasn't with Godley but with the loss of Tumblety by the surveillance officers. They all left the office to get on with their tasks leaving Abberline to pull out his bottle of single malt once on his own and take a generous shot.

Hours later Abberline was confronted by the office door being opened violently and Superintendent Arnold storming in to speak to him.

"Now look here, Abberline, the Metropolitan Police cannot take on any more embarrassment. The Commissioner has resigned, we have six unsolved murders and now you want to circulate details of a man we have failed to apprehend? You must be joking."

"Mr Arnold, we will lose a crucial suspect if we don't. He may not have killed Kelly, but oddly he has given us a name. He could well be in the frame for the others. He must be found."

"On what evidence do we do that then?"

"The handwriting we are waiting on. That will nail him."

"Abberline, is it back yet?"

"No, sir, anytime though." Abberline replied dejectedly.

"Well when you have that decent level of evidence, tell me and we will then blockade the ports to find him."

"Fine, it will be too bloody late. So you can burden that responsibility. I've done my bit and will write a statement now to that effect."

"You do that, Inspector, and look up this other suspect in the meantime. Do something useful," he spoke the last line with venom and left the room. Abberline's conscientiousness hit a new level of turmoil as he hit the bottle again.

Godley wandered back in to find him becoming drunk. He grabbed the bottle and flung it against a wall in fury; it smashed sending splintering glass all over part of the office and the remnants of the alcohol ran down the wall as Godley spoke to his troubled friend.

"For fuck's sake, Fred! That won't get you anywhere. It's not your fault if the politicians of this job get in your way. Just document it and we'll do what we can, history will be the judge in this and you are a good detective. Go home and sober up and come back with a clear head and we'll make a start on the Chapman lead tomorrow and deal with Tumblety when the results come back and the politicians untie our hands." Abberline stood up to face his longstanding friend with a tear in his eye. He needed the reassurance at that moment he had been given.

"Thanks, mate. I need some sleep and a rest. Your right, we'll crack on tomorrow."

* * *

Klosowski sat his future wife down to explain why the shop was up for sale and that they would be moving on. He spoke to Lucy Baderski in a sinister and threatening fashion that left her cold, afraid and with little choice but to obey him. She too was an immigrant but without the tenacity and survival instinct for life that Severin had so she coalesced to his threats very easily. They hadn't been together for long and by his violent nature she had always felt compelled to let him do as he pleased.

"Lucy, I have to lay low for a little while because of all this Ripper business. It's not me has committed all these crimes but the police might come calling and when they do you must tell them that I left the city at the start of November before the Kelly murder. If you don't or you threaten my liberty in the future then you shall go the same way, but not under the knife. I shall kill you in a fashion that is hard to discover. Now, my darling, do you understand?" Lucy was shaking with fear but she plucked the courage to confront him on terms he would understand.

"Look after me and I shall look after you, Severin. That is all I can agree to." She had to try the mutual help ploy to guarantee staying in London. He continued looking at her with his piercing dark eyes considering what she had said. His very survival would depend on it and he needed to ensure that she would give him an alibi, rubbing his stubbly chin he was forced to agree to her terms but the price was worth it.

"All right, I shall keep you with me here or wherever, but you must state that I spent the entire night with you on the 9th of this month. Do you understand?" She looked back him with extreme suspicion.

"Are you Jack the Ripper?" she asked quizzically.

"No, but I have a trail of guilt around the last killing. Just so you know. But don't worry, should the police come to our door it will probably be too late. I have arranged a home and work in North London from next week, new name and everything. I doubt you will really need to lie for me."

"Will I need to come there with you, or do I stay here?" she asked keeping firm eye contact with him to gauge his fortitude.

"Yes, from today the shop closes, the name board will be removed and it will be empty again. We move to Tottenham and stay there until after Christmas for the fuss around here to die down. I will be back to being Klosowski again, not using the name Chapman for now. Pack, we leave later today." Lucy eventually only broke his gaze after a long silence between them to go and gather her things with her thoughts deep in contemplation of their future together following the revelation of their conversation. Was he the Ripper or not? He claimed to have a hand in the most recent murder, but why? For now she would keep her silence and stand by him knowing that not to do so would mean she would end up like all the women so far slaughtered. Klosowski gathered his own things in preparation for the cab he had arranged to arrive late in the afternoon which would lead to one of Abberline's lines of enquiry going very quickly cold.

* * *

Apart from the revelation that Lucy Baderski had discovered on the 19th of November, it was also the day that Mary Jane Kelly was to be laid to rest following her harrowing and violent death. This would prove to be the most emotionally difficult day in Robert Ford's life, and one which would bring about a complete emotional shut down from him on a long term basis. For him, she had been the one, and he could not live his life until he had avenged her death. He waited at the Shoreditch Church along with a huge gathering of local people to pay their respects to a well known and popular local figure; sadly Robert Ford was the closest to a relative to attend, there was no member of her family there at all. Most likely because at that point none of them knew of her callous and brutal demise. The only other person there with a close connection to Mary was Joe Barnett. The crowd had begun to gather from around 10.30.a.m for a service that wasn't due to take place until 12.30.p.m. Despite the presence of a large body of police the road outside the church soon became blocked and they struggled to keep it clear for traffic. Inspector Chandler was in charge of the body of officers attempting to keep order. They managed to clear a single lane for the funeral carriage to access the front of the church when it arrived at a little before 12.30pm, time for the bearers to get the coffin into the church. It was an open carriage provided at the expense of a local businessman Mr H Wilton conveying a simple but dignified pine coffin bearing a brass plate with the inscription 'Marie-Jeanette Kelly, died November 9th, 1888, aged 25 years'.

Her body was being brought from the Shoreditch mortuary followed by two coaches ready to convey the closest of mourners to the cemetery for her burial following the service. The cost of the funeral was being borne by local business leaders and Robert had been able make a contribution from the meagre savings he possessed. He had shut himself off to the world since the discovery of her death and had played no part in the organisation of the service. He knew it would be a test simply for him to attend and try to avoid a complete emotional break down. While he was stood outside the church watching the coffin arrive he felt a hand on his right shoulder and looked round to see who it was. He was quite comforted to see that it was John Littlechild, come to pay his respects and from what he whispered to the grieving Robert Ford offer his support.

Ford was dressed in his best suit, the one he had worn when he had spent such a fabulous day with Mary back in September but this time with a black tie. He had a handkerchief in his right hand which he used to wipe away the frequent tears that were prickling his cheeks as he watched the coffin arrive and be carried into the church. As it entered the double doors it was led along the aisle by the local priest with the mourners following behind it. He found himself stood almost shoulder to shoulder as he entered the building with Joe Barnett, Mary's former lover and lodging partner. It would have been easy for there to be animosity between them on any normal day but today they were united in their grief and sense for revenge against the man who had thrown them here together. They acknowledged each other as they made eye contact, both with red and swollen tearful eyes, but once they reached the front of the church and the coffin had been placed on trestles laid out for it they took separate sides of the church, in a bizarre almost wedding party like fashion; Barnett and his supporters on one side and Ford and his, fewer in number, on the other.

Amongst the gathering were George Lusk and a lot a members of the Vigilance Committee, Detective Sergeants Godley and Thick, many members of the local community of prostitutes now living in even more terror, business leaders who had made contributions and many humble local working men and their families. Ford was almost oblivious to his surroundings lost totally in his grief; in three months he had lost the people that were dear to him on an increasing scale, first Ralph, then Del Lake and now the love of his life taken from him. He was in such a numbed condition that he barely acknowledged the service beginning or ending; he didn't sing any of the hymns, follow any of the prayers and he only stood up as an autonomous response to those around him. He sat or stood in a staring trance like state with his gaze fixed on the coffin and simply followed the procession out as the coffin was lifted by the bearers and walked behind it, again bizarrely shoulder to shoulder with Joe Barrett.

Mary was loaded onto the open carriage as the key mourners boarded the two coaches waiting behind it and within a few minutes the three vehicle procession was on route to the Catholic Cemetery in Leytonstone. Ford stared out of the coach at the streets which were lined with local people wishing to pay their last respects to the popular Spitalfields girl; the event seemed quite surreal to him as the streets resembled those of a Royal procession with the populace lining the footways. By the time the cortège had travelled beyond Cambridge Heath Road the pavements had thinned back to their normal state.

It took twenty-five minutes for them to arrive at the gates of the cemetery in Leytonstone, a leafy and very rural East London outer suburb. The gate keeper had seen them coming along the road and was expecting them moving out from his small lodge early to ensure the wrought iron gates were open for carriage use and not just the usual pedestrian access. The three carriages trundled past him over the cobbled road with the offside wheels of the first mourners coach clanking noisily over the iron ground anchor for the gates securing bolts and jolting the passengers, Robert included, heavily within. The jolt focused his mind again to where he was and what was happening and he knew the hardest part of the day had now arrived; the time when he would have to see the coffin and his love within finally placed into the ground and each person depositing earth upon on it, Robert being one of the first.

All three vehicles were allowed access on the internal road which took them right up to the plot that sat only a few yards from where all would have to alight. Being one of the first on to the coach Robert was one of the last off and he followed the throng of people in front of him to the graveside. He looked up once he got there instinctively to see Barnett stood on the opposite side of the grave, head bowed being comforted by what looked like another working type man; most probably a work colleague assumed Robert. He looked back to the internal road and the coaches and carriage to see that the pall bearers had unloaded the coffin and were being led by the priest through the myriad of scattered graves to finally lay Mary to rest. They moved slowly and gracefully, the priest setting the pace with the grim faced group following behind all in step with him. There was absolute silence across the cemetery barring the sound of some subdued sobs amongst the gathering; there was no birdsong as it was a cold winter's day with only the odd robin flitting around silently from branch to bush of the scattered greenery on the peripheries. Everyone's breath could be seen heavily in the air and the cool temperatures exaggerated their pale complexions and ruddy cheeks and noses from the tears that had been shed. Ford looked around the mourners surveying the gathering with the occasional familiar face standing out to him; Godley, Lusk, Thick to name but a few. He knew most at least by sight from the beats he had walked within the Commercial Street district.

His gaze falling back to the empty grave, it seemed like only seconds later that the priest and the coffin arrived at the graveside and the words of the final commitment began to be spoken by the priest. The coffin began to be lowered having been carefully placed over planks and strapping above the hole, the planks removed and then the straps used to lower with dignity Mary into the earth. Robert didn't sob, he contained himself but the tears streamed along his cheeks falling onto his suit jacket soaking into the wool of its weave. Thoughts of the future so cruelly taken from him played continuously in his mind along with images of Mary at her most beautiful on the boating lake only weeks before. He barely heard the closing of the priests address 'ashes to ashes, dust to dust.' He recognised those words and followed Joe Barnett's lead of throwing some earth on the coffin now at the bottom of the grave using a small trowel that had been left on the mound of earth dug out and piled alongside.

And then it was over. He was moving away from the graveside with the throng of mourners so dazed by the event he couldn't even look back to Mary's place of rest. He had it in the back of his mind that he would return privately and quietly to visit her. A pilgrimage he would make at least once a month that he was in London. There was to be no wake. There was no one to organise it and those that knew her had resigned to meet later that evening at Mary's favourite haunt The Ten Bells and raise a glass to her there. Robert just wanted to be alone and drifted away from the main group leaving the cemetery on foot and beginning a long and lonely walk back to Whitechapel on his own. That night, although not a religious man, he would go Christchurch in Commercial Street on the opposite side of Church Street from The Ten Bells and light a candle for Mary and say a prayer for them both.

* * *

Tuesday 20th November saw Abberline return to the office sober, clean shaven and feeling refreshed from a restful night at home to find Godley there ready and waiting with the rest of the immediate team including Robert Ford. His arm had become substantially stronger and he was certainly able enough to work on door to door enquiries; an area of basic police work that Abberline had gained permission for him to do. It was time to pursue the 'Chapman' angle while they waited for the handwriting analysis, so Abberline sat everyone down in the office and briefed them all on his intended plan of action for the next few days.

"Right then you buggers, I'm back, clear headed, refreshed and focused on the task in hand. Today we shake down all the people in the area called 'Chapman', and don't discount women neither. This is going to be a time consuming process but follow up leads around that name. Working in pairs I'll allocate wards to be visited and I'm keeping this within this small team to ensure thoroughness, we cannot afford to miss any leads, so dig and keep digging. Right, dividing this into parishes,

Bill Thick, work with young Robert and cover Christchurch Spitalfields and St Botolphs Without Bishopsgate." Robert looked puzzled and his scowl was noted by Abberline who almost telepathically answered the young policeman's concern. "Yes the second one is City police but I want my lads to do it. Mather and Robinson I want you to look at St Dunstan Stepney and St Mary Whitechapel north of Commercial Road and Murphy and Parish you do St Botolph Without Aldgate and St Mary's west of Leman Street and me and George will do the rest of St Mary's and St George in the East. No stone unturned boys, no stone unturned. If you shake up any other business don't take it on, whistle up for help and pass it on to the uniformed patrols. Any questions?"

"What about trades? Is it Chapman's with particular trades, Boss?" asked Mather, note book at the ready for the answer, possibly protracted.

"No, all Chapmans. The trade has to be consideration but also a side issue, could be like our friend Netley and have a sick non-professional interest." Another question came from Robert Ford.

"Sir, what about Tumblety? Are we going to do any hands on to find him ourselves? Any luck on the handwriting?"

"No on both counts. Ports have been put on alert to stop him if they find him and we're expecting the handwriting result at anytime," replied Abberline. "Anything else, gentlemen?" The gathered officers looked round at each other and were individually shaking their heads in acknowledgment of his question. "Right, unless you come up with something I'm not looking to reconvene until we've all finished our parish sweeps."

The individual teams all began getting their stationary, notebooks and outdoor clothes ready to leave to get on with their tasks. Abberline stalled ensuring everyone else had got their things and left leaving only Godley and himself as he wanted to chat to his old friend and confidante briefly before leaving to put his own mind at rest over his leadership and actions.

"George, was that all right? To the point? A good plan of action so far?" Godley nodded his head and considered his answer.

"Yes, absolutely. Not much else we can focus on right now as a small unit, so I think it's good. Tell me, why have you given us part of the largest single parish in the district plus a whole other then?"

"You don't miss a thing, old friend, do you?" he replied chuckling. "I know of a foreigner who set up a barber shop in Cable Street near Dock Street who christened the shop 'Chapman's Barbers'. I reckon a sound first port of call for us as he certainly has a background in using sharp implements. Some of these foreign barbers have a varied tradesman ship in their own places so he's my priority today."

The senior detectives were just donning their top coats when there was a knock on the door and a young uniform constable entered carrying an official looking brown envelope. Abberline and Godley looked at each other both sensing this package may contain the information they needed to start to break open the case and dropped their coats onto the desks.

"Thanks, lad," said Abberline taking the envelope from him. The constable left the office encouraged by a nod from Godley to dismiss him. Abberline tore at the seal and opening it swiftly and pulling out a neatly finished report on beige coloured paper in impeccable Victorian handwriting and began to read intently. It was what they had been waiting so long for and so overdue. Godley watched with apprehension waiting for Abberline to voice the findings.

After what seemed like an eternity Abberline looked up with a knowing and satisfied grin and spoke with a sense of absolution.

"In short, George, the writing expert says that without a shadow of a doubt the writing on the 'Dear Boss' letter and on the 'from Hell' letter are the same as Tumblety's signature."

"Bugger me, Fred! Is it worth us all going out then?" asked Godley with an air of triumph starting to read the report as Abberline finished a page and passed it to him.

"Oh hell, yes, mate. I want as much against this bloke as possible and there may be something in this Chapman connection bearing in mind that Dr T was in custody that night. But, later today we have got to go and search his last lodgings. We'll see everyone here later."

They left the office and the report on Abberline's desk to head off to Cable Street.

10.a.m. Abberline and Godley arrived by cab outside what had been Chapman's barber shop in Cable Street both dismounting from the hansom looking at the building in astonishment. What had been a flourishing small independent business only days before, something they could both subconsciously recollect, was now a newly derelict building; the name sign ripped down from above the windows and door leaving only a blank wooden panel, the windows painted from the inside with whitewash so no one could see in and the front door securely locked.

"Right, round the back, George, we need to see what's been going on here to make him shut up so suddenly." Both began strolling round the block via Dock Street to gain access, Godley speaking in response to Abberline's lead.

"Any idea of what this bloke looks like, mate?"

"No, we'll have a look round the place and then ask the neighbours."

A narrow alley way took them around to the back of the former barber shop and having counted how many it was in from the front before going round the back Abberline easily determined which rear gate they needed to enter the yard. Trying the latch the wooden gate didn't move so Godley reached over and felt for a bolt which he found securing the gate; undoing it they entered the desolate yard. It was small only about 12 feet square but not unusual for the type of building it served with a door centrally at the rear of the shop entering the yard with small windows either side of it. Nothing was present in the yard apart from a few papers blowing in the slight breeze that created a small vortex moving them in circles with the dust all around. Godley was the first to try the door which at odds with the gate was open but he discovered why as they entered; there was no lock fitted to the rear door. The building was of a two rooms up and two down layout with the front room downstairs forming the working public area with the rear room in which they found themselves as a living room. It was laid out with a set of stairs to one side and some very shabby furniture scattered around; a table with two chairs, a high backed bench against one wall with an old sideboard against another and a weathered armchair in a corner.

"Where do you want to start, Fred?"

"We'll do a room at a time together so we don't miss anything, and then see the neighbours." Abberline made straight for the sideboard while Godley went to look at the armchair.

To Abberline's utter amazement the sideboard was empty of anything except a few scraps of paper which must have been used to wrap china or glass at sometime, and he found quite a lot of dust. Godley in the meantime had pulled the equally dusty cushion from the armchair and keeping on his leather gloves he had worn because of the November temperatures, he slowly and carefully began to feel down the sides of the frame and coverings of the armchair. He did it methodically to avoid missing anything and to avoid injury on anything sharp. He could feel the usual odd coin and matchstick along the left side and around the back as well as the worn springs, but it was as he ran his hand slowly along the right that he made a discovery that would remain a matter of suppression. He could feel the rounded handle of some kind of knife which by its size he could tell it was more than a domestic table knife. He took hold of the handle fully and slowly drew the item from the chair and called to Abberline to come over as he did so. In the shock of his own actions on the night of the murder of Mary Kelly, Klosowski had dropped the knife into the chair when he slumped into it following his return from Millers Court, an action that later Abberline could only surmise about.

"Bloody hell, Fred, I think we've found where Jack the Ripper has been working from!" Abberline said nothing initially and took the knife slowly from Godley's hand, looking the blade up and down, noting the faint residue of dried blood along it. Could the doctors in some way link this blood with that of one or any of the victims? If not now then perhaps this would something they may be able to discover to aid investigation in the future; the thoughts raced through Abberline's mind for some moments before he voiced rational thought.

"Right, this bloke is a serious fucking suspect for Kelly's murder and we need to find out where he's gone, but so is that American bastard. Let's face it, he's done a runner and his signed his own death warrant with that signature. We have to set out to find them both 'cos they might each have responsibility. Tonight back in the office we get teams together to trace them."

Abberline and Godley finished their search and took the damning evidence with them, arranging for the neighbours to be interviewed by some of the junior detectives to establish Chapman's background. He hoped that they might even know where he had gone but certainly they would be able to help with a description that would then be circulated nationally on the police gazette. The most serious suspects in what was London's or even Britain's most notorious murders needed to be found urgently. Having now discovered Chapman's complicity in the gruesome events of the last twelve weeks, they now had to search Tumblety's premises to conclude once and for all who was 'Jack the Ripper.'

* * *

Wednesday 21st November; the door to Tumblety's former lodgings in Graham Road, Hackney burst open as sections of the frame around the lock's strike plate and catch shattered and splintered across the reception room as Godley forced it open with a violent kick. He entered closely followed by Abberline and Ford; all of them setting to methodically searching the premises for any clue of Tumblety's whereabouts or further guilt in the murders. The handwriting had proved to be a damning piece of evidence but there had to be more to prove his guilt unless he had been very thorough in covering his tracks. Tumblety had occupied what amounted to being the first floor of a three storey single fronted Victorian town house. It consisted of a comfortable reception or living room, a single bedroom with a sink and a kitchen. The toilet was shared with the residents of the other floors and sat at the rear of the premises.

Three rooms, three officers. Abberline took the bedroom, Godley the living room and Ford under their directions was despatched first to the kitchen and once finished there he had responsibility for the toilet. No where that Tumblety may have used was to be left unturned. They were fortunate to find that the whole place was quite sparsely furnished but every inch had to be scoured to find any clue whatsoever that would lead them to Tumblety's whereabouts or movements.

Abberline walked into the bedroom to find it laid out with a single bed, a bureau, a tall boy chest of drawers and a dining chair in a corner looking as if it was positioned for use as a clothes horse. Abberline made straight for the bureau and began with its three drawers; it was constructed from mahogany with each section available to be locked but none of it having been secured. This immediately led Abberline to assume little would be found in it but he would persevere knowing that complacent assumptions could lead to missed opportunities; something that could be ill afforded.

None of the drawers was lined and all were completely empty leaving no clue of what use the American might have made of them. He opened the writing section which activated supporting arms as it was lowered into a horizontal position revealing the compartmentalised section situated at its rear behind the leather covered blotter surface. He felt more hopeful of something here as two of the sections held papers which he pulled out and sat flat on the blotter to leaf through. At first they all seemed quite innocuous revealing only blank writing paper and some matching envelopes; the thought struck him 'could it be the same paper Tumblety had written the Ripper letters on further fuelling a case against him?' He seized it as potential evidence. The other papers turned out to be some folded sketches of sights he recognised as Parisian another more vital clue that could infer guilt. There was also a sales receipt made out for three medical specimen jars from a supplier near the London Hospital but with no client details entered on it. There was nothing else in the bureau but the discoveries were essential.

Abberline turned to the bed looking underneath it finding nothing except bare floorboards and then stripping it and turning the mattress again revealing nothing. A rug lay on the floor on either side of the bed both of which he moved and analysed the floor boards in the room to see if any had been disturbed. There was no sign of any of them having been lifted for use as a hiding place underneath but the removal of one of the rugs exposed a tiny edge of a piece of paper sticking up from between two of the boards. So little was exposed that Abberline couldn't get hold of it between his index finger and thumb so he removed the pin from his neck tie pin and gently speared the edge of the paper with it and pulled it free. It proved to be a crucial find; a sales receipt made out to 'Frank Townsend' from a company called 'The Transatlantic Line' for a first class single sea view cabin to America. The only frustrating element to the receipt was the lack of a name for the ship upon which the journey would take place. There was nothing else left for Abberline to check within the room so he returned to living room to see how Godley had been getting on there and young Ford in the kitchen.

While Abberline had been working in the bedroom Godley had been making an extensive sweep of the living room and had finished dealing with all the furniture and now went on to the floor and a walk in cupboard. Abberline was free to assist him move the rugs and the items of furniture to examine the floor boards. Between them it took another five to ten minutes to do this and check the cupboard to reveal nothing. They were passed by Ford who was now making his way to the outside toilet who said nothing on his way through.

"Anything in there then, Rob?" asked Abberline.

"No, Boss, nothing. Be back in moment just going out to the bog," replied Ford. Abberline shared his finds with Godley while the lad went outside.

Ford made his way to the rear of the premises via the communal corridor and found the rear door unlocked. He opened it and went outside to find the exterior lavatory situated next to a coal bunker; there was access to this yard from an alley way between blocks. He opened the door of the toilet and found it unusually clean for a communal facility. Looking round there was virtually nowhere to conceal anything; he moved the coarse mat on the floor to reveal only a stone floor, the walls were bare and there was no false boxing built around the pipe works. The only possible place was the toilets cistern. He stood on the rim of the lavatory bowl and lifted the lid to look in. He was hit by the smell of its rotten water with its film of scum floating on the top as he looked in, but there was nothing to be discovered.

He walked back out into the fresh air and looked around the yard. It was bare and minimalist paved with rough cobbles with a washing line stretched across it. The only place here to look through or into was the coal bunker; he pulled up the chute's shutter at knee level to reveal only a trickle of some lumps of anthracite. 'Odd?' he thought 'they must be waiting for a delivery.' He was about to walk away, but paused. He returned to it and tried the top merchant's delivery hatch but it was jammed shut. He studied it and found curiously that it had been nailed to the main bunker so he bent down and took a look in but could see little in its extreme darkness. With the absence of any lighting he would have to lean in and try and feel for anything inside.

He had to lie down prone on his front to be able to get any significant range with the small wooden structure and felt frustration in soiling his clothes. From left to right he felt his way round as far as he could his hand brushing all kinds of rough stony debris he assumed was a mixture of coal and broken rocks having found their way in with deliveries. Then his hand brushed something soft and fury but cold and still; he reluctantly took hold of what he believed was an animal's leg and dragged it toward him to get it into some light. As it began to be struck by the light from the chute he could see that it was a dead emaciated cat. Although expecting it, it still made him jump when he saw it nervously withdrawing his hand and shaking off a handful of maggots from his arm. Undeterred he put his arm back in and continued his sweep feeling more small lumps of coal and little else until he had almost reached the leading wall of the bunker by the front chute and felt an upright leather bag.

He ran his hand over it trying to find something to which to gain a purchase to pull it out into the open. He caught hold of a carrying handle, gripped it and pulled the bag out into the daylight. His heart was racing with excitement having found an item that had so obviously been hidden, but it still left him with clarity of thought. He knew that he should not open it without more experienced officers present but didn't want to drag it too far from where he found it. He called out for his superiors to join him.

"Mr Abberline! Sergeant Godley! Come outside there's something here you must see, gentlemen." Inside they had been examining Abberline's finds together and looked up at each other with a start on hearing Ford's shout. They left the lodgings and walked briskly to the rear of the premises entering the courtyard to see a blackened looking young officer with a leather arts bag in front of him.

"I haven't looked inside it yet, Mr Abberline, thought that you two ought to be present before it was opened, you know evidence and all that," said Ford as he was trying vainly to brush his clothes down with blackened palms – making the situation worse much to the amusement of the senior detectives.

"I wouldn't bother if I was you, son. Wait until you've got white not black hands!" said Godley with a chuckle. Abberline bent down to the bag.

"Right," he said examining the clasp which he found was unlocked "Lets see what's inside, what that American fucker forgot to take." Abberline pulled the top of the bag apart having released the clasp and looked onto the tops of lots of jars and varying arts materials. The bag had a solid box section to it inside which kept everything tidy and in order, but essentially stopped the jars falling over and leaking. He slowly pulled out one of the jars and stood up holding it up to the light and looked into it with disbelief.

Ford stood mouth open, aghast; Godley muttered something like 'oh my Lord' while Abberline looked into the contents with fervent hate for its owner. Even without anatomical expertise he knew the jar contained parts plundered from the Ripper's victims and looked down into the bag dreading what else was in the other jars. He put the first jar down and pulled out another, then another and then another and there were still more left in the bag; he couldn't bear to pull any of the others out and knelt in silence staring into the bag, Godley and Ford silent and still too shocked to speak.

"What the hell is that all about, Fred? What the hell drives someone to possess such a gruesome collection?" asked Godley reeling.

"Don't know, George, but this fucker is going to hang, no doubt. Rob, go off to get Llewellyn and Phillips, I want them at The Street to tell me what the fuck all this stuff is." Abberline replaced all the jars in the bag as he spoke and closed it up.

"Right, Guv." Ford made his way back through the house to run the errand while Abberline picked up the bag and he and Godley walked slowly and with further troubled minds from the lodgings in Hackney Road.

While the search had been taking place Sir Robert Anderson had ordered the attendance of Superintendent Arnold at his office that morning for a briefing, as far as Arnold was concerned, regarding information from the Home Secretary, Henry Matthews on the direction of the Ripper case. Arnold could never have been prepared for the direction he was about to be given.

"Sit down Mr Arnold please," said Anderson as he himself sat at his desk. "Now listen very carefully to what I am about to tell you."

"Yes, sir, as always. What has the Home Secretary instructed?"

"You are to dismiss the investigation against Dr Tumblety. There is apparent new evidence that sheds innocence upon him in relation to the Ripper murders." Arnold sat silent for sometime before answering.

"But Inspector Abberline has evidence against him that makes him one of the strongest suspects in the investigation. The handwriting evidence especially crossed referenced with the statement he made. He is quite certain Tumblety is the man, or one of them."

"Well I can tell you he is not. This information disputes the version of events that Abberline subscribes to and that is that. Matter closed." Anderson sat back in his chair pompously.

"Sir, there will be hell to play with Abberline. He is very tenacious."

"I don't care! You tell him from me, that man is innocent, and if he doesn't like it tell him to come and see me. I want you to pass all evidence regarding Dr Tumblety to me for safekeeping."

"That won't be easy; I'll need reason to do so." Anderson thrust a piece of paper at Arnold. It was a handwritten letter; signed Victoria R on official Buckingham Palace letter paper the rest of the content seemed immaterial. The actions had Royal approval.

"I think that should cover it Superintendent, show it to Abberline or any other obstructive minions. If they don't like it they'd better think of other careers."

Arnold was stunned. He been put in an impossible position and had to think of himself, his reputation and his imminent pension.

There really was little else to be said in the face of the weight of establishment pressure now being placed. He held on to the letter and stood up to leave with a final address to Anderson.

"For the record, I don't like it and I shall mark my diary as such and complete a statement which I shall have verified and sealed for any later repercussions. I accept I am a servant of the crown and must act accordingly. Good day to you." Arnold left the office. Anderson looked on as the door to his office opened and closed. The matter had been easier than he had expected.

Chapter Twenty-Four

Sunday 25th November; Tumblety boarded the French steamer La Bretagne at Le Havre following a journey along the coast from his landing in Boulogne having fled England. Using his favoured pseudonym of Frank Townsend, a name that he would travel under until he was well away from the coast back in America; he embarked on a seven day Trans Atlantic crossing. Wearing a plain dark blue gent's suit with a wing collar shirt and tie, he had decided to ditch his favoured uniform look to avoid attention and if the London police had wired details to the French Surete they could be looking for a uniformed man. He had waxed his distinctive handle bar moustache to change its appearance and cut his hair considerably shorter again to appear as different to his London persona as possible. He sported a bowler or 'derby' hat and carried with him an umbrella and two canes tied together, one his sword cane and the other a single shot firearm; now he was returning to the States he would again have the right to bear arms.

His luggage had been placed in his outside cabin and he entered the comfortable accommodation and walked to the opposite seaward side and stooped slightly to look out through the traditional maritime porthole. He was looking out of starboard side to a calm English Channel, or to the local people of France 'La Manche.' Tumblety eagerly anticipated a quiet journey where he would keep his need to venture from the cabin to a minimum and only after dark if at all. He was fully aware that although no one would find him if checking the passenger manifest for the name Tumblety, the police may have posted officers to watch passengers on all trans Atlantic ships calling at or sailing from Britain. He would keep any forays out onto the deck to a minimum and have most services brought to his cabin pleading sea sickness as a reason for his reclusive ness. Satisfied with his surroundings he would unpack later in the day and wanted to witness the departure from the quayside in the cool French coastal air on deck.

He ended up stood portside as the ropes were untied and cast away by the dock workers and watched as the ship moved and the heavy twill ropes made mighty splashes falling into the murky dock-side water. The decks were full of people squeezing up against the ornate iron balustrades of 'La Bretagne' waving and cheering to the crowds on the quayside mirroring their actions. Tumblety scanned the crowds idly as the ship moved slowly away his gaze eventually falling to the front of the throng of people on the quayside. There stood against the waist high railings by where the gang planks had been he noticed two very anxious looking smartly dressed men who had pushed their way forward. He unwittingly made eye contact with them as they looked up with an apparent sense of futility on their faces with the ship now many yards from the dock-side. One of them, a man of about 40 years of age wearing a bowler hat caught Tumblety's look directly, his eyes noticeably widening as he did so and immediately nudging the other younger man with him and pointing up directly at the doctor.

'Damn it!' thought Tumblety 'it's the Goddamn cops!' He instantly withdrew from the ships edge, furious he had been seen knowing now that the Metropolitan Police would wire New York's Police Department with no way now of preventing his arrival from being put under surveillance. He pulled back to the iron sides of the upper deck enclosing the first class accommodation pressing himself bolt upright out of view behind the crowds of passengers and carried on cursing heavily in his mind. 'How the hell do I get round this?' He would spend the early part of the voyage considering this matter deeply to get the authorities at both ends off his scent.

Inspector Walter Andrews spoke to the young detective constable working alongside of him with them both having spotted Tumblety.

"Bugger it! Right we've missed the boat so we can't follow him ourselves to New York. But we can send a wire to the NYPD and get them to watch him at the other end until a team can get there. Let's get to the telex office to let Abberline know. Least we know where the bastard is headed for now."

"Boss, can't we get on a smaller boat to intercept him if we go and see the Surete now?" asked the young DC.

"Why bother, he can't get off until New York. How could we miss him at the other end?"

This optimistic view by Inspector Andrews, who would ultimately head the team who travelled to New York, would prove to be unfounded by Tumblety's guile yet again and fuel the enduring enigma of the Whitechapel Murders.

* * *

Monday 26th November the very next evening and the cunning American doctor had already hatched a plan to create a deception for him to give the slip to any police surveillance. He made his way to 'steerage' and found himself wandering around the impromptu parties and small drinking groups in the communal areas of the lowest of the classes. The atmosphere was warm and actually quite humid as a result of the sheer volume of humanity in the area and smelt strongly of a multitude of scents; body odours, tobacco smoke, alcohol and fried foods. Everyone was dressed in working class clothing and all age groups frequented the communal areas with children running around playing tag type games and a group of working men playing a selection of instruments including a harmonica, accordion and banjo. They jammed together in a harmonious way that encouraged couples young and old to dance in pairs or in groups. Tumblety very purposefully observed all the males of about his own age to see who might be suitable to assist him in his plan at a price. He needed to be careful that he found someone that was not intoxicated and would therefore listen with sobriety to his proposition.

As he wandered through and away from the major throng of people, ahead of him he could see a man of around forty-five years leaning against the ships bulkhead slowly drinking from a pint glass of beer. He was of a similar height, medium build so just a little thinner but with well kept hair and a prominent dark moustache. Perfect for his burgeoning plan. He appeared to be simply enjoying the taste of the beer and not the long term volumetric intoxicating effect; he was himself watching the revellers keenly as he drank. He noticed the American approaching him and made and maintained eye contact with him, displaying to Tumblety a man of confidence and caution. He was dressed in heavy corduroy trousers, a collarless blue shirt with a neck tie, heavy black leather working boots. Despite trying to appear casual and blend in to the surroundings of steerage, the man could see it was obvious that the American who approached him was not travelling on this deck. As Tumblety neared him, he stood up straight away from the wall he had seemed to have been supporting. The American spoke to him.

"Evening, fine entertainment down here, beer and accommodation any good?" The steerage man paused looking Tumblety up and down before speaking.

"Remarkably few rats. The beer is crap as a matter of fact." Tumblety couldn't believe his luck; this man was a fellow American.

"Frank Townsend, doctor," said Tumblety extending his right hand to make an introductory handshake. The man from steerage looked down at it before raising his own to reciprocate the greeting.

"Bill Weston, carpenter and former Union soldier," he replied sternly. He continued as they let go hands. "You don't come down here to socialise, Mr Townsend, cut to the chase. What the hell do you want with me?" Tumblety looked him in the eye and then dropped his gaze down to the ground and thought heavily before conducting his answer.

"All right, Mr Weston, I will. I have a business proposition for you which will simply mean you have the chance to live comfortably on the rest of this crossing, and then for a few months on arriving in New York."

Weston was immediately suspicious, but also virtually penniless and was intrigued by the chance of some comfortable living. This curiosity stemmed from that most natural human weakness – greed. He squinted at the American doctor and sipped some more beer having to wipe froth from his moustache. He then spoke again in response.

"Carry on, but be truthful, I guess you have some trouble in your wake then, Dr Townsend." Tumblety considerd his reply and spoke far from the truth.

"There are men following me and watching me from London, due to financial difficulties. Their feelings are unfounded and they mean just to intimidate me for a while, what I need is someone to act as me for a short period to let me get away when we dock. You're a smart man; you know why I am asking you I'm sure."

"All right, go on; are they liable to want to kill you, or me?"

"No. Just scare and intimidate to try to goad me to pay them off."

"Is someone on the boat watching you now?"

"No, you are not under scrutiny until we dock, I want you to fill in for me for a couple of days before hand so you get used to the idea."

"How much then, Dr Townsend? And how long do I masquerade as you in New York?" Weston was intrigued and in need of money.

"$1000. I have an address for you to use for a month when you arrive, then you can just disappear." Tumblety felt his offer generous.

"No. $1500, you pay my expenses on the boat for whatever I want, some of your wardrobe and I take over as you tomorrow." Tumblety was not in a strong position to negotiate, but he tried.

"$1400. You can take over as me as you ask, but must be confined to your cabin complaining of sea sickness and pay for your own indulgences." There was an uncomfortable silence between them.

"$1500 and I'll pay my expenses." Weston would not be swayed.

"Deal. I will bring you a suit tomorrow and you will groom yourself down here before going to first class. I will leave a second suit for you upstairs, the cash in an envelope on the bedside table and the details of accommodation in East Tenth Street for you to use. There's no rent to pay on it. Just live there for a month and then disappear in the night in your work wear." They shook hands to close the deal.

"You have a deal then, Dr Townsend. I shall see you tomorrow."

"We will never meet again after that, Mr Weston. Enjoy your new life for a short period then."

* * *

During the morning of the 26th Abberline had received the telegram from Andrews in France informing him of Tumblety's evasion and sailing for New York. Although not pleased at this development he at least knew that, unlike the loss of their subject in Hackney, this time they were certain of where he would end up and the local police could therefore be asked to begin surveillance on him until Scotland Yard detectives could be despatched. He discovered that morning from the American embassy that the head of the New York Police Department was Chief Inspector Thomas Byrne, and as soon as Godley had passed this name to him Abberline went straight to The Yard's telex room by carriage from The Street to personally ensure the communication was sent. Godley accompanied him while the other detectives on the case were still collating and going out to obtain more witness statements. Separating the useful from the fanciful as Abberline had directed was a difficult task. By this the detective inspector implied that those that were unreliable as a result as being those of attention seekers, drunks or inveterate liars should be disregarded, but not destroyed. Many statements, some taken by Abberline himself would prove invaluable and formulate much of the Ripper legend, especially that of George Hutchinson regarding the last sighting of Mary Kelly. Robert Ford found this statement in his hands as Godley and Abberline left for the telex room. He began to read it slowly to take in its content. It had been taken at 6.p.m on the 12th November after Mary's inquest:

'About 2.a.m on the 9th I was coming by Thrawl Street, Commercial Street, and just before I got to Flower and Dean Street, I met the murdered woman Kelly, and she said to me Hutchinson will you lend me sixpence. I said I can't I have spent all my money going down to Romford, she said good morning I must go and find some money. She went away toward Thrawl Street. A man coming in the opposite direction to Kelly, tapped her on the shoulder and said something and they both burst out laughing. I heard her say alright to him, and the man said you will be alright, for what I have told you: he then placed his right hand around her shoulders. He also had a kind of small parcel in his left hand, with a kind of strap round it. I stood against the lamp of the Queen's Head Public House, and watched him. They both then came past me and the man hung his head down, with, his hat over his eyes. I stooped down and looked him in the face. He looked at me stern. They both went into Dorset Street. I followed them. They both stood at the corner of the court for about three minutes. He said something to her. She said alright my dear come along you will be comfortable. He then placed his

arm on her shoulder and she gave him a kiss. She said she had lost her handkerchief. He then pulled his handkerchief a red one and gave it to her. They both went up the Court together. I then went to the court to see if I could see them but I could not. I stood there for about three-quarters of an hour to see if they came out. They did not so I went away.'

Ford dropped the statement onto the desk having finished the last word and stared blankly into space with many unanswerable questions spinning in his mind. The conversations Hutchinson talked of made no sense as they were all half recorded. So what was she trying to achieve? Was she drunk and unaware of her actions? Had she drifted back to prostitution that night? Had she decided to turn her back on him? He knew that he would never get an answer to these enigmatic questions.

Abberline and Godley arrived at The Yard at around 11.a.m and made their way straight to the second floor telex room. The corridors and offices of The Yard were filled with uniformed and suited policemen going about they work on a busy Monday morning catching up on their many and varied investigations following the weekend lull of staff at The Yard.

The telex room was staffed by an inspector in overall charge, two roving sergeants and half a dozen constables all sat at their telex units with their headphones on all focused on sending and receiving messages mainly around the U.K, some to Europe but not normally any to the United States. Abberline on entering was met by the Inspector Thomas Willis who recognised the famed detective and availed himself immediately.

"Mr Abberline, what can we do for you?"

"Inspector, I need to send a telegram urgently to the NYPD. Can you free up one of your blokes now so I can get it done?" said Abberline.

"Certainly, this way," Willis led the two detectives to one of the terminals operated by a portly middle aged constable with a large handlebar moustache. "Smiffy, finish what you are on and then do whatever Mr Abberline requests please."

"Thank you, Mr Willis, much appreciated," said Godley as the inspector wandered back to his desk.

Smiffy after just a few seconds looked up at Abberline and nodded his head in readiness to go with fingers poised at the keyboard. Abberline opened up a sheet of paper and began to speak with Smiffy typing.

> FAO Chief Inspector Thomas Byrne. URGENT From Inspector Frederick Abberline, Chief Investigating Detective Whitechapel Murders.
>
> Requiring interception and surveillance until Yard detectives arrive: Doctor Francis Tumblety. Already of note in USA, expected to arrive from Le Havre aboard La Bretagne on Sunday 2nd December. Seen leaving France by detectives, most likely travelling first class. Smartly dressed, around 50 years old, 5'11" outlandish moustache and military dress quite frequently or at least very smart. Please reply once picked up surveillance. Thank you for co-operation.

Smiffy finished typing and spoke "Anything else, sir?"
"No thank you, Smiffy, thanks for that. Let us know over at The Street when you have a reply."
Abberline thanked Inspector Willis and they left the room and returned back into the busy corridor. Word of their presence had obviously spread around The Yard as Superintendent Arnold was waiting for them outside. He spoke to the detectives stopping them in their tracks in the corridor.
"Frederick, I need to see you and you alone in my office please." Godley and Abberline exchanged glances before Abberline replied.
"All right, sir. George I'll see you back at The Street."
"Good choice, Inspector, you maybe sometime." Both detectives looked further puzzled. Godley continued out of the building while Abberline followed Arnold to his third floor office. They entered and sat either side of Arnold's desk. He pulled a drawer open and took out a bottle of scotch and two glass tumblers. Abberline knew that by this action something serious concerned Thomas Arnold. He had known him on and off over many years.

"Boss, not for me it's too early in the day. Can you cut to the chase please," said Abberline. Arnold poured a glass and had to take a large swig of the strong tasting bitter alcohol before he could begin. The taste made him contort his face as it burned its way down his gullet and sat warmly in what felt like the pit of his stomach.

"Fred, how long have we known each other?" Abberline began to feel very uneasy as a question with sincerity or nostalgia often disguised a killer blow and looked Arnold hard in the eyes before answering.

"Well, we were sergeants together seventeen years ago. Our paths have crossed on and off ever since. Why?"

"Brace yourself for what I am about to show you." Arnold passed the Buckingham Palace letter across the desk to Abberline who studied it intently.

The Office of Her Majesty, Victoria R,
Buckingham Palace,
London,
SW1,

To all concern investigating the Whitechapel Murders,

I hereby give Royal decree that any line of enquiry regarding the above mentioned murders and the investigation of Dr F Tumblety be forthwith ceased. Any actions contrary to this Royal proclamation maybe considered Seditious and against national interests.

Victoria R.

Abberline sat in stunned silence reading it over several times. He got up and silently poured himself a large glass of scotch. Still without saying anything he walked over to the window in Arnold's office and stared out blankly. The view was across the embankment towards the south side of Westminster Bridge. It seemed like an eternity to Arnold before he spoke.

"Tom, what the hell is going on? I've slaved my guts out over the last twelve weeks within a community that is living deeply in fear and is distrusting of the higher echelons of society, and I have had to do my utmost to down play their fears. Now this? Are they going to write a Royal pardon for George Chapman too?

"It's not a pardon, Fred."

"Might as fucking well be. I have damning evidence against him, he's done a runner from the country and they are telling me to let him go. Do any of them know that he's gone, eh?"

"Old friend, please don't shoot the messenger. I…" Abberline interrupted.

"Listen. Enough of this shit let me tell you how it is, Tom. Both are as guilty as hell. My feeling is that Tumblety is responsible for most of it but for some reason Chapman killed the last one. Do they want me to fit one man up with them all, who I can't find, or do they want the killer? I know where Tumblety is."

"Fred I've shown you the official line. My job is done. It's up to you what you do. If you continue it will be on the heads of you and your men."

"This is establishment? Isn't it? This is Catholic or Masonic. Tumblety is one or the other. Well justice comes to everyone religion, class or any other fucking divide aside. I'll go underground with this if I have to."

"Good luck to you, mate. I agree. Do what you have to for those women, but you will have to turn over all you've got to me. I'll give you 24 hours to get it copied by photograph, facsimile or whatever."

"Good. Thanks, Tom. I want justice. All those smug bastards have never had to see the horrors inflicted upon those women, the fear inflicted upon the community or the trauma on all those who pick up the pieces. I tell you now, the truth will prevail." Abberline finished his impassioned response.

"Be careful, Fred. Tread very carefully."

Chapter Twenty-Five

1.p.m on the 26th; Klosowski had found employment working for a gentleman's barbers using his real name, rightly assuming there would be a search on for the former proprietor of 'Chapman's Barber Shop'. He maintained his trade albeit for someone else's benefit whilst Lucy Baderski did casual work locally as a seamstress. The premises were in West Green Road, Tottenham and they lived there above the shop not unlike their circumstances in Cable Street previously thanks to rapport he had struck up with the owner when he ventured in for a job. He did his best to engage on a friendly basis with all of his new clientele as soon as he had begun work there to create a positive impression and keep any suspicion at bay. It was quite obvious to him that the residents here would be aware of the circumstances of the Whitechapel Murders and would have read about descriptions. He was acutely aware that the night he had taken Mary Kelly's life so ultimately pointlessly, he had been seen with her in Commercial Street. This liaison must have been reported to the police and a description of him that night put forward. Little did he know the extent to which the police would be making their enquiries as a result of his abandoned premises. He decided to keep his moustache short and hair cropped following the move from Whitechapel in an attempt to avoid being associated with any of the descriptions of the murderer.

Klosowski was blissfully unaware, however, of a casual conversation Lucy had had with one of her local acquaintances back in Whitechapel. He had told her where he intended to relocate them and she had in turn innocently mentioned it in conversation before leaving to a friend who was wishing her well. This would lead the authorities to his door when he was least expecting it and force another more substantial move.

* * *

With the crushing news regarding the investigation delivered by Superintendent Arnold, Abberline hurried back to The Street to call a briefing with the entire investigation team and implement a covert plan of action against Tumblety. As he arrived at the front door of Commercial Street Police Station he was met on the steps by Chief Inspector John Littlechild. They knew each other only in passing but both were acutely aware of the skill each possessed as detectives and leaders of men. Although one rank divided them, they had always politely spoken as equals.

"Fred, before you go in, can I have a word?" asked Littlechild.

"Yes. What can I do for you, John?" said Abberline in response politely shaking hands with the veteran detective.

"You know about my department. I am the only one within it who probably knows what you have just been told. I am not going to offer a flood of secret sleuths to help you, but as I hear things at The Yard I'll let you know. Do you know Robert Ford who is attached to your team?"

"Yes, of course. Why?" said Abberline quizzically, amazed that nothing seemed to slip past the Special Branch.

"Right, he's a reliable young lad, I know he's been terribly scarred by the events of the last twelve weeks but use him over others. He won't arouse suspicion and he'll be tenacious." Abberline paused looking into his eyes. There was no hidden agenda with Littlechild; Abberline's years of interviews and instinct told him that.

"All right, John. Yes I will do. It will be him with either Godley or Bill Thick. He'll need a little guidance."

"Good choice. Remember, if you need help give me a call." They shook hands and Littlechild disappeared along the main road whilst Abberline entered the building.

Inside the police station the corridors bustled with people as always as he made his way to the incident room. Inside the room fell silent as Abberline entered; he looked around relieved to find everyone key was there: Godley had returned as expected, Parish, Murphy, Bill Thick, Robert Ford, Robinson and Mather and Walter Dew, now permanently on the team. The only one he would have to brief separately would be Inspector Andrews who was now on route from France due back at The Street the next day.

"Fellas, get yourself a tea, a smoke, something to eat or whatever but no alcohol thank you. I've got some serious news for you and you won't like it. But, we must push on undeterred. So take a few minutes to make yourself comfortable and then pin back your ears and listen." All within the office looked around at each other with concern but made sure they were indeed comfortable with fresh tea and a smoke or sandwiches that they had brought from home to eat during the day between tasks.

"Sarnies, that's a good idea, Robert get up to the canteen and get some plates done, here's a couple of shillings for them," Abberline passed the young constable the money and he scurried out of the office as directed.

"I take it the news is big then, Fred," asked Godley with Bill Thick listening in standing next to him.

"Huge. It's a kick in the bollocks too, but we'll get round it." Abberline was watching the room and gave them some direction. "Right, pull out all the chairs from behind the desks and set them in a circle facing the display board. Once Rob's back we'll lock the doors and only open them for the sandwiches."

Within a few minutes Robert returned carrying two dinner plates full of sandwiches. Unusually for policemen everyone gave him time to put them down and the entire gathered crowd only took a couple each ensuring everyone got some. Godley locked the office doors and took a seat within the circle as Abberline took up position in front of the display board to address them all. Behind him on the wall were photographs of the victims, street plans of the murder scenes, pathologist's statements and sketches and a large street map of the area with each murder site marked, except those of Del Lake and Ralph the paperboy.

Abberline coughed clearing his throat, drank from a steaming mug of tea, then took a bite out of a cheese sandwich and began.

"Mmm, anyone had the cheese, they're bloody good, Rob!" The room burst into laughter as it certainly wasn't what they expected from the detective inspector's mouth. "Right, settle down, sorry lads. They are bloody good though. You'll all be wondering what this is all about and you're going to find out and not like it. I want you all to read this brief but corrupt letter and say nothing until it's been round the room. Corrupt? Well I think so because I don't think the author would have written it without massive influence. There is establishment or society membership involvement here, maybe even complicity and we are being told to sever a key line of enquiry. But I have a plan to deal with this. Before I voice that, I welcome comments or questions from the floor." The room sat in silence as the letter did the rounds with those gathered who read it looking around the room and up to Abberline in disbelief. It forced several to light a cigarette to calm tensions that they could feel building within them. The letter returned back to the front edge of the circle and into Abberline's hands. Bill Thick was the first to speak.

"Guv'nor, what the hell is going on?"

"Bill, that's what this meeting is all about. I am forced to trust that none of you are linked to organisations such as the catholic guild or the masons. If you are I stand to end up in the Tower of London and so do some of you if we pursue a covert line of enquiry against Dr Tumblety. For that reason I ask all of you to display the loyalty and integrity that you have so far and leave the room and the investigation if any of you are members of either society." Abberline's words seemed to echo around the room as the atmosphere could be cut with a knife. Abberline quite deliberately said nothing for what seemed to all like an eternity but was in fact only half a minute as he made eye contact with all in turn looking around the office. With the assembled team still sat firmly he continued. "So from here on in officially you can all only go on the hunt for George Chapman and evidence against him regarding any of the murders. But I will be selecting a small team to continue the investigation against Tumblety. You will have the right to refuse if I ask you, but I ask any of you to say nothing of any ongoing enquiry of this nature. If you do, all of us will be at risk and I can assure you anyone that betrays the team will be taken down with us." He scanned the room again ensuring he made eye contact with all gathered. Again the detectives and those assisting looked resolute.

"Good. Chapman must be found as he most likely responsible for the murder of Mary Kelly, but motivation? That remains unknown.

That we may only discover by arrest and interview. Tumblety will be found but, gentlemen, I cannot guarantee justice for him." Robert listened intently, he was determined that both men would be brought to justice. "Saturate the area around Cable Street. I want any lead regarding Chapman followed. He must be found. To that end I want everyone visiting every barber's establishment in London to see if he's moved on or to find any trace of him having passed through, Bill and George will supervise those enquiries." He said pointing to Godley and Thick. "Fellas, any questions?"

Everyone wanted to ask, but no one dared to, who was going to pursue the Tumblety enquiry. Most realised from Abberline's as yet silence on this matter that he wanted to keep the risk to each man to a minimum. They all looked around the room shaking heads, most still stunned from the revelation of the Royal intervention in unfathomable circumstances.

"Good, you two," pointing at Thick and Godley "sort out teams to go out and do these enquiries, no stone unturned." As the gathered began to break up from the circle Abberline grabbed Godley's arm and whispered quietly into his ear. "Make sure Robert is tasked by you because I need to use him." Godley looked at him and nodded in instant recognition of what the detective inspector was implying.

Abberline then left the office without saying a word to anyone as to where he was going.

"Where do you think he's off to then, George?" said Bill Thick looking on curiously as Abberline left the office.

"No idea, leave him to it. He's close to cracking despite his front I think," replied a concerned Godley.

The detective inspector was actually making his way to a local main post office to go and send a telegram to the head of the N.Y.P.D to warn him of the latest development and contact him directly.

He arrived at the post office in Whitechapel High Street after a casual ten minute stroll south along Commercial Street. On route he passed so many now ominous sites that he once treated with nonchalant familiarity; The Ten Bells, Millers Court, Hanbury Street, The Britannia. All now permanently etched on his psyche as a result to their connections with Jack the Ripper. Abberline was determined to bring both his key suspects to justice by legal means or otherwise.

In the post office the clerk instantly recognised the celebrated policeman.

"Hello, Mr Abberline. What can we do for you today then, sir?" Abberline sometimes felt uncomfortable with his local notoriety.

"I have a brief telegram to be sent to a colleague in New York."

"Oh, really, how flattering you come here and not to your telex office in Scotland Yard." Abberline knew that the clerk would find this curious.

"I was passing and you were obviously closer. I don't have a lot of time can we get going with it?" He knew he had to get word to Thomas Byrne as soon as possible.

"Certainly, Mr Abberline." Abberline had to word the message carefully. He did it knowing it would sound a little odd to the clerk. He was sure that the almost celebrity status he had locally would prevent the post office staff taking the matter up with other officers from The Street or even Scotland Yard. He began to dictate the message to the clerk.

> Mr Byrne,
>
> Due to political conflicts you maybe asked to not pursue the investigation of Dr Tumblety. This is a cover to avoid attention. On my authority please keep this man under observation until Inspector Andrews arrives and please extend him all available assistance. Don't hesitate to contact ME directly to maintain discretion.
>
> Frederick Abberline (Insp).

"Will that be all, Mr Abberline?" asked the clerk having taken down the message on post office notation paper.

"No, destroy the copies of this telegram once it is sent, a matter of national security," replied an official sounding Abberline.

"Yes, sir. I understand. Thank you."

Abberline left the Whitechapel post office and began to stroll casually back towards The Street. As he walked he was aware of a carriage pulling up alongside him; looking round he saw it was John Netley.

"Hello, Mr Abberline. Can I give you a lift?"

"Ah, Netley," Abberline paused for a moment "Yes, thank you." He climbed aboard and Netley set off. There was design in taking this opportunity. He knew Netley seemed to always have an ear to the ground and was all too aware of what was happening in the area.

"So, Netley, how's business?"

"Very good thank you, Mr Abberline. Where to then?"

"Commercial Street nick, but there's no rush. What's the word around the streets then about the murders?"

"Well. That American surgeon did a runner so I hear," Netley would not be so foolish to incriminate himself saying he had assisted, the job had paid well. "Seems old George Chapman had something to hide. Shop closed straight after the last murder and seems to have pissed off."

"Yes, so I heard," said Abberline innocently. "Any word around as to where."

"Well, I have heard somewhere in north London. But no one knows for sure."

"Hmm, interesting. Know anything else. What about the Vigilance Committee. Heard what they're up to?"

"Naah, gone very quiet they have. I think since they got their knuckles wrapped for not helping your boys they try and steer clear, know what I mean?" Netley waved his crop at the horse as he spoke.

"Yes, I do. Look, hear anything about anyone, even it's something or someone that seems disconnected from what you've heard, let me know. It'll be worth your while, old son." Abberline watched Netley's back for any obvious body language reaction. He seemed impassive.

"Yes will do, Mr Abberline. Will do."

They arrived at The Street barely ten minutes after leaving the post office. Abberline alighted and offered Netley the fare. He politely declined and tipped his hat to the famed detective and set off towards Bishopsgate. Abberline stood and watched him drive off with a feeling of distrust of the obliging coachman. He returned to the incident room to find it empty apart from Godley and Robert Ford busy with desks full of paperwork.

"Excellent. George, lock the door. Rob, listened very carefully. As far as we are concerned you are the only member of the team now beyond corruption. Sadly you have a vested interest in the investigation so I will be tasking you to do some very discrete jobs. Do you understand?" Young Robert stared at him intently and with a concerned frown.

"Yes, Mr Abberline. I think so. What do you want me to do?"

"Good. First off I want you to take all of the documents that relate to Tumblety and get them photographed by a local bloke. His name is Morley and his studio is in Stratford. It's not far so get a cab and get them done first thing in the morning. Wait with them and then get a cab back to here, come and see me and then we'll get the originals passed on to Mr Arnold." Abberline looked across at Godley as he finished.

"Very well, sir. What time?"

"Leave here at six and he'll be expecting you. Now bugger off for the rest of the day, lad and we'll see you tomorrow."

"Thanks, Boss." Robert grabbed his top coat and left the office.

"He's a good lad that one, Fred," said Godley looking on.

"Yeah, he is and like I said reckon he's only one we can trust totally."

"Yes, mate, he has but we need to keep an eye on him. He's tough but he's also vulnerable." Added a concerned Godley. They both got back to examining the Tumblety documents that day before they would be taken on the next to be copied by the photographer. It would be the last time either of them would have hands on them.

* * *

Tuesday 27th November 6.a.m; with a sizable cardboard box under his arm Robert Ford left the front steps of The Street into the cold morning darkness and had to wait several minutes to hail a cab to take him south in Commercial Street and on to Stratford. He didn't know the easily corruptible John Netley who was driving the cab and neither did he know, nor Abberline and Godley for that matter, that the conversation with Robert's directions for this morning had been deliberately overheard at The Street. Parish had been coerced by Sir Robert Anderson's office to inform on developments regarding Tumblety. Promised a promotion, he had been stood the other side of a door in the office that had been blocked off from inside by the need for additional desk in the room.

"Where can I take you to, guv'nor," asked a jovial Netley.

"Just head towards Stratford for now, mate," replied a cautious Robert Ford as he climbed into the cab. Netley had been contacted the previous night and bribed by Parish and already knew the destination anyway. Parish was not foolish enough to be involved in the interception of the material that Robert was carrying and neither were his masters who had already warned him off. Two local thugs had been paid by Parish to ensure the material didn't make it by whatever means necessary.

The cab carrying Robert trundled across the cobbles of Commercial Street southbound towards Whitechapel immediately followed by another at a discreet distance containing the two thugs and a third man. Robert would have expected the journey to progress along Whitechapel High Street, Whitechapel Road, Mile End Road and onto the Bow Road eventually to the outskirts of Stratford. So when Netley turned from Whitechapel High Street to Commercial Road Robert was a little confused. He leaned forward and spoke to the driver.

"Why are you going this way, mate?"

"Oh, er, been a crash with an omnibus outside the hospital. Thought this way would be quicker." Robert was instantly suspicious. He looked around in the darkness and could see the light of a cab behind them. He decided to keep quiet and watch it to see if it maintained pursuit of his cab. Sure enough over the next few minutes the same light stayed with them as they reached the junction with Yorkshire Street and the edge of the Regents Canal Dock. He was not happy and felt vulnerable; he pulled out his police whistle ready.

"Stop the cab now, mate." He said with menace to Netley. He also had his truncheon with him in the outer pocket of his top coat.

"Sorry, what Guv'nor?" Netley replied trying act in a confused and innocent state.

"You fucking heard, cabbie. Stop the cab now!" Looking round Netley found himself staring at Robert who was brandishing the truncheon with some purpose. Netley was a natural coward so he did what Robert said and pulled over by the north kerb facing to the east opposite the Canal Dock. Before Robert could alight the other cab had pulled up next to them with the two local thugs onboard. Robert looked across to see them just beginning to alight. Without hesitation Robert reached up and gave Netley the hardest blow he could with his truncheon knocking him off the drivers perch. He made no sound as he hit the pavement as he was completely unconscious; the injury would play havoc with him in years to come and ultimately lead to his death under the wheels of a coach as he was taken by a grand mal seizure whilst at the reigns.

The horse reared up and began galloping off in Commercial Road towards its change to East India Dock Road. Taken completely by surprise the thugs jumped back aboard their cab which lurched off in pursuit. Robert had been thrown into the seat and lost the grip of his truncheon but not possession of it as the wrist strap slide up his forearm. "Fuck!" he shouted following a sharp pain in his elbow as the flailing weapon struck him on the elbow. He regained his balance and struggled onto the perch as the horse still continued with fright along Commercial Road. Looking over his right shoulder taking control of the reigns he could see the other cab in pursuit. The streets were still relatively quiet and empty as it was only just approaching 6.15.a.m. The pursuing cab was closing on him driven by an experienced cabbie so Robert was forced to consider what he could do to get away. A quick plan came into his head; he would turn right into West India Dock Road and head towards Blackwall Police Station on the edge of the Isle of Dogs.

However, as he made the turn the other cab pulled along his outside and began to force him wide towards the pavement and the buildings. Robert pulled hard on the reigns to try to slow the horse or even, he hoped, stop it completely before running off the road and potentially killed. As he did he was aware of the box containing the Tumblety papers make a loud banging sound as it hit one side of the cab. In the chaos of the chase he had almost forgotten about it. He got a chance to see his potential assailants again as the pursuing cab overshot him as he managed to pull his cab to a halt and could see they were both very heavy set but slightly over weight East End men. There was also the third much more slight figure in the cab that he couldn't make out properly. A fight even with his truncheon didn't look like a good option but running away, despite the handicap of the precious box, might be. He jumped down from his perch the instant the cab stopped and reached in to the passenger section and pulled out the box. With the box under his left arm, now only strapped with a bandage for support and the bones feeling significantly stronger, and the truncheon still in his right he ran for his life back towards the main junction from which he had just turned. He ran across it into Burdett Road and it was then he heard the first shouts. One of the thugs was on foot trying to give chase but struggling to keep up; but where was the other? As he made the first fifty yards of Burdett Road he could hear a horse pulling a wheeled unit behind it on the gallop; it was the cab with the other thug on board was his guess as the sound came nearer. Just as the sound was on him he had Farrance Street on his right and he darted across the road in front of the pursuing cab missing it by a whisker as it shot straight ahead. He could hear it pulling up hard to come back. He kept up his pace knowing that the other foot borne thug was still plodding along behind him.

Robert made a wrong assumption at this point. He had imagined that the cab would have tried to turn around and come back to Farrance Street as he turned left still running into Calcutta Street which led to the next road parallel; Dod Street. As he came into Dod Street he could see the cab to his left only yards away still at almost full pelt. He turned immediately right and crossed on to the other pavement now running along by the wharf warehouses which sat on the banks of the Limehouse Cut waterway. At last a chance to outsmart the cab too as he ran down an alley way between buildings barely five feet wide. He was breathing hard and despite the cold sweating profusely from the exertion of making his escape with the precious documents; he assumed that this whole incident was about the box. Robert could hear the cab pull up for sure this time and knew that there would be a fresh set of legs behind him now as he came to the water front. With arms full he had not been able to get to his whistle and now looked for somewhere to hide as he was momentarily out of sight to all three of the men in pursuit of him.

Ahead was another alley way but it wasn't an option in case they decided to come up from the other end of it too. He had one choice; most of the filthy stinking canals were no more than five feet deep so he could climb in and wade across. They would see him but may be slow to follow giving him a little edge on the other side to blow his whistle to try to summon help. Placing the box on the waters edge momentarily he then jumped in from the side managing to avoid getting his head under as he did so. He was right the water was only just over five feet deep, but that was enough to force him to wade across holding the box above his head. The shock of the entry into the icy cold water drew the breath from his lungs momentarily, but he calmed himself and began to breathe normally. He was about half way across the canal when he could see both thugs on the south bank he had just left now trotting towards him.

"Stop there, you stupid fucking copper, or else you'll not only get beaten but fucking drowned too," said one of them with genuine malice. He ignored him and silently continued wading. He was about twenty feet from the other side. He had his back to them now as he slowly made progress aware of the fact that there could be an unexpected deeper section or dumped items on which he could loose his footing. Behind him he heard a massive splash; one of them had dived in and if he was swimming he could be on him before he got to the other bank. He looked round to see one man still on the bank looking as if he was trying to find missiles to throw at him whilst the other one was swimming surprisingly briskly towards him. 'These bastards must be getting well paid' Robert thought as he tried to up his pace.

He did manage to make the other side before the swimmer caught up with him so he was able to put the box down on the canal bank. As he did so the swimmer came to his feet and got hold of Robert in a headlock and pulled him under the water. The shock made him draw in some of the cold, filthy water into his lungs and momentarily his mind went blank as he sensed he could die. Then he jabbed the truncheon below the surface as hard as he could into the swimmers slightly portly stomach. In the silence of the water he didn't hear the swimmer groan but the brief release of grip it caused was enough for him to struggle free and resurface coughing and gasping for air as he ejected the rancid water he had swallowed. He quickly re-focused on the swimmer who lunged for him but Robert himself jumped out of the way and then swam to the middle of the canal to draw his assailant away from the box. The swimmer now prone in the water from the failed lunge saw where Robert had gone and swam round to get to him stopping short to avoid getting in truncheon striking distance.

Robert sensed he was dealing with a seasoned fighter and got ready to strike as the swimmer squared up to him. He then heard a quieter splash than the first he had heard from the swimmer now engaging him and quickly glanced behind to see the other thug had lowered himself from the bank into the water and was about to begin to wade towards him. Looking back the swimmer lunged at him but Robert was equal to this swinging hard and fast with his truncheon and striking him a glancing blow on the left side of his head.

"You scrawny little bastard! You're fucking dead, mate!" shouted the swimmer stepping back and rubbing his head. He was initially looking Robert in the face but then momentarily appeared to look beyond him and then he suddenly turned and began wading quickly away towards the box. 'Fuck!' thought Robert, he knew what was happening; the other thug must be feet away from him freeing the first one up. Robert turned quickly to see the second thug about to swing with a large piece of wood at him. Robert raised his truncheon to meet it in a kind of sword parry. They exchanged several blows each in an almost fencing type fashion both keen to defend themselves and try to inflict injury as soon as possible. The thug wasn't equal to Robert's speed and stamina being much older and a little overweight from alcohol abuse. He became slow to defend a blow to his ribs from Robert who connected with his left side forcing him to bend over clutching his ribs in pain. Robert took further immediate advantage of this placing a well aimed and fearsome blow to the thug's skull sending him then underwater.

He turned towards the north bank to where he had placed the box after neutralising this first immediate threat to see the second thug about to lift it from the bank side.

"Put the fucking box down now if you know what's good for you!" shouted Robert with real aggression but doing little to dissuade him. The second thug, a broad but squat man with a mutton chop beard and hands like a navvy's shovel, ignored the threat and placed his enormous hands on the box lifting it from the bank then turning to look at Robert with a toothless smile on his face.

"Bring it back over here," called out a slightly muffled but well spoken voice, unusual for the company that he was obviously with.

The voice was coming from the south bank of the canal and it seemed somehow familiar to Robert. He turned to look in its direction to see a well dressed gentleman in a deerstalker hat and heavy top coat pointing a revolver in Robert's direction. His face was masked by a scarf that was up over his nose leaving only his eyes below his hat very narrowly exposed.

Robert knew that the salvage of the box and its safe transit was imperative so without thought he turned his back on the gun man and waded quickly towards the squat thug who was making his way across the canal carrying the box high out of the water. He looked fearful as Robert approached him; a shot rang out making Robert flinch autonomously as if he had been struck by a bullet. It took him a second to realise that he in fact had not been shot, a second that seemed to last a life time momentarily with the thought of facing death in the festering water. The fearful look from the thug had been due to the fact the revolver had been aimed higher and at him. Robert noticed the man stopped in his tracks and bloody began pouring down his forehead from under his flat cap. The gunman had shot him in the hairline at the top of his forehead covered by the hat. He seemed to freeze upright for a moment and as he did Robert moved forward with a dive to get close enough to rescue the box. Another shot rang out but it splashed harmlessly in the water next to him as he grabbed for the box now falling from the thug's arms as he crumpled vertically into the water like a collapsing chimney stack. The box landed with a heavy splash and initially bobbed about on the surface momentarily. As it did so Robert made a grab for it to lift it out; another shot rang out and whizzed close by his right ear and splashed into the water sending up a small plume of spray. He now realised that the masked man whose voice struck such a chord with him was out to kill him or anyone that interfered with the box or more importantly what was inside.

It was a difficult judgement call for him knowing the importance of the documents inside held the chance of conviction of the man directly or indirectly responsible for Mary's murder. Dead, he could do nothing to seek justice for her at all. With that fact in mind he took a deep breath and forced himself under the water and swam as hard as he could below the murky black surface given that appearance in the moonlight. Two more shots came by him underwater, not terribly close, and bizarrely very silently. He knew he had to go as far as his lungs could carry him to get away from the danger of the gun toting stranger. Within seconds in the cold darkness of the water he felt as if he had travelled hundreds of feet and his lungs seemed to be straining; mainly an effect of the cold. He made in the direction of the north bank where at least he felt that at some distance he could surface fairly covertly and at least momentarily to catch his breath.

In the intervening seconds, the first thug with whom he had fought with his truncheon and felled surfaced in a dazed and spluttering condition. The gunman immediately shouted instructions to him.

"Grab that box before it goes completely under and empty it all into the canal." The thug just stared back confused for a moment. "Now!" screamed the gunman. The thug looked around and saw the box beginning to disappear below the water; he grabbed it and up ended it and the contents came spilling out into the canal. The Victorian ink instantly began to run and blur and then paper began to pulp. No hard work was needed to destroy any of it including Tumblety's hand signed statement, the most crucial piece of evidence against him. As the thug was doing this the gunman was loading new rounds into the drum of his revolver very casually. He clicked the drum back into the body of the gun as the thug looked up at him. As he did so the gunman aimed the revolver directly at him.

"Well done, you," he said condescendingly to the thug as he then shot him three times in the chest.

Robert had surfaced thirty yards away in the darkness by the north bank and could not be seen but was able to observe the last seconds of his first assailant's life. He clutched his chest and looked up in total disbelief and astonishment at the man who had shot him and then with a groan collapsed into the water. Robert looked on in horror at two bodies now floating in the canal shot by this familiar masked man. The gunman walked casually along the canal bank observing the hundreds of decaying sheets of paper and then turned on his heels and walked along one of the alleyways back, Robert assumed, to the cab.

In fear of being shot Robert stayed silently where he was; cold now hit his body with chilling aggression. To this point he had been physically and mentally engaged in the canal and past the initial shock of the cold water as he entered it and had not had time to realise he was beginning to get dangerously cold. The sensation of coldness now hit him fiercely and he had to get himself out of the water as he could feel himself shivering with an intensity he had never experienced before. He was delaying getting out initially for concern over the masked gunman coming back maybe having only disappeared into the shadows to encourage him to come out. This man probably did not make an assumption that Robert might be dead from the shooting and had not surfaced.

He forced himself to wait for what he thought was a couple of minutes. He had no way to tell what time had elapsed as his watch had stopped as a result of being in the water. Feeling mostly confident the gunman had gone and in fear of passing out and drowning he began to pull himself out by the north canal bank; as he did so he heard the crack of a riding crop and a cab or carriage pull off on the cobbles. From what his hearing allowed him to determine in the awkward wharf side acoustics the cab's sound was from the south side somewhere gradually fading away. He lay out shivering on the canal bank for a minute or so before pulling out his police whistle and blowing as hard as he could until fatigue took him over and he began to pass out from the cold in his soaked condition.

Chapter Twenty-Six

Wednesday 28th November 1888; aboard La Bretagne the exchange of identities was about to take place between Tumblety and Weston to throw any observers either on board or when they arrived in New York off the scent. Tumblety had packed a carpet bag of his most vital belongings and now found himself back in steerage confronting Weston in his meagre accommodation. Weston's cabin was located inside of La Bretagne and sounded as if it neighboured the engine room as Tumblety entered and was hit by the austerity of his new surroundings. It contained a simple iron bed, a chest of drawers and a wash bowl on a table in a corner, below which was a chamber pot. It was somewhat less grand than what he was used to. His facial expression obviously displayed the sense of dismay he felt and Weston read it well.

"Well, Doctor. Better get used to it. You've only got a short cruise with the rats though," said Weston looking Tumblety up and down. He liked the look of the suit the American was wearing that he was about to take possession of.

"Yes, I'm sure I will. Shall we get changed then?"

Both men began to take off their outer clothes and placed them in separate piles on the bed ready to exchange, each eyeing the others garments as they did so but with completely different emotions. Tumblety reminded himself this temporary down classing was a necessary evil to ensure his survival. He knew that capture and return to London would mean the gallows if his Masonic ploy had failed so the discomfort and lack of privacy of steerage was a worthy sacrifice. Weston eagerly pulled on Tumblety's suit trousers, and then grabbed the shirt clumsily fastening the buttons. He had given himself a good wash and picked up his new dapper expensive shoes and overbalanced as he pulled on the first, falling onto the bed and looking up embarrassed.

"Hey, fella, don't rush so much, you'll have plenty of time to enjoy first class over the next two days," said Tumblety casually as he more slowly and almost with disdain dressed himself in Weston's very proletariat clothing. Weston picked up the neck tie having pulled on both shoes.

"Before you put that on get some of this inside your shirt, just so you smell a little more first class." Tumblety offered him a bottle of cologne. Weston looked at him with an air of offence. "Look, if you're going to pass as me you have to smell like me. The people bringing me cabin service are used to it." Weston took the bottle and eyed it with annoyance but quickly considered the American's point valid. He loosened the upper buttons of the shirt and sprayed a generous amount around his neck and upper chest.

"Well done, you'll grow to like it," said Tumblety. Weston could sense some condescension in his voice but chose to ignore it when he considered what he was going to make out of their agreement.

Tumblety fitted very naturally into his new working class role having learnt during his many travels and especially around Whitechapel to be able take on many personas. He looked Weston up and down and felt he couldn't necessarily say the same for him. He looked a little uncomfortable in his new finery and would need a few tips for his public appearances.

"Mr Weston, you look good, but relax a little. Make sure your cuffs are pulled down below your jacket sleeves, don't wear your trousers so high and just hold yourself a little more upright. Do those and you'll carry it off. Just try to speak politely but a little low, even hoarsely so you make an excuse about your throat to not arouse cabin service staff's suspicion."

Weston had to admit it was all good advice and nodded his head acceptingly. "Yes, Doctor you are quite right." Tumblety offered Weston his hand.

"Well, Mr Weston, good luck and enjoy your brief foray into the upper echelons. Remember allow a little time at the lodgings in New

York before moving on. Enjoy, and thank you for this great personal service."

They shook hands firmly making positive eye contact as they did so.

"Whatever you've done, Doctor, good luck."

Weston turned and made off finding the stairs to take him to the upper decks; without hesitation he placed a foot on the first step, briefly looked round back to steerage without making any eye contact with Tumblety. He looked gleeful to be leaving it all behind and then turned carrying on up and out into fresher air. Tumblety was left surveying his austere surroundings and the meagre possessions he temporarily now carried, most important of all being the jewellery case. In his potentially more volatile and less secure accommodation he sat and unpacked the contents and laid them on the bed. From his carpet bag he removed a leather money belt and began unbuttoning his shirt and then pulled it from his shoulders. He carefully placed the various precious stones into the leather belt ensuring that they were turned to avoid getting the sharp edges digging into his abdomen as he had several days of keeping them concealed. He repacked the empty jewellery case into the bottom of his carpet bag and packed some of the retched clothes left by the man with whom he had swapped identities on top to avoid even the case, although devoid of treasure, being seen.

* * *

Thursday 29th November 10.a.m. Constable Philip Rowntree walked his usual beat along West Green Road in Tottenham passing the many shop keepers he knew giving each other a polite 'hello' eventually reaching the 'Tottenham Barbers Shop' owned by William Blake, a distinctive corner premises. He looked in and saw that the shop was quiet with just one person in a chair and no other men waiting for the barber's services. His vision fell to his reflection in the window and he could see that his mutton chop moustache and his hair could do with a little bit of tidying up. He walked by the barber's distinctive red and white horizontally striped rotating pole and opened the door setting off the hanging door bell to alert the staff. Bill Blake who was cutting the hair of the seated, overweight client looked round recognising Phil Rowntree straight away and smiled.

"Phil the filth! How are you, mate! Not come in for me new bloke have you?" He said jovially. The ears of the 'new bloke' pricked up who was waiting for work reading a newspaper at the rear of the shop. By the comment he realised a policeman must have entered and he felt uncomfortable with the visit so soon. But Klosowski realised that with the words his new employer had spoken he would have to front the visit out.

"Not unless he's bleedin' Jack the Ripper, Blakey. I've come in for one of your Sweeny Todd specials, you bugger!" he said taking off his helmet and placing it under his arm. The only person who saw the irony in the remark was the man now emerging from the rear of the shop. Rowntree looked him up and down as he walked cautiously, it seemed, towards him with his head slightly bowed and piercing eyes looking up from a furrowed brow. This man fired his 'policing sixth sense' into action as he looked like a man with a dubious past who didn't relish the company of the police. He spoke to Rowntree with a foreign accent.

"Morning, Constable, what can I do for you?" he was drying his hands on a clean white towel as he spoke.

"Quick trim please, Mister....?"

"Klosowski. Severin Klosowski." He spoke uncomfortably.

"Right. I'll sit here," Rowntree said as he got into the other barbers chair in the shop. Klosowski then put a barber's apron over his chest and shoulders tying it behind his neck as was standard to avoid soiling his clothes with cut hair. There was silence for half a minute or so until Blakey renewed conversation in the shop.

"So who they looking for then, Phil, in this Ripper case?" Rowntree could see in the mirror before him the foreign barber begin to work on his hair and felt distinctly nervous being asked this question with this man close to him with sharp objects in his hands. He considered his words carefully.

"Well, as far as I know they're looking for a, er...... fellow from overseas, dark, average height maybe. Good with a knife. Bit of anatomical knowledge."

"Sounds like fucking you, Sev!" replied Blakey laughing as he spoke and causing his client to laugh but no one else. Rowntree made eye contact with Klosowski in the mirror. He looked furtive and not keen to engage in any conversation himself. Rowntree was compelled to force him to speak to get some sort of background from him. He suspected whatever he said would have to be what he had already told Blakey.

"So, Sev, where you from then?" There was a pause before he answered.

"I come from Poland." He wouldn't expand.

"Nice. What brought you here then?"

"Work."

"Barber there as well then?"

"Yes." This was very much like conducting an interview with a criminal suspect. But he was dangerously hooked by the intrigue of who this man was.

"So, did you come straight here from Poland? Have you worked elsewhere in London? Married perhaps?" There was a pause.

"Look, Constable, I work. I don't like to talk. You suspect me of something, eh?" Rowntree was confused by the response. Was this man actually a potential suspect and being difficult, or was he an innocent and protesting his innocence and dislike of being treated as a potential criminal.

"All right, mate. Sorry. I'm a local bobby and I like to get to know people. Shan't ask you anything else then, fellow. But if you can't be civil don't expect me to be either." Silence then descended again over the barbers shop.

This lasted for several minutes. Blakey was about to try to lighten the atmosphere when the carnage began. Having continued cutting Rowntree's hair silently Klosowski then acted swiftly and in a deadly manner. He lifted his right hand clasping the scissors quickly high above his shoulder and then plunged it down into the back of the constable's neck. They sank deep into his trapezius up to the handle as Rowntree screamed out with the searing and blinding pain. He tried to clutch his wound but as he did so he was pushed by Klosowski out of his chair and landed on the floor in a limp heap.

The calculating Klosowski left him to writhe on the floor as he then approached the witnesses to the attack. From the front of his barber's apron he pulled out his cut throat and folded out its blade then swiftly and silently swung out at Blakey with it as he turned to face his new employee. The cutthroat struck as Klosowski intended severing Blakey's windpipe, jugular and carotid artery and he slumped to the floor unable to speak and without the strength or wherewithal to retaliate. Blood sprayed from the wound and stained the mirrors of the shop running slowly down to the counter below. The seated client in the meantime had jumped to his feet and was making for the door which for him unfortunately opened inwards, therefore slowing his potential escape.

The fast moving and callous Klosowski grabbed the back of his shirt collar as he attempted to open the door and pulled him down to the floor. The terrified fat man looked up shaking in absolute fear and then wet himself.

"No don't please. I'll say nothing. Please, please, no!"

The cutthroat first struck diagonally across his face from the left side of the fat man's forehead down to just below his nose. It opened up his face deeply, split his left eyeball and slashed the bridge of his nose down to the cartilage. He screamed incessantly for just a few seconds as this first wound was inflicted but it was cut short as his throat was cut in the same way as Blakey's. He stayed silently on the floor his body shaking in erratic spasms as death took hold and within half a minute was limp lying in an expanding pool of blood, overlapping and mixing with that of the old and now lifeless prostrate barber.

Klosowski was then startled to hit the floor facedown as he was struck from behind. 'Who the hell was that?' Was his first thought as he was taken totally by surprise. But then he recognised the hissing voice in his ear and became aware of the police truncheon as it missed his head as he and his assailant clattered to the floor.

"You fucker! I'll have you!" said Rowntree in a pained low voice drawing his truncheon back to have another go at Klosowski. The Pole, who had been pinned down by Rowntree, rolled to his left as hard and quickly as he could managing to partially free himself from the policeman's weight. It gave him a free left arm too. The truncheon came down towards him again but he blocked the strike with his left forearm striking the policeman's right wrist. Looking up at the policeman who was now kneeling over him, he could see the top of the scissors handle sticking out of the back of his neck. He was stunned this man had recovered so soon as he had hoped to have punctured his brachial nerve. Rowntree then delivered a punch with his left hand taking Klosowski completely off guard as it connected with right side of his jaw. It hurt and for a couple of seconds his vision blurred but not so much as he didn't see the truncheon again coming down at him until it was about to strike. He moved his head to one side and the wooden weapon struck hard against the stone floor. So hard that it shattered, leaving only a stump in Rowntree's hand. He stared at it in disbelief; the moment's inattention was enough for Klosowski to throw him off. He landed heavily on the floor on his back which winded him. The Pole was up briskly to his feet and as Rowntree looked up he had grabbed a broom and struck the policeman around the head with the brush end. As were all Victorian brooms, its head was made of a heavy piece of wood with a wad of coarse bristles attached. It connected harshly and with force to the left side of Rowntree's head knocking him backwards and to the floor.

Looking to his right he saw an iron bucket only a few feet from him. He sat up and reached across for it then sprang to his feet. The adrenaline surging through his system had dulled the pain of the scissors buried in his back and as the broom was swung at him again he countered it with the bucket. The broom head caught in the buckets handle and mouth and Rowntree pulled it from Klosowski's grasp. For a moment the Pole stood confused and motionless. Rowntree took advantage of this moving forward quickly and swinging at him with the iron bucket. It hit him in the chest as he tried to take avoiding action. The Pole kicked out striking the policeman's right shin hard which put him to the floor in pain.

Klosowski moved forward and kicked him squarely in the jaw sending him backwards unconscious. He stood motionless surveying the carnage within the shop and then noticed he was heavily stained with blood. Quickly, he moved to the door and locked it and turned round the status sign from open to closed. He grabbed the cord for both the door rolling blind and the window blind and yanked them down to ensure no one passing could see what had happened. He blocked the door further with one of the chairs and then made for the back of the shop.

Lucy Baderski was upstairs and he knew time was of the essence. They had to escape. He washed his face and took off all of his soiled clothing before he went up to see her so as to keep her suspicion to a minimum.

"We're leaving now. Pack your things." He tried to sound nonchalant in his demand.

"Why? Where are we going?" Was Lucy's reply not unsurprisingly at this sudden demand as he had appeared upstairs. He went up to her grabbing her by the throat and pulling her close to his face and scowled.

"I am your husband and your meal ticket. Do what the hell I say or I shall cast you into the streets. Pack the minimum you need for us to go away. You have five minutes." She was choking as he spoke and tried to release his grip but without success. She fought for breath and tried pointlessly to speak as he grasped her for several seconds once he had finished speaking. He then flung her away and she landed on the floor clasping her throat and fighting to regain her breath; she looked up hatefully at him but knew this vile and cruel man still, at that moment, had a hold over her. She got up turning her back on him not wanting him to see her eyes welling up with tears of fear and left the room to follow his demand.

In reality she possessed little so to pack the essentials in a few minutes was not a difficult task. Klosowski was soon in the room with her packing his own belongings hurriedly in preparation for what to her was going to be an imminent departure. He put on his suit as he got to it. She had wondered why he had come up having discarded his working clothes.

"What has happened, Severin? Why are we going now?"

"Shut up and do as I say. I will tell you when we are far from here."

The rooms above the shop were bland and austere and not at all homely. They had no furniture of their own to be discarding so clothing was virtually all they owned. A fire was burning in the main living room so Lucy felt the cold as they retreated to the unheated cold bedroom with its battered wardrobe and chest of drawers. Emptying her clothing into the old case didn't take long.

"We have some food left in the pantry as I only bought us some yesterday. Should I take that with us?" Klosowski thought for a moment. It would save them stopping too soon to eat if they felt hungry.

"Yes, put it in a muslin sack, but only what we can eat without preparation. We'll be getting a bus and then a train I think. I need, err… want to leave London. There is no future for me here."

He knew he was certainly right in that assumption. Having killed further the only future he faced was that at the end of a rope. He pulled up the mattress and grabbed a leather satchel from under it. It contained his savings, a not inconsiderable amount of cash, and it would be essential to get away.

"Are you done?" He menacingly demanded of Lucy. She was clutching the muslin sack now containing some bread, cheese and ham.

"Yes," she said with dry eyes and ready to pick up her case.

"Good. We must go."

He grabbed her case and ushered her with a nod of his head out of the door.

"Do not go through the shop. Leave via the back gate. We will go straight into West Green Road from there and down to the High Street to catch a bus to the railway station." She knew that it was pointless to ask any question as to why so ruefully nodded her head in recognition of the instructions.

Within ten minutes they were on an omnibus and heading off, little did Lucy know, as fugitives. As he sat down a cold chill hit him as he realised the huge and potentially fatal mistake he had made. The policeman was probably still alive and the only living witness to attacks in the barbers shop, the only witness to any of his atrocities. He was a professional and word would be around the authorities fast; word of his description but also his name and his nationality. He knew they needed to be out of not only London but also England within the next twenty-four hours before his details were posted at all ports. He remained deep in thought as the horse drawn bus passed rhythmically over the cobbled Tottenham streets.

* * *

Friday 30th November 9.a.m; Robert Ford was lying in his bed still recovering some two days after the fight of his life when he heard a heavy knocking on his lodgings door.

"Rob, you in there, lad?" called Abberline. Then the door opened and Abberline and Godley strolled in. When at home Robert rarely kept the door locked. "How are you then, boy?" brashly asked Abberline.

"All right now, Guv, thanks to the local Stepney boys. They got me stripped off and into one of their cells wrapped in blankets. Took me a good few hours to warm up but then I was all right. I told Inspector Chandler what happened. S'pose he told you too?" Abberline gave a knowing glance at Godley and nodded.

"Yes. He did and I'm sorry you took the brunt of it again. Do you know what happened to the box?"

"I can only guess. Sorry, sir."

"The whole bloody lot pulped. Nothing recoverable at all. Well, as you can imagine our hand has been completely forced where Tumblety is concerned. We have no evidence and no case. The lads are pursuing this Chapman bloke now. He might help us further of course. Want anything here?"

"No thanks, Guv, I'll be back in tomorrow."

"Good, lad. I need you." Abberline nodded at Godley and they had left no sooner than they had arrived it seemed.

Feeling a little lost, Robert decided to have a sort through in his room, something he had not had the chance to do properly for weeks. He persistently had been throwing discarded clothes into the base of the wardrobe an area which had been obscured by several hanging garments so he had not seen the very bottom for some time. The doors were only pushed to and not properly shut; they couldn't be because of the pile of clothing obstructing the doors from closing. 'Bloody hell' he thought as he pulled the doors apart and the pile spilled out on the floor. It included uniform, police shirts as well as some worn casual clothes of his own, all of which appeared to need laundering. He bent down and pulled them all out and now low down he could see virtually to the rear of the wardrobe, but not quite with the poor lighting and shadow cast by the hanging garments. He leaned in with his right arm to sweep for odd socks or anything that may be left and was surprised to feel something paper which felt quite thick to touch.

He took hold of it and pulled it out and found it to be a thickly stuffed white envelope. He had never seen it before and was suspicious of its contents; he reached in and could feel it was further paper items and pulled out to his amazement a thick wad of bank notes in large denominations. At the top of the pile were the beginnings of a hand written note. It must have been penned by Mary by its opening sentiment, the writing was poor and quite uneducated but he treasured the few words upon it as they were the last communication from her.

> Deer Robert,
>
> Pleese find here mony that will be for us
> When we move from london. When we
> Next meat face to face I will tell you where
> It is form but leave this note so you know it
> is for Us. I look forward to

And the note ended. It appeared that she may have run out of ink as the last word seemed to fade out. Robert on his knees initially collapsed back onto the floor in a seated position as one hand held the letter while the other one came to grip his forehead in total disbelief. Where had the money come from? What it was for seemed more than obvious, but how had Mary obtained just short of £3000 seemingly from no where. His hand ran from his forehead through his hair, his fingernails brushing his scalp at the rear of his head as he fell into deep thought. He rubbed his unshaven face as he considered how he could use the money to perhaps avenge her death; the only thing he knew for certain was that it would help secure his own immediate future if he needed it to. He placed the money back in the envelope which he then put in an old beaten up leather satchel bag he had and put it back in the base of the wardrobe. He mind numbingly carried on sorting out his clothing as he thought about the money and its origins.

* * *

Abberline and Godley went directly to the Whitechapel post office for a fresh message to be sent to the New York Police Department via telex regarding the Tumblety investigation, and away from the prying eyes in Scotland Yard. If caught, they were both acutely aware that their careers would be hanging by a thread.

"Well you know what the definition of a career is, Fred?" joked Godley on the way, "A head long rush down hill, mate!"

Abberline needed to inform Thomas Byrnes of a particular passenger to check when La Bretagne arrived as a result of the events of the night of the Kelly murder. Tumblety had of course been taken into custody over the false allegations of indecent assaults and had foolishly given the name Frank Townsend when first interviewed; the name that Abberline had found on the receipt for the Atlantic crossing. The Transatlantic Line had not yet provided a passenger manifest to Abberline and in the wake of the events regarding the Tumblety investigation he could not really pursue it further, but he at least knew the names that his American counterparts should look for. He would have to word his message carefully so as not to arouse too much suspicion in Thomas Byrnes when requiring that he replies only be to himself personally via the post office. Before going to the telegram operator he worded the message methodically with Godley reading over its contents.

> Chief Inspector Byrnes,
>
> Be advised of the possible presence of a Frank Townsend arriving with the Transatlantic Line on Sunday. If he is on board he is a key suspect in the Whitechapel murders and must be traced for questioning. Please ascertain if he is present, which I am sure he is, as any address he ventures to is crucial pending the arrival of Scotland Yard detectives. Please reply to me via this postal address, Scotland Yard too busy to give me prompt service. Townsend/Tumblety are one and the same.
>
> Frederick Abberline, Inspector.

Abberline looked up at Godley once finished who gave him an accepting nod of approval. He took it to the clerk and within a few minutes it was gone. They returned to The Street to discover the latest on the Chapman enquiry and were in for some extremely mixed news.

Over one hundred additional policemen had now flooded into the Whitechapel area to assist in door to door enquiries and to try to calm the general feeling amongst the populace by providing even more patrols. It was the enquiries of one of these officers drafted in during a casual conversation with a worried local woman in Cable Street that had brought some vital news. Constable Ben England from Forest Gate division had engaged a woman resident from Cable Street in casual conversation when she had asked him if anyone was as yet in custody.

"No, madam, afraid not. But we're working on it, like."

"So, where's old Chapman gone then, or ain't you a local bloke?" asked the woman.

"Don't know who you mean, love. I'm from Forest Gate just brought in to help, like."

"Oh. Do you want to know where he is?"

"Every thing helps of course....?"

"Well. His wife, Lucy, said he were in a bit of trouble. Don't know what sort, but she said they was going off to Tottenham to stay away for a bit. He's a right shit. Horrible to her, and always impolite to his customers. Good job he's fucked off." The constable listened to all that she said intently; he knew that the detectives would relish hearing this information and he was keen to get back and report it.

The dire news of the brutal events in the barber's shop had also reached the Ripper incident room. This was a massive development and needed to be acted on immediately along with PC England's intelligence which only confirmed that their second key suspect must be in Tottenham. The wounding of the constable and the murder's of the two civilians needed the intervention of Abberline's team immediately with it's relevant links to the Whitechapel events; a foreign suspect, in a barber's in Tottenham, the missing Cable Street barber having gone to Tottenham and the wounding of a constable who had been asking the right questions of the wrong person when he had been in a vulnerable position. With this news Abberline and Godley immediately left with Bill Thick and Murphy for Tottenham, all of them deciding to draw revolvers and join the manhunt.

Chapter Twenty-Seven

Friday 30th November and Richard Mansfield's 'Jekyll and Hyde' had closed. Initially embittered by the closure of what was hailed as a spectacular performance and theatrical success, he had lifted his own spirits by throwing himself wholeheartedly into a new version of Shakespeare's 'Richard III'. Mansfield was a believer, as were many of the age, in spiritualism and had decided to seek the guidance of a noted London psychic again. He had decided to convene with Robert Lees at the Café Royal at the bottom of Regents Street just prior to Piccadilly Circus. They were aware of each other's notoriety and formally introduced themselves for a second time in the foyer before taking their table for afternoon tea.

They were shown to a comfortable table on the first floor overlooking the bustling thoroughfare outside surrounded by many others of London's upper class society. They both knew some of the other diners that were also taking tea there that afternoon; Philanthropist Dr Thomas Barnado, colourful London Coroner Dr Wynne Baxter, Miss Lilly Langtree, and painter Walter Sickert who was taking tea with and at the request of the Duke of Clarence and Avondale, Prince Albert Victor. They perused the menu and ordered a selection of sandwiches, scones with jam, cream and Cornish butter and a pot of jasmine tea to be served without milk between them.

"How very civilised and English, Robert." Remarked Mansfield glibly.

"Well, you know. When in Rome and all that, old boy. I thought you might appreciate sampling our traditions."

"Certainly. I have sampled so much of your culture so far. Your overbearing police, the misleading and ill reporting press and the fickle London audiences."

"Well, one can apologise for the fact that fate did conspire to bring these forces together against you."

"Well I am glad you bring up the matter of fate. You obviously received my letter regarding my request for further clairvoyance on my career. Have you as yet seen anything in your psychic sessions?" Mansfield was pleased he had managed to guide the topic of conversation so soon.

"Well, Richard, my visions of recent have been many and varied in several matters. But in your life, I see many things. Some of which you may not wish to know about."

"All right, if there's good news and bad news I guess I'd like to start on a high. Besides, paying money for such a service where ones life is foretold, it can't be all roses and parties." Again his remark was glib bordering on flippant.

"Very well. Firstly, your next role is of a regal nature, yes?"

"Yes it is. Shakespeare's Richard III."

"It will play for a successful run in London, but more importantly for you it will be well received in a Lincolnshire port."

"Goddamn Lincolnshire! I've never been there and don't intend to go. You sure on that?"

"Well, there could be a double meaning; there is a Boston there and of course your own country."

"Well, that's more like it. What's the bad news?" There was a pause in the conversation. Lees looked around the room before bowing his head and speaking without making eye contact.

"I can see nothing past your 50th year, Richard. Please see a physician regularly at the turn of the century." He lifted his head and made eye contact with Mansfield who was nodding his head in grave thoughtful acknowledgment.

"I see. Got anything else?"

"Not of note, my friend."

Their afternoon tea arrived and was placed on their table by an attractive young waitress. Mansfield looked her up and down and made eye contact and smiled. He was renowned as a discreet womaniser. She returned the smile shyly and then bowed her head and left, back towards the direction that led to the kitchens.

"Anything to brighten my humour or titillate then, Robert? What of the Whitechapel murders then?" This was a topic on which Robert Lees felt great passion, though resentment of his treatment by the police. He was more than willing to comment on what had come to him recently but what he had vowed never to take to Abberline or anyone else.

Lees composed himself before speaking. He lifted the tea pot and poured them each a cup. He sat back and took a deep breath.

"Where should I start? That common fool detective Abberline had the audacity to call me a fool and a lunatic for trying to provide them with information regarding the killer. He failed to understand that my visions are frequently symbolic and not always directly precognitive. They sent me away but I was proved right by what I told them. But, I have the 'last laugh' for want of a better metaphor. I have foreseen that the men who have committed these crimes will never be caught by the law and the detectives will be prevented to do so by powerful men in society; so their efforts will be fruitless." Mansfield looked on in stunned silence following the outburst. He considered Lees' words which provoked questions in his mind. 'These men' he spoke of, who were they? Was there more than one killer?

"Robert, of what do you speak?"

"Ah, I knew it would get someone's attention. One man is **responsible** for the true murders on the whole. Others became involved either by design or accident. But one who has fled the land is responsible. Trust me."

"Who the hell is this man?" asked a stunned and transfixed Mansfield.

Again Lees fell silent, seemingly reluctant to speak further. He sipped his jasmine tea and lifted a sandwich and took a bite.

"One of your countrymen is culpable for these acts. He commissioned them himself and committed three. Of the other three one other man of greater evil is responsible or associated with them. He killed through lust and greed." Mansfield was feeling cynical about such in depth information, especially concerning a fellow American.

"Oh, really," he tried not to let his cynicism sound in his voice. "Pray tell me what this American's motivation was?"

"Hatred fuelled by curtailed passions," replied Lees with conviction. "You seem no better than Abberline, Mr Mansfield?" said Lees making eye contact with him.

"Look, Mister, you tell me Jack shit in depth information about my future but you know all about Jack the Ripper. You must have gipsy blood in you and read a goddamn crystal ball knowing all that stuff. No wonder the cops don't take you seriously. Give me a bill and we'll be done." Lees stood up outraged and was about to speak but was interrupted by Mansfield finishing his diatribe.

"In fact, here's £20 of your crappy money, I can afford it having been given compensation for the show closing early due to you limey bastards." The room had now fallen silent with everyone transfixed by the confrontation taking place. Mansfield now got to his feet.

"You know, I understand your future crap about me. My play is too good for here so I shall take it back to the states at the earliest opportunity. And that shit about me having no future after fifty, that's because I won't be here in the U.K so you won't be able to see it either way."

He threw the money at the sensitive Lees who watched aghast as it bounced off of his chest into his tea and Mansfield stormed off. Lees looked around the silent salon of the Café Royal to see everyone staring at him. He took another deep breath and sat down as he heard the conversation around the room restart, albeit he could tell about what they had just seen, he had his pride. He continued to take his tea and forced his now churning stomach to accept sandwiches. Another such humiliation in London would drive him to leave the capital sooner rather than later.

* * *

3.p.m; Abberline, Godley, Bill Thick and Murphy arrived at Tottenham to follow the trail from the scene. The bodies of the victims had long been taken to the mortuary but the barber's premises had been left as it was following the attacks. Constable Rowntree was back having been tended to at the hospital and been fortunate to have lost little blood. He was keen to impart anything he could that may prove of use to Abberline. The problem for the detectives when they arrived at the scene was that there was no trail to follow. Rowntree had been unconscious when Klosowski had escaped. No one near the premises seemed to have seen anyone leave. The alarm had only been sounded when the other constable patrolling in the vicinity hadn't met Rowntree during his own rounds. He found the wounded policeman unconscious still behind the closed doors of the Shop.

"So, Constable Rowntree," said Abberline, "who was this man then?"

"Well, Guv'nor, he was Polish, average height dark hair and a slight moustache, with 'orrible piercing eyes full of hate."

"I see. Did you get a name for this fellow then? And what was he wearing when it happened? Has he been here long?"

"They called him Sev which was short by all accounts for Severin. I found some papers here that gave his name as Klosowski. He had a barber's apron on and clothes underneath must have got covered in blood. I've got to say he didn't answer many questions before it all kicked off."

"Did he say anything beyond that?" asked Godley listening intently.

"In fact, no he didn't. I asked him a couple more but he got really offish. It all went quiet for a while until he plunged the scissors into my back."

"How old was he?"

"Mid to late twenties. Looks just like any other Polish immigrant really. Nasty bastard though." Abberline moved away from him and wandered around the interior of the shop. There was a lot of blood on the floors and on the walls which without even seeing the corpses of the victims indicated to Abberline the ferocity with which the attacks had taken place.

"Right, then." Abberline addressed the gathered officers. "I want all local bus conductors and cab drivers interviewed over the next few days to see if they saw anything. He's left with the girl that blabbed in Cable Street so have descriptions of both available when you talk." They all looked on at him waiting for him to continue. He looked around back at them with a scowl. "What you waiting for, you're still here; get out there before the streets close!"

Bill Thick, Murphy and all the gathered local uniformed officers hurried out and dispersed to get on with his instructions.

"Right, George. Telex all ports and main railway stations. Get them all on alert to find this man. I'm not fucking losing this bloke as well."

* * *

Saturday 1st December 10.42.p.m and DC Parish found himself back at The Street about to enter the locked incident room having just had a couple of quiet drinks locally still with an ear to the ground for information. No one came forward in The Ten Bells or The Britannia with any thing new so he had decided to return to the office for a cup of tea to warm himself up, and to try to reduce the smell of alcohol on his breath before returning to his wife. As he got to the door he noticed that it was already ajar. It should have been locked. He could see candle light burning inside and assumed, dangerously wrongly, that some one else from the team must be in there. He pushed the door open and saw a figure with his back to him at one of the desks.

"What's going on here then, matey?" he said expecting the figure to turn and for him to recognise him. The figure remained at the desk looking through a file. Parish took another step further into the office which proved his down fall.

A figure stepped from behind the door and lunged at his face with a hot burning candle. It struck him hard in the right eye with immediate and agonising pain. He collapsed with a scream and almost throwing up from the agony the attack inflicted. His scream was quickly muffled as the figure then shoved the candle into his mouth which did cause him wretch and vomit ejecting the candle at the same time. He was powerless to react through pain and illness disabling him as he was then kicked with ferocity several times in the stomach. The two figures left the office; the one that had been at the desk he did manage to notice was carrying a bag of some sort, leaving him writhing in silent agony on the floor. His throat burned from the acid bile being forced up from his stomach and from melted wax having also contaminated it. His eye was causing him indescribable pain and he sensed he may not see out of it again. He now realised that those powerful men to whom he had sold himself previously to supply information were ruthless in the extreme; they cared not for who got in the way of their plans and any loyalty or assistance they had been shown. He suddenly and guiltily resented having sold out the investigation. Then the pain in his eye socket seemed to escalate and it wasn't long before he passed out and sensed nothing.

In the parade room they had heard his stifled scream and the initial thoughts were that it was another drunkard or madman in the custody office or cells. It wasn't until Taffy Evans found the limp body of Parish in the doorway of the open incident room that anyone realised it was an occurance 'in house' where an officer was the victim. Fortunately, Dr Llewellyn was in the station tending a prisoner in the cells and he was immediately sent for to come and deal with Parish. He got him sat in the incident room washing his face with cool water which brought him round and cooled the burning in his eye. He drank some of the water to sooth his throat as Inspector Spratling arrived.

"He'll never see with that again," said Llewellyn as he examined Parish's eye. It was deeply blood shot from the burning with the candle and it's wax.

"What the hell has been going on here?" said Spratling scowling at all gathered with anger and confusion. In a broken voice Parish spoke.

"Someone has just been in to make sure there really is no link to Tumblety ever again."

"What?" said a confused Spratling.

"The fucking bags gone, Guv." Parish croaked in obvious pain.

"Oh, bloody great," said Bill Thick arriving on scene. "Bloody great. Rob gets duffed up and the case papers relating to Tumblety get destroyed. We get to Tottenham to find fucking Chapman has give us the slip, and now the bags been nicked and he's been blinded. Abberline's going to fucking love all this."

The question was, who was going to be sent to tell him, and when.

In the meantime Parish's assailants had slipped out of The Street and into their waiting carriage; the driver cracked his crop and the horse lurched off heading for their offices in the Special Branch section at

Scotland Yard. Having followed his direct orders, Dr Robert Anderson head of the C.I.D and often keen to bribe the lower paid ranks to do 'jobs' for him, would be pleased with the recovery they had made.

* * *

Sunday 2nd December 1888 and despite the strong desire to observe La Bretagne's arrival in New York from upon deck Tumblety kept himself down in steerage in the hope that watchful eyes would be drawn to Weston now in his place. It was a hard decision as he had been away from his 'homeland' for many months' and missed its security terribly; the opportunity to disappear due to the sheer size of the country. Even from as far down as he was he could hear the cheering on deck from the mixture of excited passengers, some wealthy and returning home from perhaps a European Grand Tour and for others it was their first sight of a new world full of opportunity and promise.

Bill Weston on the other hand was fully enjoying his new found comfortable life as Mr Frank Townsend despite having been confined mostly to his cabin for the latter part of his crossing. He stood up by the railings looking out over the lower promenade decks at the New York dockside building line, happy in the thought that he even had some comfortable lodgings to use on arrival, something that his normal life would never had provided. He was somewhat surprised as he casually gazed over the view to see a small official looking launch approach, especially since the ship had not yet been met by tugs, with people on board who seemed to have purpose and interest in coming aboard. As it got closer he could see that there was a scattering of men on board both in smart civilian clothes and others that appeared to be in police uniform. The ship seemed to be noticeably slowing too co-incidentally and he began to sense that this event must be linked to the mysterious American doctor.

The launch pulled along side and kept pace with La Bretagne and Weston could see a line being thrown down to it. A uniform policeman took hold of the line and strangely tied it around himself and was then lifted up from the launch and began to be hoisted upwards towards the lowest of the open decks. The launch pulled away and headed off towards the docks leaving their colleague to come aboard. Weston saw the policeman pulled over the railings but then lost sight of him as he was ushered inside. He was left wondering what was going on. Tumblety remained unaware of the event but quite secure below decks in steerage.

Officer Thomas Quinn was met by the captain, such was the importance of this policeman's visit, and escorted him to the purser's office to check over the passenger manifest. La Bretagne had been cabled the day before from the NYPD informing them of the need to come aboard prior to landing to check the manifest before anyone could leave. Quinn was handed the crucial list by the purser on the captain's directions and began with the first class passengers: the most obvious class in which the curious Mr Townsend would be travelling. Although wanting to know that he was aboard it was also imperative that he did not get sense that he was being watched. It didn't take long scanning the list to discover that a Mr Frank Townsend was on board and indeed a first class passenger.

"Are you staying with us until we dock, officer?" asked the captain.

"Yes, sir, I am. But I will stay out of sight. Watching this Mr Townsend is not my job."

It was about another half an hour before the ship was on the quayside and the gang planks were down allowing people to slowly alight and make their way through to immigration. On the dockside watching those departing from first class were two of the plain clothes policemen who were on the launch and were also two of Thomas Byrne's best detectives; Crowle and Hickey. They stood slightly back in the gathered crowd to avoid being seen at the front scrutinising the passengers as they disembarked. Weston now suspected from what he had observed on board and his liaison with the enigmatic Dr Townsend that he may either be arrested or followed as he stepped foot on the American dockside. A porter from La Bretagne carried his cases for him as he strolled nonchalantly along the gang plank expecting the worst of the two; arrest. If this was the case he would immediately declare to the police what had happened.

He passed along the lines of the cheering gathered crowd made up of some well wishers but mostly expectant relatives unaware of the two detectives keenly watching him.

"That's the guy there, next to the porter with the glasses," whispered Hickey to Crowle leaning slightly to speak into his colleague's ear.

"Yeah, Goddamit, you're right. Just let him move up a little way then I'll shadow him from the crowd, you go and get the coach, bud," replied Crowle. They already began to feel satisfied that there were not on some limey wild goose chase.

Crowle eased his way through the crowd as his colleague made straight to the city outside of the dock gates. Weston was blissfully unaware of being followed from the crowd, feeling relieved and comfortable that having now been on American soil for a couple of minutes and one hundred or so yards he hadn't been deprived of his liberty. The porter humbly followed on behind waiting for, he hoped, a generous tip from his client. They then joined a queue that took them through the immigration control; however, it was a short specialist queue for those travelling from the upper class. Their check was somewhat cursory as it was taken as written that they harboured no diseases and, as moneyed people, no ill intent to the New World.

The other side of the immigration control was a new troop of porters as those from the ship were not allowed through. Weston handed the young man with glasses two dollars as he placed the cases down at the cusp of the dockside/city side in the most convenient place for one of the native porters to take over, which one readily did as the immigration official ushered Weston as Tumblety through with no check whatsoever. Crowle showed his detectives badge to another official to get through and maintain surveillance of his quarry.

Outside of the terminus, Hickey was ready with their transport as Weston emerged with his porter who took him to the horse drawn cab rank and loaded the cases onto the vehicle at the head of the line. Weston was forced to tip another porter begrudgingly with only a couple of one dollar bills and climbed aboard.

"Where to, sir?" politely asked the New York cab driver.

"East Tenth Street, please, driver." Weston replied in a very satisfied manner. This unusual work Townsend asked him to do was going to be a 'piece of cake.'

With the crack of the cab driver's riding crop they set off into New York City with Crowle boarding a second cab with Hickey and then following together at a discreet distance.

Whitechapel

Forty minutes later and Tumblety walked ashore as the crowds had subsided and walked straight up to the immigration control with no queue of hopefuls to hold him up. The exchange with Weston had been thorough all the way down to immigration papers and passports. He was unshaven with his moustache trimmed back from the norm dressed in Weston's best working clothes and clutching a single case. His hat helped to disorientate the view of his face.

"Mr Weston," said the immigration officer from behind his high desk, "what do you bring back to the United States?"

"A lot of fond memories of visiting the old countries, sir," said Tumblety in character.

"What is your trade, Mr Weston?"

"I am a carpenter; I've worked in some of the fine hotels in London and in some of the Thames ship yards. I return to settle in a log cabin in the woods near Buffalo." He spoke far from the truth.

"Anything in your case, sir?" asked the immigration official eyeing the case curiously.

"Oh, just a small treasure case of valuable gem stones, sir," Tumblety replied heartily with a chuckle to try to break the normal ice of officialdom. The immigration official stared back impassively.

"If that be true, Mr Weston, watch your step with the portside gangs. Good day." He stamped up the passport and handed it back to Tumblety who tipped his hat and smiled and walked casually back in to the United States of America.

He left the port for the Grand Central Station. Once there he enjoyed a coffee on the concourse having bought his train ticket. The entire metropolitan atmosphere of New York was very different to him than that of London. The smells, the noises and the accents all now made him feel very safe and at home. Abberline and his cronies would never find him with his decoy in place and whenever they discovered that it was Weston and not him it would be too late. Once his train left for Rochester, New Jersey no one would find him. He would be able to enjoy fine living again as a bachelor; he had no intention of being anything else now the voices had gone away, and tour the United States now he had regained his fortune and discover the places he had not as yet seen. That would help him decide on where he would eventually live out his days. He sipped from his steaming cup and enjoyed the scent of the freshly ground beans that emanated from the coffee vendor. He'd missed the taste of America and savoured it along with his new sense of freedom.

Chapter Twenty-Eight

Druitt did not know what to do, or where to turn in the wake of the court decision of two Friday's ago. He read the press coverage for the fifteenth time in the fortnight old Saturday edition of 'The Times' following the aborted court case.

AMERICAN DOCTOR FREED IN COURT

Following the collapse of the trial of Doctor Francis Tumblety this month, failed barrister but currently serving school master Montague John Druitt is sought under a police warrant for his part in fabricating the scandal against him....'

The article expanded beyond these points to further besmirch Druitt's character and thereby ruin any semblance of reputation he had. He had been simply waiting for a knock on the door of his room from either the police or the headmaster of the school, both to remove him from the site. He decided to pre-empt this by dressing simply to walk out as if just to visit the local High Street on that first Saturday morning of the headline, leaving all his possessions in situe; there seemed little point in waiting for the inevitable disgrace and wanted to save himself from public humiliation. He made for Central London from Blackheath using his season ticket and then spent the next two weeks dwindling his savings by staying in a comfortable lodging house in Wapping close to The Steps. This found him wandering down to the river's edge most days at least twice to ponder his future staring listlessly into the icy Thames. He had lost weight and was looking significantly gaunt living mainly on whiskey and tobacco, smoking his pipe most of the day and paying visits to a local opium den in Limehouse almost every other day; this only fuelled a delusional state in his mind that he was living no more than a nightmare.

He read the deteriorating copy of The Times at least once everyday seemingly in some psychologically misguided state as if believing that one day the news would be different and in his favour. Reality was now striking home that circumstances were set in history and were never to change and he was an object of public disgrace and humiliation. A mild depressive as a result of his latter schooling as a youth, he was now in a full blown manic depressive state.

Leaving Wapping around eleven o'clock he made for Tower Hill and the main thoroughfares where the reduced Sunday omnibus services ran to travel along to Charing Cross station. He was dressed in a now dishevelled navy blue suit with no tie and his wing collar shirt undone, scuffed leather brogues, face unshaven and hair un-brushed and he was smelling unwashed, he himself unaware of the reactions of those nearby as he boarded the bus and his odour became overpowering in a confined space. The conductor winced at his breath as he paid for his ticket and moved briskly away from him and back to the running board of the bus and the cool icy fresh air. Druitt stared wide eyed without focus out of the right hand window of the bus sightlessly watching the world go by with no recognition of it. Passengers jostled past him as the bus stopped along the way to Charing Cross knocking into his shoulder but it drew no reaction from him; he just swayed to one side and then rocked back to his upright seating position like some kind of circus puppet.

Like an automaton he alighted at the stop along the Embankment at the junction with Northumberland Avenue. He walked slowly along the pavement in the direction from which he caught the bus pulling a leather bound hip flask from his inside suit pocket as he did so. He unscrewed the stop and placed it up to his mouth throwing his head back with it and gulping heavily on the burning liquid inside; he had become accustomed to it's strength so it's hotness as it slid down his throat which was an effect he was almost impervious to. He emptied the contents of the flask which was enough combined with cold air to bring a lightness to his senses and a slight stagger to his walk.

He wandered blindly and carelessly across the Embankment carriageway; fortunately the traffic was light and he had a near miss with only one hansom that was travelling east.

"You drunken wanker!" shouted it's indignant driver as he swerved his horse and cab to miss him. Druitt was oblivious to the danger narrowly missed. He walked slowly and with uneven footing along the cobbled Villiers Street which led him to The Strand and the front of Charing Cross station. Reaching the main junction at the top he looked with glazing eyes to his left and the direction of Trafalgar Square. He could make out the spire of the Eleanor Cross outside of the station and recognised through his drunken state that he had got himself to his intended destination.

He walked across the forecourt at Charing Cross and made for one of the arched entrance ways over which hung the sign 'entry and tickets'. As he passed through the arch he barged between a young courting couple making their way out not striking the young woman but heavily shoulder checking the smartly dressed young man and knocking him against the side wall.

"Oh, bloody hell, mind your step you drunken sot!" shouted the young man after him as Druitt staggered on ignoring the rant completely. The young man looked to his fiancée with disgust, brushed his clothes straight and they exited to the forecourt, muttering about incivility and the need for drunks to be taught manners. Druitt found his way to one of the ticket kiosks and with slurred speech, the cashier protected by a slatted grill; he bought a 2nd class return to Hammersmith. His intention was to take himself further west to jump into the Thames and end his tortured existence thus, he hoped, ensuring that his body would be found before being carried too far east and out to sea. His troubled mind at least rationalised that there was a chance his body would be found to be given a decent burial although unable to be buried in a churchyard due to suicide being the cause of death.

The cashier instructed him as to which platform to take to which Druitt responded without any gratitude wandering away from the window dropping change as he did so and leaving it rolling around the floor. He made his way to the platform and onto the waiting train, all the time with continued unsteadiness on his feet and dropped himself unceremoniously onto a seat knocking into a youth sitting by the window.

The train from Charing Cross was slow but not crowded being a Sunday and bizarrely he enjoyed the journey taking in sights of London that he had not seen before as the train crossed the Thames as soon as it left the station and followed a line for a time on the south bank. It didn't take long to reach Hammersmith and he was the only one of the train's few passengers to get off there. With little conscious thought he alighted from the train and wandered along the platform handing his ticket to the barrier attendant to be punched and oddly retrieving it from him; he was not intending to have need of it again. He stuffed it into his overcoat pocket and left the station.

He made his way to Furnival Gardens alongside of the River Thames just west of Hammersmith Bridge. There he walked amongst the ornamental flower beds to look for heavy border or rockery stones to help weigh him down. He enjoyed the fresh smell of the hardy annuals that were still present as he trod some of them down to collect several stones and place them in his overcoat and suit jacket pockets. He could feel the significant additional weight they provided and he knew that coupled with his enforced resistance to try to swim they would help speed his desire to sink effortlessly and soundlessly below the murky surface of the river. He left the riverside gardens and walked up to the start of the bridge joining it from Rutland Grove.

The wind felt cooler and fresher as he walked along the bridge approach over the bank side land below before actually reaching its span of the river. He pulled a second hip flask from a pocket in his suit and began to drain its contents as quickly as he could; the first had long since been finished and he had discarded it on the train shortly after having boarded. The lower temperature over the river as he made his final walk onto the bridge and heading south made him shiver and subconsciously pull his weighted overcoat round himself just a little tighter. He made his way to about half way across on the west side of the bridge all the time looking over the side watching the fast flowing Thames below with it's strong under currents. It looked cold and dark as he walked and being a Sunday there was little river traffic apart from one or two pleasure craft meandering up and down stream. As the alcohol took effect and continued to dim his senses he very quickly became oblivious to the cold chilling breeze as he reached the half way point and paid no heed to the deserted footways of the bridge. He had never wanted an audience but had the bridge been populated at any level he had the inward resolve to go through with his intended course of action regardless.

He placed his hands around the circular iron tube that topped the metal balustrade running along the length of the bridge on both sides. It did feel exceptionally cold and it sent a renewed shiver down his spine. He gripped the tubing and looked down at the white knuckles of his hands as he increased the pressure of his grip upon it. He was getting ready to vault it now and allow himself to be sucked under in the cold dark muddy Thames water at the earliest opportunity. Suddenly he felt an epiphany; he visualised his family at his graduation, he recalled himself scoring his first six in colt's cricket as a boy, he recalled his first day at grammar school with his mother straightening his tie as he got ready for the carriage to take him there, he recalled looking up from a soft warm bed into the eyes of his young mother. Then, nothing but cold and darkness.

Without conscious thought he had jumped; vaulting the balustrade and dropping the fifty-five feet from the bridge into the icy black waters of the River Thames. He felt the plunge and severe shock to his body as he entered the water and kept sinking within it silently deeper and ever deeper. The extra weights in his pocket were doing their trick. In a reflex action he breathed in and swallowed hard filling his lungs with the cold and mucky river water and chocking upon it. The ensuing panic his body experienced filled his lungs further and further with water. He felt somehow at peace as he gave up the fight for life in his heavily intoxicated state. He closed his eyes and his body fell limp and sank to the floor of the Thames. Montague John Druitt was dead.

* * *

Tuesday 4th December 10.45.a.m and Dr. Robert Anderson sat in one of the comfortable lounges of the Masonic Halls in Great Queen Street awaiting the arrival of Sir William Gull, the Queen's personal physician. He sipped a large 12 year old single malt whiskey produced in distillery on the Isle of Skye from a heavy crystal cut glass tumbler savouring its distinctly peaty taste. He was becoming content that the potentially embarrassing loose ends concerning the Whitechapel Murders were now being wrapped up and Abberline would be forced to take the investigation in only one direction. Glancing down at the side of his high backed leather armchair he looked at the leather arts bag that his paid detective thugs had recovered for him. He had taken a look briefly inside it and was disgusted by its contents. He had also felt quite ill having pulled out one its macabre jars and looked inside and knew that its owner was obviously one of these 'succession' or 'serial' murder victims that Sir William had spoken of. Lost in his thoughts, he hadn't noticed Gull appear from over his left shoulder and stand slightly offset in front of him. His attention was eventually drawn to him as Gull shuffled towards the leather chair opposite Anderson, the other side of the low mahogany drinks table from him.

"Deep in thought there, eh, Sir Robert?" Said Gull in a softly spoken voice. Anderson looked him up and down before he spoke and watched Gull lower himself into the chair opposite him. Anderson had only seen him once since his stroke and he could see how physically weakened the famous surgeon had become. But, his impaired health from his slow movements and much quieter voice belied the sharpness that his mind still possessed.

"Yes, I was. Thoughts of how depraved the owner of this bag must be. It's only for the benefit of the Brotherhood that I am happy to ensure it is disposed of or returned."

"Well not being a medical man I guess you would find it hard to understand, sir," replied Gull as he settled into the chair. He was approached by a steward who dutifully stood by the two men to take a drinks order.

"Same again for me," said Anderson.

"And for me please," followed Gull promptly. "Now, Sir Robert, what can I do for you?"

"Lets dispense with the formalities, William, I thought you would want possession of these items," said Anderson pointing to the bag, "and while we are at it, perhaps you could explain this murder theory of yours to me, and help me feel more comfortable as to why we should let this Tumblety man get away."

Gull unbuttoned his jacket and took a deep breath casting his eyes around the room before beginning to speak. "Well. First of all he is a brother and the Movement must not be compromised or scandalised. You of all people know that, no matter what the events; we must protect. Secondly, I need to examine the status of the samples that have been collected to see if I can put some rational thought to Tumblety's actions. After all, he was some kind of doctor so he may have been trying to discover something about sexual diseases, or the effects of class on prostitution or even ethnicity. He may have just been completely insane of course, but whatever the cause he pursued we are duty bound by the words of our degrees and the status of our offices to protect our brothers. If you can't live with simple aspect of the honour of our organisation then you perhaps should think twice about your own membership."

Anderson was offended by Gull's words. He took a deep breath and leant forward in his seat slamming his glass down on the table and hissed a lowly spoken reply to him, trying to avoid their conversation being overheard. "How dare you! How bloody dare you, you senile old goat! I don't care who you are and what standing you may have, don't you dare speak to me like that or question my Masonic integrity. I am proud of who I am what I have done but I am not comfortable in protecting a mass murderer. There can be no justification for what he has done."

"Don't get too excited, Robert. Look at the class of those involved. It hardly matters. Having looked at the post mortem reports most of them would have been on the morticians table in months anyway."

"You class conscious soulless snob! A human life is a human life. They are all of the same value even if they can't all make the same contribution to society. I suppose you would endorse any medical experiment he may have been conducting then."

"Only if the women had already been dead, and made available for it. You misunderstand my intention; I am merely trying to understand the justification in the actions within a troubled mind. The pattern of the actions from the nature of the specimens may help me do this. I don't condone it so just calm down before the Duke arrives."

They both sat back in their chairs in silence as the steward then arrived with the round of drinks, again in fine crystal cut glass tumblers.

They continued sitting without conversation waiting for the Duke of Kent to arrive.

"Gentlemen, good day," said the Duke as he took the third seat by the table. Anderson and Gull both looked up and nodded acknowledging his arrival. He could tell there had been tension between them.

"I take it you both find it hard to agree then?" Anderson spoke first.

"Well you hit the nail on the head there, Grand Inspector. This obsessive sees it only from the upper class medical perspective. He seems the feel the murders are less serious as they are low class unfortunates."

"No you misunderstand. I shan't explain again. Needless to say I am taking the fool Tumblety's bag for examination," replied a condescending Gull.

"I must stop you there, William. That will not be the case. It is damning evidence that I would like Assistant Commissioner Anderson to ensure it is disposed of by The Yard appropriately." The Duke was resolute.

"But, Grand Inspector," began Gull, "they will not arouse suspicion in my possession. I am a doctor and entitled to specimens. They may help me pursue my research on the matter of succession killing." Gull protested.

"William, the reputation of the Brotherhood is more important than anything. They will be disposed of by the police and that is final. And while I am at it, get along to Abberline and tell him to disengage from this Tumblety matter and surrender anything else. From what you tell me he persists and must be stopped." Anderson was quick to defend the Duke's obvious feeling of inaction on his part.

"Grand Inspector, Abberline has been spoken to. His attempts to retain copies of papers relating to this Brother Tumblety have been thwarted, by my direct intervention. I have had this bag," indicating to the leathers arts bag "recovered from Commercial Street Police Station and the Ripper incident room. These actions I have taken at great personal risk so please do not intimate that your precautions have not been enforced."

Silence now fell amongst the three of them creating an uncomfortable pause. The two less prominent masons both took a drink from their tumblers nervously as the Duke pulled a cigar from inside his suit jacket and lifted one the halls packets of matches from the low coffee table. He un-wrapped the large Cuban cigar and ran it end to end under his nose twisting it as he did so. It smelt fresh with a rich tobacco aroma which conjured up visions of exotic native women rolling them on a sun drenched coast, as he had indeed witnessed on his travels in the Americas. He placed the cigar in his mouth and using the small packet of matches from the table casually struck one. Everyone got a brief hint of the phosphorous in its strike as he then placed the burning wooden stick to the end of the cigar. He sucked in several times and quickly the end of the Cuban was glowing. He shook the match out and dropped it into the ash tray. Enjoying a large draw on the cigar he tasted the bitter sweet smoke; it engendered him with taking it into his lungs before lifting his head a little to exhale it. He looked to Gull and Anderson and spoke calmly but menacingly.

"Gentlemen. Whatever needs to be done to protect Brother Tumblety, but most importantly the Movement, will be done. Assistant Commissioner you will go today and speak to Abberline personally and take the bag and have it disposed of. And you, Royal Physician–in–Ordinary, will ensure that the name of the Royal family through your connection, and fellow masons within the medical profession does not bring us into disrepute over this debacle. Do I make myself clear?"

Neither of them spoke, feeling their standing had been fiercely attacked. As the Duke looked at them each in turn they nodded in acknowledgment of his directions and authority. "Now then, another large malt, gentlemen?" They dare not defy him in any way again and agreed to another drink.

* * *

Early afternoon and Abberline, Godley, Robert Ford and most of the Whitechapel murder team were all present in the incident room in Commercial Street Police Station as Sir Robert Anderson arrived there in person to execute the Duke's wishes. Everyone looked up as the door burst open without a knock and he briskly and angrily marched in. Robert Ford's blood ran cold as he heard this man now standing in the room speak. He had not seen his face before and initially did not know who he was until the apparent drama of the visit unfolded;

but the voice was unmistakably the same as the one he heard from the masked gunman on the canal bank.

"Now, all of you listen up, you especially, Abberline. I am Assistant Commissioner Dr Robert Anderson for those of you who don't know me, head of the detective branches of this force. We will have no more of this subversive nonsense regarding these murders here and you have all been told to desist from pursuing the case against Dr Tumblety. I want anything else you are in possession of surrendered now, or so help me I will have anyone guilty of retaining this information tried for sedition!" There was silence across the room for some seconds until Abberline stood up from his desk and spoke. He cared nothing of the consequences; obsessed with seeing justice done he spoke his mind and the feelings of his team to counter this unexpected high ranking visit and outburst.

"So, Assistant Commissioner, why is that, sir? Hmm? One of my men has been blinded following a burglary here and seizure of valuable evidence against an obviously guilty man. A man who had it not been for the destruction of written evidence in a Limehouse Canal and the attempted murder of another of my officer's would be convicted by any court in the land. So tell us all, what the hell is so important that you come down here in person and shout the odds."

Anderson was now red faced with rage with the impertinence of a mere detective inspector standing up to him. It took him several seconds embarrassingly to compose himself to launch a retaliatory tirade.

"You common little man! How dare you challenge the integrity of the upper echelons of the police service. With our superior knowledge of the workings of the force we know where the truth lies and it lies obviously with the man Klosowski or Chapman as we all know he is also known. His guilt is most evident, he attempts to kill a constable and kills two innocent people to escape so don't tell me an innocent American doctor is guilty."

"Oh really?" replied Abberline folding his arms and now prepared for a head to head confrontation, "so tell me why his handwriting matched that of some of the Jack the Ripper correspondence."

"Abberline, that is science of pure charlatans. Comparing writing, such nonsense, many of us write in the same way."

"And what about the arts bag and specimen jars. Somewhat damning evidence, considering the parts missing from some of the victims."

"Abberline, he is doctor. Why shouldn't he have anatomical specimens?"

"Or is it because he is perhaps a freemason, and you are obliged to protect your own in your so called charitable and benevolent order?"

With this barbed and difficult to refute comment Anderson flew into an even greater rage and now shouted at the top of voice.

"Abberline GET OUT! How bloody dare you make such an unfounded accusation. I'll deal with you outside in a moment." Abberline for some seconds stood firm. There was silence across the office with all the other officers stunned by the confrontation. Then calmly and slowly Abberline walked out of the office keeping eye contact with the enraged Assistant Commissioner all the way past him. He stood out in corridor some feet away from the office door.

"Now the rest of you hear this. Find the real murderer and don't dare consider there to be any basis in the slanderous comments of your Inspector. Anyone I hear of repeating such comments or being involved in any case or pursuance of a case against Dr Tumblety will have me to answer to. That will not be a pleasant experience. Do I make myself clear?" The room remained silent and with no verbal response from any of them as Anderson wheeled and left the room shutting the door behind him. Everyone remained quiet looking around the room at each other in a somewhat dazed condition. They all listened out for a further outburst from the corridor but heard nothing.

Anderson confronted Abberline in the corridor and spoke quietly and menacingly to him face to face with only a few inches between them having squared right up to the defiant inspector.

"Don't expect much more of a career, Abberline. I can't take you off this case because the press like you and the public like you and there is already too much dissent amongst them for me to cause anymore by removing the so called trusted, sympathetic local man. Cross me again publicly like that or pursue Tumblety and you will have nothing, and I mean ***nothing.***" They stared hard at each other for several seconds neither seemingly prepared to give up. Taffy Evans appeared along the corridor unnoticed by Abberline and Anderson. He felt unsure as to whether to try to pass and coughed to gain their attention. This action made Anderson feel uncomfortable; it forced him to give up the confrontation and leave. Abberline for once actually felt disturbed with Anderson's parting words thinking not only of his police career with the threat but perhaps it's greater meaning to his personal life.

Chapter Twenty-Nine

That same day following a directive from Abberline, Inspector Walter Andrews arrived in New York having travelled directly from France with the young Detective Constable Arthur Bentham. They were met beyond the immigration control by Detective Hickey sent on the directions of department head Thomas Byrne. The New York Police Department still had the man they thought was Tumblety under observation following the request from Abberline, a request that as yet had not been over-ridden. Both English officers were familiar with Tumblety having followed him in France and seen him during the investigations when he was still in London in custody on the night of Mary Kelly's murder. They were both more than happy to take over much of the surveillance on the Ripper suspect freeing the NYPD officers to return to their duties.

Hickey shook hands with Andrews and Bentham as they met.

"It's an honour to meet you, gentlemen, real Scotland Yard detectives. I look forward to assisting in your enquiry in any way I can."

"That's very flattering of you, Detective Hickey. We're very pleased to meet you too," replied Andrews returning the vigorous handshake.

"Call me Hicks. I'm your official liaison so anything you want or need then please ask."

"We will thank you, Hicks. First thing we'd like to do is to take a ride past the lodgings I understand you have traced him to," requested an enthusiastic Andrews, keen to start to watch their quarry as soon as possible.

"Sure. It's East Tenth Street. A pleasant enough carriage ride, so you'll get to see a fair bit of the city. My colleague Detective Crowle is running the current surveillance. Tumbelty or Townsend hasn't been out since he got here apparently."

The relationship between Andrews and Bentham with the NYPD was to become positive and very cordial despite the disastrous results that would soon emerge. They walked out of the dockside buildings into the winter sunlight to a plain enclosed carriage that belonged to the NYPD and was used for detective duties. They climbed aboard having passed their minimal luggage up to the driver who stacked it on the roof of the carriage and tied it down. They made themselves comfortable out of the sharp sea breeze within the carriage as the driver secured his load and then within half a minute or so they heard the crack of a riding crop and the carriage lurched off across the bumpy New York dockside cobbles.

The officers observing 79 East Tenth Street had not seen 'Mr Townsend' since his arrival in the city and his lodgings for very good reason. They were very comfortably furnished and the hospitality offered by Mrs McNamara was second to none. He had the use of four rooms, excluding a kitchen which was no disadvantage as the landlady was more that willing to cook, albeit for a fee. With his new found wealth, being cooked for and having a supply of quality alcohol on hand for a fee was the life of luxury for Bill Weston. His rooms consisted of a large lounge furnished with a leather sofa and armchair, a mahogany writing bureau, a glass topped coffee table, a large mirror with an ornately carved wooden frame above a large tiled Victorian fire place. The walls sported a picture rail with beige plain painted plaster above it and ornately patterned red and beige wallpaper below it. He had a large bathroom well appointed with a free standing Victorian iron bath, a large wash basin on a pedal stool with an oversize mirror above it, a toilet and a wooden cabinet that held personal toiletries. He also had two bedrooms. One with a large, soft double bed covered with a traditional Ida down above sheets and blankets, a wooden dressing table, a wooden chest of drawers and a wardrobe. The other bedroom had two double beds with furniture not dissimilar to the first, a room where as he got to grips with his new lifestyle he could accommodate guests, although he'd also use his own room for that purpose with female callers.

Having never enjoyed such luxurious surroundings with the service provided by the landlady, Weston had decided to stay in and eat, drink and bathe. All things that he had been unable to do freely and wantonly. He would start his day in the large and comfortable deep iron bath, the room filled with steam from the hot water he lazily wallowed in. A generous breakfast of pancakes and syrup with sausages would follow and leave him replete until around 1.p.m when he would enjoy a cooked lunch with a good bottle or two of beer. A read and sleep during the afternoon lead up to a sumptuous evening meal with more alcohol, wine and port, all this more than happily supplied by Mrs McNamara at a price. She found the tastes from her lodger the same as his usual lifestyle, but due to her short-sightedness it was only his voice that seemed to have a different sound to it.

The English detectives took a slow drive past with Hickey looking the property up and down; it was very different to London premises. The front door was reached by a steep set of steps going up known locally as a 'stoop' which was not a regular feature in London with its considerable height. It was a pleasant looking three storey premises that was obviously well maintained and certainly didn't look to be the kind of place where their quarry would have plied his work. The carriage rattled and bumped over the cobbled street as it passed number 79 and the English detectives were cautious not to be seen to crane their necks looking back as they passed it arousing suspicion from the occupant or neighbours. They pulled up around the corner out of sight at the first junction they met where the driver brought the carriage to a halt by the right kerb.

Inspector Andrews alighted from the carriage and walked back to the junction and peered carefully around the building line having removed his very distinctive English wide brimmed trilby hat. There were residential properties on both sides of the street. The street itself seemed to be fairly sparsely populated by either pedestrians or horse drawn traffic. Men in the street would therefore 'stick out' so any following of Tumblety, masquerading as he believed as Frank Townsend, would have to be done by officers exiting the premises from where the surveillance was being conducted from cautiously. He sighed and walked back to Hickey and Bentham who were informally talking by the carriage. He put his hat back on as he approached and they turned to face him.

"Hicks, where are your men that are keeping watch?" asked Andrews.

"We've got two guys opposite in number 80, and one guy in the house in the next street that backs on to it," replied Hickey.

"And how co-operative are the local residents with that, can they be trusted to not try and tell the occupants of number 79?"

"Well, yeah. We told them all that we were watching a suspect in the Jack the Ripper murders in London and to keep their Goddamn mouths shut, or get implicated in aiding and abetting a felon." Andrews was a little concerned by Hicks apparently gung ho response; he didn't like the threat to people and he didn't like people to know that someone had been pursued here. If it hit the press then Tumblety would probably try to run again or at the very least be cautious in his movements. Andrews rubbed his chin and for several seconds stared into space saying nothing. As he gathered his thoughts to form a plan of action he looked up and spoke.

"All right. Say nothing to anyone else about the true nature of the investigation. Not even in your department. The less people know the better to keep it potentially out of the press. Don't threaten anyone it only serves to alienate. We'll try to spin a new cover story about the surveillance in the meantime and I'll need to keep on a couple of your blokes until more of mine arrive…" Hicks interrupted.

"What's 'a bloke'?" he asked somewhat bemused by the term.

"A man. I have five more men imminently arriving then I won't need any of your fellows for the surveillance."

"But you won't have any jurisdiction to arrest, Mr Andrews."

Hickey had a good point. They would have no official power of police arrest in New York, unless they got sworn in, but could detain someone as a private citizen. He thought long and hard on this matter and was quiet for sometime as he considered options. He had wanted to keep the NYPD's involvement to a minimum, which now seemed impractical in the best interests of the investigation.

"Good point. I want you, if you will, to stay working with us on the investigations as a liaison, which you have told us you already are, but more importantly for your police powers." There was a pause and looking at Detective Hickey Andrews noticed that he looked a little unfulfilled. He took stock of what he had just said and quickly addressed it.

"And of course and most importantly, for your law enforcement experience, especially your local knowledge of New York City."

"Mr Andrews, when do you want to start taking over the majority of the surveillance?"

"Well. Tomorrow would be good if we go off to our accommodation now to get rid of a luggage and get a fresh start then."

"Great. Let's go, the hotel is comfortable and it serves good beer. The welcome drink is courtesy of Chief Inspector Byrne."

"Splendid," replied Andrews who put his hand in a comradely way on Hickey's shoulder allowing him to board the carriage first. They all boarded and the driver snapped his crop and they lurched off along the cobbles.

* * *

Abberline re-entered the room to find everyone looking at him in stunned silence. He looked around at his loyal team and it took him some minutes before he could compose himself to speak. He was genuinely unsettled by Anderson's visit and looked at the faces of these trustworthy, decent men and felt humbled in their dedicated presence. Before he was about to speak Robert Ford broke the silence.

"Guv'nor, this all stinks. That man who was here was the same man that led the attack on me and the papers I was getting copied. I recognise that voice anywhere, he's the one that fucking killed his own and was going to do me. I'm sure I speak for all of us," he said looking around the room as he spoke, "but what the hell is going on?"

Silence again descended over the room as Abberline coughed to clear his throat before speaking. He looked down at his feet, then up in the air, scratched his forehead and then spoke.

"Gentlemen, we are in the hands of a conspiracy that runs deep into the heart of the British establishment. It has roots within the judiciary, government, an unsuspecting Royal family and of course the police service. It is more powerful than any of us and we are all fucked if we attempt to take the Tumblety issue any further; and it makes me sick to the stomach." There was silence across the room again which was broken by Ford.

"Who are these people? What is going on, Guv?" There was a long pause before Abberline then spoke expressing his ill feelings.

"Freemasons were responsible for corruption in the detective department before and it's happening all over again and it makes me sick. For those of you that don't know, back in 1877 it was discovered that virtually every officer in the Yard's C.I.D was in the pay of vicious swindlers. It all started in 1872 when John Meiklejohn, an inspector and a mason, met William Kurr another mason and head of a bogus betting agency. This crook needed someone in the force to tip him off as to when the police were gaining enough to nick them for their business. Meiklejohn accepted £100 bribe to keep the old bill off their backs. Trouble was all the blokes in the C.I.D were masons, except the Boss, Superintendent Williamson; all the senior detectives, Clarke, Palmer and Druscovitch all fucking masons. None of them were fussed therefore about Meiklejohn and his carry-ons. He was known in coded messages from his criminal mason friends as '**countryman**,' and I say friends in plural as it included not only Kurr but a dangerous madman called Harry Benson. Benson was known as a lunatic from an incident where whilst in Newgate he set light to himself on his bed leaving himself scarred and crippled. Meiklejohn introduced all the junior detectives into the payroll but they were all found out when Benson and Kurr pulled off one job too big when they managed to swindle £10,000 out of a French noble woman. Williamson put Druscovitch in charge of the investigation, not knowing of the corruption involved; but when he made no headway Williamson took action. Eventually all the corrupt officers, all bloody masons, were brought to justice leaving the C.I.D in ruins. It was after that I moved into the department and I swore that they would never get that sort of hold again." He was silent for a few seconds before finishing. "But look what's happened. The bastards have got control again and they are so powerful there is nothing we can do."

Robert Ford thought long and hard on Abberline's words and knew from that day the masons would never get the better of him, his future investigations and in his pursuit of justice for Mary. "Guv, Anderson was prepared to kill me, one of his officers. I mean, to whom does he give the greatest loyalty? Law and order, or these freemasons?"

"Simple answer to that, lad. To the Brotherhood and never forget it. You'll never be able to, in their eyes, out smart them. You might win a battle, as they say, but never the war." Abberline paused and then spoke again. "George, come with me down the post office we've got to contact Wally Andrews and call him off. Gentlemen, the pursuit of Tumblety ends here. Let's try and salvage something and find this Chapman or Klosowski bloke."

Abberline left the office followed very quickly by George Godley as everyone else looked around the room at each other and silently got on with their tasks; some leaving the office, others back to the dull process of sifting the various statements and their content.

* * *

Wednesday 5th December 8.a.m, Andrews and Bentham arrived at number 80 East Tenth Street via the rear to take over the day shift from the NYPD men. They were quickly left there by themselves, save for a lone local cop watching the rear of the premises, and settled in to watching from the behind the net curtains of the bay window. The occupant already knew who they were looking at being familiar with Mrs McNamara's regular lodger and his less than wholesome reputation. Andrews's hopes of the investigation being discreet were more than compromised and hoped the path of it would not lead to more bad news for Abberline. At this stage he was unaware of the events of the week in London and the fact that he shouldn't even be pursuing Tumblety. He was blamelessly oblivious to the fact that Abberline had, at that point, not told The Yard's hierarchy that men were on a mission in America.

The distance across the street was such that they didn't need to use an implement like a telescope. The occupier had very happily and hospitably served them coffee and American cookies but then left them to it. Little did they know that the day's events would be relayed to the local press by their apparent host. The weather outside was grey and overcast, and being the time of the year it was only just a little beyond dawn as they began their vigil. The odd carriage passed by outside with condensed breath visible from the mouths of the hard working horses pulling them. Many of the passing pedestrians too had sharply visible breath as they came by wrapped up for the cold with many rubbing their hands or wrapping their arms around themselves to keep warm.

They had been watching for nearly two hours when the front door opened and they waited almost holding their breath for an occupant to emerge. They weren't disappointed. A well dressed man emerged sporting a dark brown bowler hat and a cane. He had a large moustache and looked to be the height and build of the man they were after. Certainly at the distance they were, both seemed sure that this was their man. He looked up and down the street almost as if he was aware he might be being watched before he set off down the stoop to reach the street. Weston certainly was somewhat surveillance conscious as a result of the deal he had struck with the curious Dr Townsend and was indeed looking for local cops on the watch for him. It had been a secondary reason why he hadn't ventured out for several days in the naïve hope that they might have got bored and left. He could see no one so felt unsure either way. The air was crisp and cool and he was pleased with the gloves he had also brought out with him along with a heavy astrakhan overcoat. He quite fancied a walk to work off some the excesses he had indulged in and turned left at the bottom of the stoop.

"Right. Bentham, stay here and see who else comes and goes. I'm off after him to see where he is going." Andrews was totally unaware that the subject they were observing was not their man who was now long gone to Rochester. He emerged cautiously from the front door of number 80 and had Townsend in his sights now some fifty yards or so along the road, a distance with which he was happy, and began his surveillance following on foot. He had one concern right at that point. The traffic was sparse and if Townsend hailed a cab he could lose him as they didn't seem common place along the street. Inspector Andrews observed that Townsend walked briskly as he made his way along East Tenth Street almost as if he sensed that there was danger to him and he inconspicuously wished to distance himself from it. With a mind to the crimes that Scotland Yard believed he was guilty of, that notion was no surprise to Andrews as he walked quickly himself to maintain his distance and keep his quarry in sight. Weston, aware that he was still in the guise of Townsend gave a couple of furtive glances behind him as they made their way to the junction with Lexington Avenue.

He didn't pick up on Andrews following him with a group of three Irish migrants walking in-between laughing and chatting loudly and catching Weston's attention instead. A very fortunate circumstance for the English detective, in an otherwise fairly quiet residential street.

On reaching Lexington he turned towards Central New York and again began looking over his shoulder. At the corner Andrews had slowed and peered cautiously round shielded by a stoop to observe Townsend's actions. The Irishmen had crossed straight over the junction but fortunately for the detective Lexington was a much busier street. It appeared that Townsend was looking for a cab as he kept walking and glancing much more frequently over his shoulder at the approaching traffic. Andrews was forced to let the distance between them increase to avoid being spotted and allowed Townsend about 100 yards on him. Townsend eventually stopped and stood at the kerb side to watch the traffic in more detail approaching him. From his ad-hoc manner when he had first entered Lexington he had already missed two empty cabs that had been travelling in the same direction. Andrews stopped and was looking in the window of a corner store as he saw a cab stop for Townsend.

He looked along the avenue beyond the now boarding Townsend in the hope that there was another empty cab not far behind. He couldn't see anything other than a few loaded delivery wagons. He looked back to the cab to see Townsend now sitting back comfortably within it and he began to feel anxious. There was still no following cab in sight and he could certainly not hear the destination that Townsend was shouting to the driver who was leaning back to hear his passenger's directions. The cab driver snapped his crop by the horse's ear and the cab lurched off. A desperate situation required a desperate measure. The last of the delivery wagons in the line was just passing him; he began to run to match its speed and grabbed hold of the hand rail on its side to gain purchase to climb aboard next to the driver. He pulled himself up explosively to match the vehicles movement and then landed awkwardly next to the driver bumping into him, knocking him slightly left of his perch.

"Goddamn, mister! What the hell is going on?" screamed the astonished wagon driver.

"Sorry, old man," said Andrews at the same time pulling out his leather wallet holding his police warrant identity. He showed it to his new found associate as he straightened his position. "Inspector Walter Andrews, on the trail of Jack the Ripper. In the name of Queen Victoria her Britannic Majesty I ask you to follow that cab up the in the distance." The driver looked at him open mouthed, completely aghast of this Englishman's arrival and his dramatic assertion. As it slowly sank in and he looked ahead to see the cab in question and then looked back at Andrews.

"You a real Scotland Yard detective, fella?" asked the stunned American.

"Yes, and on the most infamous case in Europe. Please help out, old man. I need to follow this man's movements," he replied, almost pleading now as he could see the cab with Townsend starting to make some ground on them.

"All right, buddy, you bet ya. Let's go!" He snapped the crop again with the horse picking up a little more speed and beginning to pass the other goods wagons. Within in few seconds Andrews was happy that they were keeping pace with Townsend and he was able to relax a little. They continued towards Central New York.

* * *

Klosowski and Lucy were now a significant way across the Atlantic bound for America themselves following the immediate and cunning escape orchestrated by him. He had got them out of London and up to the port city of Liverpool to gain the earliest passage that he could to America which was a ship bound for New Jersey. It sailed on the evening tide of the 29th November which had proved the last opportunity by sheer chance for them to have fled as the news hit the ports first thing on the 30th following Abberline's directions. The speed of their escape was enhanced by payments to carriage drivers and bribes to railway and port officials that meant they were well able to flee the country long before word had reached the ports of their descriptions and immediate detention. The vessel they had boarded was purely commercial and he had obtained a cabin that was comfortable but Spartan. To him it mattered not as he was pleased to have evaded capture and to Lucy she was grateful of an opportunity to 'start a new' as he had put it and the promise of starting a family. She did live in fear of him as a result of his overpowering and intimidating personality and because of the violent secrets she suspected that he withheld from her.

They would both end up back in London in years to come. She would leave him and returning on her own some months before him and giving birth to what would be by that time their second child. The new life she had wished for would prove short lived in New Jersey, but she would at least prove to be one of the only unfortunate women to come into Klosowski's life and survive. She sat alone in the cabin staring out of the salt stained porthole at the grey and swelling, ominous North Atlantic while Severin ingratiated himself amongst the crew to curry favour. He especially kept himself in with the wireless operators to get to hear of any of the mainland communiqués that were received. His ability to persistently bribe those who crossed his path on this journey continued with the suppression of the wire regarding the Tottenham and Whitechapel murders. It allowed him their safe passage and disembarkation in the New World. For the conscious free Klosowski, however, justice would eventually catch up with him after a new murderous spree of a different kind back in London.

* * *

Andrews and his ride found themselves following Townsend all the way to Grand Central Station where he saw the Ripper suspect pay off his cab driver and alight into the station.

"What now then, buddy?" asked the wagon driver tipping his hat back as he spoke. Andrews watched him enter the station and pulled out his wallet as he did so. He pulled out a couple of dollars and gave them to his temporary companion.

"Courtesy of Queen Victoria, my friend. Your service is appreciated." Andrews then jumped down from the wagon.

"Anytime, Fella. You take care now. Maybe see you around," replied the smiling American as he fingered the notes. Andrews nodded to him in a very polite English way and followed Townsend into the station by the same door.

The station in 1888 had been built some seventeen years previously by shipping and railroad magnate Cornelius Vanderbilt. Designed by John B Snook it cost $6.4 million to construct; it served four separate railroads each one containing their own waiting rooms, baggage and ticket facilities in the grand building. It sat between 42nd and 48th Streets, Lexington and Madison Avenues with a distinct gothic appearance over its three main floors, with additional levels below and above, within its European style towers that finished its magnificent façade.

Inside the station concourse was bustling with people from all classes, colours and religious backgrounds and within the few seconds that Andrews had temporarily lost sight of Townsend through the door into this crowd he had disappeared. He stopped in his tracks only yards into the building and frantically began to scan the environment desperately trying to spot his man and in so doing found himself frequently jostled by the passing throng. The crowds of people were so different to those that he had observed in London stations; there men dressed like cowboys, a phenomenon to which he had become accustomed from the American circus's visiting England, women dressed not unlike those at home, a few black men and women, a sight he had as yet not seen commonly in London, native Indians, again familiar to him for the same reasons as the cowboys. There were soldiers, the odd policemen patrolling, well dressed men in bowler hats, cowboy hats, wide brimmed trilby hats and bare heads. He hoped that the overcoat and head gear that Townsend or Tumblety was wearing would stick out; at that point it didn't. He began to walk in no specific direction wandering the wide crowded area around him whirling around to desperately try and pick up sight of his quarry somewhere; the action quickly began to disorientate him along with high volume of noise and the constant passing of humanity close to. Andrews very quickly reached the conclusion that he had lost him.

Depressed by losing sight of Townsend so soon he walked along the concourse to the natural centre of the station and decided to sit down and have a coffee, he knew tea would not be the norm and he wished to try to blend in just in case his man came back into sight. He noticed that on the next level up running around the edge of the main concourse and looking over it were small cafes where he could gain refreshment. This elevated view he felt would afford him a greater opportunity to possibly re-acquire sight of Townsend. He found the main set of stairs leading up there and made his way up against what seemed to be a heavy flow of people coming down towards him. The whole area suffered with a perpetual faint smell of coal burning smoke and steam from the ever transient trains.

Walking around the first level he found the perfect spot that over looked the entire concourse below and was opposite the main stairs he had just climbed. He hoped that this would offer the ideal view especially if Townsend decided to make use of the first level also. The coffee cost him a few cents and was served in a heavy ceramic cup which he carried to a table overlooking the area he was desperate to survey. He placed the steaming cup on the rough wooden table and sat down in the accompanying chair pulling himself forward, all the time keeping watch as he did so. The coffee was very hot and steamed in a discouraging fashion as a result; he was quite happy with his job in hand for it to take it's time to cool. He busily scanned the area below looking for the astrakhan coat and the brown bowler hat that was being worn with it by Townsend, or Tumblety as he now kept saying in his mind. Sat down, he started to feel the cold that had sunk into him during the goods wagon ride and he instinctively wrapped his hands around the steaming cup. People came and went from the coffee kiosk he had used and all paid little or no heed to those passing around them; apart from him through force of habit as well as current duty.

He had been there nearly an hour and was onto a second cup of coffee and also a dry sandwich when he spotted a brown bowler hat on the first level. Amazingly the wearer had come from behind him and was now walking around the course of the first level to where he had himself come; heading it seemed for the stairs. Looking him up and down as he dropped the unpalatable sandwich onto the plate, he also wore an astrakhan coat and carried a cane. The height, build and gait all seemed to indicate it was the man he had lost earlier. Andrews stood and began following him from a safe distance within the crowds and as he observed the man turn and head down the stairs, although his head was down he could see that the individual was sporting a moustache; it was him.

He closed the distance between them as they reached the main concourse comfortable with the proximity finding the crowds were shielding him. He noticed that Tumblety, as he again reminded himself this man was, seemed totally unconscious of any surveillance. This he hoped this would be to his advantage. Tumblety headed for the same door by which he had entered, passed through it and approached the cab rank climbing aboard the first free one in the line. It pulled off quickly as Andrews jumped on board the next one and instructed the driver to 'follow that cab, please.'

"So you're a limey then, eh?" said the cab driver as they moved off. Andrews was keeping a keen eye on the cab ahead and seemed initially distant. He then spoke as he became happy they were keeping pace.

"Yes I am. And I don't like that turn of phrase thank you. Please keep up with that cab in front and there'll be an extra $3 for you in it."

The financial encouragement was enough for the driver to accept his passenger's curtness and get on with the task in hand. They were already heading along Lexington again and Andrews suspected back to East Tenth Street.

In the bay window of number 80 East Tenth Street Arthur Bentham sat in a comfortable dining chair behind the net curtains looking out upon the quiet residential street as he had done for the past few hours. He was struggling to stay awake with frequent 'neck breaker' nodding bringing him back to the world of the lucid. The kindly home owner plied him with good strong coffee almost every three quarters of an hour which he hoped was reducing the effect of the boredom and fatigue of his duties. It was as he began his next cup of coffee, steaming hot with its bitter chicory taste, when Tumblety's cab arrived outside in front of number 79. He remained seated but leant forward to reduce the effect of the nets obscuring his vision. It was definitely their man alighting and paying the driver and then hurrying up the stoop and into the house. The cab pulled off and as it did so he noted a second one go past with Inspector Andrews on board. He too climbed down and then walked briskly into number 80 to reduce his time out in the street.

"Well, Guv? What did he do?" asked Bentham having now turned to split his attention between looking from the window and looking to Andrews coming into the room.

"Nothing. He went to Grand Station or whatever they call it; I lost sight of him temporarily in there. Did something and then left again."

"Was that it?" Bentham seemed disappointed.

"Yes. That is bloody well it." He sat down next to Bentham and they both stared silently out of the window.

Inside number 79 Weston, aware that he could still be under surveillance, took off his hat and top coat and then he too looked out of the window into the street. He could see nothing out of place but already began to feel constrained by the limitations of living some else's life. He craved female company and tonight he knew that he could go out and buy some at a better quality than usual. 'Hang it' he thought. He would go out, maintain the outer façade, but enjoy the way he liked to live.

Chapter Thirty

Chief Inspector Thomas Byrne head of the New York Police Department looked at the telegram he was receiving from Inspector Abberline from London with disbelief. Tumblety, who had been so adversely reported on in the press on both sides of the Atlantic, was suddenly having the case against him dropped. What the hell had happened? Before informing his men and the English detectives he would have to reply to Abberline's communiqué, which read:

> C/Inspector Byrne,
>
> Apologies. The case against Dr T has to be dropped by orders of powers that be within the Metropolitan Police Force. And beyond. Please inform officers currently deployed and arriving to gain passage back to U.K at earliest chance.
>
> Professional regards. F Abberline D/I

In it's simplicity it was disturbing. 'Powers within and beyond?' What the hell did that mean? Before he would pull anyone off of the case he had to contact Abberline. He replied:

D/I Abberline,

Confused? Thought this was your man. Please expand on issue before I pull off surveillance.

T.B

Many more hours would pass until Byrne understood what was going on, which by the early evening gave the man under surveillance the chance to get out and about in the harbour side of Manhattan.

* * *

Abberline had decided to send the telegram from The Yard; having sent a telegram to Chief Inspector Byrne, as he couldn't face returning to The Street and the faltering investigation as yet following the recent confrontations. He sat silently with Godley drinking a hot cup of tea looking out from the magnificent red and white brick building that had an aspect over the Thames affording some excellent views. He sat there staring out of the window towards Hungerford Bridge almost with the eyes of the blind not registering any of the movement across the bridge, along the river or the Embankment. Within his own mind he now doubted that he would ever bother seeing his thirty years out; if the right opportunity came along he would leave behind the high level corruption of the Force where it seemed his best efforts for the common good were of little consequence. How could an organisation be prepared to shelter someone guilty of such hideous crimes of utter cruelty and depravity? He occasionally looked at Godley to see his gaze also far away perhaps contemplating many of the same things or maybe just trying to get into Abberline's mind. The silence was broken by a uniform sergeant coming up and coughing loudly to get the attention of the distant detectives. Godley looked round and spoke to him.

"Yes, Sergeant, what is please?" He noticed the sergeant had a piece of paper in his hand. The sergeant spoke and proffered the paper.

"For Inspector Abberline. From America." He handed it over and walked off leaving them to read and digest it. They both looked at the short and direct telegram from Byrne. Abberline spoke first.

"Do we send him a message telling him the truth?"

Whitechapel

"Well. What if he is one of them? Is it worth the risk?" replied Godley.

"If it comes from me, what else can I possible lose now? All I can do is write it in a bit of their code and hope for the best, mate."

"All right, Fred. Your call lets go."

They made for the telegram room and Abberline carefully sat at a desk and worded a message to pass to an operator for instant transmission. It took him some time recalling the events of the 1870s and many of the turn of phrases used. He then slipped the telex operator a few pound notes and held his index finger to his lips to indicate silence and secrecy. The message read:

> A journeyman told me to check if you were an apprentice on the square or on your way to be a Knight of the East and the West or beyond. I will level with you, do you understand the Juwes are the men that will not be blamed for nothing? Do you understand the relevance of 'Alpha' in a written message? Prompt reply.
>
> Abberline.

"Bugger me, Fred. What does that all that mean?" Godley was as confused as the telegram operator.

"I'll tell you. 'A journeyman' was one of the original terms for a second degree mason. 'On the square' or 'on the level' refers to identifying if someone is a mason. An 'apprentice' is a first degree mason and a 'knight of the east and the west' is a 17th degree mason. You'll remember that the term 'Juwes' is a collective for the three men who murdered Hiram Abiff in the original Temple of Solomon, and finally a capital 'A' can be hand written to look innocuous but will represent secretly the compass and set square, the famous tools of a masons trade. If he is a mason, well I'm in the shit. If he isn't he'll be very confused."

"And so if he isn't 'on the square'?" asked Godley.

"We go to an outside post office and send a reply telling of a conspiracy and to get our men out before masons out there step in."

It was now mid evening in London. The day was passing by and the dejected Abberline had hardly even noticed.

* * *

It was early evening and Andrews and Bentham were still watching the street from their snug bay window when the front door of number 79 opened up again. Dressed in the same way as earlier in the day Tumblety emerged and again walked off in the direction of Lexington Avenue.

"Right. There is no one else in there to worry about, Arthur. Lets both go this time," said a determined Andrews. They both left the building and followed Tumblety at fifty yards or so towards the bustling main thoroughfare towards the centre of town. He turned into Lexington and kept walking for quite sometime showing no interest in any form of transport.

"This is odd? Maybe he's going to walk all the way?" said Andrews. Bentham remained silent as they kept walking.

Tumblety had walked nearly a quarter of a mile before he stopped to hail himself a cab. Andrews and Bentham were ahead of the game this time; moments before, Bentham had remained on foot whilst Andrews had hailed a cab and followed slowly from further back. Tumblety climbed aboard his ride as Bentham jumped into the cab with his boss and the driver snapped his riding crop to keep pace as instructed. The English detectives had no idea where they were going towards as they fairly quickly turned off of Lexington Avenue on the left hand side.

"Driver, where do you think he's going?" asked Andrews.

"Could be the harbour side on Manhattan if he keeps going," replied the helpful driver.

"What's down there then?" asked Bentham.

"Well, where should I start? Ideal for a night out. Bars, dance halls, restaurants and in the right places a woman at all budgets."

The two Englishmen fell silent and looked at each other. Andrews spoke first.

"My God. Perhaps he's starting all over again over here!" Bentham stayed quiet as they both remained transfixed on the cab ahead. Both carriages rumbled over the cobbled streets lined with a mixture of buildings with very distinctive smells in different areas as they journeyed.

"Guv'nor, do you really think that's going to happen." asked Bentham.

"If it does, we're going to stop him," replied a determined Andrews

* * *

Byrne received Abberline's latest telegram and read it over several times. He sat with the paper flat on his desk with his head supported by and in his hands with his elbows resting either side of the telegram. Crowle was in his office with him having brought the telegram in.

"Goddamn it, Crowle! What the hell does all this crap mean! Has he gone mad? Journeymen, knights of the compass, levels and squares. It's all hogwash." Byrne grabbed a piece of paper and composed a hurried short reply. He then handed it to Crowle. "Right, send this back to him. I don't know what the hell he means and I need straight English!"

"Abberline's reputation, sir, is as a smart man. He's one of Scotland Yard's best detectives. This has to be a coded message and if you don't understand it that might be deliberate. Why would they drop such an investigation unless there is some corruption or pressure. Whoever the Ripper is he's killed six women and an officer. What would stop you investigating such a case other than pressure from above?"

Byrne digested what his subordinate had said. He stood up and walked up to the window in his office and looked and rubbed his chin as he considered this scenario. He stared out of the window with his arms crossed. Crowle silently watched him. After what seemed like minutes but was in fact only 30 seconds or so he turned and spoke.

"Give me that paper." He took it from Crowle and screwed it up throwing it into his waste paper basket. He took another piece from his desk and composed a new message.

Frederick,

An interesting message that sadly means little to me. But I understand there maybe connotations. Please send me a straight talking answer so we can understand the need to disengage from the case. Hope to meet one day.

Thomas.

"Get it sent now please. It's late there but I'm staying until there is a reply." Crowle left the office and made for the telegram room passing many officers on the way that had been engaged on the initial surveillance but now re-assigned; none really had a care in what was now happening. It concerned events such a long way that they felt unaffected.

* * *

Tumblety arrived at the dock front in Manhattan watched closely but still at a discreet distance by the Englishmen. Unaware of this alias, Weston stood still on the pavement as his cab rode away looking the street up and down for anyone who seemed to be taking an unhealthy interest in him. Sensibly the Englishmen had instructed their driver to continue a little way past before they alighted by which time their subject was on the move again. It was dusk on the harbour front with the lights all coming on making the whole place look appealingly attractive.

Weston crossed the road under the gaze of Andrews and Bentham and entered a lively and well lit bar. As they were about to cross the road to follow him, Andrews stopped abruptly on the kerbside and put his arm up across Bentham's chest as he did so stopping him in his tracks.

"What?" said Bentham frowning at Andrews. Andrews took a deep breath in and turned to face is subordinate.

"You go in and watch him and I'll stay out here." He had put his arm down and Bentham began to cross the road. Suddenly he grabbed Bentham's arm. "No. I've changed my mind. You stay her and I'll go in." He felt he needed to burden the responsibility of apprehending the murderer, whilst engaged in a new crime, personally.

He entered the smoke filled bar, 'The Jefferson', with a piano playing noisily in the background. It was full of the cross section of people he had seen in the station except for a large number of elaborately dressed women in typical American saloon-bar wear. They ranged in age and attractiveness quite greatly, but then so did the clientele and undoubtedly so would the price. Unlike in the station he spotted his quarry up at the bar already buying a drink for himself and with a lady next to him. 'He wasted no time' thought Andrews. Tumblety was still sporting his bowler hat pulled well down to his eyebrows as before making it difficult to clearly see his features unless you were close to him. He didn't want to close that sort of gap to him as yet. He wanted to catch him in the act, and of course Andrews and Bentham were both completely unaware of the Masonic conspiracy and the termination of the investigation.

Weston particularly liked the smell of the twenty-two year old buxom blonde prostitute he now courted as well her impressive and well displayed bosom. He found it especially difficult to always look her in the eye as they made conversation his gaze drawn to her voluptuous breasts. She was very pretty too, with an attractive hour glass figure and he knew that the cost to have sex with her would be much greater than he could normally afford. Then again with his clothes and new found wealth she was much better than he could usually choose. She was from the deep south of the country and her soft 'southern drool' on top of all of her other physical attributes really aroused his desire. He would have her, whatever the cost. At the opposite end of the bar Andrews was buying himself a drink and keeping a close eye on Tumblety whose back was to him. He too could see why he had chosen this woman to talk to as she was very attractive. He had only ever seen prostitutes like her in the West End of London, with the bizarre exception of Mary Kelly, never would women of that class frequent the pubs or streets of Whitechapel.

At times he almost found it difficult to see to the other end of the bar due to the thickness of the smoke which was beginning to make his eyes feel quite sore. The constant noise level from the piano and the loud bawdy conversations ever trying to compete with each other already made Andrews ears start to ring; he could understand how the woman and Tumblety were so close to each other. She seemed charmed by him chatting freely and almost constantly smiling as he plied her with drink. Andrews only wished he could hear the conversation that was taking place between them.

"So, pretty lady, what's your name then, huh?" asked a smiling Weston.

"S'April, named after the month you know. Do you like it then, sir?" She smiled back at him lifting her right leg and brushing it along his left calf and then slowly going a little higher.

"It's lovely. Call me Frank. None of that formal bullshit. You got somewhere quiet we could go to, huh?" She brushed his thigh as he finished talking. She looked down all innocently and then back up into his eyes with a glint and spoke again.

"Certainly have, Frankie if your money is right. It's private and warm and comfortable and we can fool around as long as your money allows."

"Lady, April honey, I can pay to fool around all night." Away from prying glances he opened up his coat and showed her a wad of notes in an inside pocket. The English detective looked on in puzzlement of what was going on. What had he shown her? She nuzzled into his neck and then gave the man Andrews perceived as Tumblety a light kiss on the cheek.

Andrews looked on at the intimacy of the situation between them feeling uncomfortable that the Whitechapel murderer could be able to shortly strike in New York. Suddenly his blood ran completely cold as the two linked arms and walked away from the bar. He looked on in horror to see if they were leaving the building before making any moves himself. They made for the stairs which led up to a landing with an ornate balustrade around it with, he could see, several doors running off of it. He felt pangs of the Kelly murder; if this was Jack the Ripper he would again have privacy to commit terrible crimes undisturbed and without time constraints. Andrews walked slowly through the crowds keeping his eyes transfixed on them as they reached the bottom of the stairs and began to make their way up the wide carpeted staircase. Despite the Ripper obsession and the desire to prevent any further bloodshed Andrews rationalised that he also had to consider that Tumblety was about to embark on a simple business transaction with a prostitute. He reached the base of the stairs as the still laughing couple were at the top and turning right onto the landing arm in arm with their faces often close to each other exchanging what appeared to be many words of innuendo.

April and Weston only walked a dozen feet or so reaching a door which she opened and showed him in. He tipped his hat to her and took it off but his back was to Andrews observing him from down below. He couldn't get a good look then at what he still perceived was Tumblety's face as the couple entered the room and the door closed behind them. Transfixed and unconscious of how conspicuous he was about to become he climbed the stairs himself too, watched from the crowd by a large set, overly tall, dark skinned American employed by the establishment's owner to deal with trouble makers. He too made his way to the stairs watching Andrews who he assumed was a thrill seeker of some sort now reaching the landing and looking to the door were he had seen April taking her client.

Andrews walked up to the door and placed his head next to it with his left ear pushed up against the wood to hear what was going on inside. As yet all he could hear was muffled and hushed conversation oblivious to the large menacing American now almost at the top of the stairs keeping him under fierce observation. He could still hear nothing different as he felt a tap on his right shoulder and he wheeled round to be presented at eye level with the chest of a veritable giant. He looked up into the eyes of the man mountain that now bore down on him.

"So, little man, what the fuck are you doing?" said the giant of a man as he folded his arms looking down sneeringly at Andrews.

"Err, I'm, err, I……….." Andrews fell over his words completely surprised by what he was confronted with.

"You've got seconds for a good answer, you little pervert." The giant unfolded his arms and began limbering up his fists.

"I'm Inspector Walter Andrews from Scotland Yard on the trail of Jack the Ripper, the Whitechapel murderer." He straightened up as he spoke and was about to reach into his suit pocket for his identification.

"Bullshit, limey bastard! You expect me to fall for that crap!"

Angered by what he thought was a contrived excuse and on his guard to having a gun pulled on him, the Giant grabbed Andrews by the throat and pinned him up against the wall next to the door to April's room. Andrews struggled for breath as he did so and the banging sound of him hitting the wall with force disturbed the occupants of the room.

"What the Goddamn is going on out there, buddy?" shouted the male voice from the room.

"Nothing, sir," replied the Giant American as he prepared to get Andrews in a wrestling lift and eject him from the premises. Andrews tried to pull the hand inflicting a vice like grip on his throat but his resistance was futile. He felt the giant's other hand pass between his legs and grab the back of this trousers and he was suddenly and almost effortlessly lifted into the air. He began to be carried downstairs still fighting to loosen the grip on his throat.

Within seconds his feet and head were being used to force the doors of 'The Jefferson' open and he found himself in the street. The giant then lifted him above his head giving Andrews an elevated view of the footway and passing carriages.

"Mister, don't give me that bullshit. At least be truthful. Next ti…" The giant's words were cut short by a scream from a room above them from the first floor that faced out over the street. Unknown to Andrews the room it emanated from was April's and the scream was instantly recognised by the Giant American. "Goddamn it! Don't tell me you were right!" He lowered Andrews and unceremoniously dropped him from at least only from waist height as he turned to run back into the premises. Oblivious to the impact with the ground Andrews sprang to his feet and followed him.

All this was observed by Arthur Bentham who crossed the road and ran into 'The Jefferson' after both the men. As Andrews got into the main bar he could see the giant making his way up the stairs ahead of him. He pushed his way through the jostling crowds and sprinted up the stairs himself. As he reached the top the giant was already forcing the door in to the room open and then froze in the doorway as he did so. Andrews, looking over his shoulder as he reached the top could feel his heart racing more through the fear of what he now expected to be greeted with rather than the physical exertion. The few paces he needed to take from the top of the stairs to the door of the room seemed to take a an eternity in slow motion as he saw the giant who had so easily man handled him standing still and speechless in the doorway. He expected the worst; another Kelly murder scene. His auditory functions had shut down unable to hear Bentham's calls for caution, who was now on the stairs warning him that the killer might still be there with a fearsome knife.

He reached the door and was stunned by what he saw; it was not a scene that he could ever have expected to be greeted with. The girl was naked on her knees as she had leant back in shock of the door being opened shouting at the giant stood silently in the door. The man he had thought was Tumblety was stood with his back to the door and his trousers around his ankles and bare chested. He now looked round as Andrews reached the door and both he and the giant understood why she might have made such a scream. This man, who facially he now realised close up was not Tumblety but someone who looked very much like him, was indeed in possession of a weapon but it was an extremely large natural one. So exceptionally, that it had caused the girl to scream out in apparent shock.

"What the Goddam hell are you men doing?" She screamed indignantly, "can't you see a girl trying to work!" The giant replied sheepishly.

"Sorry, April, I thought you was being attacked, baby."

"Well Hell I ain't! I just haven't seen anything this big before and it gave me a goddamn shock as I dropped his trousers and it flopped out!"

Weston seemed amused by all this and looked at the men in doorway in a very proud fashion. He smiled and spoke to them.

"Sorry, guys it's curse. But I can live with it. Now fuck off and leave us in peace!" He turned away from them back to the girl who stared at her eye level at him still with some obvious trepidation in her face.

The giant turned away sheepishly forgetting that Andrews was stood just beyond him in the door jam with Bentham in the corridor. He brushed shoulders with Bentham on the landing as he moved past. Andrews stared at the man's back in disbelief. If this wasn't Tumblety where the hell had he gone? Weston was aware of a man still stood behind him especially as he hadn't heard the door close. The girl was about to begin the activity, a little nervously, her profession demanded when Weston spoke turning his head to face the man in the doorway.

"Do you mind? The lady and I have some unfinished business." Andrews felt a wave of anger wash over him and he stepped menacingly towards Weston. "Steady, fella, I'm a lover not a fighter," said Weston raising his hands in a defensive gesture responding to the threat, although not moving away from the girl. "But if have to..."

"Who the hell are you, you... freak?" Hissed an incensed Andrews, Bentham had walked in behind him somewhat lost as to what was going on.

"Well, what the hell is it to you, mister?" replied Weston, indignant that his long awaited expensive carnal pleasures were being interrupted still.

"I am Detective Inspector Andrews from Scotland Yard. I was pursuing a man called Tumblety over the Ripper murders in Whitechapel. You are dressed as him, living at his address and spending like him, but you're obviously not him."

"Look, do you mind, can't this wait until later?" said Weston flippantly. This reaction pushed Andrews over the edge. He grabbed Weston's right arm and forced it up his back and pushed him face down on the bed. He screamed in pain as his elbow was forced high up towards his shoulders in an awkward twisted position. The girl also screamed, Bentham looking on somewhat hypnotised by her swinging breasts as she stood up and stepped quickly backwards. Aware she was being looked at she covered her upper body with one arm and her lower parts with the other. Andrews looked around seeing her stood by the window.

"Miss, get dressed. Bentham, compensate her please from your impress money." Bentham stared on at her for a moment. "BENTHAM!" His attention returned to Andrews.

"Yes, sir. Sorry, sir. Miss, please take your clothes, how much do you need?" April was surprised by this reaction from these, she noticed, not local men. Perhaps her time wasn't wasted after all.

"Ten bucks please, mister." Andrews nodded in agreement still with Weston pinned to the bed whining in pain. Bentham paid the girl who then fled the room having picked her clothes up to get dressed in privacy.

"Get off of me! I ain't done nothing! What the hell do you want!" Andrews noticed Weston's eyes watering with the pain he was still applying to the prostrate almost naked man.

"Right. I'm going to let you go. When I do, pull up your trousers, put you shirt on and then sit in that chair," Andrews pointed to a wooden captain's style chair sat in one corner of the room next to the window. "Then you are going to tell me everything, or so help me God, I'll find the evidence to take you back and have you hung, you bastard." Weston fell silent. He had a dozen thoughts spinning around in his head. That son of a bitch Townsend had really framed him. Although pleased of the money and the comfort, he now wished he could find Townsend himself to get a real answer to all this. He was also frustrated that he had paid the girl at the bar and she had now received double the money with absolutely no sexual gratification for him at all. His shoulder and arm being used to pin him to the bed were burning with pain. He decided to acquiesce.

"All right, all right. I won't struggle and I'll tell you everything. That son of a bitch Townsend has really played me for a fool." Hearing the name Townsend and with Weston agreeing to co-operate Andrews released the arm lock he had applied. He felt sick to the pit of his stomach with the realisation that Tumblety had again outwitted the powers of law and order. Weston knelt up and then got to his feet on the bed and pulled up his trousers. He stepped off and grabbed his shirt which was amongst a pile of clothes on the floor and pulled it on beginning to then button it. Tucking it in, he sat himself in the captain's chair and sighed heavily running his hands through his hair.

Andrews took a good look at him; it was easy to see why at a distance he had been mistaken by himself, and by Bentham, for Tumblety; but now in a study close to it was quite obviously not their man. Bentham was still stood in the open doorway; Andrews turned to him and spoke.

"Come in, lad and shut the door. Right, Mister....?"

"Weston, Bill Weston," he replied disparagingly.

"Mr Weston, tell us all about your friend Francis Tumblety from the very start of your association with him. You do know he is the key suspect in the Whitechapel murders?" Weston buried his head in his hands. He should have guessed that the whole issue for Townsend in London was more than money related; after all he had introduced himself as 'doctor'. Weston was also very well acquainted with the events in East London; he had been in the English capital for most of the year.

"He told me his name was Townsend and that there were some guys after him as he had got into financial difficulties as he put it. I guessed there'd be trouble ahead but not a murder rap. He just asked me to be him for the majority of the crossing and for a month here in New York. He made it well worth......er."

"Paid you did he, Mr Weston?" Andrews didn't have to work hard to maintain the upper hand. Weston had to think on his feet or he would end up broke again.

"Yes. $200. That's all and some new clothes. I really needed the money." Andrews remained silent staring at him. "I tell you that's all!"

"All right, Mr Weston, You will of course have to forfeit that money as it is involved in the escape of a known criminal suspect."

"Oh, for God's sake! Give me a break!" He was in truth happy to forfeit that money as he still had over a thousand dollars.

"Mr Weston, it's a small price to pay to maintain your liberty. Now, where did 'Dr Townsend' say he was going?"

"He didn't. I have no idea. I really don't." Andrews looked him in the eye for some seconds and then turned to look at Bentham. He pulled down the sides of his mouth in a begrudging manner of cynical acceptance of Weston's story.

There was a knock on the door; Bentham opened it up to see a breathless Detective Hickey outside leaning on the door frame. He looked at both the English Detectives and then stepped in with a piece of paper in his hand. Abberline had replied to Byrne's last telegram. Hickey held it out to Andrews as he looked at him in astonishment and then looked at the paper in his hand at the same time taking hold of it. It was folded in half but he recognised it as telex paper and opened it to read. The message was simple but damning. From its content he knew that their work was over.

> C/I Byrne.
>
> There is an apparent Masonic involvement in these murders and I have forthwith been instructed to discontinue the case against the suspect in your city. I am grateful for the professional courtesy you have shown.
>
> F Abberline.

Andrews was mortified by the telegrams implications. It struck him that an alleged benevolent organisation was party to murder. He, like all the other key detectives on the Ripper case and the London based Masonic order involved, would never know that they had been duped by a clever and resourceful man who it seemed was destined to evade justice. It would reflect badly on both organisations. He looked up staring blankly at the walls in the room and then walked out, passing Bentham and handing him the telegram as he did so.

"What's going on, huh?" asked a puzzled Weston. Bentham was reading the telegram still. He then looked up and exhaled a large breath puffing his cheeks out before breathing in and replying to Weston.

"Mr Weston, I think you're free to go." Weston looked puzzled. Hickey looked on at him impassively.

"What? What the fuck do you mean?" He now began to speak angrily.

"You're are free to go, sir." Bentham then walked out to.

"You lousy, limey bastards!" He jumped out of his chair and began to stride towards the door, enraged by the change of tack and confused by it. Before he could get to the door he was stopped by Hickey with a firm hand placed in the centre of his chest.

"I think you've done quite well, Mr Weston. Let's leave at that, eh?" Bill Weston was momentarily lost for words and then having found some composure was about to launch a verbal tirade. He opened his mouth to speak and then stopped himself; they had left and he still had all of his money. The American cop was right, he was better off cutting his losses.

Chapter Thirty-One

Friday 7th December 7.30a.m: Abberline and Godley were in 'The Bull' an 'early house' in the Smithfield meat market area drowning their sorrows. The case against Tumblety had finally been discarded by them through no choice of their own and there was no trace anywhere of the second main suspect Severin Klosowski also known as George Chapman. The public house was full with meat porters and butchers who had just finished their hours of early morning toil in the market. The butchers were easy to distinguish from the porters in their white aprons and work coats heavily stained with blood from the dozens of carcasses they had dealt with through the night; either cattle or poultry, the effect on their work clothing was the same. They took little notice of the two now shabbily dressed detectives stood at one end of the bar by an external wall being served without question by the landlord. He knew who they were by reputation and familiarity although the market lay deep within the City of London Police's jurisdiction.

"Another Ale, Mr Abberline?" politely asked the publican of the noted detective. Abberline was using the both the bar and the wall for support. He and Godley had only been in there for a little over an hour but they had sunk nearly seven pints each on virtually empty stomachs. Abberline was reaching the end of his seventh hence the enquiry. They were both drinking a thick, dark ale almost black in its colour, called 'Hells Teeth'. It was strong and bitter and perfect for the intentions of the great East End detective; to become as drunk as possible in the quickest possible time. Godley had barely started the seventh and was in little better condition than Abberline but he was aware that one of them had to ensure a safe journey home and avoid any actions leading to major embarrassment personally or for the beleaguered Metropolitan Police. Godley watched Abberline sink the last of his pint draining the glass as if it were the last request of a condemned man. He saw how glazed his friend's eyes were becoming and as he spoke he could tell his speech was beginning to slur.

"Tell me, George, how do you reckon this will go down in annals of the history of the Metropolitan Police? Do you think that they'll use us as scape goats to justify an incompetent investigation? Eh?" Godley looked his friend in the eye and thought long and hard about an answer. He looked into his nearly full pint glass still considering his words and then drank about a quarter of it before beginning to speak.

"Well." Godley paused and looked around the crowd of market drinkers who were paying them little or no attention. "I think that history will judge us well and find out those who obstructed the investigation. This was a slaughter of the innocent drawn from the masses and the papers love to champion the under dogs in favour of knocking the establishment. You will be hailed as the people's hero who did his best but failed while trying through no fault of your own. All the blokes on the case from you down will be judged that way. Problem is, Fred, that you'll have to be careful not speak out. Keep any memoirs to a minimum, keep interviews vague and for the time you have left in this job keep your head down. If you can get another rank then at least the pension will be better."

"Funny you should say that, old friend. I already got that inducement from Arnold, or was it Anderson? I'm getting too drunk to remember."

"I did notice that you're beginning to go, mate. Sure you should have any more?" Abberline picked up the eighth pint just served by the publican and laying on the counter.

"I'll be the judge of that. But you're right this had better be the last. Then we're off." He began to sink some of the thick, dark and richly alcoholic ale. He managed about a third of the glass before he banged it back down on the bar spilling some of it as it lapped over the sides of the glass with the force of the impact. "I need a slash." Abberline began to move away from the wall just supporting himself against the bar with Godley paying close attention. He looked up across the saloon to the opposite side where the toilets were across a sea of white clad, blood soaked humanity. Squinting, he located them and let go of the bar and began to stagger towards the toilet door. He managed three unsteady steps before collapsing in a heap on the floor, Godley making a desperate but failing lunge to catch his fall.

Two of the burly butchers had seen what happened and downed their pints quickly and put the glasses on a table then going over to help the now struggling Godley attempting to lift the uncoordinated drunken Abberline. Almost pushing Godley aside quite by accident and not design, each of them got hold of an arm and hoisted him effortlessly up onto his feet; a strength born out of years of carting livestock carcasses around the market. Godley stood to one side himself unsteady on his feet too as the butchers headed for the door of the pub leading out into the crisp cold morning air. Contact with the air outside sent Godley's head spinning accentuating the intoxicating effect of the ale and he looked at Abberline to see what unfortunate results befell him too. He seemed impassive to it just groaning with the ill effects of the excess alcohol. A familiar voice called to the butchers from a parked carriage on the opposite side of the road.

"Over here, lads, stick him on board." It was Robert Ford climbing down from a waiting carriage with a look of some concern on his face. "Is he all right, sarge?" He asked enquiringly of Godley who was following slowly behind the butchers and Abberline.

"Yes," fighting for the right words to come out "we've both just had too much, son. Get us home for Christ's sake." He supported himself against the carriage as the butchers unceremoniously lifted the now completely limp Abberline into the passenger compartment. He groaned as he was placed onto the floor and then pushed in by his legs to clear the door, his head hitting the opposite side provoking no reaction from the dull impact of skin and bone against light wooden door.

"Thanks, lads," said Ford handing the butchers a few shillings each for their trouble. "Keep it to yourselves, eh?" They looked at each other and nodded in recognition of his request.

Ford helped the increasingly unsteady Godley onto the carriage and then jumped in himself with the driver who snapped his riding crop as he did so with the horse moving the whole thing off with a lurch. Godley sat with his head in hands as Abberline remained silent on the floor with the noise of the carriage over the cobbles seeming to pound in his head. Rubbing his eyes he looked up at Ford quizzically and spoke.

"You know it's over, don't you?"

"For now. Chapman or whatever his name is will pop his head up again. We'll get him. Least we are allowed to do that," replied Ford.

"There is no 'for now' about it, son. It's OVER!" Godley said agitated.

"Officially and for now. What I choose to do is my choice, sarge." Ford was calm and calculated in his reply and not phased by his superior.

"Listen, if you value your career and your life, you'll leave it."

"Yeah, whatever. I've a lot more time left in this firm than you." He also had financial means which was unusual for a young policeman; that was his business and his alone. They were both silent for some minutes as the carriage travelled on through familiar streets. Godley then quizzically spoke.

"How did you know where we were then?" Ford looked at him and smiled. "Well, you don't think I've spent all this time on the team and not learnt the art of detection do you, sarge?"

"Well done, son. Glad some positives are coming out of it."

In just a few hundred yards more both Godley and Abberline were snoring heavily as Ford directed the driver to their home addresses to drop them discreetly off.

* * *

Everyone finally enjoyed a long weekend with the trails having gone cold, at least for now. That was everyone other than Robert Ford who had decided to begin to take matters into his own hands. It was Sunday, late afternoon and he had spent most of the weekend hatching a plan to start to gain justice for Mary and the others. He was being eaten up inside by the conspiracy of fellow police officers working divisively against their brothers to defend a cruel and tortuous killer from justice. He felt personally aggrieved from the attack he had received led by Sir Robert Anderson who he now felt certain was the mastermind of all the operations to break the investigation into Tumblety. As a uniformed officer he should be able to gain access to Scotland Yard with relative ease but once inside it was the domain of the detectives and wandering the corridors of the upper floors he would need to be in a suit. Neither fact presented a problem; he wore a dark suit under a police tunic so once inside he would only need to remove the tunic and helmet to blend in. By the time he would arrive at The Yard from his lodgings in Bethnal Green it would be at its most quiet, an early Sunday evening, with no one restarting in the offices until around 8.a.m the next morning.

His plan was simple, perhaps naively so; he would break into Sir Robert's office to find any remaining evidence against Tumblety, most likely only the arts bag. Dressing as planned he left he lodgings without any of the local people batting any eyelid, all of them familiar with him and his profession. The only thing that seemed at odds with the norm was seeing him hail and board a hansom cab further south in Bakers Row.

"Whitehall please, driver." He confidently instructed the cold looking driver perched on his exposed padded leather saddle sporting a thick blanket over his knees. The gaunt and pale old man driving the cab nodded in acceptance and wiped away mucus dripping from his nose with the back of the sleeve of his crop bearing hand. He cracked the crop and the cab rumbled off along the cobbles in the now dark gas lit East End streets.

The journey took a little over twenty minutes; the cab pulling up in Whitehall just a little way beyond Whitehall Place and Great Scotland Yard. Ford jumped down and paid the driver his fare and watched blowing warm air in into his hands as the cab drove off. It had become bitterly cold following sunset and he wished he had brought his police beat duty cape or an overcoat to deal with the drop in temperature, especially pronounced with the proximity of the location to the river. Still, he would be outside for a minimal period of time as he began to walk briskly along Whitehall to turn into Whitehall Place leading up to Scotland Yard and to the entrance to the hallowed Metropolitan Police headquarters located there. As he walked towards the red brick and white edged building he considered the international reputation that it commanded for its crime fighting prowess and right now how undeserved it seemed in the face of such illicit corruption. If he pursued his police career beyond this night he vowed that he would never let such practices and associations influence his resolve or investigations in which he embarked.

He reached the steps in the deathly quiet early Sunday evening street to see the reception desk inside the double wooden doors illuminated by a desk lamp but the rest of the open hall in darkness. Few officers came and went; he decided that he would show out entering in uniform so he walked past to try to find somewhere to stow his helmet and tunic safely until he had finished. Near the junction with Victoria Embankment he found an open doorway in darkness in building that seemed largely disused. He rolled his helmet inside the heavy blue serge tunic and placed them just inside the door jam pulling the tatty pine door closed behind him. He turned to walk back still with no one in the street and began to climb the steps to the entrance to 'The Yard'. His movement as he approached the door must have been picked up by the desk sergeant's peripheral vision as he looked up from the desk just as Ford was about to push the door open. He entered gauging the type of officer he was about to have bluff his way past examining him without giving the fact he was away.

The desk sergeant was a seasoned veteran by his age and his bearing. A balding well built man with big thick hands, a greying moustache and, as Robert Ford was about to discover, of a direct nature; truly he thought the sergeant a wily old campaigner. Immediately the sergeant could see that he was going to be dealing with a young officer, possibly by the mode of dress a young hot shot detective. He sat back and upright in his chair and spoke with ferocious probing eye contact.

"Yes, son. Can I help you?" Ford could tell getting past him would be challenging and considered his words carefully before speaking.

"PC Ford, attached to the Whitechapel murders, sarge..." before he could continue he was interrupted by the seemingly anti C.I.D. sergeant.

"Oh, yeah? And what do you want at this time on a Sunday then, son?" He used the word 'son' in a very condescending fashion. There seemed little point fabricating a complicated story with this man so Ford decided to remain as truthful as possible to try to keep some kind of control of the conversation. "Inspector Abberline has tasked me to collect some case papers from the office here for examination by him personally tomorrow morning. Early."

"Really?" The sergeant folded his arms and looked him up and down. He was annoyed the story seemed so plausible. To satisfy his boredom and verbose nature he would just make the lad feel a bit more uncomfortable. "And these papers relate to whom then?"

Robert Ford knew he didn't have to answer that question, but decided to be equal to the obtuseness he was meeting. "Jack the Ripper, sarge." The sly smile that the sergeant had been giving him fell to a completely stony look of annoyance. The lad had given a smart answer and one he couldn't contend. His sport with him was over.

"Cheeky, bleeder. You know where the office is then, lad. Bugger off and get what you need." He settled down to read the newspaper in front of him again as Ford walked past him hurriedly into the building and breathed a sigh of relief.

The corridors were only marginally lit as it was a Sunday, a day when activity in the building was fairly dormant. He made his way up the main staircase having ignored the building guide on the wall by the stairs on the ground floor deliberately so as not to arouse anymore suspicion in the desk sergeant. He knew where the Whitechapel Murders office was but had no clue as to where Sir Robert Anderson's office was. On reaching the first floor landing he studied the floor guide there; he was in luck, Anderson's office was only one more floor up. He moved briskly up the stair case in the seemingly deserted building. He passed through the double doors to enter the second floor corridor, breathing just a little heavily now from having run up the two flights nervously; he was presented with a wall plate in front him with a guide to the offices. Anderson's was room 2.09, a right turn from the doors along the dimly lit corridor. The walls were panelled in a dark oak; this was the floor where many important senior officers had their offices. He reached 2.09 and the door to the office was equally ornate to match the walls.

The door was four panelled in the same wood as the walls with a large brass door knob with a Chubb lock key hole underneath. Ford looked at the door; surely it would be locked and a door like this would not be soundless to put in. Before simply trying the door knob he placed his ear to the door to listen on the off chance for any activity inside. It was, as he expected, silent. He wrapped his right hand around the door knob and gently and quietly tried to turn it. It moved, so he turned it fully and pushed and the door opened into a dimly lit but sumptuous office.

It was again decked out in oak panelling, bookcases, a drinks cabinet and a leather topped desk with a high leather backed office chair behind it, and above a small fireplace in the room hung a portrait of Queen Victoria. The wooden floor was highly polished with a rug in the centre on top of which sat the desk and chair and two less comfortable looking wooden almost dining type chairs in front of the desk; obviously for subordinates to sit in uncomfortably and receive the fury of the Assistant Commissioner when necessary. But why was the room lit? He looked around the room more closely and saw behind the door was an iron hat and coat stand with, he noted with dismay, a hat and coat on it. Anderson couldn't possibly be here this evening? He cast his vision again around the room and spotted on top of the drinks cabinet two whisky tumblers, one empty the other with about three quarters of inch of light brown coloured spirit in it. He was still stood close to the office door when he heard the double doors from the stairway open and the sound of a man and a woman laughing as they sounded as if they had barrelled through them. 'Christ!' Ford quickly shut the office door and tried to see where around the room he could hide. There was no where other than behind the office door when it opened. He had come this far; he was now going to have to see through an extreme course of action.

Robert Ford was not prepared for what he saw when the door opened. Anderson walked with a young woman holding her by his right hand. He led the female up towards the desk where the she stopped and turned round to face him. He couldn't believe it, it was the pretty East End prostitute Julia Styles. She was smiling and leaning back against the desk reaching for Anderson's trousers. She spoke as she did so.

"Want a suck before your fuck then, sir?" Anderson batted away the girl's hands with his own and spoke.

"Just turn round and lift your skirt, girlie, and bend over the desk. I'll see to me." Julia began to do as she was told as the office door slammed shut.

Robert Ford could have never seen that he would be in such a position of strength against, or so he thought, the establishment and all of its corruption. Neither Anderson nor Julia had seen him in the shadow behind the door as they had entered but now both looked at him aghast as the door closed loudly and both seemed momentarily frozen in time. Julia said nothing but began to pull her skirt back down as Anderson stood silently regarding the young man he had previously tried to kill.

"So, Assistant Commissioner, we meet again, sir," said a confident Robert Ford.

"What do you want?" muttered Anderson, obviously in a compromised position. Julia looked on nervously and tried to begin to walk away, speaking as she did so.

"I better be going, sir."

"Stay where you are, Julia," said Ford. "I'll tell you what I want, you bastard, re-open the case against Tumblety. That's what I want. Give me back the remaining evidence against him too." Anderson spoke immediately.

"I can't do that."

"Really? Is this because of your damned 'Brotherhood'?"

"You know all about that do you, Ford?"

"Yes. I don't give a shit. Re-open the investigation, or I go public with this about you," he said gesturing to the nervous unfortunate. Anderson casually turned his back on Ford and walked round to his chair behind the desk and sat down. He opened a drawer of the desk and pulled out a large thick cigar and a box of matches. He rolled the cigar by his left ear and then placed it in his mouth. Pulling a match from its box as he opened it he struck the red phosphorous head against the striking plate on the box and lit the cigar and coolly and slowly drew on it until it glowed brightly and evenly. Julia and Ford both looked on incredulously at the casual calmness of his actions in such a compromising scenario.

"Ford, come and sit down. You, girl," said Anderson to Julia "Go and pour two large malts please. Then you can fuck off." To Ford the use of such coarse language from one so refined and eloquent seemed very out of place. He was shocked by Anderson's confident and calm actions and had no immediate reply. Trying to get a grasp of the situation, he did as he was told and came and sat down opposite Anderson in one of the austere wooden chairs. He gathered his thoughts as Anderson spoke.

"This is bigger than you and anything you can imagine. There is no investigation to be re-opened because there is no longer any evidence."

"But, the papers maybe gone; there are still the jars and the bag. You can't keep this suppressed, not when I now know you use the services of prostitutes, being exposed as a cheap thrill seeker will destroy you." Robert was certain that he must still have an upper hand as he spoke.

"No. The bag is gone; I passed it onto the burgeoning forensic department to destroy once they had examined it for their own experience. You can't magic up the hand writing evidence against Tumblety. So you destroy my reputation? Two things on that, one, do you think that people will believe a lowly street constable in our society, grieving over the loss of his best friend and love and racked by emotion over a respected senior police officer? Hmm? Just look at my reputation, it is glowing. And second, do you think with all I have done to protect The Brotherhood I will be scared to become a scape goat of some kind? I would have to retire from public life but I'd be looked after. Would you?

Julia approached the table and placed a generous tumbler full of single malt whisky in front of each of them.

"And what about her, surely it concerns you that she could blow the whistle on you or black mail you?" asked Ford watching the young woman step away from the table.

"Not really." In a rapid movement Anderson reached back into the drawer he had used earlier and pulled out a revolver and pointed it at Julia. He pulled back the hammer action which set with a loud click. He pulled the trigger. To Ford the room for a fraction of a second froze as he tried to comprehend what he had just seen in relation to the sounds. There had been a another loud click only and no sound of a shot so he realised that everyone still sitting or standing was the right picture he should be seeing. He could hear running water; looking down at Julia's feet he could see fluid running onto the floor from under her skirt. He had to confess to himself that Anderson was indeed a ruthless and determined man. Events from the canal back flooded back to him to re-enforce this view.

"Do you honestly think that there would much of an investigation into the murder of a prostitute? They are hardly unusual these days are they? Don't underestimate me or what I am prepared to do. You have nothing. Go away, enjoy your career, or what you may have left of it, and live a sad unfulfilled working class life."

Ford felt belittled, exactly as Anderson had intended. But Anderson had said nothing about him entering his office.

"But, what about tonight?" He asked Anderson who was gradually filling the room with more smoke.

"Granted, you have that on me. I shan't pursue that matter, not having bribed the sergeant to let my friend in. Think of it as a battle won against us. But as you know, a battle and not the war." Ford couldn't believe he was hearing those words again. He grabbed the tumbler and emptied it. The bitter powerful liquid burnt his throat and he could feel the sensation all the way to the pit of his stomach, which as it began to line it he felt his head go a little light. He got up to leave, lost for words and intending to say nothing and further give Anderson the upper hand.

"Take her out with you, and shut the door when you go," said Anderson with more self assurance than ever referring to Julia.

Ford had turned towards the door as Anderson spoke. He stopped in his tracks and faced his adversary and replied.

"Fuck you."

"Oh, no. That's my job as you may have noticed when you saw us come in." Stunned by the sheer gall of the man to rebut him in such a manner at the last, he walked out and said nothing further. He realised that for now he had won the only battle he was ever going to win.

Chapter Thirty-Two

1903

Tuesday 7th April 6.a.m; Severin Klosowski had not had a restful night in his cell on death row in Wandsworth Prison. On the 19th March he had been convicted at the Central Criminal Court in London, colloquially known as 'The Old Bailey', of 'The Borough Wife Poisonings'. The presiding judge had been Justice Grantham who had donned the black cap to sentence Klosowski to death following the unanimous guilty verdict on the death of Maud Marsh and two other acts of fatal poisoning on Bessie Taylor and Mary Spink. His plea for clemency to the Home Secretary had failed and he was wakened by guards checking on his condition prior to his last meal who all saw real terror in his face. Klosowski, alias George Chapman, now himself faced death following the reign of terror his own existence had wrought. When arrested by Detective Inspector George Godley in October 1902, Godley's former colleague and mentor the now retired Chief Inspector Frederick Abberline was reported to have commented to him "I see you have caught a Jack the Ripper at last."

His cell was a meagre ten feet square with a Spartan harsh cot on which he attempted to sleep. This evil man at last had no control over his own life or that of others and therefore the manner of his death. He had at last become a shell of a man with his only method of escape from his incarceration being the hangman's rope. A catholic priest arrived at the cell and entered to find Klosowski on his knees and praying on his arrival – a massively uncharacteristic display of religious conviction.

The confession that was taken by this priest would be of a remarkable nature and the contents of which would go with both men to their graves.

"My son, do you wish to make a confession and be granted absolution?" Klosowski was sobbing with all colour from his face drained. He felt sick and found it hard to speak. During this silence the priest administered last rites which when finished had given the evil Polish multiple murderer enough time to compose himself and find a voice.

"Father," he spoke in a low tone in close proximity to the priest to ensure no one else could hear. "May the Lord forgive? I have sinned greatly and fear that I am only destined to burn in hell. Though I don't consider myself to be Jack the Ripper I am guilty of some of those killings. One was premeditated and the others spontaneous through violent rage. I have also killed in Paris, on the way to London from Europe. I killed outside of London to affect my escape and I killed in America. If the Lord can find it in his heart I wish to confess and be granted entry to his kingdom." Tears were rolling down his cheeks from his heavily bloodshot eyes.

The priest, although a man of God, had as human a sentiment as any decent man. He found it hard to speak the traditional words of comfort when he heard such a sickening confession to a multitude of evil unpardonable sins. As he considered his own feelings that this man should indeed burn in the fires of hell, he composed himself to speak the accepted reply that this loathsome individual on his knees before him expected to hear.

"My son, God is an angry God but a forgiving God. You will be granted entry to the Kingdom of Heaven, but never forget when the day of judgement comes, you will be held to account and you will meet your victims again. You must be resolute in your denunciation of your own evil acts. There is no penance I can set you other than the fate you are about to meet. Dare I say it, but my son the Old Testament talks of an 'eye for an eye'. What do you yourself think? Do not be trite in your request."

The priest's words struck home quickly and hard with Klosowski. But he knew he was right. He began to shiver in fear of what was approaching and the harsh comfort that he had been given and felt constantly sick. He was a little deaf to some of the words the priest was now speaking but caught the tale end of the delivery as he saw the priest make the sign of the cross.

"In the name of the Father, the Son and the Holy Ghost, may God bless you and save you. Amen." The priest then walked out leaving the shivering wreck on the hard cold stone floor. Klosowski knelt alone and terrified, his face buried in his hands, his forehead on the cold floor. He was sobbing.

Just before 7.a.m and shortly after the priest had left, the guards brought in a last meal; a breakfast consisting of bread, butter and coffee. He had become a withdrawn nervous wreck in the face of imminent death and the slightest movement or sound saw him move in startled way like a terrified animal. He made eye contact with everyone who came into contact with him now looking for hope, help and rescue from his fate. He knew that this was really a pointless expression of emotion and merely fear controlling his psyche. He could barely bring himself to eat anything; he was starting to rock backwards and forwards in whatever position he was in, seated, kneeling, standing or otherwise. He was mumbling to himself and only managed two bites from the bread before he threw it into the corner of the cell and kicked the enamel mug holding black coffee across the floor in an act of futile defiance or so it seemed. He was not unsurprisingly slipping into a moody and depressed humour.

Elsewhere within the walls of Wandsworth prison had slept Mr William Billington the executioner for that part of London and his assistant Mr Henry Pierrepoint. This act of sleeping within the prison was a long held tradition and one that both men were happy to adhere to; not because of any sense of joy in their work but through a sense of solemn duty. On the Monday evening before, William Billington tested the gallows with an appropriately weighted sand bag which also had the effect of taking the stretch out of the rope. Billington had been born in 1873 and came from a family of state executioners holding this office from 1902 to 1905. It was a position that he had taken over from his father James who resigned office having been the executioner for the Wandsworth jurisdiction since 1884. He himself also became the London executioner in 1892 having succeeded the famous James 'Hangman' Berry.

Perhaps knowing that ultimately his fate would lead to a rendezvous with the executioner, Klosowski had obtained a rare copy of Berry's book on his work. Being all too aware that he faced a front seat in the proceedings, he feared the remaining hour and minutes of his life having read about what was in store for him in great detail.

Henry Pierrepoint was also an accomplished executioner in his own right despite only being an assistant in these proceedings. He held office from 1901 to 1910 and despatched 117 prisoners in his tenure. Both he and Billington were known for their brisk and efficient work in the hangman's shed and this morning would prove to be no different. Oddly they were also known for their abilities to keep the prisoner calm in the minutes they were led from their cells to imminent death with a softly spoken and almost caring demeanour in their spoken word.

The prison governor Major Knox gave the orders to commence the execution procedure around 8.a.m. Following his signal the grim face execution team entered the cell lead by Henry Pierrepoint and all observed how terrified Klosowski had become by his shaking and pallor. He was ordered to stand and knew that time to leave this world had come. Attempting to stand, at first he faltered and leaned back against the back wall of the cell in a slump. But before long he was slowly able to stand and with quiet brisk efficiency, born out practice and experience, the team moved forward and prepared him for the gallows with Pierrepoint briskly completing the task of 'pinioning'; the practice of pinning the condemned man's arms by their side. This practice was developed from the previous method of tying their arms in front of them which seemed to allow resistance from the prisoner. Klosowski looked on at the work being done around him wide eyed and in an almost trance like state numbed with fear.

Major Knox entered the cell with the pinioning having been completed.

"Prisoner, I don't know what you said to the padre," he said pacing the cell in his characteristic black suit and with a lit pipe in his right hand, "this is your chance for some honesty. There are some who believe you are guilty of several others murders, but in the main those perpetrated in Whitechapel fifteen years ago. Your next trial which it has been decided not to go to public expense with would have been for those murders and an attempted murder in Tottenham that same year. Now tell us, we can all bear witness to your confession, are you Jack the Ripper?" The cell was deathly silent. Klosowski's head was bowed and he was gently sobbing. He looked up slowly into Knox's face with an expression of helplessness. He appeared unable to speak. After a few seconds, that seemed like an eternity his mouth opened as if to speak.

He began to wretch, then cough and within another few seconds of this accompanied by a violent convulsing movement by his torso he vomited profusely. He wept loudly having ejected the meagre food he had taken in for breakfast and as the execution team held him upright he urinated in his trousers; it running down the inside of his trouser legs onto the floor. He never spoke in a language any of them recognised from that point until the rope dropped.

"Get over to the shed please, gentlemen," said the Major in a somewhat disappointed tone.

The colour had now drained completely from his face and he was led by two prison guards out of the cell on his slow final death walk. Once out into the open air his true ashen pale colour showed through in the subdued morning daylight and he stumbled on numerous occasions having to be supported by the two guards. When he eventually looked up having taken his first unsteady steps out in the open he noticed the executioners wooden shed now less than fifty yards away from him. He fell to his knees immediately dragged back up by the two guards and began sobbing loudly again and screamed for mercy in Polish, a language that none of the gathered officials could understand. About ten yards from the shed door he collapsed one last time and was then physically carried into the building and to the base of the steps of the scaffolding.

In Polish, as they began the walk up the thirteen steps to the point of the executioners '6-6' drop, he cursed those that would 'take his miserable life' under his breath. He was centred on the wooden trap door, which gave slightly as it took up his weight, by Billington and would soon drop away.

"All right son, nice and steady, nice and still that's it," said Billington as he neared the completion of his work. He strapped his legs together tightly and said nothing else to the clearly terrified and violently trembling Klosowski.

The white hood was then placed over his head and adjusted accordingly. The rope with thirteen turns constructed of hemp and silk was placed over his head and tightly pulled. Billington quickly found the right place for the knot to be placed for best and swiftest effect. With the shock of having had the rope placed over his head Klosowski seemed to raise his body as the final reality of it struck home. The thirteen foot rope, now stretched from the night before by Billington, would allow the proper force to be transmitted to the prisoner's neck for the maximum and quickest effect. Klosowski was muttering incessantly below the hood while Billington gave a swift look to the officials gathered with Major Knox. Billington always tried to make the procedure within the shed as brisk as possible to keep the massive fear of imminent death to the minimum.

Almost as Knox gave a nod Billington pulled the lever for the trap doors. They opened with a small banging sound and 37 year old Severin Klosowski dropped the 6'6" from the trap door to the end of the rope's fall. As the rope almost instantly reached the end of its drop it snapped the prisoner's neck and his head jerked backwards ending his life with an incredibly loud audible snap of bone and vertebrae tissue. The sound of the trap doors banging open would have been the last sound Klosowski heard. His body twitched and shook for a moment and then swayed silently as bodily fluids drained out of it. There was silence across the scaffold amongst the execution team and the gathered witnesses, most of who despite not being strangers to these events were still shocked by the controlled brutality of the procedure.

Attending as a government official was a local doctor called Beamish who now stepped forward from the witness gallery to certify that life was extinct. Placing a stethoscope on Klosowski's chest there was a faint heart beat that very quickly faded away to nothing and Dr Beamish was indeed able to pronounce him dead. He was then left hanging in the shed, which was secured to prevent theft of the body, for one hour which ensured that there would be no mistake in his death.

An hour later the execution team led by William Billington returned to the locked shed and removed the body to be taken to the district coroner Mr Troutbeck. Under his examination and following a short inquest it was noted that the dead Klosowski's neck was now elongated by about one inch. The traditional black flag was raised above the prison to signify that an execution had taken place. Gathered outside the prison gates was a crowd of about 150 people consisting of journalists, the curious members of the public, a small group of relatives of the victims of Jack the Ripper and curiously, with her brother Stanislaus and her sister, was Lucy Klosowski, formerly Baderski. They were comforting her as the flag was raised as Severin had refused to see her or anyone else prior to his execution barring the compulsory visit of the priest. The rest of the crowd cheered as the flag moved up its pole, especially those with family links to the victims who had gathered following the reported speculation that Klosowski was the infamous Whitechapel Murderer as a result of Abberline's comment to Godley. There were some women who then broke in tears who had a close link to either Tabrum, Nichols, Chapman, Stride, Eddowes or Kelly. Photographers with the journalists took a few still pictures of the throng and of the flag above the prison. As the wave of macabre euphoria passed among the crowd the journalists got to work interviewing the most vulnerable or vociferous.

Stanislaus gave his grieving sister a hug having introduced her to Severin many years before. Despite his monstrous acts he was still her husband and the father to her three children and she therefore felt affection for his part in this family group. Seeing a journalist and photographer approach them, Stanislaus ushered all three of them away and they disappeared through the crowd and then out of sight.

Klosowski was buried in an unmarked grave within the walls of the prison with the rope still tight around his neck. He would be one of only 763 hung throughout England and Wales during the 20th century upon the last working gallows to be dismantled in England. They were last used on September 8th 1961, the anniversary of Annie Chapman's murder and dismantled on the 31st July 1992.

* * *

St John's Hospital situated at 307 South Euclid Avenue, St Louis, Missouri had been established in 1871 by Mother M de Pazzi Bentley as a charitable hospice for the care of the old and infirm and terminally ill. It had been run for sometime by the Sisters of Mercy and as

Francis Tumblety reached seventy years of age with failing health he had decided that it would be a good place to die. The fight, resilience and resourcefulness within him had long since gone and he found it difficult to look after himself. He had become particularly fond of Sister Mary Theresa the red haired pretty Irish nun who treated him with a tenderness for which he had always longed. She knew him as Francis Townsend the name under which he had registered when he had arrived at the hospital on Sunday 26th April 1903. He was fond of shuffling around the grounds with his walking stick for support in his faded red and threadbare military tunic. He had few possessions all of which he was open about as none of them held a clue to his evil past.

On Monday 25th May he had become very weak and he realised with the medical knowledge he possessed that had little time left owing to a serious heart condition he had developed in the last twelve months. That day he insisted on dressing for his usual walk and showing his old and normally subdued strength of will and independence he went for his walk alone. The air smelt fresh and cool during that morning and its fantastic summer nature reminded him of when he had first met Mary Kelly. The aggression and bitterness that accompanied their relationship was something that he failed to recall with halcyon images of their times together before Paris, and the renewal of his faith in womankind. He strolled amongst the leafy orchard of peach trees with it's fantastic fruit laden scent, the sumptuous lawns and the finely laid ornamental gardens with their elegant topiary; it was here he concluded that this was a fitting last place on earth in which to exist.

He had walked for quite sometime tiring himself greatly but not really aware of the flat footed nature with which he was shuffling around the grounds. He made it back to the steps at the rear of the hospital which ran down from a set of fine oak carved ornamental double doors that opened out onto this idyllic vista. He sat slowly and awkwardly on the steps, his every muscle and joints in his legs straining to get himself seated to take in the view. He was unaware that his stick was only teetering on the edge of a step to give him support and as it tried to bear all of his body weight it slipped forward off of its precarious perch. Tumblety fell forward completely losing his balance and toppling down several of the steps his face striking hard on one of the steps breaking his nose. He was fortunate not to break any other of his fragile bones as he lay concussed at the base of the steps.

His strolling of the grounds and now this drama was being observed by a middle aged well dressed stranger. He was lean in his build with marginally greying hair, and looked on with concern from the orchard as he saw the old man fall. 'Bollocks. Not having come this far. He can't collapse without the chance of a question being asked.' The thoughts of disappointment rushed through his mind. He looked on to see two of the nuns rush down the steps to tend the frail old man. They gently lifted his limp body between them and got it sat on the steps; his face lifted to look out over the grounds which showed the old man's face streaming with blood. He looked seriously distressed but he was at least alive. 'Still a chance to speak to this man about his past'. A third nun came into view at the top of the steps with a heavy wooden wheel chair. She then descended the few steps to join her colleagues and they eased the old man up the steps and into the wheel chair. He looked ill and winced as one of the nuns tried to gently wipe the blood from his face. The stranger hoped there was still time to have his questions answered. He would use the guile that he knew the old man had used many years ago in London to evade justice. The old man was turned around into a wheel chair and taken back into the hospital building. One of the nuns walked back down the steps and picked up the old man's stick. The stranger had seen this stick many years before and knew it had itself born witness to the terrible acts committed by the one who now left it lying at the base of the steps.

* * *

Thursday 28th May; the weak and ailing Francis Townsend lay in his bed in a private room with the warm summer sun streaming through the window. His squinting eyes were able to make out the deep green leaves of the peach trees in the orchard having been propped up in the bed by Sister Mary Theresa when he had first woken. With his sins playing over in his mind along with the thoughts of the life he had led he knew that his time was drawing near. He stared around the comfortable though austere room and felt sad that he had so little to show for his seventy years from an intrinsic point of view that he could willingly pass on. In reality, however, he had no one to benefit from any mementoes he would leave behind.

He heard the door to the room open and turning his head slowly he looked across the room toward it. Closing the door behind him was a smartly turned out, middle aged, lean, slightly greying catholic priest carrying a bag that had a familiar look to it in his failing glance. He had thoughts of requesting absolution but had felt almost too guilty to do so for fear of the sisters discovering his secret; not that a priest would pass on his secret. Seeing the priest he knew he must seize the opportunity to do so and die at least he felt with a clear conscience.

Tumblety's eyes were failing and he could not really distinguish the finer points of the priest features, yet when he spoke he sounded familiar and certainly hadn't been a local man by birth.

"Father, how fortuitous for me to see you. Thank you," said Tumblety weakly, his mouth feeling dry and his heart seemingly labouring.

"You are welcome, my son. The sisters had informed me you had not been well these last few days." The priest's voice was that of an Englishman and had a colloquial quality he recognised.

"Are you from London, father?" He asked quietly.

"Yes, my son. From a London parish but I am here as a missionary. Tell me, what can I do for you?"

"Forgive me, father, I have sinned." Tumblety began with a rasping voice and with a struggle for breath. "I have done terrible things and I seek absolution. I have fuelled the commission of terrible things too."

The priest sat at the side of the bed with seemingly an air of curiosity over any other emotion. As he sat Tumblety could hear the knocking of the priest's rosary beads; as a formerly devout catholic during his formative years it was a sound that took him back to his childhood.

"Be calm, my son, and speak. God is here to hear your confession. His greatest gift is forgiveness." The voice and even the priest's presence were familiar to Tumblety. In his condition though, he was more concerned in seeking forgiveness.

"Father, in 1888, fifteen years ago in London I committed some unspeakable acts of wickedness and I pursued a sickening agenda." He stopped speaking and began coughing violently. As the coughing died down the priest passed him a glass of water. He slowly drank it, very gladly soothing his throat, and then continued.

"Father, it is very simple. I was Jack the Ripper." Stunned silence fell between them; Tumblety sensed that the priest was seemingly waiting to hear more. He swallowed hard and continued.

"Father, I was driven into it by jealousy and provocation. Voices possessed me and drove me on and all because the two true loves of my life sinned against me so developing a mistrust and hate of woman kind. This hate drove me to kill and obtain unspeakable trophies from them, the possession of trophies was a vice I developed before the killing began because of the hate inside. But after committing so many of these crimes I found salvation when I met the second woman I had loved in my life again whilst I still felt driven to kill her. She made me realise I was weak; I couldn't do it, I couldn't kill her so I sinned further; I coerced someone else to do it."

Sobbing from the cathartic out pouring of guilt, Tumblety was unaware of the priest's demeanour. He was leaning up closely to him scowling with hate, knuckles white from gripping the beads and seemingly hanging on to his every word. He was transfixed on what the old man had to say and hadn't even noticed for quite a few seconds that the confessor had paused and was struggling to compose himself. The priest snapped out of his fixation to speak to the old man.

"The Lord is forgiving, my son," consoling words were so hard for the priest to speak. "And you shall be absolved as I come to perform your last rites. Who was this poor and unfortunate man that you engaged in your ungodly enterprise?"

The old man fell in to a fit of almost uncontrollable sobbing as the priest waited for him to answer. The priest with uncharacteristic reserve for his office slowly and tentatively held the old man's right hand and felt a shiver run through him. Holding the hand of such a man was not comfortable but in return for this gesture of support the old man clutched his very tightly, fearing death was near.

"His name was Chapman, George Chapman. I then tried to stop him when I realised how wrong I had been but I was too late. I also killed a policeman in London and wounded others to evade capture. Father can the Lord ever forgive me? Could you? Please…" his voice was breaking heavily. "Please forgive me!" He sobbed uncontrollably.

For a moment the priest was very distant. He knew this man Chapman had been hung for other crimes in London. A comment he once heard by the great detective Frederick Abberline to George Godley back in London regarding the arrest of Chapman, 'you got a Jack the Ripper then?' had to have been true. He blurted out a question to the old man without thinking. "So who did this man kill then?" The priest already knew the answer. He wanted confirmation from the true Ripper's mouth on his cowardly crime committed by proxy. Tumblety fought for breath to try to answer the priest's question.

"It was Mary Kelly," Tumblety again sobbed and could feel his heart beginning to race. His eyes were tightly closed as he wept so he never saw his end coming. He was unaware that the priest had let go of his wrinkled and heavily veined hand.

Next to the bed was a plain functional pine bedside cabinet on top of which was a jug and glass of water, a small vase with some red and white roses wilting within it and a cotton handkerchief. From the cabinet as he watched Tumblety sob the priest pulled out a spare pillow and held it in both hands pulling it quite taut. He stood and leaned forward and while Tumblety's eyes were still screwed tightly shut he placed the pillow over the old man's face. He then pushed down hard cutting off the air supply to the old man's weakening lungs and driving his head deeper into the pillow below his head. For a few seconds there was a weak struggle; Tumblety grabbed the priest's arms in a futile attempt to push him off, but his frail arms were no match for the strong and more youthful arms of his assailant. Very quickly the old man's grip loosened from the priest's arms and fell limply onto the bed and his entire body became still. The priest held the pillow in place for a good half of a minute when the struggling had stopped just to be sure. He moved it aside and checked for a pulse; there was none and no sign of any breathing activity. Francis Tumblety, alias Frank Townsend the instigator of the Jack the Ripper murders was dead. Justice, it seemed perhaps, had at last been done in that both he and Severin Klowsowki had met with either a vengeful or capital death before nature could take its course.

With that in mind Detective Inspector Robert Ford put the pillow back in the bedside cabinet feeling, at last, satisfied that he had brought justice for Mary Kelly and the other murdered East End women. It had taken him several years to amass the leave he needed to take from his position with the Metropolitan Police in London. He had always had the financial resources to do it as a result of the money he had invested that had been left in his lodgings fifteen years before by Mary Kelly. Ford had moved into the Special Branch at Scotland Yard and one day when casually inspecting exhibits in storage for the crime or 'Black' Museum he had found Tumblety's arts bag. To have seen it again after so many years had brought a chill through his body and he was stunned that Sir Robert Anderson had failed to dispose of it, although in fairness to Anderson a man he had come to despise, he ultimately had left it's destruction to others. For the first time he had decided to look the bag over in some detail and it was the manufacturers label on it that had brought him to the state of Missouri. It did, however, mean he could bring final shame upon Tumblety and a historical inference of guilt. He had been in the United States for nearly a month tracking Tumblety's movements via the archives of the press and the judiciary since his return there. He was grateful he had at least been able to start in the right state of the union with the clue the bag had given.

He stepped back from the bed and looked down on the lifeless aged man who lay there. He looked remarkably peaceful and strangely innocent under the crisp white linen sheets of the convent hospital and seemed far removed from the man who had killed so many including his own true love and best friend. He felt no remorse for his actions. Due to the interference of the Freemasons within the Police Force he knew that justice was never to be done if left to the legal system as the years had proved. He had left no bruises no sign of obvious foul play with the lack of forensic evidence that existed in 1903. He looked around the room. It was quite sparse but had a cupboard and a wardrobe either of which would prove appropriate to deposit Tumblety's bag of 'trophies' from the years gone by.

The wardrobe held only a few hanging garments; a suit, some breeches, a hunting jacket and a military style tunic. He moved across to the plain wooden cupboard and opened its double doors. It seemed to be the best place to leave the bag for which Detective Constable Parish had lost the sight in one eye for at the hands of the determined thief who had burgled the incident room at Commercial Street Police Station to clear the last traces of Tumblety's guilt. He had always found it hard to bring himself to touch it. He would leave it here to bring shame upon the dead man when the nurses discovered it. For the final time he picked up the tatty leather arts bag, with memories flashing through his mind of when he had discovered it in Hackney fifteen years previously, and placed in the cupboard. The final physical connection with it made his blood run cold as it had when he had first seen it again in the Museum store. Shutting the cupboard door, curiosity got the better of Robert Ford and decided just to check the single drawer above the doors of the unit slowly pulling it open. It was empty barring what appeared to be a battered photograph laying face down in its centre. It seemed odd that it was the only item that it contained so he picked it and turned it over very casually. He could not have been prepared to see the image it contained.

Staring back at him was a beautiful sepia image of a youthful Mary Kelly. She was dressed in a fine costume like the one she had worn on the day they had gone boating together fifteen years previously; probably the happiest day of his life he could remember. She so looked perfect and to find this image of her was the most miraculous emotional experience he had undergone since that halcyon day. With an even greater sense of fulfilment he placed it carefully in his jacket inside pocket with tears running down his cheeks and a lump constricting his throat.

At last in Robert Ford's mind justice was done; it was time to go. He had to leave. Now. He had completed his life's pursuit. He walked to the door, cautiously grasped the handle and slowly opened it and looked out. No one in the corridor; just the smell of clinical sterility from the obsessive cleanliness of the religious nursing staff, and the brightness of the lightly coloured walls echoing the light along it. Closing the door behind him he entered the corridor leading to the main reception where one of the sisters was sat busily writing at the desk. The nun working there looked up, although he had silently walked along the corridor, as if she possessed a sixth sense.

"Are you leaving now father?" she spoke to him with familiarity, obviously used to the frequent presence of priests at the hospital.

"Yes, my work here today is done," confidently replied Ford, looking very natural in his religious garb. A result, no doubt, of his years within the detective department and the hard lessons he learnt during the Whitechapel investigation.

"Good day to you, father. We hope to see you again soon. You all bring such comfort to our patients." Ford was a little taken aback by this reply. Not being a real priest and with the nature of his visit he felt uncomfortable at deceiving someone so honest. He felt trying to answer would be unfair to her and inappropriate and said nothing. He nodded and gave a faint smile and exited through the double doors out into the open air.

Walking out along the cinder path that led from the front of the building to the main street, the warm May Missouri air he felt was comforting on his face having committed such a cold and calculating deed. But, despite of the nature of his actions he felt that a weight had been lifted from his mind and he could press on and live his life. An aspect of the day's events did, however, trouble him. No one would ever know that today in relation to the crimes of fifteen years ago justice had finally been done. The other publicly suspected Ripper murderer had been hung just before Ford had left for America and now The real Jack the Ripper had finally been brought to task for his crimes. It made him feel somewhat unfulfilled that the public could never know. He turned out of the grounds of St John's Hospital into South Euclid Avenue and disappeared into the city, absorbed by the crowds of people on the pavements and the rattle of the traffic on the cobbled streets.

EPILOGUE

Fact: Frederick George Abberline was promoted to Chief Inspector in 1890. He retired on a full police pension in 1892 (a year short of official pensionable service) having received 84 commendations and awards during his service. He then worked as a private enquiry agent including three seasons in Monte Carlo. In 1898 he accepted the European agency of Allen Pinkerton's famous detective company. He died in 1929 in Bournemouth and left little in the way of memoirs. No photograph of Abberline has ever been discovered.

Fact: George Godley eventually gained the rank of Detective Inspector and retired in 1908 after 31 years service. He arrested Severin Klosowski alias George Chapman in October 1902 for the 'Borough Poisonings' of three women.

Fact: Francis Tumblety died in The St Johns Hospital, South Euclid Avenue, St Louis on Thursday May 28th 1903 having failed to recover from the shock of a fall in the grounds.

Fact: According to Masonic tradition Hiram Abiff, the architect of the Temple of Solomon, was murdered by the 'Juwes' (Jubela, Jubelo and Jubelum). The events of his murder form part of Masonic ritual which include 'the Fellow Craft [Mason] to have his heart torn from his breast; the Master Mason to have his bowels burnt to ashes.'

Fact: Aaron Kosminski has been considered a strong suspect by many retired senior detectives of the period in their memoirs. In 1891 he was placed in the Colney Hatch Lunatic Asylum from where in 1894 he was moved to Leavesden Asylum following a violent attack on an attendant. He died of gangrene of the leg in 1919 following a period where he suffered from 'aural and visual hallucinations'.

Fact: Inspector Walter Andrews did lead a team of detectives to New York in late 1888.

Fact: John Netley was a self employed cab driver during the time of the Whitechapel murders. He died in a road accident in Park Road near Baker Street after a wheel of his van hit an obelisk and he was thrown under the horse's hooves and his head crushed by a wheel.

Fact: Sir Charles Warren did, co-incidentally, step down as Commissioner following the Mary Kelly Murder.

Fact: The investigation into the Whitechapel Murders was continued until 1892, the same year that Chief Inspector Abberline retired.

Fact: Many original papers from the investigation are missing; some there are still facsimile copies of. No one has, as yet, been conclusively identified as 'Jack the Ripper'.

Glossary

Bang-tail – harsh slang term for prostitute

Beat – the posted area patrolled by a constable

Black Mariah – a secure carriage made specifically for the transportation of prisoners

Bloke – An English slang term for man

Bobby/bobbies – slang term for policeman/men derived from Sir <u>Robert</u> Peel, founder of the Metropolitan Police Force

Brief – slang term for lawyer or solicitor

Charge room or custody office – the area in a police station were prisoners are received and charged with offences.

Chinese whispers – slang for rumours

C.I.D – the Criminal Investigation Department

Copper – slang term for policeman

Cunny – coarse slang term for vagina

Drop of bail - slang for granting a prisoner bail to return to a police station or to appear in court

Early house – a pub that opens early in the morning to service the night workers of the markets

Freebie - slang for something given without charge

Ground – a colloquial term for the catchment area of a police station

Hansom – a horse drawn cab

Lipski – harsh slang term for Jew

Mucher – a person who robs from drunks (verb - muched)

Mucker - colloquial term for friend

Nick – slang for a police station

Old Bill – slang for police

Piece of cake – colloquialism meaning easy

P.M – short for post mortem (also known as an autopsy)

Pogrom – term referring to the wholesale murder of Jewish people

Pub – short for public house a licensed drinking establishment

Relief – term for team of police officers working a shift together

Shag – slang term for sexual intercourse

Squaddie/s – slang term for a soldier or soldiers

Square him up – a slang expression for getting even with someone or putting them in their place

Whitechapel

Steerage – poorest class available on Trans-Atlantic shipping lines

Tom – slang for prostitute

Unfortunate – a low class prostitute

Wanker – coarse term for someone who masturbates, usually used as an insult

Wicket – small lockable window in a police cell door

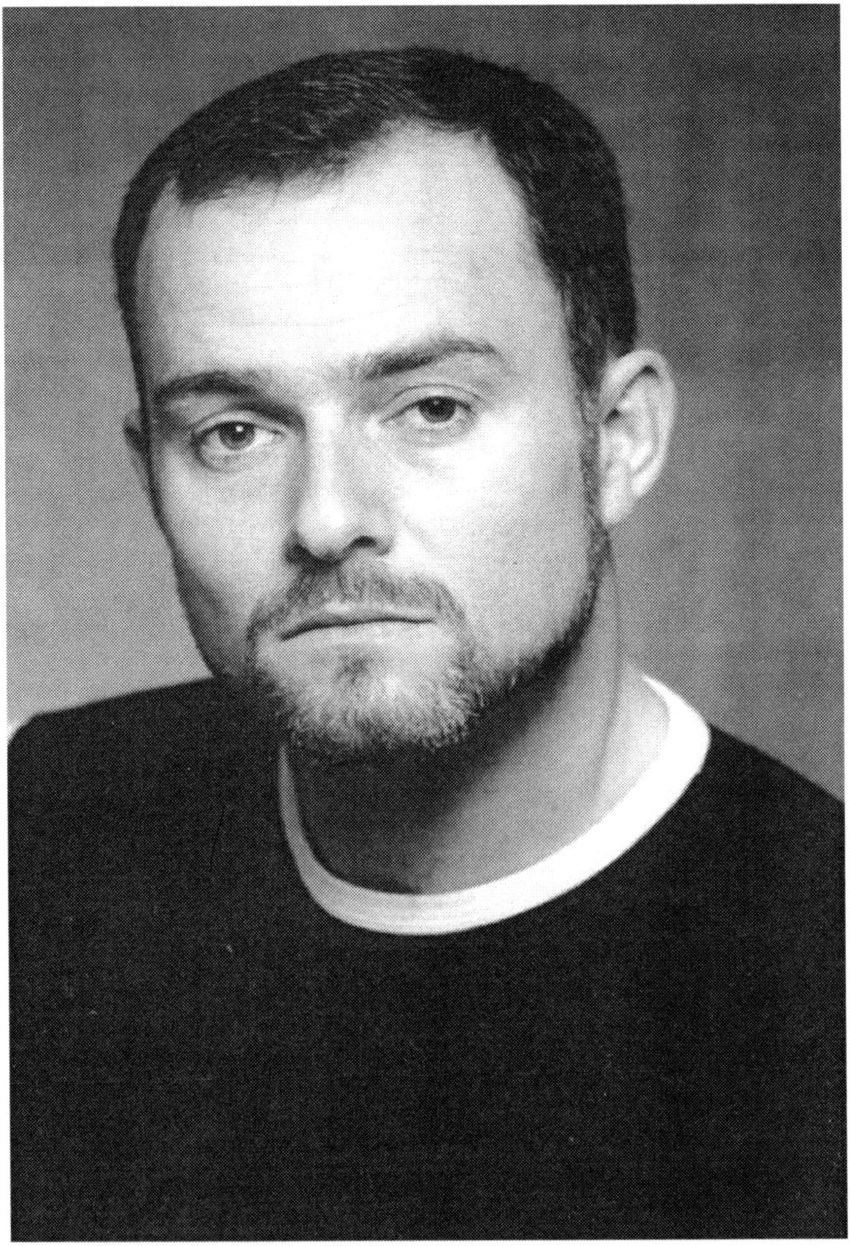

BRYAN LIGHTBODY

Born in 1968, Bryan Lightbody the son of a police officer and a teacher has been a member of the Metropolitan Police since 1988, co-incidentally the centenary year of the Whitechapel Murders. Inspired by coverage of this fact, he began avidly reading as much as he could on the subject and also watching relevant films and documentaries. This led to a good working knowledge of the crimes, and in 1993 he transferred to duties that brought him to work directly in the area in which the crimes were committed. This allowed the opportunity to observe the area regularly by night in its most atmospheric 'Ripper' sense. By the end of 1998 having left the area to move again to other duties he was inspired to consider writing a book. There are numerous reference books on the subject but few fictional period thrillers, and inspired by books such as Anthony Grey's 'Saigon' a historical novel, he began to tentatively put 'pen to paper.'

With eighteen years police experience behind him in various uniform departments, he felt that he could write a thriller with the central character as a humble uniform constable and his interactions with those involved in the investigation. On an informal basis with groups of friends he has toured the area which on the whole no longer reflects the East End that either 'Jack the Ripper' or the police attempting to apprehend him knew.

Bryan Lightbody has worked in the Borough of Redbridge, engaged in traffic duties around the East End of London, worked as a car and motorcycle instructor at the police driving school at Hendon and currently works within the Royalty Protection department.

Outside of work he is married with two dogs, two motorbikes, a scooter and two cars – motoring is a passion, and enjoys theatre, Roman history and archaeology, travel, cinema and of course writing.